AF771448

CRIMINALIZING CHILDREN

Indigenous and non-Indigenous children have been subject to detention in institutions in the name of welfare and of justice in Australian states and territories from the beginning of colonisation. Countless government and non-government inquiries and initiatives have attempted to address the problem of increasing criminalization of children with little success. The rates of child removal and incarceration of children is rising rapidly throughout Australia, with Indigenous children most at risk of removal from their families and of imprisonment. Taking the Australian state of Victoria as a case study, David McCallum traces changing rationalities of governing Aboriginal and non-Aboriginal children over a period of one hundred years. The book challenges our assumptions about the role of both law and the human sciences in determining the conduct of child welfare and juvenile justice, under specifically liberal forms of governing.

DAVID McCALLUM is Emeritus Professor in the Centre for International Research on Education Systems at Victoria University in Melbourne, Australia. His publications include *The Social Production of Merit* (1990), *Personality and Dangerousness* (Cambridge, 2001), and *Inside the Child's Head* (2009) co-authored with Jennifer Laurence. He is a past convenor of the Crime and Governance Thematic group for The Australian Sociological Association and a member of the International Sociological Association.

CAMBRIDGE STUDIES IN LAW AND SOCIETY

Cambridge Studies in Law and Society aims to publish the best scholarly work on legal discourse and practice in its social and institutional contexts, combining theoretical insights and empirical research.

The fields that it covers are studies of law in action; the sociology of law; the anthropology of law; and cultural studies of law, including the role of legal discourses in social formations; law and economics; law and politics; and studies of governance. The books consider all forms of legal discourse across societies, rather than being limited to lawyers' discourses alone.

The series editors come from a range of disciplines: academic law, socio-legal studies, sociology and anthropology. All have been actively involved in teaching and writing about law in context.

Series Editors

Chris Arup
Monash University, Victoria

Sally Engle Merry
New York University

Susan Silbey
Massachusetts Institute of Technology

A list of books in the series can be found at the back of this book.

Criminalizing Children

WELFARE AND THE STATE IN AUSTRALIA

DAVID McCALLUM
Victoria University, Melbourne

CAMBRIDGE
UNIVERSITY PRESS

CAMBRIDGE
UNIVERSITY PRESS

University Printing House, Cambridge CB2 8BS, United Kingdom

One Liberty Plaza, 20th Floor, New York, NY 10006, USA

477 Williamstown Road, Port Melbourne, VIC 3207, Australia

314–321, 3rd Floor, Plot 3, Splendor Forum, Jasola District Centre,
New Delhi – 110025, India

79 Anson Road, #06–04/06, Singapore 079906

Cambridge University Press is part of the University of Cambridge.

It furthers the University's mission by disseminating knowledge in the pursuit of education, learning, and research at the highest international levels of excellence.

www.cambridge.org
Information on this title: www.cambridge.org/9781845656676
DOI: 10.1017/9781316535028

© David McCallum 2017

This publication is in copyright. Subject to statutory exception and to the provisions of relevant collective licensing agreements, no reproduction of any part may take place without the written permission of Cambridge University Press.

First published 2017

Printed in the United Kingdom by Clays, St Ives plc

A catalogue record for this publication is available from the British Library.

Library of Congress Cataloging-in-Publication Data
NAMES: McCallum, David, author.
TITLE: Criminalizing children : a history of welfare and the state in Australia / David McCallum, Victoria University of Technology, Melbourne.
DESCRIPTION: Cambridge, United Kingdom ; New York, NY : Cambridge University Press, 2017. | Series: Cambridge studies in law and society | Includes bibliographical references.
IDENTIFIERS: LCCN 2017043876 | ISBN 9781845656676
SUBJECTS: LCSH: Child welfare – Australia – History. | Juvenile delinquents – Australia – History. | Children – Australia – Social conditions. | Children, Aboriginal Australian – Government policy – History.
CLASSIFICATION: LCC HV802 .M33 2017 | DDC 364.360994–dc23
LC record available at https://lccn.loc.gov/2017043876

ISBN 978-1-845-65667-6 Hardback

Cambridge University Press has no responsibility for the persistence or accuracy of URLs for external or third-party internet websites referred to in this publication and does not guarantee that any content on such websites is, or will remain, accurate or appropriate.

Contents

Preface

This book has been written at a time when both child welfare and juvenile justice are matters of concern for many Australians and those in the legal, welfare and justice fields. Incarceration of both Indigenous and non-Indigenous people continues to rise in almost all parts of Australia, despite efforts to address it. Recent scandals in Queensland, the Northern Territory and Victoria testify to a system which appears to be at breaking point in many areas. Indigenous children especially continue to be removed from parents and communities at extraordinary levels.

The State of Victoria was chosen as the main focus of this historical and sociological study in part because Victoria regarded itself as more progressive in its social policy outlook, including in relation to Aboriginal peoples. However, rates of child removal and incarceration continue to steadily increase while policymakers face ongoing management issues in child protection and juvenile justice. The aim of this book is to seek greater understanding of how these present problems came into being. It uses historical and sociological analysis to address a series of questions: how did the categories used by Victorian welfare and justice authorities to classify at-risk children come into existence? What do their conditions of emergence tell us about their present operation? How do these forms of knowledge inform and organise placement in welfare and criminal systems, for both Indigenous and non-Indigenous children?

The book contains aspects of the history of many Indigenous men and women who were affected by government policies in Australia. It could not have been written without recognising their involvement and existence. In some Indigenous communities, seeing the names of dead people may cause sadness and distress. Indigenous peoples are warned that the names of such people appear in this book.

The author acknowledges with thanks the contribution of Jennifer Laurence to the research of this project. Thanks are also due to the Moondani Balluk Indigenous Unit, and the Community, and Displacement Research Network at Victoria University, Melbourne, for their collaboration and support. The author is grateful for the support provided by Victoria University through research funds and study leave, and to my colleagues in the College of Arts. Thanks are also due to Oz Child for permission to access the historical manuscripts of the Victorian Children's Aid Society and to the staffs of the State Library of Victoria, the Public Records Office of Victoria and the Melbourne branch of the National Archives of Australia.

1

Child Welfare and the Australian State: An Introduction

A decade ago the Australian government announced the Northern Territory Emergency Response, within days of a public report raising issues of sexual abuse of children in Aboriginal communities in the Northern Territory (NT). The Intervention, as it came to be known, was announced in June 2007 in the lead-up to an Australian federal election and contained widespread restriction of alcohol, compulsory and intrusive medical checks of Indigenous children, the quarantining of income support to restrict spending to basics such as food, enforced school attendance and the abolition of the permit system on Aboriginal lands. It was accompanied by the arrival of doctors, police and army personnel. The Intervention was at odds with the recommendations of the *Little Children Are Sacred* report by Wild and Anderson and released a few weeks before, which although it addressed the allegations of child sexual abuse, emphasised that any evidence of this was largely a symptom of 'a breakdown of Aboriginal culture and society', and the extent and the sources of this breakdown were summarised in the report.[1] It was the claims of child

[1] Northern Territory (R. Wild and P. Anderson) 2007a (Summary Report): 'Most Aboriginal people are willing and committed to solving problems and helping their children. They are also eager to better educate themselves . . . Aboriginal people are not the only victims and not the only perpetrators of sexual abuse . . . Much of the violence and sexual abuse occurring in Territory communities is a reflection of past, current and continuing social problems which have developed over many decades . . . The combined effects of poor health, alcohol and drug abuse, unemployment, gambling, pornography, poor education and housing, and a general loss of identity and control have contributed to violence and to sexual abuse in many forms . . . Existing government programs to help Aboriginal people break the cycle of poverty and violence need to work better. There is not enough coordination and communication between government departments and agencies, and this is causing a breakdown in services and poor crisis intervention. Improvements in health and social services are desperately needed'; Northern Territory (R. Wild and P. Anderson) 2007b: 12–13: 'Programs need to have enough funds and resources and be a long-term commitment . . . Our appointment and terms of reference arose out of allegations of sexual abuse of Aboriginal children. Everything we have learned since convinces us that these are just symptoms of a breakdown of Aboriginal culture and society. There is, in our view, little point in an exercise of band-aiding individual and specific problems as each one achieves an appropriate degree of media and political hype. It has not worked in the past and will not work in the future . . . What is required is a determined, coordinated effort to break the cycle and provide the necessary strength, power and appropriate support and services to local communities, so they can lead themselves out of the malaise: in a word, *empowerment*!' (emphasis in original).

sexual abuse that provided the main impetus and political rationale for the Intervention, which also included the suspension of the Commonwealth Racial Discrimination Act (1975) to enforce, among other things, income quarantining and the taking of lands. The national newspaper reported extensively on allegations of abuse of children and the sickening state of the remote communities in the northern parts of the South Australian desert, but few column inches were devoted to the historical accounts contained in the report or the impact that the legislation would have – how did this problem come about? How would this policy provide a solution? The suspension of the Racial Discrimination Act allowed the government to force Aboriginal people to live in areas approved by the government through the removal of social security benefits when a child was considered to be in need of protection, or when the parents resided in specific areas or when a child had an unsatisfactory attendance record at school.[2] Suspension of the act was accompanied by acquisition of Aboriginal lands through compulsory leases, the abandonment of the existing Community Development Employment Program and the prevention of the courts being able to observe customary law and practices in sentencing offenders. A submission to the UN Committee on the Elimination of Racial Discrimination argued the following:

> The legislation was based upon a nuclear family assumption, which has little or no relevance to many Aboriginal communities. It also ignored the fact that through years of neglect of basic services to Aboriginal communities, many children would be living in situations where the provision of education services is inadequate and unattractive.[3]

With the defeat of the conservative Liberal/National government, a new Labor government appointed a panel of experts to review the Intervention, which in turn recommended the reinstatement of the Racial Discrimination Act and changing the compulsory income management to voluntary income management. Instead, the new government introduced an amended Racial Discrimination Act to maintain compulsory income management while also extending it to include targeted non-Indigenous welfare recipients throughout Australia. The government claimed to have carried out its own extensive consultations across seventy-three communities. Indigenous communities disputed the government's claim that it acted in accordance with their wishes and Indigenous leaders still continue to challenge the government's claim to have consulted with affected communities.[4]

AUTHORITARIAN LIBERALISM/'RACE' WAR

A group of Indigenous and non-Indigenous people called Concerned Australians submitted a report in 2010 on the Northern Territory Emergency Response to the

[2] Australia. Racial Discrimination Act (No. 52) 1975. [3] Nicholson, Harris and Gartland 2010: 17.
[4] Concerned Australians 2010.

UN Committee on the Elimination of Racial Discrimination, arguing that some of the worst human rights violations in the Western world were taking place in the NT.[5] In keeping with the post-9/11 descriptions and analyses of extraordinary governmental interventions in which 'normal law' was apparently suspended, such as the US establishment of a prison at Guantanamo Bay, the NT intervention was described in the language of 'special measures' and 'martial law', a mission to 'stabilise', 'normalise' and 'exit'.[6] Members of the government under Prime Minister Howard spoke of the situation in the Northern Territory as a 'national emergency', Australia's version of Hurricane Katrina.[7] The Intervention was 'operationalised' under military command and the language of strategy and tactics was used to describe its activities. The majority of the measures in fact required new Commonwealth government legislation to proceed.[8] The Social Security and Other Legislation Amendment (Welfare Payment Reform) Act mandated that 50 per cent of income support and family assistance payments to Indigenous people living in remote parts of the Northern Territory be managed by the government.[9] The funds could only be used for items considered essential by the government, such as food, clothes, rent, electricity, medicine and basic household goods. Not only did this law underpin the government's activities in the NT, it was then extended to non-Indigenous welfare recipients across Australia, to satisfy requirements for revising the Racial Discrimination Act (1975), which prohibited legislation discriminating against groups on the basis of race. Income quarantining for welfare recipients was initiated under so-called emergency circumstances and its 'exceptionality' as a legal provision under social security legislation became a legal 'norm'. It is in this sense that the 'exceptional decision' came to affirm law's normality – 'that the exception to the law is itself of the law and that the exception's attendant sovereign rule is constituted by law'.[10]

Three weeks after the announcement of the emergency response, the affected NT Indigenous organisations asked for a two-staged plan to address problems of child abuse in remote Aboriginal communities, including an emergency response agreed quickly between governments and community leaders, and a more comprehensive plan and costed financial commitment for more resources for communities, police, child protection and health services; tougher restrictions on sale of alcohol; community-based family support; improved access to mediation, treatment and

[5] Nicholson, Harris and Gartland 2010: 5. [6] Tedmanson and Wadiwel 2010: 7–22.

[7] Australia (M. Brough, Min. Families, Community Services and Indigenous Affairs) 2007.

[8] Australia Northern Territory National Emergency Response Act (No. 129) 2007; Australia Social Security and Other Legislation Amendment (Welfare Payment Reform) Act (No. 130) 2007; Australia Families, Community Services and Indigenous Affairs and Other Legislation Amendment (Northern Territory National Emergency Response and Other Measures) Act (No. 128) 2007; Australia Appropriation (Northern Territory National Emergency Response) Act (No. 1) 2007–2008 (No. 126) 2007; Australia Appropriation (Northern Territory National Emergency Response) Act (No. 2) 2007–2008 (No. 127) 2007.

[9] Australia Social Security and Other Legislation Amendment (Welfare Payment Reform) Act (No. 130) 2007.

[10] Fitzpatrick and Joyce 2007: 65–76.

rehabilitation services; and better access to primary health care and education services.[11] Aboriginal community organisations commented on issues of the safety of children and families in the following terms:

> Effective child abuse prevention and child protection occurs where local community agencies, police and child protection staff work in a collaborative and coordinated manner ... The emergency measures announced by the Australian Government lack insight into effective child protection interventions and in effect seek to strengthen only one partner in the three-way partnership – the Northern Territory *police*. Whilst the allocation of increased police resources for Aboriginal communities is a priority, other key elements of the child protection system also require immediate additional resources. Only by providing additional resources for police, local Aboriginal agencies and statutory child protection staff to all play their part in child protection interventions will we see a significant improvement in how abuse is reported and dealt with.[12]

This advice was echoed in the Australian Human Rights Commission (AHRC) Report on the intervention,[13] and by the Wild and Anderson report itself.[14] The AHRC reiterated what Wild and Anderson had recommended, 'a radical change in the way government and non-government organisations consult, engage with and support Aboriginal people'. Wild and Anderson stated that it was 'a common theme of discussions that many Aboriginal people felt disempowered, confused, overwhelmed, and disillusioned with this situation leading to communities being weakened to the point that the likelihood of children being sexually abused is increased and the community ability to deal with it is decreased'.[15] On the question of law, however, evidence forwarded to the UN Committee on the Elimination of Racial Discrimination showed that the consultation and consent, which was required before any 'special measure' was introduced, had not taken place. According to Concerned Australians, this meant that the legislation introducing the special measure 'appeared to be inconsistent with the Racial Discrimination Act'.[16]

The recommendations provided to government in the *Little Children Are Sacred* report stressed the fundamental importance of consultations with Indigenous communities before any action was taken on its findings. Instead, as this book argues, the NT Intervention and other similar forms of intervention by Australian governments continued the tactics of government that have characterised the management of

[11] Combined Aboriginal Organisations of the Northern Territory 2007.

[12] Combined Aboriginal Organisations of the Northern Territory 2007: 10, emphasis added.

[13] Australia (Human Rights and Equal Opportunity Commission) 2008.

[14] Northern Territory (R. Wild and P. Anderson) 2007b: 21: 'In the first recommendation, we have specifically referred to the critical importance of governments committing to genuine consultation with Aboriginal people in designing initiatives for Aboriginal communities, whether these be in remote, regional or urban settings. We have been conscious throughout our enquiries of the need for that consultation and for Aboriginal people to be involved.'

[15] Northern Territory (R. Wild and P. Anderson) 2007b: 50.

[16] Nicholson, Harris and Gartland 2010: 9.

'Aboriginal Affairs' from the beginning of colonisation. For example, the Aboriginal and Torres Strait Islander Commission (ATSIC) had been campaigning since the early 1990s for funding to implement child abuse prevention strategies. ATSIC itself was subsequently closed down, with a previous minister for Indigenous affairs in 2007 describing it as a 'fraud'.[17] An example of good governance often provided by Indigenous organisations was the National Aboriginal Health Strategy in 1989, which has been described as 'the first occasion in Australian history since 1788 that Aboriginal peoples and Australian governments had worked together under the Aboriginal decision-making process of consensus', but the policy itself remains unimplemented.

Many Australians recall the Northern Territory Intervention as an overwhelmingly punitive response to a report which in fact highlighted the need for a series of ordered social policy responses that had been sought by Aboriginal communities for decades, and to economic and community disintegration wrought by the appropriation of land and the imposition of invaders' law and culture. Some researchers argue that present-day conditions for many Indigenous Australians are linked to assemblages of power located in the partisan victories around sovereignty and white interpretations of Aboriginal resistance to rule;[18] that particular formations of administrative knowledge around concepts of family abuse interpret economic and social dislocation as intentioned perpetrations of child abuse and sexual deviance;[19] that a 'freedom' of the victor is to perpetually subjugate through the normalising power of legal mechanisms that seek to control sex, sexuality, reproduction and Indigenous identity.[20] But the NT Intervention displays another historical element observed by Paul Muldoon – more general criminalizing of the population by means of its exclusion from the social sphere: the blue billboards announcing the alcohol restrictions, the intense power through the shaming of the people. An Indigenous leader in the NT wrote this in summary:

> [S]o as far as we're concerned, it's too much exertion brought to bear on naughty children. We are not naughty children. We are very deep thinking people and we utilize our law of the land to assist us to where we want to get. The biggest thing that we have an argument with the government is, we're not white people. We have our own language. We have our own ceremonies. We have our own land. What we want from government is *real* help and *real* funding rather than putting law on top of our Law.[21]

The significance of these events was to turn the history of the raw violent colonising of Aboriginal people living in the outback, detailed in countless appeals for resources to stem the economic and social disintegration, into a story of the collapse and failure of Aboriginal culture and way of life. Such disintegration was now supposedly so dramatic, so hopeless and helpless, that the people had

17 *Canberra Times* 2007, June 2: 8. 18 Muldoon 2008. 19 McCallum 2008: 41.
20 Tedmanson and Wadiwel 2010. 21 Concerned Australians 2010: 21.

turned to violence on their families and children, a performance played out on news services across Australia in ways which could only be met with revulsion and outrage. Such strategic preparations made the eventual police and military strike a highly predictable event, and in historical terms, anything but exceptional.

This book is about child welfare, justice and the Australian State. It is a comparison of the ways in which one state, Victoria, on the southern tip of the vast continent that was invaded and gradually occupied by the British from 1787, governed children of Indigenous peoples who had lived on these lands for millennia, and the children of the white settlers who arrived in the lands initially called Port Phillip District (later the colony of Victoria) from about the 1830s. Besides a comparison of ways of governing these peoples, it is also a historical account that seeks to address a contemporary question: what were the conditions of possibility for the present high rates of incarceration of children in Australia, as well as the removal of children from families and communities in the name of welfare and 'the child's best interest'? This latter, modern term to describe the principles underpinning interventions in the so-called private sphere of the family, refers to a continuing focus in this study on the way in which the state seeks to intervene and shape conduct in the social sphere by means of specifically 'liberal' forms of governing. The term 'criminalization' is used by criminologists to refer to social processes in which certain conduct or events are defined as crime or criminal.

By way of introduction, three aspects of Australian legal history and the history of European-Indigenous relations are compared from the point of view of the evidence of relations between welfare, justice and liberal political reason: first, the conduct of the British in the early period of white occupation and dispossession in the neighbouring territory of New South Wales, in their claim to sovereignty over Indigenous lands; second, the conduct of 'actually existing liberalism' in the context of the white invasion of the lands occupied by Indigenous peoples; and third, the establishment and operation of encampments – missions and stations – to hold those who had been overpowered in the taking of the country. In the first instance it is asked how it may be possible to map these events, in the colonial period and in its wake, onto a history of liberal practices of governing Indigenous and non-Indigenous children. This overview will establish the basis for a comparison, in Chapter 2, with early moves to govern children in white 'settler society' in Victoria. These latter forms of legislative and institutional oversight of white 'problem children' in welfare and justice legislation began in 1864, at about the same time that Britain took these legislative steps in England.[22] This review suggests that the problem under consideration historically in Australia is not 'the Indigenous problem', but rather a problem that needs to focus on white liberal governance. In essence, the book is a study of white rule.

[22] Victoria Neglected and Criminal Children's Act (No. 2016) 1864.

A conceptual framework is developed to examine a series of powerful events and includes notions of 'authoritarian liberalism' and 'race war', where power is understood to refer to the way in which relations of force are deployed and given concrete expression – that is, the way in which the exercise of power 'is war, a war continued by other means'.[23] This framework presupposes that liberal government, with its injunction to govern through freedom, will attempt to protect individual liberty through such mechanisms as representative government and the rule of law, but the arts of liberal government also will attempt to specify the content of individual freedom and turn it to various goals. In some cases liberal government will seek to enforce obligations among those parts of the population considered to be incapable of governing themselves. With liberalism so framed, this book aims to explore a somewhat unsettled opposition between power and domination on the one hand, and individual freedom on the other.[24]

These elements of historical analysis are directed in turn to understanding matters of the present – the effects of large-scale placement of generations of Indigenous peoples in encampments on those people's capacities and dispositions ('habitus') and on their descendants, in relation to government and self-government.[25] Social worlds organised around compulsory acquisition of lands, and the management of everyday life, identity, subsistence and bare life circumstances by means of these forms of rule, were to be maintained with minor deviations throughout the period of this study (from the 1860s to the 1960s). A fundamental starting point is to examine whether the criminalization of Indigenous children relates to a problem of white governance rather than black criminality. Here an argument is developed that the springboard for the massive increase in official counting of Aboriginal child criminality from the 1960s derives in part from the increasing appearance of Indigenous children in the formerly white children's welfare/justice system, and from the intergenerational effects and 'cultural bereavement' produced in the social worlds of the encampments.

On the other hand, white children in the welfare and justice systems – systems of oversight rarely applied to Indigenous children during most of the period under review – were managed in penal-type institutions guided by the developing sciences of childhood and penal reform, and their management acts as a counterpoint to the treatment of Indigenous children. Here attempts in the social, psychological and medical sciences to capture 'truths' of wayward and recalcitrant youth are traced. These attempts are backgrounded through the constant turnover of methods and theories on the nature of the 'delinquent' amid a series of governmental exhortations to maintain the clear distinction between the two separate categories of children announced in the 1864 Victorian Neglected and Criminal Children's Act.[26]

23 Foucault 2008: 90. 24 Dean 2002: 31; Dean 1999. 25 Bourdieu 1997; Mauss 1973 [1935].
26 Victoria Neglected and Criminal Children's Act (No. 2016) 1864.

LIBERAL FORMS OF GOVERNING INDIGENOUS PEOPLE

The historian Henry Reynolds described the Northern Territory Intervention as an act of power which showed the world that the Australian government could interfere with the smallest details of domestic life in a blatantly discriminatory way, 'regardless of the country's international obligations and professed belief in racial equality'.[27] Australia is a long-standing signatory to the UN Covenant on Human Rights and the Convention on the Rights of the Child.[28] Although the previous Howard government opposed signing it, Australia has now also endorsed the UN Declaration on the Rights of Indigenous Peoples, which among other provisions acknowledges rights to fundamental freedoms, self-determination and freedom from any kind of discrimination.[29] These affirmations of liberal democratic rights and equality before the law are commonly contrasted with government actions, most recently Australia's policies on asylum seekers and its conduct of certain investigations under the Commonwealth Anti-Terrorism Act (2005) as well as the Northern Territory Intervention.[30] Historical investigation of the 'liberal promise' of Indigenous rights will often acknowledge attempts to extend formal equality to Aboriginal peoples while recognising the limits of this promise and the failure of rights discourse to achieve civil and economic rights.[31]

It is one thing to commit to the liberal principle of equal worth of all individuals; it is quite another to equate the liberalism in academic political theory with liberalism as a 'powerful historical phenomenon'.[32] So while theoretical versions of liberalism may be wedded to claims about individual freedoms and equal worth, these claims do not necessarily reflect 'actually existing liberalism', such as the versions of liberal rule under British imperialism and other versions of 'authoritarian liberalism'.[33] For example, claims concerning freedom under liberalism are often qualified by the claim that such freedom is not possessed at birth but is acquired through discipline and moral progress, and that liberal government might sometimes aim to assist in the moral development of members of subject populations.[34] Further, this historical argument might also entail a coming-to-terms with a Eurocentric 'developmental

[27] Reynolds 2010. [28] United Nations 1948b; United Nations 1989.

[29] United Nations 2007; see especially Article 1: 'Indigenous peoples have the right to the full enjoyment, as a collective or as individuals, of all human rights and fundamental freedoms as recognized in the Charter of the United Nations, the Universal Declaration of Human Rights, and international human rights law.' Article 2: 'Indigenous peoples and individuals are free and equal to all other peoples and individuals and have the right to be free from any kind of discrimination, in the exercise of their rights, in particular that based on their indigenous origin or identity.'

[30] Australia Anti-Terrorism Act (No. 127) 2005. [31] Thornton 1990; Chesterman 2005.

[32] Hindess 2004: 23–39.

[33] Hindess 2001: 93–111; 2008: 347–52. Foucault's approach to law and sovereignty as overly tied to outdated, negative forms of power has been much discussed. In this context, the term 'authoritarian liberalism' has been described as a 'seeming oxymoron' in considering the importance of law and sovereignty in balancing powers required to achieve individual freedom and security. See Wickham 2006: 604.

[34] Hindess 2008: 348.

view of humanity' and acknowledgement by such nineteenth-century liberal theorists as J. S. Mill or Alex de Tocqueville that non-Western peoples were 'not yet ready for self-government'.[35] The developmental story among educated Europeans was that humanity was divided into societies and that these could be ranked along a development spectrum, with Western Europe at the top. In addition, among these 'more advanced' societies, some people – the educated and prosperous minority – have advanced further than the rest.[36] If this meaning of liberalism is applied to the present Australian government's relations with Indigenous Australians, the NT Intervention displays not so much a contradiction of liberal political reason, or a cynical disregard for individual worth or a mistaken exercise of the rule of law but rather a historical instance of authoritarian liberalism in relation to the governance of peoples who, for present purposes, are regarded as either 'not yet ready for self-government' or as having 'failed' at self-government.[37]

Authoritarian forms of government can be seen as a characteristic feature of the history of liberal political reason in a number of ways. Here liberalism is understood as a distinct form of political reason that is concerned with the practical implications of the belief that members of the population are endowed with or capable of acquiring a capacity for autonomous, self-directing activity. Liberalism understands the social milieu as involving both government regulation and the self-regulating activity of free interactions between individuals capable of agency.[38] Government may make use of this freedom and has tended to focus on the ways in which individual liberty may be recruited for governmental purposes. But how has liberal political reason dealt with those in whom the capacity for self-government is thought to be insufficiently developed? Barry Hindess points to Locke's discussion of what should be done about the 'native' inhabitants of North America, that some people are so far from acquiring the capacity for self-government that they 'should simply be cleared out of the way'.[39] For a second group, the capacities for self-government may be developed but only through the compulsory imposition of extended periods of discipline, a view most influential in the history of authoritarian versions of the welfare state and in the history of colonial administration. A third group might be seen as lacking the capacities required for autonomous action for 'external reasons', such as ill health, poverty or lack of education, and accordingly the role of government should be to build up these capacities by establishing a supportive environment. Hindess suggests that in Western societies before the middle of the twentieth century, the vast majority of people were thought to belong to the second category:

> the category of those who would benefit from being subjected to authoritarian rule: the subject peoples of Western imperial rule and, throughout the nineteenth and early twentieth centuries, substantial groups in Western societies themselves. In spite of liberalism's undoubted commitment to liberty, only a minority were

[35] Hindess 2009: 2. [36] Hindess 2009: 4. [37] Hindess 2001; Howard-Wagner 2010.
[38] Foucault 2008; Hindess 2001. [39] Hindess 2001: 101.

actually governed as free individuals. Another minority – whose size is, for obvious reasons, difficult to estimate – consisted of those who were more or less successfully cleared out of the way.[40]

Reynolds's treatment of Aboriginal sovereignty, particularly in his *Aboriginal Sovereignty: Reflections on Race, State, and Nation*, has attracted historiographical commentary from a number of sources that seek to debunk the assumptions underpinning particular kinds of critiques of settler sovereignty.[41] For example, Ian Hunter argues that many of the critiques contained in Indigenous-rights historiography in the genre of the 'history of the moral nation' embody the principle that, in its origins, the nation failed to produce a just outcome and that the injustice of this act can be objectively judged in accordance with a moral-juridical principle common to both modern Australians and their colonising forebears.[42] But an alternative revisionist view of the culture of the common law is linked to this 'history of the moral nation' perspective through its shared commitment to 'presentism' – the view that past actors were governed by the same norms and purposes as their present counterparts – which permits the law to function as the transhistorical frame against which the moral history of the nation can be judged. Hunter shows how these assumptions permeate recent history writing of the British occupation and the functioning of legal reasoning within it.

The events discussed in this book allow some examination of the place of law in 'actual existing liberalism' and the discussion rejects a view of liberal political reason as containing fundamental moral principles that carry through the period since British occupation. Neither, it is argued, can these events be understood to follow a continuous advance of ideas and practices, over almost two centuries, according to some essential governing principle, or towards some final point of arrival or according to a supra-moral regime spanning the history of the nation. Rather they point to a set of contingent practices relating to specific problems of governing specific populations and the conditions under which these problems appear, from a point of view of the liberal task of governing. Events are understood as demonstrating modes of governance that accord with liberal political reason along with, over time, a rebalancing of law with discipline, regulation and normalisation.[43] Central features of this reasoning under examination here are the functioning of 'informal law' in the approaches to the regulation of children in family life, the functioning of the human sciences in constructing 'categories of persons' as a condition of governing and finally the avoidance of law and legal process in implementing administrative decisions particularly in relation to governing Indigenous peoples.[44]

In a similar vein, sociologists have sometimes argued that positing Australia as an advanced liberal state would only be possible by ignoring the 'profoundly illiberal manner' in which Indigenous Australians have been governed, such as

40 Hindess 2001: 101. 41 Reynolds 1996. 42 Hunter 2007: 139. 43 Hunt 1992: 1–38.
44 Van Krieken 1992; Hacking 1986: 222–36.

nineteenth-century protection and assimilation policies, forced dispossession, child removal, segregation and denial of land tenure, or by overlooking complex hybrid links to other mentalities of governing, such as neoconservatism.[45] Similar statements could equally be made for the manner of governing certain parts of non-Indigenous Australia. But as the elements of 'authoritarian liberalism' listed earlier suggest, liberal political reason may not necessarily demonstrate an observance of forms of rule such as autonomous citizenship. In studies of the conduct of liberal governing, autonomous individuals and individual liberty can be seen as a governmental product – the effect of interventions concerned to promote a specific 'form of life'. Hindess, for example, suggests that different conceptions of liberalism derive from a fundamental ambiguity in the liberal project. In the discourse of liberal politics, the figure of a community of autonomous individuals may appear as a given reality, serving to identify the character and limits of legitimate government, while it may be confected as a 'yet to be realised positivity, serving to define the objective for a variety of governmental projects'.[46]

It is in these conceptions that any opposition between liberal and authoritarian rationalities of governing might be regarded as highly unstable.[47] This is particularly the case when legal powers protecting liberal freedoms are given normative content by specialist knowledges in the formally non-political domains of civil society. Mitchell Dean argues that the liberal project of 'governing through freedom' entails divisions between and within populations in such a way as to require authoritarian or despotic forms of governing. Liberal government encompasses a defined legal-political order as well as a 'liberal police', a feature of liberalism that has long been noted by intellectual stances found in postcolonialism, feminism and the governmentality literatures. It is by examining 'liberal police' that we come to understand the substantive content of the self-governing individual and its 'others', which then provides a basis of liberal divisions within populations. The liberal conception of government as arising from knowledges of civil society 'feeds the authoritarian dimension of liberal government':

> [L]iberal government encompasses both the constitutionally defined legal-political order and a liberal police established by a knowledge of spheres, processes and agencies outside this domain, eg. civil society, economy, population, etc. In order to understand the authoritarian potential of liberal government we need to comprehend both aspects of the liberal order.[48]

With these formulations in mind, it is now time to look at some of the literature on the functioning of a legal/political order and the systems of knowledge that came into alignment in early governmental moves against the Indigenous owners of the country as it was being occupied. This may well prove pertinent when coming to the specifics of the architecture of state and civil society in the later establishment of the Port

45 Hogg and Carrington 2001: 58; Pavlich 2001: 6. 46 Hindess 1996: 66. 47 Dean 2002.
48 Dean 2002: 57; see also Hindess 2000; Dean 2007.

Phillip District and the colony of Victoria, which is introduced in the final section of the chapter. In the meantime, discussion of introductory conceptual presuppositions may be useful in understanding the functioning of different modalities of power exercised in relation to the Indigenous inhabitants.

DISCOURSES OF SOVEREIGNTY AND DISCOURSES OF WAR

A glimpse of Indigenous peoples in their accommodation of and resistance to the early settlers of New South Wales provides one standpoint on the exercise of power. In her account of attempts to impose sovereignty on the territory in the earliest period of occupation by British authorities, Lisa Ford documents the way colonial authorities used diplomacy as the basis of state-Indigenous relations – but when negotiation and conciliation failed, 'the colony made war'. In the period 1790–1816, military campaigns sent out to kill or capture Aborigines contained no declaration of martial law, as this would have assumed an assertion of sovereign authority over subjects or citizens.[49] In 1805 Judge Advocate Atkins suggested that though Aborigines were 'within the Pale of H.M. Protection', they could not be legally tried because they were 'totally ignorant' of the 'meaning and tendency' of British legal proceedings. He advised the governor to meet Indigenous depredations with decentralised violence 'through the formation and deployment of local militia' while the settlers were excused, in law, of charges of murder for shooting Indigenous people who stole their corn.[50] Ford argues that 'if imperial protection of Aborigines in New South Wales did not equate to jurisdiction over them, retaliation might be a legitimate response to Aboriginal violence under European principles of natural law . . . [T]he government of New South Wales did not equate settler sovereignty with territorial jurisdiction. Indigenous people marked the juridical boundaries of the colony.'[51] Instances of legal pluralism included an 'Aboriginal highwayman' who in 1815 was incarcerated for two weeks to induce him to return the money he stole, without any intervention by a court. The following year, Governor Macquarie asked outlaw Aborigines to surrender so they could be 'forgiven and pardoned', an offer Ford described as a 'jumble of diplomacy and jurisdiction' but also a recognition that Aborigines 'had yet to submit themselves to His Majesty's protection [and] had some corporate or individual choice in the matter'.[52]

At this time, in both Australasia and North America, settler administrators and judges began to understand Indigenous jurisdiction as a threat to settler sovereignty. Governor Macquarie's 1816 proclamation stated that armed individuals or groups of

[49] Ford 2010: 45. [50] Ford 2010: 47.

[51] Ford 2010: 47. Ford observes that 'protection' was a vague term used to describe the status of foreigners residing in Britain or the status of a weak sovereign under the thrall of a stronger one: 'Neither status necessarily implied the loss of individual liberties or of corporate sovereignty.'

[52] Ford 2010: 52.

Aborigines appearing near towns would be considered 'enemies' of the colony and would be treated accordingly. Macquarie asserted that Aboriginal jurisdiction could be geographically (not juridically) displaced by a new special category – the Public Peace – and that barbarous Aboriginal customs might be displaced by British law. On these terms Aborigines could not bring arms near farms or congregate in family groups without risking summary execution. Indigenous violence near farms was clearly regarded as an act of war. According to Ford, Macquarie's argument invoked a particular liberal (but nevertheless, by 1816, anomalous) iteration of the ancient laws of conquest, whereby local law subsisted until displaced by the king, although British conquest would automatically invalidate any local customary laws that were 'barbarous' or against natural law. Much of this position was enunciated in the form of an opinion from the chief justice and other sitting judges, requested by legal officers such as the attorney-general; in many cases the opinion was acknowledged as such; in many instances it was referred to as an expression of 'mere principle'.[53]

By the end of the eighteenth century, Ford suggests, Enlightenment philosophy had created a new ideological universe in which Aborigines were a people 'so savage that they were unable to claim property or to constitute political society'.[54] Throughout the nineteenth century, narratives of peril and 'fear of one's life' continued to have salience as a justifiable homicide defence in settler killings of Aborigines in the more distant Australian peripheries, when the colony could not or would not exercise jurisdiction over Indigenous peoples. The settlers had a monopoly on legal evidence, as legal practice privileged the words of 'respectable men' and relegated Aboriginal testimony to rumour.[55] At the end of that century, 'race science' constituted yet another ideological universe to buttress policies of separation and exclusion of Aboriginal populations, the effects of which are still being experienced.

So until 1836 in New South Wales, and after the settlement of Port Phillip District in 1838, law was used both as a method of 'civilising' Aborigines and an instrument of terror, but, as Ford observes, the gradual establishment of settler jurisdiction did not

[53] See for example Australian Legal Information Institute, 'R. v Ballard or Barrett [1829] NSW Supreme Court 26: Source – *Sydney Gazette* 23 April 1829': 'The Chief Justice observed, that, sitting alone, he should not like to prouounce [sic] any opinion upon a matter of so much importance; and, indeed, it would be much more advisable that an opinion should not be rendered necessary. He would state, however, that he could easily imagine cases in which the Aboriginal natives would clearly come within the provisions of the municipal law, and in which he did not consider that they would. If, for instance, a dispute arose amongst a tribe, and that they dedided [sic] it according to their own customs, and what was, in fact the ancient law of England – namely, by battle, and that one or more of the combatants were slain, such a case would, clearly not be cognizable by our law. If, on the other hand, a native, living in the town, and who, by such residence, had placed himself within the protection of the municipal law, was attacked and slain by any other native, then he conceived the native by whom he was slain would be rendered amenable to our law. These remarks, however His Honor stated, were only made in passing, and upon mere general principles. Should the case require to be raised in a formal manner for the consideration of the Court, he would have an opportunity of conferring with, and taking the opinion of the other Judges on so novel and so important an enquiry.'

[54] Ford 2010: 74–75. [55] Ford 2010: 103.

displace either Aboriginal customary law or frontier settler violence. In 1836 the complicated jurisdictional story around the case of *R v Murrell*, and particularly the decision of the jurist William Burton, finally determined the common-law status of Indigenous jurisdiction and sovereignty. Aborigines were entitled to be regarded as a 'free and independent people', but the various tribes had not attained 'to such a position in point of numbers and civilization . . . as to be entitled to be recognised as so many sovereign states governed by laws of their own', which Ford describes as 'a mix of Enlightenment stadial logic with law'.[56] Using the work of political philosopher Emer de Vattel as his main source, Burton argued that Aborigines had no property or dominion in land because, as savages and barbarians, they had not appropriated it to themselves through cultivation. He assumed also that the British sovereign protected Aborigines as individuals, not as corporate groups, and as such, under the law of nations, they fell within the jurisdiction of colonial courts and governance.

Paul Muldoon argues that if one views the Murrell case from the perspective of war, it is possible to see the extent to which the unity proclaimed through the discourse of sovereignty was in fact the victory of one 'race' over another.[57] Rather than the problem of justice in the postcolonial state lying with issues around custom and giving it proper recognition through a system of law, as some critics have argued, Muldoon's focus instead is on the discourse of sovereignty itself and the question of the so-called universality of sovereignty as a system of rule. The real problem is not so much that the 'barbarians' have not been recognised as 'sovereigns' but rather that sovereignty, conceived as a specific territorial system of rule, continues to be the measure of politics. Hence Muldoon seeks to displace the 'discourse of sovereignty' in favour of a 'discourse of war' as the main grid of intelligibility in understanding relations of power that endured in the wake of the initial colonisation of Australia. Sovereignty functions as a stratagem by which one 'race' achieves domination over another. It is in this sense that the institutionalisation of British sovereignty does not so much represent the beginning of the reign of law but rather a 'partisan victory' – a victory of a modern Western conception of politics over another system of governance that did not rely on the figure of the sovereign or the principle of territoriality.[58] So Muldoon treats *R v Murrell* as a sign of a historical conflict over law – a conflict in which sovereignty emerges as one of the tools to subjugate Indigenous inhabitants. Indeed, the Murrell case re-enacted the foundation myth of political community:

> By turning New Holland into a political nothingness and then filling it with law, Burton completed the Hobbesian metamorphosis in which the sovereign reclaims

[56] Ford 2010: 200: 'According to stadial theory, often ascribed to Adam Smith, peoples pass through four distinct stages of development based on the sophistication of their means of subsistence or economy. The means of subsistence were held to shape "manners", conduct, and the "moral" progress of a people as they passed from primitive savagery (hunting and gathering), to barbarism (pastoralism), agriculture, and finally to civilized commerce and foreign trade.' See Buchan 2005: 10.

[57] Muldoon 2008: 59–74. [58] Muldoon 2008: 61.

the state of nature for 'society'. Not only did this deny the act of conquest that was underway, it robbed the Aborigines of both the justice and intelligibility of the war they waged against it. After Murrell, *their resistance to settlement had no other language in which to speak than that of criminality*.[59]

The instructions given to Cook in 1770 were to cultivate good relations with the inhabitants and to take possession 'with the Consent of the Natives'. But consent was not really attempted, and certainly not gained. The British failure to negotiate is often attributed to the legal doctrine of *terra nullius*, but, as Kercher has shown, this doctrine was applied long after the initial occupation.[60] Buchan points instead to British efforts to represent the Indigenous inhabitants as lacking an effective form of government by drawing on particular aspects of European thought around concepts of property, society and government.[61] In seeking to determine whether Aborigines were 'uncivilised' or 'savage', and hence lacking effective forms of government, the British 'were not simply aiming at factual description but were engaged in the linguistic and conceptual representation of these peoples as subjects who could legitimately be dispossessed:

> [B]y representing the Indigenous inhabitants of Australia as lacking effective government, the British did not simply mistakenly or perfidiously fail to acknowledge pre-existing Indigenous forms of government. Rather, the very structure of their thought, and the language used to articulate it, led them to deny the possibility (at an official level) that Indigenous people could indeed possess their own legitimate forms of government.[62]

Other more political concepts of a nation such as a self-governing community were available to the British but were rejected. In 1841 Justice Willis attempted to adopt the concept as it was applied in the United States, but authorities in Sydney opposed this. Further, in *R v Murrell* (1836), defence counsel argued that Aborigines had 'manners and customs of their own' – 'in point of strictness and analogy to our law, we were bound to obey their laws not they obey ours'.[63] But notions of a more advanced, superior civilisation enabled the mainly British political thinkers to portray Indigenous peoples, especially as a consequence of their 'primitive' means of subsistence, as being in want of effective government or indeed any government at all.[64]

Much later, in the early twentieth century, the bare-life conditions of Aboriginal peoples were such that the Australian national and state governments took it upon themselves to attack Aboriginal culture and communities as a matter of policy. By that stage not all of the massacres had stopped. But the shift in relations between black and white turned in a concentrated way to the destruction of cultures, ways of

59 Muldoon 2008: 69, emphasis added. The term 'criminalizing' refers to processes whereby an individual becomes institutionally recognised as being criminal.

60 Kercher 1995. 61 Buchan 2005: 1–22. 62 Buchan 2005: 12. 63 Muldoon 2008: 67.

64 Buchan 2005: 4.

living and familial and community relations.[65] In the first instance the newly formed national government revoked the citizenship rights of Australia's Indigenous peoples in those territories where they had been left intact. Then the state welfare boards removed thousands of children from their parents and placed them in foster homes or institutions:

> The watershed cases of the 1830s ... redefined settler sovereignty as a territorial measure of authority that left little or no space for indigenous rights to property, to sovereignty, or to jurisdiction. They re-crafted plural settler polities into modern nation-states whose legitimacy was predicated on the subordination of indigenous rights. The many acts of dissolution, oppression, and marginalisation that followed were all performances of sovereignty. State legislation displaced Aborigines from their country to missions – a systematic attempt to erase indigeneity through spatial, social, and legal domination.[66]

It is possible to observe, in these manoeuvres of displacement, glimpses of a merging of sovereign and disciplinary forms of power that were made bare by the presence of the white overlord. We may also observe the category of race as becoming central to a series of questions around the constitution of political power in the colonial period, but which are occluded as these questions begin to merge around disciplinary forms of power based around science, rationality and specialisation.[67] 'The people' is replaced by questions of population and a series of questions about its wealth, health, distribution and biotechnical existence, while its attachment to 'race' becomes submerged. The constitution of specifically liberal forms of governing moves beyond the binary of 'them and us', 'Europe and its Other' to cluster around a more complicated set of concerns about life based on 'statistical probabilities and rational normative discourses'.[68] As Dutton observes, there is contained in Foucault's conception of governmentality an elaboration of a 'warlike relation' that still is 'rumbling away ... beneath political power'.[69]

CATEGORIES OF RACE AND CHILDHOOD

A recent editorial in *Ethnic and Racial Studies* by Ann Morning on the continuing use of categories of biological race in the social sciences is a timely wake-up call to researchers that not everybody 'knows race is a social construct'.[70] Given the evidence of under-theorised and ahistorical research papers appearing in high-profile social science journals arguing that 'racial categories are linked to genetically distinct clusters' in populations, Morning warns of a certain complacency among sociologists that we had 'moved beyond all that'. She notes that sociologists may well acknowledge that 'the racial and ethnic categories we live by are social constructs', while claiming there also exist '"objective", genetically distinct clusters of human

65 Broome 2005. 66 Ford 2010: 205–6. 67 Dutton 2009: 306. 68 Dutton 2009: 306.
69 Dutton 2009: 305; Foucault 2003 [1976]. 70 Morning 2014: 1676.

beings that we can impartially measure, and that serve in some degree as templates for our socio-political labels'.[71] This theoretical dichotomy echoes the commonly deployed conceptual distinction between biological sex and socially constructed gender. Yet as Morning points out, feminist scholarship offers a quite different lesson – that is, that the 'most earnest approximations of the natural world are always shot through with the social ... [T]he clusters we infer statistically are as beholden to cultural beliefs about groups, similarity and difference as the socio-political classifications enshrined on [sic] the US census.' The categories that we use 'are always ones that we fashion; they are not simply "out there"'. Morning argues that contemporary claims 'about races somehow arising out of biological groupings tell us less about our bodies than they do about the tenacity of a centuries-old search in the West to attribute social inequality to forces outside the social sphere'.[72]

This point is amply demonstrated in existing Australian research on the social and historical conditions of possibility for classifications and categories of Australian Indigenous peoples, in the period often referred to as the 'protectionist era' of Australia's colonial interventions upon the original inhabitants. Tim Rowse examines the effect of changes in the categorisation of Aborigines – from 'peoples' to 'populations' – on their demographic representation, and he takes note of how a more recent 'reformed' census from 1976 allowed comparisons between all-Australia and all-Aboriginal people for the first time.[73] He observes the manner in which social categories (such as the 'half-caste') excluded certain groups from earlier government data collections pertaining to Indigenous populations 'as they conceived them'. In a comparative study of official statistics and Indigenous peoples, Rowse and Smith identify a particular idiom of public reasoning around a concern for justice that quantifies injustice by drawing on official statistics.[74] Features recorded by colonial administrations during the protectionist era included age, sex, births, deaths and health, and whether Aborigines were from settled areas or 'beyond settlement and enumeration'.[75] Accordingly, statistics were used to problematise particular fields of governing. In this case they defined and classified as a means of exercising power over Indigenous peoples, described by Rob Watts as 'the imbrication of statistical techniques with modes of social regulation informed by social interests'.[76] Studies of this kind question whether we are confined to considering these instruments of power/knowledge as determined by the pregiven social interests that make use of them, or whether the instruments themselves shape the form and character of social governance.

Other Australian research on welfare, policing, the sciences and race provides evidence of the role of expert knowledges in governmental interventions, the specificity of institutional welfare and justice over time and the importance of

[71] Morning 2014: 1678. [72] Morning 2014: 1679–80. [73] Rowse 2012. [74] Rowse 2006.
[75] Rowse 2006: 2–4. [76] Watts 2003, cited in Rowse 2009: 195; Rowse 2006.

regional differences in governing populations. Stephen Garton's extensive social histories of New South Wales (and elsewhere) study the historical antecedents of government interventions involving medicine and madness, eugenics, policing and child welfare as contingent on the social and political requirements of the time. He shows how certain categories of personhood are historically contingent and how categories of welfare cases in particular can be shown to reflect the manner in which counting takes place and categories are produced.[77] This research provides a model for further investigating statistics and categories as historical artefacts, produced by the circumstances of their formation and use. In Queensland and other parts of Australia, as Finnane and Garton show, the creation of centralised police forces ensured a substantial state involvement not only in the business of public order maintenance but also in the business of generating knowledge of 'problem' populations.[78] For this reason historical understanding of the police role is not simply a matter of looking at criminal justice statistics. The 'contingent determinacy' of official statistics included legislative provisions which laid a large emphasis on the government of particular populations for specified social and political ends. Hence, interventions by police could include responsibility for ensuring school attendance, monitoring the fate of illegitimate infants, removing Aborigines to their assigned mission stations or reserves or in observing, restraining or battling 'juvenile larrikins'.[79]

Instances of 'making up' categories of Indigenous peoples are demonstrated in studies of the assumptions accompanying the removal of Aboriginal children from family and community through the powers of the Victorian Board for the Protection of Aborigines (BPA) delegated to it under the Victorian Aborigines' Protection Act 1869.[80] The initial colonising of Victoria was in some ways distinctive in that there were far fewer convicts compared with the colony of New South Wales and the occupation was swift because of fewer geographical obstacles (such as the Blue Mountains west of Sydney) and the abundance of rich grasslands for sheep grazing. At the time of settlement of Port Phillip District, the Whigs in government in Britain and also the Clapham Sect, an influential group of humanitarians and evangelicals, were pressuring the then Liberal government to assist emancipation of African slaves in the British West Indies. The Clapham Sect then looked to Indigenous peoples throughout the British Empire, establishing a select committee to call for better protection and attempts to ameliorate the effects of British colonialism on those peoples. Their influence in Victoria was to try to protect Aboriginal people from the 'murderous onslaught' experienced both in Victoria and in other parts of the country.[81] The Victorian Aborigines' Protection Act (1869) was the first protection legislation drafted in Australia or anywhere else in the British Empire, and it was used as a model in other Australian colonies and Indigenous populations in Canada and New Zealand.[82]

77 Garton 1988. 78 Finnane and Garton 1992. 79 Finnane and Garton 1992: 63.
80 Hacking 1986. 81 Broome 2005: xxiii; Davies 1987.
82 Victoria Aborigines' Protection Act (No. 349) 1869; Nanni and James 2013: 46.

STRATEGY, TACTIC, MANOEUVRE, COMBAT

In Victoria during the mid- to late nineteenth century, the colonial government established a series of encampments in the form of church-run missions and stations for Aborigines. Almost forty years after the settlement of the Port Philip District, they had become sites of rigorous and systematic attempts to destroy families, economic independence and Aboriginal identity. The missions produce evidence of a disciplinary regime, along the lines of a reformatory or prison, as well as evidence of a resistance to white sovereignty, which, to use Muldoon's phrasing, had no other language to speak than that of criminality. The activities of the Board for the Protection of Aborigines in the colony of Victoria, built around disciplinary routines and penalties, were framed in language deriving from various Victorian acts pertaining to Aborigines.[83] The board's actions, and those of its officers at the coalface of day-to-day implementation of administrative decisions were consistent with the conduct of war – strategy, tactic, manoeuvre and combat. This is evidenced in the machinations of the BPA as it sought to implement a series of measures, imposing categories which denied Aboriginal identity to some, in turn closing off their access to the missions and hence dividing families and communities, and breaking up familial relationships. Moreover, these actions were willed rather than determined by contemporary ideological shaping, as statements of political adversaries evidence. Many contemporary observers understood the claims to British sovereignty over the country to be a fiction.

The encampments or missions were established ostensibly to 'protect' the remaining survivors of the British occupation, which had reduced the original inhabitants from more than 15,000 in 1834 to fewer than 3,000 in 1851, and by the 1920s to about 500 people.[84] Students studying early 'massacre maps' of the killings in the 1830s in the Western District and in the vast sweeps of Gippsland in eastern Victoria peer in disbelieve as there remains so much silence about the human cost of taking the land. Keeping in mind the previous qualifications about interpreting the results of the counting, official statistics are premised on accounting for a range of definitional issues regarding Aboriginal identity, including the counting of Aboriginal children, since after the passing of the 1886 Aborigines Protection Act, known colloquially as the 'Half-Caste Act', most people of mixed Indigenous and non-Indigenous parentage were no longer formally categorised as Aborigines.[85] There were an estimated thirty cultural-language groups made up of hundreds of clans or land-owning groups composed of perhaps 60,000 people before the European arrival.[86] The policies of protection after the mid-nineteenth century were seen to be motivated in part by what was seen to be the inability of the authorities to safeguard Aboriginal people from settler violence and secure access to schooling and other services in the face of

83 Hunt 1992: 1–38; Hunt and Wickham 1994; Rose and Valverde 1998: 541–51.

84 Campbell 1994; Broome 2005: xii.

85 Victoria The Aborigines Protection Act (No. 912) 1886; Read 2003.

86 Broome 2005: xxi.

European resistance. On the other hand, as Richard Broome suggests, the motive may have been to convince the British government to allow pastoral settlement to go ahead on the southeastern coast. Sandor observes that a major objective of placing on reservations a population of tuberculotic and otherwise unhealthy Aborigines was to minimise the health risk to Europeans – the Port Phillip Association had set down its aims for protection as 'the civilization of the native tribes ... and pastoral pursuits'.[87] But whatever the motives, at least three-quarters of the Aboriginal population in the Port Phillip district died during the period of 'protectionism'.[88] Broome claims the influence of so-called humanitarians and evangelicals led to the only treaty ever offered to Aborigines in Australia, later retracted by the Colonial Office, and to the establishment of the first protectorate legislation enacted by a colonial government, a unique Aboriginal administration and a network of Aboriginal reserves and missions.[89]

A Central Board to watch over the Interests of the Aborigines in the Colony of Victoria was established in 1860, based on an earlier protectorate formed in 1838, to act as guardian and protector of Indigenous people in the colony. With the passing of the 1869 Aborigines' Protection Act it became the Board for the Protection of Aborigines (BPA). The 1869 protection act provided a legal definition of those to be deemed 'an aboriginal' and hence who fell under the remit of the BPA: 'Every aboriginal native of Australia and every aboriginal half-caste or child of a half-caste, such half-caste or child habitually associating and living with aboriginals, shall be deemed to be an aboriginal within the meaning of this Act.'[90] In 1877 a royal commission was appointed to investigate increasing rates of Aboriginal mortality as well as allegations of mismanagement at the mission stations. A new Aborigines Protection Act of 1886 redefined Aboriginality, giving the board new powers to discriminate against those subsequently classified as half-castes, who were increasing in number and cost. Only according to a list of exceptions were half-castes 'deemed to be aboriginals'.[91] Thus began a period of governance of the Victorian Aborigines,

87 Sandor (unpublished) 1990: 3. 88 Andrews 1963. 89 Broome 2005: xxvi.

90 Victoria Aborigines' Protection Act (No. 349) 1869 s 8.

91 Victoria The Aborigines Protection Act (No. 912) 1886:

> 'The following persons shall be deemed to be aborginals within the meaning of the Principal Act: –
>
> Every aboriginal native of Victoria.
> Every half-caste who habitually associating and living with an aboriginal within the meaning of this section has prior to the date of the coming into operation of this Act completed the thirty-fourth year of his or her age
> Every female half-caste who has prior to the date aforesaid been married to an aboriginal within the meaning of this section and is at the date aforesaid living with such aboriginal
> Every infant unable to earn his or her own living, the child of an aboriginal within the meaning of this section, living with such aboriginal
> Any half-caste other than is hereinbefore specified who for the time being holds a licence in writing from the Board under regulations to be made in that behalf to reside upon any place prescribed as a place where any aboriginal or any tribe of aboriginals may reside Victoria.'

lasting until at least the 1970s, which Broome describes as culturally the most dangerous: the breaking up of families, removal from land, denial of Aboriginal identity and closely supervised surveillance and correction.[92] The takeover of land and the spread of European settlement continued across the colony of Victoria; at the same time, rates of morbidity and mortality among Aborigines increased and remained very high into the present day. The costs of maintaining mission stations rose. Public utterances of officials during this period reflected the racial thinking of the period but as Broome and others have shown, a number of political leaders privately confessed to the 'usurper's anxieties about ownership' – as recently as the early twentieth century Victorian Premier John Murray wrote that 'though the white man may have a legal right to the land, we must not forget that, after all, in a higher court, the blackfellow would be able to establish a much stronger moral right to the land than any of our white friends who own them today'.[93]

However, in the absence of this 'higher court', the imagery of liberal government was to maximise the freedom of subjects and to govern through this freedom – a freedom which we will discover was full of caveats. One of the many effects of the missions was to deny sovereignty in relation to Aboriginal peoples, or at the very least maintain a certain ambivalence by means of a 'protectorate', while establishing relations of force over populations considered part-Aboriginal. As an element of a genealogy of self-determination,[94] liberal governance thus set about defining and separating out a so-called half-caste population and then obliging this population to be free to join the labour force and compete in the marketplace. This obligation to observe the discipline of the market was founded not on a discourse of sovereignty and law but rather on political economy and the discourse of norms. A code of normalisation refers in this case to the field of human sciences, which incorporated theories of race.[95] Underpinned by the designation of some Aboriginal populations as non-Aboriginal, and achieved through the establishment and expansion of the system of encampments and subsequent separations within them, the fate of Aborigines could appear as an expression of individuals' actions in the world rather than as an expression of race war. And resistance to these attacks on identity and culture similarly could appear as individual, isolated and non-political – for example, an expression of individual criminality – if the resistance referred to the 'action of the norm' rather than a response to political domination.

The more mundane management of Indigenous peoples on the missions provides glimpses of how resistance came to be translated according to liberal forms of governing.[96] The office of the BPA was located in the City Bank Chambers in central Melbourne; in 1890 its chairman was the chief secretary in the Victorian government, and the members consisted of members of the Victorian parliament, educationists and an assortment of senior public servants. Albert Le Souef, for example, was director of

[92] Broome 2005: 185–206. [93] Broome 2005: 199. [94] O'Malley 1998: 159.
[95] Foucault 2003 [1976]: 38. [96] O'Malley 1998: 158.

the Zoological Gardens, and Alexander Morrison was headmaster of Scotch College, a leading Melbourne private school. The board exercised close and ongoing connections with each of the missions spread around the colony and provided detailed instructions and guidance on matters of staffing, funding and rules over the movement of the inhabitants of the missions. A minister of religion usually held the position of manager of the mission and reported to a general inspector and secretary, though into the twentieth century, management would be secularised. Schooling, religious services and work on the mission were the daily routine, and a daily 'roll call' was conducted.

From the 1886 act and its regulations, and in the records and correspondence of the BPA, it is clear that a number of strategies were put in place during the last decades of the nineteenth century and the early twentieth century to try to draw the different Aboriginal groups into a dependent, perhaps supplicant relationship with settler society. This was attempted through a range of strategies that problematised fundamental elements of life-politics – the constitution of Aboriginal identity, the control of bodies and spaces in which Aboriginal people would live and labour and the placing into 'darkness and silence' the possibility of alternate powers to assert Aboriginal possession and occupation of the land.[97] As in the first protection act of 1869, the 1886 act stipulated that the government had the authority to make regulations 'for prescribing the place where any aboriginal or any tribe of aboriginals shall reside'. The board was given full power to execute the regulations. Regulations under the act stipulated that Aborigines on the mission were required to perform work in order to draw rations: 'Every able-bodied half-caste and aboriginal, residing on a prescribed station shall do some reasonable amount of work, and any one persistently refusing to do so when required shall have his supplies stopped until he resumes work.'[98] The board instructed its managers and agents on the missions that Aborigines were required to 'provide for their own wants': 'it is not intended that the Aborigines should derive their subsistence wholly from the liberality of the Government and, indeed, the sum voted for the supply of stores each year is inadequate to provide for their wants'.[99] By the turn of the twentieth century there were six missions spread across the colony. The board tried with limited success to close many of the missions and transfer 'the blacks' to a single station in a remote area of the state at Lake Tyers. Regulations pertaining to the 1886 act forbad people deemed half-caste access to the mission stations and their families, which had the immediate effect of separating family groups, reducing the productiveness of the missions and denying Aboriginal identity. The purpose was to 'merge' these Aborigines with the white population. With the anticipated 'dying out' of the so-called full-bloods, this tactic

97 Foucault 2003 [1976]: 70.

98 Victoria The Aborigines Protection Act (No. 912) 1886 s 8; Victoria 1890b (BPA): 24, Appendix II, Aborigines Act 1890 – Regulations (Reg. 6).

99 Public Records Office of Victoria (PROV) VPRS 1694 Unit 1: Circular, Board for the Protection of Aborigines (BPA) to Station Managers and Agents 19 Sept. 1896.

would remove the Aboriginal population – it would, to recall Hindess's words, 'simply be cleared out of the way'.[100]

The records of the BPA indicate that one of the first signs of 'trouble' and criminality to emerge in the context of a policy of removing those deemed half-caste from the missions was the young half-castes 'hanging about' the missions when they were supposed to be 'merging'. Evidence from the board's records on this and related subjects will be discussed more fully in Chapter 4 and will show that trouble making was consistently depicted as the kind of activity that put at risk the government's aim of reducing the size and number of missions. Aborigines who challenged the imposed divisive categories of aborigine/half-caste as inscribed in the 1886 act (neither is afforded the status of a proper noun) – young half-castes, for example, who refused to leave the mission surrounds, and their families who supported them – acted contrary to this or that regulation pertaining to the act. And regulations pertaining to the act were amended and supplemented periodically so as to 'capture' this or that kind of behaviour to bring troublemakers under the remit of the law. For example, a new regulation might be brought in to prevent families from sharing their rations with youths who were 'sent off' the mission as half-castes, but who persisted in 'hanging around' the mission boundaries. It is in these terms that the reader might begin to interpret Muldoon's claim that Aboriginal resistance to white settlement 'had no other language in which to speak than that of criminality'.[101] Throughout the period, systems of security underpinned by law (in the case of the Northern Territory, the 'legal' segregation of persons defined as Aborigines beginning with the Northern Territories Aborigines Act 1910) established a juridical combination of law and regulation that gave protection officers direct powers over basic life circumstances and, in particular, attempted control over procreation.[102]

Scientific views of the superiority and inferiority of races had become prominent among some Europeans as a rationale for the 'clearing away' of those referred to as the full-bloods. Once again, the translation of race science requires a local, practical engagement with the particular circumstances of the Australian colonial setting.[103] What came to be taken as a given in science shifted in the nineteenth century to accommodate a range of perspectives on the origins of Australian Aborigines and their likely destiny. There is evidence that environmentalism influenced early nineteenth-century ethnographers' views on the condition of Aboriginal people, indicating that their supposed lack of sophistication and civilisation was due to the inadequacies of their environment, while towards the end of the century the view that Aborigines were different in their 'natural' capacities and were remnants of an about-to-be extinct race became more prominent.[104] But throughout the nineteenth century, the focus of scientific attention was on the origins and significance of racial differences in Indigenous people as these might

100 Hindess 2001: 101. 101 Muldoon 2008: 69. 102 Howard-Wagner 2010: 221.
103 Anderson 2009: 4. 104 Hindess 2001: 103.

affect the future of the white race in the new settlement in Australia. In the lead-up to World War I, many scientists were convinced that Aborigines were the remnants of an earlier Caucasian invasion which had either eliminated or absorbed the first inhabitants and hence provided the groundwork on which to speculate about the white race in the antipodes. Anderson observes that the doctors who were drawn to Aboriginal studies seemed to be more interested in discerning racial types and tracing human genealogies than in recording the 'pathophysiological mechanism' that led to Aboriginal demise on contact with the white invader. But many did not countenance the continued deterioration of the Aboriginal population. Scientific inquiry may have accepted that culture derived from inherited racial capacities rather than historical circumstances, and that 'race struggle' shaped history. But many were also alert to the Lamarckian dynamic evidenced in Aboriginal peoples' rapid adaptation to local needs. Rarely were early Australian doctors driven to an uncompromising hereditary view of the Aboriginal condition, and most supported and argued for the view that 'a change in environment would change the race'.[105]

Nevertheless, contemporary observers were appalled at the effects of white policies on Aboriginal health. In the 1870s both the chief medical officer and later the premier of Victoria argued that appalling sanitary conditions were causing the high sickness and death rates on the Coranderrk mission, rather than the preferred explanation that Aboriginal diseases were unique to Aboriginal people, or that the people themselves were responsible because they could not look after themselves.

There was an international scandal about Australia's policies of Aboriginal child removal in the 1920s and 1930s when mission educator and activist Mary Bennett, in her 1933 paper to the Dominion Women's British Commonwealth League in London, denounced the removal of Aboriginal women and girls as 'akin to slavery' and as contravening the League of Nations Covenant and Slavery Convention.[106] At a number of different times and places from the 1860s, the racism shown to Victorian Aboriginal peoples was acknowledged, called out and opposed by significant members of the Victorian establishment. But at the same time, in many governmental circles and administrative elites, the situation of Victorian Aboriginal peoples was treated with wilful blindness.

In the following decades, the government sought to construct rationalities of rule shaped from ideas of assimilation, and then self-government, in contexts of continuing dissent. For example, the period between 1967, when a constitutional amendment allowed Indigenous people to be counted as citizens and new policies advocated self-determination, and 1996, coinciding with the election of a conservative coalition government, is regarded as a 'discursive break' in the history of Indigenous affairs. Language changed; new entities and categories were brought into being. But the language of self-determination and autonomy, as Howard-Wagner observes, was largely a federal government 'construct', which

[105] Anderson 2002: 67. [106] Paisley 1997; McCallum 2007: 29–40.

in effect allowed any tentative moves towards Indigenous self-government to be declared later as simply a failure.[107] These moves helped provide the political conditions for attempts to turn agency (or blame) for the circumstances of their existence back upon Aboriginal peoples themselves.

107 Howard-Wagner 2010: 223.

2

Knowing the 'Neglected' Aboriginal Child

A precursor to the first Aborigines' Protection Act (1869) was a Central Board to Watch Over the Interests of the Aborigines of the Colony of Victoria, constituted by a vote of the Victorian Government Assembly and by command of the governor. The board was set up to

> Advise the Government as to the amount of public moneys to be voted . . . to control the expenditure of such moneys . . . to recommend the proclamation of reserves . . . to supply rations [etc.] . . . to recommend the appointment or removal of all agents, officers or local committees in connection with the said Board; and to direct and control the duties of all such persons.[1]

The board operated without the benefit of an act for the first decade or so. It first met in June 1860 and its first annual report was published in the 1861–62 session of Parliament. At first it consisted of a Central Board and a number of reporting local committees, but this proved unwieldy; by the time of the first report, the local committees had been replaced by a number of 'honorary correspondents' appointed 'in those districts most frequented by the Aborigines'.[2] The recommendation of a Select Committee in 1858–59 led to a new era of Aboriginal missions and reserves established on Crown lands during the 1860s under the control of the Central Board, which was given authority to prescribe where Aboriginal people could reside, the work contracts in which they could be engaged, how their earnings might be distributed and how the care and custody of their children should be managed.[3] The board was answerable to the chief secretary (a position equivalent to a present state premier), but it had little ministerial oversight; even though it had little contact with or knowledge of Aboriginal peoples, it had virtually free reign over their lives on the reserves.[4]

A fundamental issue facing the newly appointed Central Board was that of population – in particular, how many Aborigines resided in the lands then occupied by the settlers, as well as those supposedly residing outside these occupied lands.

[1] Victoria 1861 (BPA): 34. [2] Victoria 1861 (BPA): 3. [3] Nanni and James 2013: 12.
[4] Attwood 1986.

Early on, the board had received a suggestion from the duke of Newcastle to carry out Florence Nightingale's plans to obtain 'accurate returns as to the diseases, sanitary condition, or the progress of education' to ameliorate the condition of the Aborigines in the various colonies under the British Crown. But the board considered such an endeavour premature, and perhaps too unreliable:

> The Board could give a statistical statement, but it would probably mislead. As the honorary correspondents in most cases have enough to do in relieving the physical wants of the blacks, it would be impracticable to obtain accurate returns as to the diseases, sanitary condition, or the progress of education; and it is not proposed, therefore, to call upon them to furnish returns in the form suggested by Miss Nightingale.[5]

The board was concerned that previous counts had possibly overestimated the 'decline' in the Aboriginal population. The first count, in 1862, reported 2341, the following year, 2165 and the year after that, 1908 Aborigines. However, for reasons not reported, and with a curious use of language, the board noted that a careful reading would perhaps show that the decrease 'is not very rapid, *considering the position which the Aborigines occupy in the colony*'.[6] The first was a very 'rough' count and the board conceded that some tribes were included in the survey that should have been omitted. The report instead recommended a study be conducted by the board's honorary correspondents, who had 'a number of Aborigines under their control' and were hence more reliable: 'This method will show that, having regard to the past circumstances of the blacks, the decrease is not startling.' Nevertheless, a one-off scan of births and deaths across several regions gave some cause for concern and set in place a pattern that would continue: 'amongst 642 Aborigines residing in the area, there had been thirty-nine deaths and thirteen births. This decrease is alarming, and very painful to contemplate, but there is reason to believe it has received a check.'[7]

Immediately following its constitution, the board, finding itself confronted by a dearth of information about 'the black population', distributed a circular to a number of honorary correspondents, including 'wardens, police magistrates and respectable settlers', for information 'as to the numbers, condition and location of the Aborigines'.[8] It was effectively a census of the Aborigines in certain defined areas, which distinguished adult males and females and children, the names of their tribes and where they frequently congregated. The board asked its correspondents questions about whether inducements would encourage 'the natives' to follow pastoral or agricultural pursuits and whether the settlers would recommend 'a reserve for use of the aborigines: if so to what extent and in what part of your locality'. Replies in some cases listed the numbers of men, women and children. A table summarising the information was published in the board's second report. Responses about the names of tribes were deemed fairly useless. The circular asked for information on 'their

[5] Victoria 1864b (BPA): 12. [6] Victoria 1864b (BPA): 13, emphasis added.
[7] Victoria 1864b (BPA): 13. [8] Victoria 1861 (BPA): 4.

moral and social condition' such as their means of livelihood, whether or not any of them were 'employed as servants by the settlers', and whether or not such servants resided during the whole of the year by their employers, and if during only part of the year for how long. And had means been used to impart religious, moral or secular instruction, and if so with what success. As noted, this first census revealed 2341 Aborigines:

> In nearly every case the correspondents state that they congregate around public-houses, in towns where there are public-houses and on the goldfields. Where there are neither goldfields nor towns they frequent the stations of the squatters. They appear to neglect to a great degree hunting and fishing, and prefer the populous districts of the white man to the solitude of the forests and plains.[9]

Replies from the honorary correspondents recorded that schooling was seldom offered and generally had failed. Some 'black children' had received instruction, 'but as they become older their indolence and carelessness prevented anything like improvement'.[10] Health problems were thought to result from 'sexual excess' which rendered the Aborigine 'weak in constitution and deficient in stamina, and consequently more liable to disease and less able to bear it ... [It] is a painful but well-known fact, that about townships and gold fields prostitution is their too frequent mode of obtaining a livelihood, as a proof many of the children are half-castes.'[11] The only means for benefitting Aboriginal people was 'to induce them to part from their children and educated them in Melbourne'.[12] A settler named Chauncy spoke from his experience bringing up an Aboriginal child in Western Australia – no attempt would prove successful 'unless the children be completely separated from their own people, by sending them to the school at Bombay or some other place where colored [sic] children were taught and the climate was suitable'. Another, George Russell wrote the following:

> [T]he young of both sexes should be removed from their tribe, educated and taught industrious pursuits in establishments for the purpose, situated in a distant part of the country from where they had previously been located. I think from 2 to 12 years of age would be the most suitable time of life to carry out the system if adopted.[13]

Lewis Gilles recommended the formation of a depot in connection with an already existing government establishment, at which Aborigines could receive occasional supplies of stores and make their wants known: 'the moral condition of the young half-caste and other natives could only be better by their entire separation from their native friends'.[14] The reference to Aboriginal health was never far from a discussion of morality:

[9] Victoria 1861 (BPA): 14. [10] Victoria 1861 (BPA): 18 (J. Wileski).
[11] Victoria 1861 (BPA): 30 (T. Goodwin). [12] Victoria 1861 (BPA): 20 (C. Hughes).
[13] Victoria 1861 (BPA): 19–22 (P. Chauncy, G. Russell). [14] Victoria 1861 (BPA): 20 (L. Gilles).

> The present generation is not equal to the former; the old people are finer, stronger, and better able to endure fatigue; as one remarked to me a short time since, in former times, 'before whitefellow come, blackfellow could run like emu; but now, supposing big one run, then big one tired, and plenty heart jump about; and always like that blackfellow'. Many of their best customs and most stringent rules, in regard to the young people, have been weakened and broken by the introduction of the evil habits of vicious white men; and the young men, being more intelligent, pay less regard to the old men, and follow their own sexual desires to the full extent. The young women are even more sensuous, and reckless of future consequences.[15]

In this early surveying exercise, the board requested no specific information on 'half-castes' even though the term was used often in the settler responses. Nor was the term applied in the Governor's Command under which the board was constituted. Half-castes at this point were not distinguished in any of the tabulated statistics or figured as of particular concern. In the context of the information received from its honorary correspondents, the board made a number of recommendations, including that the governor be given 'full power to order . . . as to the disposal of orphan and deserted children'. There was no mention of this specific cohort among the correspondents' replies to the board, but some settler-correspondents were particularly concerned about half-caste children, as shown in the responses of settler-correspondents Strutt and Glass:

> They have neither the wish nor the application to learn anything requiring much trouble. The half-caste children might possibly be improved, if placed in an early period under European influence exclusively, but if left as at present, to their own inclinations and mode of life without any restriction, the whole race will speedily become extinct. The great difficulty experienced in bringing up and teaching a young aboriginal is occasioned by the interference of the older blacks in taking away their younger relatives from the Europeans who have been endeavouring to educate them. If this interference could be effectively prevented, the efforts of individuals to improve the condition of the young blacks and half-castes might be more successful. It would however be difficult to prevent the older blacks from intimidating those who are under European care, as they would not hesitate to kill those natives who refused to accompany them in their wanderings.[16]

The view of the Aborigines as vulnerable was consistent with reports from the 1830s on establishing early protectorates, such as the one established near the Goulburn River at Michellstown, where Assistant Protector James Dredge had reported 'great difficulty in keeping drunken policemen and other Europeans from having intercourse with Aboriginal women'.[17] But thirty years on, the white settlers' views as reflected in the board's survey held the Aboriginal people themselves responsible for their 'moral' problems.

15 Victoria 1861 (BPA): 11, 30–31 (T. Goodwin).
16 Victoria 1861 (BPA): 22 (C. Strutt and R. Glass).
17 Clark 2013: 1.

The settlers' language was used to name and describe almost every aspect of Aboriginal people's lives including Aboriginal identity itself, to be inscribed in governmental terms. Recall from the previous chapter the definition provided in the first protection act:

> Every aboriginal native of Australia and every aboriginal half-caste or child of a half-caste, such half-caste or child habitually associating and living with aboriginals, shall be deemed an aboriginal within the meaning of this Act.[18]

Nanni and James observe that the 1869 act defined Aboriginal people culturally as a 'shared way of life, rather than 'racially'.[19] Also, a regulation pertaining to this act, which for years had been urged by the board, now permitted the forced removal of children: 'the Governor may order the removal of any Aboriginal child neglected by its parents, or left unprotected, to any of the places specified in Regulation I, or to an industrial or reformatory school'.[20] As becomes clear, removal of Aboriginal 'neglected' children was facilitated by a categorising of the entire Aboriginal population as neglected. But a caveat added to the clause on who was to be considered an Aborigine stipulated that 'at the hearing of any case the justice adjudicating may, in the absence of other *sufficient* evidence, decide on *his own view and judgement* whether any person with reference to whom any proceedings shall have been taken under this Act is or is not an aboriginal.[21] Hence the caveat allowed 'evidence', 'view' and 'judgement' as to who was and who was not to be deemed an Aborigine. Justices were permitted to read 'signs' of Aboriginality; discriminations could to be made. This imperative might well have provided the conditions of possibility for a more fully fledged 'science' of colour to emerge – as a methodological way of distinguishing who was Aboriginal and who was not, or perhaps even degrees of Aboriginality.

So while it is possible to say at the time of the board's formation at the beginning of the 1860s that little was known about the Aboriginal population in Victoria, in another sense the Aboriginal population was already known. The board and the honorary correspondents regarded the population through an anthropological or quasi-anthropological lens that had emerged in the preceding decades; the lens provided a quasi-scientific authority to its reasoning and affirmed its practices. The texts of these early reports are 'shot through' with allusions, some more direct than others, to an already anthropologised 'race',[22] although the question of just where it 'fitted on the scale marked out by the ethnologist' might be open to question.[23] A pivotal question of the *degree* to which the Aborigine could be civilised, given 'his' nature, had already been established. Answers to questions on the health, morality, education and life chances of the Aboriginal child were contingent on a judgement of Aboriginality. That was now *the* question – the (scientific) ground from which to

18 Victoria Aborigines' Protection Act (No. 349) 1869 s 8.
19 Nanni and James 2013.
20 Victoria 1871 (BPA): 33, Appendix X, Regulation 13.
21 Victoria Aborigines' Protection Act 1869 (No. 349) s 8, emphasis added.
22 Morning 2014: 1679.
23 Victoria 1864a (BPA): 11.

proceed – and the board explained its operations and aspirations within the bounds of that question. It featured in its first reports the story of the futile attempts to civilise a 'pure Australian': the child named Bungeleen, providing an illustration of the likely 'fate of the blacks'.

TESTING FOR THE 'CIVILISED CHILD'

Thomas Bungeleen was the son of 'the celebrated captive chief of Gipps Land' who had survived a massacre – an 'aweful destruction of Aboriginal life' – wrought in the name of rescuing a white woman. She was not found, and the chief and his 'two lubras' were taken hostage and put in the native police barracks at Narree-Narree-Warreen, whence the chief was chained to a tree for several days and nights, imprisoned, and then 'died of grief'. The two women and two children were sent to Merri Merri Creek Mission School very close to Melbourne: 'The young lubra inhumanly went away from the mission station, with a mob of blacks, leaving her two children behind. She soon became diseased, and died about eighteen months afterwards at an encampment at the junction of the Diamond Creek and the River Yarra Yarra.'[24] One could possibly identify some irony in the selective description of 'inhuman' action in this account. But an administration's actions upon this group, civilised or otherwise, were not the subject of the board's scrutiny – the baby Bungaleen was. The story of the baby, taken at six months, was presented as a test case for the question of the potential of the 'pure Australian' to become civilised:

> Thomas Bungeleen presents all the marks of the pure Australian, and in mental capacity, disposition, and character, is probably a fair type of the race . . . Before the Board undertook the care of him, some attempts had been made to teach him drawing . . . but all the gentlemen who had kindly taken an interest in his welfare, and endeavoured to teach him, concurred in stating that his want of application rendered any improvement quite hopeless: he was found to be averse to labor, and all those inducements which operate on the European were wanting in him . . . Here, in the case of this young Aboriginal, an opportunity seemed to be presented to the Board of proving to the world that the Aborigines of Australia are degraded rather by their habits, than in consequence of mental capacity.[25]

Perhaps, as the board's report suggested, a stint at the Grammar School in Melbourne would make Bungeleen an Aboriginal leader ('the highest usefulness as an agent in dealing with the Aboriginal race'), but the school refused to grant him a place: 'Nearly all the Aborigines are . . . prone to amusements, and they dislike work and restraint of every kind: of a happy, playful, kindly nature, it is questionable whether any of them are capable of sustained labor, such is a requisite to obtain knowledge to fit them for the business of civilized life.'[26]

[24] Victoria 1861 (BPA): 8. [25] Victoria 1861 (BPA): 18. [26] Victoria 1862 (BPA): 8–9.

Young Thomas was then sent to the hulk C.S.S. *Victoria* under the care of Captain Norman, but his conduct continued to be 'most unsatisfactory'. He was 'wholly deficient in the qualities which belong to a sailor'. When it was necessary to inflict punishment, he exhibited 'the mental peculiarities of some varieties of the African race – stolid indifference': 'He "sulks"; and however severe the punishment might be, it would produce no effect. This characteristic, if joined to other qualities, would not be a mark of inferiority; but he lacks the *amour proper*, that personal pride and desire to be thought well of, without which mental progress is impossible.'[27]

By 1865, Thomas 'Bungelene' (the spelling had changed in the board's report) was pronounced dead from 'gastric fever'. He had worked in the board's office in Melbourne – 'a hope was entertained at one time that he would become a useful member of society; but owing to defects in his early education or a natural propensity to evil, he became nearly as troublesome in the office as he was on board the *Victoria*'.[28] Such was his epitaph!

Throughout the rest of the decade, the board reported on knowledge of the 'customs and habits' of the Aborigines that reflected living at close quarters and a kind of well-meaning, amateur anthropology. Mr Thomas as guardian of the tribes around Bourke, Mornington and Evelyn furnished an account of their 'customs and habits' and honorary correspondents were requested to furnish 'complete sets of native weapons and utensils, so that records of this interesting people may be preserved for the ethnologist'. It seemed the die was cast. The secretary of the board promised to furnish a report which embraced 'a concise account of their customs, with drawing of their nets, utensils &c.; a description of their warfare, with drawing of their weapons &c., and advantage will be taken of all facts collected by physicians and surgeons who have examined the frame of the Aboriginal'.[29]

The board's quasi-anthropological knowledge of the Aborigines as a 'race' was fed by the responses of its honorary correspondents to its requests for information regarding their moral and social condition. Mr Chauncy reported that the moral and social condition of the Aborigines 'can scarcely be worse than it is':

> In their pristine state the natives were a merry, independent, thoughtless race, but with few temptations to vice. Thieving was scarcely known among them, and intoxication not at all. Among their virtues personal courage and affection for their offspring were common. I have often known them to be generous, patient, and attentive to each other's wants, and in Western Australia they are noted for being remarkably honest and trustworthy.[30]

Mr Edgar reported: 'The moral condition is low; the men addicted to intemperance, the women to prostitution, thus contracting and fostering disease which forbids increase, and is fast hastening their extinction as a race.'[31] C. A. Reid wrote:

27 Victoria 1862 (BPA): 14. 28 Victoria 1866 (BPA): 18. 29 Victoria 1861 (BPA): 10.
30 Victoria 1861 (BPA): 14. 31 Victoria 1861 (BPA): 15.

> Their moral and social condition has never been improved: they are no further advanced in civilization at the present time than they were fifteen years ago, and I am afraid, owing to their stupidity and ignorance, and their great desire for a wandering life, that they will be no further advanced in fifteen years to come. In fact I am of the opinion that, in the course of a few years, the race will become almost totally extinct in this district.[32]

A. M. McRea wrote:

> I would beg to call attention to the half-castes – a very interesting race. When Police Magistrate in Gipps Land, in 1852, I saw one there in her 18th year, who had been taken from her parent – the mother an aboriginal – at 8 or 9 years of age, by an excellent lady ... in Gipps Land. This girl was of a good size, well made, and of a very prepossessing appearance. Mrs Davis had herself given her a good plain education, and had made her, as I was informed, a very efficient house servant. In the witness box, where I first saw her, she satisfied me that she was perfectly well acquainted with the obligation of an oath. She gave her evidence honestly and clearly, and in a long and trying cross-examination never once contradicted herself. As this girl is, I believe, *a fair specimen of this race*, it is surely most desirable that they should be separated, if possible, from their aboriginal parents and assigned to persons known to and approved of by the Board. I would not recommend that any of the half-castes should be sent to stations, unless after the strictest enquiry, and then males only. The females, I would suggest, should be assigned to private families in or near towns, or away from the haunts of the aborigines and the contaminating society of old hands.[33]

Last, Rev. Speiseke from Lake Hindmarsh had furnished 'a very interesting diary ... showing the occupation of the blacks on the station from sunrise to sunset' and the board commented that it was 'gratifying to observe that habits of industry are inculcated and encouraged, lending probability to the hope that at no distant day the young Aborigines may become so far civilized as to be able to maintain themselves in decent comfort without much help from the Government'. The board concluded:

> [I]n their native wilds ... they possess the qualities and affections which lead to the exercise of humanity and forbearance ... but once attempt to bound them within the restraints of civilization, and all their weaknesses appear. They are idle, beyond the ordinary sense conveyed by that description, when to work is not an immediate necessity; they are careless, uncertain, under circumstance wanting in true courage; and they have no self-respect. It is not, therefore, to be expected, that in two years the Board should have produced any marked change in their condition. *They are, indeed, but helpless children*, whose state was deplorable enough when this country was their own; but is now worse, for they have adopted all the vices of the superior race, and gained nothing from the exhibition of its virtues ... If the Aboriginal is destitute of the qualities required for a higher position amongst his fellow men, his

[32] Victoria 1861 (BPA): 16. [33] Victoria 1861 (BPA): 22, emphasis added.

> race will soon disappear, and the burden will grow lighter year by year. But if the young can be trained to the habits of industry, there are numerous employments which they can follow with advantage to the State.[34]

The euphemisms eventually fell to one side and designation of 'Aboriginal' and 'half-caste' started to appear in the reports of the Board for the Protection of Aborigines. It was the usual practice of the board, in its early years, to afford the term 'Aborigine' the status of a proper noun in its reports, though not in the correspondences between the board and superintendents of the missions. The practice was not common among the board's honorary correspondents, as can be seen from their responses to the board's questions. It was also common practice for the words 'aborigine' and 'aboriginal' to be used interchangeably, the latter inscribed in both protection acts of the nineteenth century, though as discussed in this and the previous chapter, the two acts differed in their definition of 'an aboriginal'. In later decades it was common for the board to revert to using the lower case in its reports. It was not until well into the second half of the twentieth century that 'Aborigine' became standard nomenclature within all reports and correspondences of what was then the Aborigines Welfare Board. Shifts in nomenclature testify to the initial and ongoing instability of these administrative categories.[35]

Questions around identity – who was an Aborigine – continued in the counting regime of the nineteenth century. The BPA in Victoria was required to report to the government on the control of moneys voted for Aborigines and to appoint local agents to administer them. The board in fact was given very little money and initially no specific legislative powers, issues it constantly urged the government to rectify throughout the 1860s, especially regarding matters concerning Aboriginal children.

The board called for further information from its correspondents on the need for medical assistance and 'whether or not in your opinion (having regard to their habits) such assistance would be generally beneficial'. Several correspondents, we recall, considered education to be of little use to Aboriginal children given their ostensible indolence and again, a majority of respondents reported that medical assistance was of little avail 'except in extreme cases where the patient is prostrate'. As with education, correspondents reported that Aborigines' habits were the underlying cause of their health problems. As noted previously, 'sexual excess' was purported to render the Aborigine more susceptible to disease. Sometimes a native doctor was called in, 'who, by charms and the use of native herbs, induces the blacks to believe that their diseases may be cured'. In sum, opinions received across the colony 'bear testimony to the awful mortality amongst them'. Tables of mortality and birth rates in the Yarra and Western Port districts (those areas closest to Melbourne) from 1839

34 Victoria 1862 (BPA): 6, 14–15, emphasis added.

35 The term 'Aborigine' when used by the author is, unless otherwise indicated, an inclusive term and refers to a people upon whom colonisers attempted to impose various confected distinctions: aborigine/aboriginal/black/Black/native/half-caste/quadroon/octoroon/full-blood/part aborigine and so on.

to 1859 recorded 210 deaths against 28 births. The respondents were undecided on whether people should receive rations – 'what good can we do by making them beggars? I think none' – while responses on pastoral pursuits were divided: 'The evidence of the correspondents is conflicting . . . Some suppose that their indolence and carelessness would prevent their following pursuits requiring attention and labor: others believe that they would readily engage in agriculture if facilities were offered.'[36] The few specific references to children from these correspondents beyond those already cited are similarly varied: a boy working as a cow-herd, a female aged about ten adopted by a respectable townsman, 'a most intelligent and good girl'.[37]

Following its presentation of information from its correspondents, the board provided a list of its own opinions, concluding with the view that 'permanent reserves should be made for blacks' and that the act relating to Aborigines should be amended to 'give Your Excellence full power to order as to their residence and maintenance', and 'to order also, as to the disposal of orphan and deserted children'.[38] The kinds of information gathering through census and the reports on 'the condition of the Aborigine' from those on the ground served to underpin interventions formally placed into legislation. The following section shows how these legislative moves in turn authorised decisions about removing children from families and communities, setting the conditions later in the century for the construction of a specific problem of the 'neglected Aboriginal child'.

THE ABORIGINAL AND NON-ABORIGINAL NEGLECTED CHILD

There is scant reference to any Aboriginal children in the pages of correspondence from 'respectable settlers' of the colony of Victoria at this time, and strangely almost no reference at all to the matter which the board said required urgent attention – 'orphan and deserted children'. A general consensus seemed in place for programmes to remove the young for training in 'habits of industry', sometimes with special reference to the half-caste and some success stories about bringing up an Aboriginal child in European ways were recounted. There had been 'troubling cases' about 'orphans' even before the board was appointed, such as repeated applications to the government for land by a man named Banfield in Benalla 'on behalf of an aboriginal or half-caste girl living in the locality'. The board investigated, discovering that she was living in a public house, but when attempts were made to have her removed to 'an asylum', the board found because she was 'an orphan' it had no control over her whatever.[39] Lack of legislative clout to act on children was recognised from the outset. The problem of the Aboriginal child took another turn regarding 'the orphan and destitute', when the board responded to the news that the government had struck down funding for schools. This measure had

36 Victoria 1861 (BPA): 18–26. 37 Victoria 1861 (BPA): 16. 38 Victoria 1861 (BPA): 11.
39 Victoria 1861 (BPA): 9.

been intended for Aborigines to be taught 'useful occupations, so as to have fitted them for employment as servants':

> [T]here are many neglected black and half-caste children throughout the Colony, who are utterly uncared for, and in all probability, if steps be not taken to rescue them, they will become as idle and as depraved as the worst examples of the white population. The latter element in our population, the half-castes, though numerically small, are increasing, and it is a serious duty to interfere at once to prevent their growing up amongst us with the habits of the savage, as they possess the instincts, powers of mind, and altogether different constitution of the white man.[40]

Importantly, the word 'neglected' was used in reference to the Aboriginal population as a whole, such as 'the neglected condition of the blacks in Victoria'[41] and 'the neglect and cruelties which, in past years, have reduced the number of Aborigines'.[42] In this sense the neglected Aboriginal child features as a condition of being Aboriginal, a point made by Robert van Krieken in his study of children during the early settlement of Sydney.[43] As will be shown in Chapter 3, the non-Aboriginal neglected child was marked out as different from the rest of the non-Aboriginal population, but not so the Aboriginal 'neglected child'. Hence, while the vocabulary of 'neglected child' might be shared in reference to both populations, there are differences in the way neglect was figured from the very beginning of governmental attention to the problem.

It is worth exploring this differentiation a little further, given that the board was raising its concerns on the eve of the implementation of the first piece of child welfare legislation directed at white children in Victoria, where categories of vulnerable children were formally differentiated.[44] Neglect was being thought out and defined in the settler city, a number of acts were introduced and then fell by the wayside, and numerous inquiries were carried out.[45] Although at the time contentious and unsettled, the term 'neglect' for the whites was increasingly being thought about in terms of the government's management of the vagrant and the offender, and principally in the context of the prevention of crime. A problem was framed that saw the 'innocent' destitute and orphaned child bracketed off as an object of philanthropy. Jaggs's account distils the 1862–63 Municipalities and Charitable Institutions Report, whose recommendations she claims were to be definitive for government policy for the rest of the century. It recommended strongly against the introduction of any provision which might offer financial support to impoverished people as a right, and in favour of discretionary relief through local charity. However, it exempted from this the general categories of 'neglected' (i.e. vagrant and uncontrolled) and 'offending children', on the grounds that 'ignorance occasions crime' and the peculiar circumstances of the colony 'made it necessary for policing and

40 Victoria 1861 (BPA): 10–11. 41 Victoria 1864a (BPA): 11. 42 Victoria 1864b (BPA): 14.
43 Van Krieken 1992; Attwood 1989.
44 Victoria Neglected and Criminal Children's Act (No. 216) 1864. 45 Jaggs 1986.

education to be administered by the central government'.[46] For the settler population, the problem of neglect was produced out of a problem of parental abandonment – one of the ways of knowing the white 'neglected' child is that it will bear the signs of parental abandonment, inscribed in the 1864 Neglected and Criminal Children's Act as 'found begging . . . found wandering . . . not [having] any home'.[47] As foreseen in the Charitable Institutions Inquiry and by a range of critics of the establishment of government institutions for neglected children, the problem which the management of neglect would have to confront and overcome was the impediment of the parents' all-too-readiness to put their child to government care: 'parents would be encouraged to abandon their children if they knew the state would provide for them'.[48]

So the governing of parents in the white settler society assumed the need to prevent abandonment of children, adopting policy settings that discouraged such action by providing evidence of the negative consequences of parental abandonment. In contrast, in the contemporaneous figuring of the problem of the neglected Aboriginal child, the 'giving up' of children was actively encouraged by government; parental refusal to abandon the child was a serious problem and an impediment to governmental aspirations. Evidence hardens also of increased differentiation of Aboriginal and half-caste children and on the question of 'disposal'. The board later reiterated its desire for information from its honorary correspondents on 'any neglected Aboriginal children amongst the blacks under their care who should be maintained and educated by the Board'.[49] It reiterated a call for legislation authorising 'the removal of half-caste girls and orphans against the wishes of those persons who may have assumed charge of them'. It acknowledged that 'the blacks are reluctant to give up their children. They are, usually, very kind to their offspring, and they are jealous of any interference with them by the whites.'[50] By the time the board finally received legislative power to act, in the form of the 1869 protection act, the half-caste girl had emerged as a particularly morally charged subject, existing in more ways than one as a 'borderland' figure.

THE ROYAL COMMISSION 1877: COLOUR, BLOOD, ABSORPTION

A royal commission was established to answer questions about the continuation and sustainability of the Aboriginal stations and indeed to questions about 'the future of the race' – its 'absorption' or 'extinction'. Its agenda reflected the morbidity and mortality rates of the time but begged comparisons between systems of managing Aboriginal and non-Aboriginal children. As discussed in the Chapter 3, by 1877 the white child was subject to a policy of 'boarding out' with other white families, along with a critical attitude towards children's homes, especially barrack-style institutions. Establishment

[46] Jaggs 1986: 175. [47] Victoria Neglected and Criminal Children's Act (No. 216) 1864 s 13.
[48] Jaggs 1986: 175. [49] Victoria 1864b (BPA): 10. [50] Victoria 1864b (BPA): 10.

of free, compulsory and secular education was also well in hand, and the commission was to explore the question of the suitability of extending this to the Aboriginal children. Related questions about extending state education to the Aboriginal mission stations were examined, including the problem of children seeking work beyond the missions and how their education fitted them for this work. How much and what type of education did Aboriginal children need? What were their learning capacities? In terms of educability, how did the half-caste compare to the 'real aborigine'?

Perhaps the overriding question for the Royal Commission was whether and how to 'responsibilise' the Aborigine, and this would lead the commissioners to pursue questions about Aborigines' attitudes to their children – in particular their degree of 'attachment', their bonds of affection and their willingness to be separated from them. The commissioners appeared to be curious as to whether or how an Aboriginal 'family' could be spoken about, and if so, how it was constituted. Were there advantages in encouraging adult men to seek paid employment outside the missions and stations? What were Aboriginal attitudes to children's schooling – were the parents responsible enough to recognise its advantages? Though the commission presumed 'we are bound . . . to encourage family life amongst them', it seemed also to recognise the multiple contradictions involved in various managerial aspirations. How to encourage a patriarchal family structure when there seemed little of this – with only poorly paid work on stations, supporting a family likely meant separation from wife and children.[51] Forceful separation was an ongoing topic of investigation – we are told more than once that nobody (or very few) wanted to force understandably painful separations – and the commission questioned how willing Aboriginal parents were to be separated from their children for the sake of education. So the management of the 'natives' would need to be a balance of persuasion and inducement. The commission talked about trying to induce Aborigines to abandon their 'wandering life' and come onto the mission stations, which could be encouraged by taking their children and providing food and clothes at the station only if people remained there. The impatience of the royal commissioners is palpable:

> [COMMISSION:] What hope, then, can you entertain of their coming on the station if you continue to pander to their desires and hold out inducements to them to continue their wild and savage life, and remain off as they naturally would? What reasonable hope can you entertain of their coming to these new stations if they were established? – [C. OGILVIE:] They might look on it as a benefit for their children, and if once you get hold of the children, the old people might come to visit them.
>
> [COMMISSION:] Is it not a greater cruelty to get hold of the children, and then force the mothers to come and visit them: would anything justify the separation of the mother from the child? – [C. OGILVIE:] That is another question.[52]

[51] Victoria 1877 (Royal Commission [RC]): Minutes of Evidence (ME) 3.

[52] Victoria 1877 (RC): ME 6 (Christian Ogilvie, pastoralist and former inspector and secretary to the BPA).

Mission manager Reverend F. A. Hagenauer was questioned about why Aborigines from the Murray River region would go to Gippsland, so far away from their home country. Hagenauer agreed it was difficult – 'it takes years to persuade them'– but the idea of placing them faraway in Gippsland 'would dissuade them from returning to the Murray'.[53] He described the movement of people onto the stations as a power to 'break off bad associations'. Parents 'wandered about' with children and the amount of red tape involved 'to get such a child back again, to appoint a place for it' was a bugbear for the superintendents of the stations. Rev. John Bulmer, manager of Lake Tyers station, gave evidence that many men had been induced to come to his station because they were 'dying off in the Manaroo by the measles ... and thought they would be safer on the station, and, also, that they wished to bring their children to school'.[54] Rev. Alex Mackie had been regularly conducting services at Coranderrk mission and was questioned about Aborigines' attachment to their families:

> [COMMISSION:] Do you think from your experience of them, they have a great attachment to the wife and child? – [MACKIE:] I think they have a very great, but not the same kind of attachment as civilized Christians have. I think it is more a blind sort of attachment. I do not think they would agree on any consideration to separate from their children. For instance, the girls, who are either black or half-caste, if they have children, what would be called illegitimate children, I think they would never dream of exposing them or abandoning them ...
>
> [COMMISSION:] You think any scheme which involved the separation of mother from child would not be justifiable? – [MACKIE:] I think not.
>
> [COMMISSION:] And opposed to the natural feelings of both mother and child? – [MACKIE:] I think so. At the same time, those children who have very little black blood in them, being reared in Coranderrk, the father of them ought to be made to support them, and they may not be a burden on the State. There are cases there where the children are almost white, and the mother nearly white, and where the mother knows the father very well.
>
> [COMMISSION:] Youths approaching manhood? – [MACKIE:] I think when they get three or four years old they are left very much to themselves. I think the attachment I spoke of between mothers and children only extends to infants. I think after they are weaned and independent of the mother there is not the same attachment.

Mackie hinted, perhaps, at possible agreeable separations, at the behest of a question from the commission:

> [COMMISSION:] Does that attachment exist between the father and the child? – [MACKIE:] Well, there is a good deal of affection between the father and the children, but not nearly to the same extent (as with the mother).

[53] Victoria 1877 (RC): ME 40–50. [54] Victoria 1877 (RC): ME 50.

> [COMMISSION:] When you speak of 'would not desert them', are there instances where they have, and, apparently, if they are satisfied with the person to whom they can entrust them, they appear to let them go willingly? – [MACKIE:] My experience is that they are very attached to their children, the mothers even where the father is not known.[55]

Murdoch MacDonald, convener of the Presbyterian Church Committee on Missions to the Heathen, acknowledged that he had little acquaintance with the stations – he visited one station Ramahyuck for eight days. He produced evidence for the commission arguing for a 'village' structure, divided into small farms 'and allotments assigned to each family'. Heads of families would then elect an 'overman' to manage the station under the oversight of the superintendent. A Rev. Hamilton told the commission that Aborigines had abandoned their own tribal law regarding marriage. Coranderrk's collection of various tribes 'from the force of circumstances have cast aside their marriage laws'. However, when the commissioners enquired whether Rev. Hamilton was aware what their marriage laws were, he replied, 'Their tribal law I am not very clear about; I have looked into it, but not for a considerable time.'[56]

John Green, superintendent of Coranderrk since its opening in 1861 until 1874, gave the commission his views on persuading parents to give up their children:

> [GREEN:] In some cases at Coranderrk I got the children even freely given up by the mothers, and then afterwards they followed themselves.
>
> [COMMISSION:] From infancy and childhood, because after that the children would be of use to them? – [GREEN:] No, they would never give up a girl if she was ten or twelve years of age readily.
>
> [COMMISSION:] No, nor a boy either, I should think? – [GREEN:]Yes, a boy readily.
>
> [COMMISSION:] At any age? – [GREEN:] Yes, at any age if he was away from suckling, when he was weaned.
>
> [COMMISSION:] Do you think they have any strong or any very strong affection for their children? – [GREEN:] Yes, very strong.
>
> [COMMISSION:] Up to what age? – [GREEN:] Even to manhood.
>
> [COMMISSION:] It is difficult to reconcile what you state with their giving up those children aged from four to six if they had strong affection for them? – [GREEN:] Yes, because I persuaded them that they were better off with me than exposed to strong temptations as they would be there.
>
> [COMMISSION:] How do you reconcile your getting the child away from the mother with the assertion that they have very strong affection for the children? We have evidence that they have very strong affection for their children while infants, then it seems to weaken again, and we then understand that that affection must strengthen again on approaching the age of puberty? – [GREEN:] No, the girl is generally betrothed, and hence the influence to keep her.

55 Victoria 1877 (RC): ME 53. 56 Victoria 1877 (RC): ME 71–75.

[COMMISSION:] Do you think it is injudicious to supply them with rations and clothing off the station? – [GREEN:] Yes: coax them on and get them on, and get them to work and earn their food and clothing. They will work well if they are well led, and they will not be driven. No man can drive them; you must lead them.

[COMMISSION:] Do not you think they would be more content in the neighbourhood where they were bred and born, than having to go 200 or 300 miles? – [GREEN:] Yes; but there are so few in any locality. If you form a station at Wodonga there are perhaps only ten or fifteen blacks there.[57]

Testimony given to the royal commission around the disposal of children also revealed some of the assumptions relating to Aboriginal children and their place in families and communities. Those in charge of inspection or superintendence of Aboriginal stations presented the commissioners repeatedly with the assertion that when it comes to Aboriginal children, the categories of 'orphan' and indeed 'destitute' were misnomers. The commission had to entertain the possibility that Aboriginal orphans were not orphans at all. Rev. Bulmer said the station Aborigines did not regard orphan children any differently from other children:

[BULMER]: There is no fear of an orphan child being destitute, because when a child loses its father it has another father, who takes up himself the care, and loves the child as much as the parents. They would not like to see that child removed from the station. They call it their own child. A child always has two fathers and two mothers, or five or six, perhaps.

[COMMISSION:] He is not an orphan really? – [BULMER:] He is not an orphan, not in that way. In fact, they are more indulgent to him, from the fact that he has lost his own father or mother. They are very kind altogether to their children, so that, according to the views of the natives, there are no orphans at all.

[COMMISSION:] Was their answer unanimous disapproval to that? – [BULMER:] The blacks disapprove of their children being taken.[58]

Here too, the inquiry was confronted with the limits of attempting to shape responses within a framework of 'family responsibility', with all its attendant non-Aboriginal assumptions of practices and understandings, and it found itself grappling with the resultant confusions and contradictions. On the disposal of 'orphans', the problem of how to understand the status and nature of the half-caste came to the fore. Terms such as 'real aborigine' and 'pure-bred' pepper responses to questions as to the wisdom of boarding out. But what were the consequences and effects of this kind of assertion (or admission) that there were 'no orphans'? It would seem, should they have cared to reflect on management practices to date, that this kind of assertion would seriously question the legitimacy of the board's own management practices – which was its emphasis, from the time of its first report in 1862, on collecting the 'orphan and destitute' as an important reason for its existence.

57 Victoria 1877 (RC): ME 83–85. 58 Victoria 1877 (RC): ME 49.

The attitude of Aboriginal adults towards so-called orphans, given that it was voiced by station superintendents, would seem to suggest that they themselves invested in this lack of distinction. The suggestion is strengthened by references in the reports of the BPA throughout the 1870s to 'orphans' houses', 'children's houses' and 'dormitories' attached to schoolhouses. These references reveal that station management itself did not clearly distinguish between how it managed 'orphans' and how it managed other children. That is, non-orphans inhabited orphan's houses and orphans inhabited 'children's houses'. Rather, the emphasis was on separating all children from parents as much as possible within supervised living and schooling accommodations.[59]

The commission entertained the possibility of adopting a practice of 'boarding out' orphans, a practice well established for white children. Christian Ogilvie had been a settler and pastoralist for thirty-five years when he appeared before the commission, having agreed that he had observed the habits and customs of the Aborigines 'in their natural state' and also held the office of general inspector and secretary to the BPA for more than eighteen months. In the minutes of his evidence, Ogilvie was asked questions that pointed to the line of inquiry on 'boarding-out':

> [COMMISSION:] Have you known, in your experience, a single instance of a young native adopted, if I may so speak, by a person and educated and trained and taught, who did not relapse into his savage habits, one who continued steadily pursuing the life of a civilized European, after being taught and trained as well as any European in his station would have been? – [OGILVIE:] No.
>
> [COMMISSION:] How would you deal with the women and the girls? – Something the same as the orphan schools. Boarded out? – [OGILVIE:] No, educated on the station and made fit for service in a very good house; she would be hired out to some highly respectable mistress.[60]

Rev. Heinrich Stähle, superintendent at Lake Condah station in the western part of Victoria, on whether orphan children should be boarded out from the station: 'I say, "No, unless it can be proved that they are not properly trained and cared for on the stations. Besides this, they have relations among the aborigines on the stations who are almost as much attached to them as if they were their own children."' Boarding out of Aboriginal children was opposed by the station superintendents because of the dangers forecasted from previous experience. Stähle said 'they should be self-supporting on each station; and if part of them were raised on the station, and others brought up outside, they would not agree well together, in their future life'. According to Stähle, those brought up among the whites 'would consider themselves superior in such cases – the young men from outside selecting wives on the station or the young women getting husbands'. Besides, he noted, there was sufficient proof

59 See Victoria 1872 (BPA): 6; Victoria 1875 (BPA): 5, 9, 16; Victoria 1878 (BPA): 8; Victoria 1879b (BPA): 8.

60 Victoria 1877 (RC): ME 3.

that Aborigines who had been taken away from their 'native countries' and their own people, and educated among whites, had, in the course of time, been sent back to the mission stations, or else they had fallen into the hands of the lowest class of the population. Stähle concluded: 'An aboriginal will always be considered an aboriginal, and have too little chance to rise in any respectable society, so he must fall back to the lowest class. It is the same with a half-caste.'[61] The children simply would not prosper away from the stations. Hagenauer, the superintendent from Lake Wellington, gave a couple of examples:

> Colonel Anderson had a little boy, who for a little while was a pet in the house; but he grew disobedient, and after a time they could do nothing with him. He was a very wild child. His parents had been shot in Queensland, where he was rescued. I was asked to receive the boy, and he is now getting on very nicely in every respect; and the arrangement is that after he has passed the standard he is to be given back again; and no doubt he will go on very well after that . . . Captain Phillips, a squatter in the western district had one. The child was prospering very well; got a good education, and was in every way looked upon as a child of the family, but when she came to a certain age – thirteen or fourteen – the black nature got so strong in her that her mistress was glad to get her to my place out of temptation, away from the men on their station. I could give many other similar instances.[62]

The view that Aborigines on the mission stations were almost as much attached to orphans as if they were their own children was amplified several times by the superintendents:

> [HAGENAUER:] I remember one case of a little child who had been adopted by a white family which turned out at eight years of age a wicked little child, and the man who adopted it brought it before the police and wanted it sent to Sunbury [Industrial School]. I went to the police court and saw the child, and the natives whom I had explained it to besought me not to let the little black child be sent to Sunbury. The child was handed over to me on the guarantee that it would be cared for.
>
> [COMMISSIONER:] How did the natives know of this? – [HAGENAUER:] They know of every one [sic] in the district.
>
> [COMMISSION:] Did they themselves speak to you? – [HAGENAUER:] On every account they begged me to go and get the child, and she is turning out a useful girl.
>
> [COMMISSION:] There cannot be a doubt that it would be a mistake not to cherish that affection? – [HAGENAUER:] Yes.[63]

Hagenauer's account of his successful intervention, in this case, in an attempt to have an Aboriginal child placed in an industrial school raises the question of how

61 Victoria 1877 (RC): ME 14–17.
62 Victoria 1877 (RC): ME 35.
63 Victoria 1877 (RC): ME 39.

many other Aboriginal children found their way into children's institutions by indirect means, and other than at the behest of the board.

The Rev. Carl Wilhelm Kramer at Ebenezer Station in the Wimmera received his instructions from the Moravians headquarters in Saxony, Germany. Kramer had been in charge for fourteen months and was of a similar view about boarding out orphans. On the stations Aborigines would adopt orphans as their own, whereas if boarded out they became 'unmanageable' and wanted to get married. William Goodall, superintendent of Framlingham Station claimed they would not like to have the children taken away: 'They feel it very keenly . . . they would protest against it very loudly, and it would also tend to the dismemberment of the station.' In fact, it was the children who were the principal attraction to the old ones: 'I have had old ones wandering out till I got children they had an interest in.'[64]

Murdoch MacDonald returned to the commission with a prepared response from his Presbyterian Committee:

> [T]he committee have the strong conviction that it would be unwise, in view of the weakness of moral purpose still characteristic of the aboriginal race, to board out the orphan children. It would be extremely difficult, they apprehend, to find persons who would take an interest in their spiritual and moral well-being as would justify their guardians – the Board for the Protection of Aborigines – in entrusting them to their care. In the most favorable circumstances there would be great danger of the girls going astray; and even in the case of boys, the probability is that they would grow up with the feeling that they were regarded as aliens, if not as inferiors, and thus be tempted to contract pernicious and degrading habits.[65]

Mr Edward Curr, chief inspector of sheep in the colony, was considered adequately experienced and knowledgeable about why boarding out would be unsuitable:

> [CURR:] Those who have gone through the process have learnt to copy rather the vices than the virtues of the white man, and have become less desirable citizens than they were. Persons who advocate boarding out do so, I believe, with a view to that measure aiding in the absorption by the whites of this colony of the remnant of our black population ... This absorption to my mind is a mistake – there is no absorption in the case and I think never can be; substitute eradication for absorption, and I think you will be correct. The history of other similar races points to this conclusion. Where are the fifteen thousand blacks who inhabited this country forty years ago? Have they been absorbed? You cannot make the blacks like us. A black can never become one of us; his color will not alter, nor his propensities.
>
> [COMMISSION:] Until they die out? – [CURR:] That they must die out is, I think, a foregone conclusion. Were they as valuable as short-horned cattle, or merino sheep, there would be no fear of their dying out. The fact is we have pretended but never really wished to save them from extermination. The Anglo-Saxon in Australia, as elsewhere, does not foster weakly races. He wants their lands.

64 Victoria 1877 (RC): ME 65. 65 Victoria 1877 (RC): ME 74.

> He is thinking of riches. He tramples them under foot without noticing what he does. But I know no physiological reason why our blacks should die out.
>
> [COMMISSION:] They are changing color very fast at any rate? – [CURR:] That may be.[66]

Finally, John Green, former superintendent of Coranderrk, presented a prepared paper arguing against boarding out 'unless they were quadroons, in that case I think it would be well to try the boarding-out of orphans':

> In many cases the quadroons are so white and so unlike the aborigines that none would know them (but an expert) to be related to the aborigines. I have two in my family, and any stranger coming to my house never thinks but they are my own children; they are very likely to get amalgamated with Europeans.[67]

QUESTIONS OF COLOUR, DISPOSITION, RACE

The 1877 royal commission was dealing with the future of the younger generation of Aborigines – 'youths' or 'lads', 'girls' and among them an increasing number of 'half-castes' – some of whom a decade and a half on from the board's inception had grown up on the mission stations and were approaching or had reached adulthood. What was to be done with them? Running through the whole inquiry was a question of where and how to locate Aboriginality. In the board's assessments and statements at around this time, 'color' had come to the fore as a consideration and a means of categorising where it had previously been subordinated. Now, whatever the specific topic of discussion, questions of colour were increasingly entertained, concentrated in those parts of the commission that turned to the disposal of older Aboriginal children. Did Aboriginality lie in colour so that the absence of colour associated with so-called quadroons would allow them to pass as 'whites' and hence to be absorbed; or did Aboriginality lie hidden beneath deceptive appearances, at some deeper more fundamental level of 'nature', such that despite appearances they would eventually reveal their Aboriginality? Was half-caste-ness to be understood, in an emergent discourse of absorption, as a virtue, a potential?

An ambivalence came to the fore throughout the inquiry. The question for the commission was about the vitality of the Aborigine, and it was asked often about comparisons between white, 'half', and 'full', with race itself increasingly expressed in terms of quantity. At other times responses were couched in the language of what, for want of a better term, could be called disposition – character, morality, savageness. Human vitality was concerned with essential elements and powers to sustain life as an organism and was used to define and quantify race. The commission asked for (and sometimes received) quasi-scientific comparative measures of vital capacity – voiced in terms of energy,

66 Victoria 1877 (RC): ME 77. 67 Victoria 1877 (RC): ME 82.

capacity for sustained effort, power of endurance, steadiness of character and so on – that *sound* quantifiable, measurable, and it seemed to beg for confirmation that these capacities existed in isomorphic relation to the *full* black, the *half*-caste and the *three-quarter* white:

> [COMMISSION:] You complain of want of steadiness and application. Do you find this defect existing as strongly in the half-caste as in the blacks? – [STÄHLE:] Yes ... When I drew the average of our aborigines I could produce as many aborigines as half-castes who showed a certain intelligence and improvement.[68]

The period was one where there were signs emerging of a set of measures of Aboriginality, measures which in many instances were inseparable from concerns about economics and productivity. These signs appeared around the question of sending out young Aboriginal people for work and apprenticeships. Old hands such as Inspector Ogilvy at the board wanted all adults to leave the stations to search for work, and thought that it should be compulsory for youth of both sexes to be apprenticed to 'responsible masters and mistresses' once their education was completed. The stations should never be closed, so as to deal with sickness or distress, or with the young when wishing to visit their parents or friends during the holidays: 'I think by apprenticing the youth a great advantage would be made toward the absorption of the whole race into the general community eventually.' Ogilvy would not recommend closing off any opportunity for learning a trade, treating Aboriginal children in the same way as white children. On the children who took up education and then returned to the station losing what they had gained, Ogilvy claimed this was because they were 'still in contact with savage life on the station'. But others calculated the situation differently, arguing no Aborigines would be capable of carrying on a business on his own account, unless with a responsible party. Stähle added that when they came home, 'they would most likely consider themselves superior to the others, but yet they would be obliged to marry an aborigine and would at the same time consider them below them, and this might create unhappiness in family life'.[69] The commissioners wanted to know whether a 'want of steadiness and application existed as strongly in the half-caste as in the blacks'. Some of the officers and superintendents thought it all depended on the families they were allocated to, some thought the whites were as 'unsteady' as the blacks and half-castes. Halliday at Coranderrk regarded the girls as good cooks and seamstresses but if sent out as domestic servants they would require 'very good' overseers, such as clergymen. Parker at Echuca considered they would always require supervision 'as long as the original natives are in existence. It may not be so as regards the half-castes.'[70] Pressed on why the half-castes would not succeed on their own, Parker claimed they did not have the 'perseverance'.

[68] Victoria 1877 (RC): ME 18. [69] Victoria 1877 (RC): ME 1, 2, 18.
[70] Victoria 1877 (RC): ME 24, 33.

Hagenauer remained doubtful that the present generation would be able to live independently:

> [COMMISSIONER:] I refer to the possibility of the native himself going out and supporting himself off the station altogether, and living as a European would do, maintaining his family from his own work, and bringing them up properly, educating and training them? – [HAGENAUER:] I answered that yesterday, to the effect that I do not think it could, because he has not sufficient stability in his character; on the stations they are under continual care.[71]

Hagenauer also considered the half-caste was often worse than the full-black Aborigine 'in the want of energy' but there was not much difference – 'we have some very good half-castes on the station, and I believe by-and-by they will be superior'.

Most of the superintendents believed the disposition and habits of the Aborigines would prevent most of them from learning trades, running businesses and becoming self-supporting. These kinds of aspirations would result in serious effects on their health and stood against their being 'naturally and instinctively of a restless nomadic habit'. The argument mostly put forward to the commissioners was that Aborigines would find the whole business difficult and would require supervision, especially 'after hours', and that because middle-class people shunned Aborigines and would not associate with them, the Aborigines would be driven to associate with the 'lower grade ... and the tendency is to degrade them by the company they have to keep'.[72] There were few significant differences between the full blood, half-castes and quadroons when it came to schooling, but Green at Coranderrk thought the quadroons might be boarded into 'nice families where they are orphans, for I think in some cases they might ultimately get amalgamated with Europeans, for they are so white and so unlike the aboriginal in caste that they cannot be readily detected, and hence they can associate with Europeans freely':

> [COMMISSIONER:] They may be more than quadroons, they may be octoroons? – [GREEN:] No, I know the family well; the father was married to a half-caste woman.
>
> [COMMISSION:] But can you trace the line back? – [GREEN:] Yes, I know the whole line; her mother was a real aboriginal.
>
> [COMMISSION:] You attribute the probability of their relapsing into bad habits to their being shunned by the ordinary white class, and thus being driven to low company? – [GREEN:] Yes, that is principally it.
>
> [COMMISSION:] Then their physical appearance is of importance, with the quadroon or the octoroon, the less he is like a native the better the chance of success? – [GREEN:] Yes.[73]

[71] Victoria 1877 (RC): ME 44. [72] Victoria 1877 (RC): ME 66, 84.
[73] Victoria 1877 (RC): ME 84.

EDUCATING THE ABORIGINE

The previous discussion looked at the ways in which measures of Aboriginality could be produced around the idea of disposition and habit – conduct exhibiting energy, effort, steadfastness and so forth. Here, the commission was most interested in the Aboriginal child's capacity for learning, in the 'power of learning' and 'intelligence', especially in relation to the white population. Clearly, once there was a state system, with state inspectors reporting on progress across the whole system, a system was then in place that allowed for standardised comparative measures, a calculation referred to in the bureaucracy as the 'Inspector's Percentage'. School and schooling were understood as means of drawing children and adults into the confines of station life. The BPA noted that the school-cum-boarding house was increasingly understood as a means of separating children from Aboriginality as it was variously understood, within the confines of the station. That is, separating children from parents seems largely to have been worked at by means of the school. Schooling and compulsory education were also implicated in the responsibilisation of Aborigines – especially how compulsory schooling could impinge on relations between adults and children, older and younger generations. Schooling also raised questions about the comparative educability of the Aboriginal child.

Many of the commission's witnesses observed that Aboriginal children made as much progress grasping the elements of education as those of English parentage. The superintendents of the stations and their wives clearly took some pride in their pupils and their results 'which we are warranted to expect from earnest Christian work and skilful management'. But religious influence on morals aside, the superintendents were supportive of having state schools take charge of schooling on the stations because it provided a vantage point to assess the educational development of the Aboriginal children on the stations compared with other children. Hagenauer explained that once the Victorian attorney-general made appropriate legislative changes, 'black children can be educated like any other children'. The benefits of state education were that an inspector would come to examine the children, relieving the board and its officers of this responsibility, but also that the schoolteacher would be accountable. He was confident that state education would also pose no challenge to religious teaching carried out on the stations under the authority of the superintendent. Bulmer at Lake Tyers queried the need for a teacher to be proficient in native languages since most of the blacks understood 'broken English' and claimed the blacks developed understanding more quickly than European children. However, 'they do not care about books as a rule, and unless they are forced to write they are sure to lose what they have learned'.[74]

In answer to the commission's question, 'What distinction do you observe between the half-caste, the simple half-caste and the aborigine?' Alexander Mackie reflected on

[74] Victoria 1877 (RC): ME 36, 51–52.

the impressions he had formed of different levels of intelligence between a black woman and half-caste man, in an account of a recent marriage at which he had officiated: 'he had received no instruction, and could neither read or write, but he was a very intelligent man naturally. He knew what he was about in everything that I told him; but the woman herself seemed thoroughly dark, could comprehend hardly anything.' At the same time he perceived few differences between young half-castes and Aboriginal children, and between Aboriginal and European children: 'I find they answer as well as any white children in any of the common schools in the colony.' Kramer, with seven years' experience teaching at Ramahyuck station, reiterated that the native children would reach a standard of 'white children of the labouring classes' and the 'half-caste are [sic] a little smarter'. Superintendent Goodall's wife taught at Warrnambool and Goodall himself found 'the blacks much more intelligent than the whites'. The schoolmistress at Coranderrk said the same thing in her examination by the commission, adding that the Aborigines did not have the strength of mind to withstand the temptations of living with white families 'where they would be watched like young children. I count the oldest of them just like a child of four of five years.'[75] The commission became intent on pursuing the question of the relative educational success of various levels of Aboriginality as this was defined by the ancestry of the children – full-bloods, half-castes, quadroons and octoroons – with the implication that skin colour affected their acceptability to white educators and hence their educational progress. How else to make sense of this conversation with James Deans, schoolmaster at Coranderrk:

> [COMMISSION:] There are a number of half-castes amongst the children? – [DEANS:] A great many.
>
> [COMMISSION:] Are any whiter than half-castes? – [DEANS:] Yes, decidedly.
>
> COMMISSION:] How many that you could consider quadroons? – DEANS:] About a dozen I should think.
>
> [COMMISSION:] Any whiter still – octoroons? – [DEANS:] One or two I should think . . .
>
> [COMMISSION:] What I want to get at is how many of those children might be casually mistaken for white children? – [DEANS:] I think there are only one or two who might be.
>
> [COMMISSION:] How many of them could mix with white people without attracting observation as aborigines? – [DEANS:] Very, very few.
>
> [COMMISSION:] How many do you think? – [DEANS:] Well, I should have to think that well over.
>
> [COMMISSION:] Take your time? [sic] – [DEANS:] Amongst the orphans as well?
>
> [COMMISSION:] On the station altogether? – [DEANS:] I think there may be a dozen that are nearly quadroons.

[75] Victoria 1877 (RC): ME 52, 62, 79.

> [COMMISSION:] Who might be taken, say, for southern Europeans? – [DEANS:] Yes, decidedly.[76]

The half-caste girl emerged as a particularly charged and problematic identity. As explained in the board's reports to Parliament, it proposed to send the half-caste 'lads' back onto privately owned pastoral stations but there was much greater ambivalence about 'sending her out' when it came to disposal of an older girl. Much the same ambivalence was reflected in the commission's inquiry. Even those who endorsed the idea usually noted that special caution was required in the case of girls. So, in the previous discussion, we see a gendered response to questions of the Aboriginal child's fitness for life beyond the station – as boarded out, as in service or as in apprenticeship. A number of witnesses and correspondents suggested boys and girls should be managed differently – the girls and the half-caste girls in particular having greater 'moral' vulnerability. The school was understood as a means of drawing children and adults into the confines of station life, and it was also a mechanism for separating generations. The schoolhouse was not just a school, but also a 'boarding' institution for many of its pupils, where children often ate and slept separately from parents residing elsewhere on the station. It is also noteworthy that with regard to girls, the school functioned to protect them from the 'badlands' beyond the Aboriginal station. The pubescent Aboriginal girl or, rather, the pubescent half-caste girl was a highly anomalous figure. The half-caste whatever the gender was anomalous at this time, but this was especially the case with regard to the half-caste girl. The commission entertained the idea of the (white) country homestead as a destination for Aboriginal children boarded out or put into service. As will be shown in Chapter 3, within the white welfare system the 'good country home' featured as the desirable alternative to barrack-style accommodation and to the badlands of city life – the back alleys and squalid abodes full of grog and brothels whence lurked the vicious criminal and dissolute.[77]

But here, in the commission's inquiry and in the BPA's reports of this era, 'country' was rarely referred to as 'the country' and rarely with any reassuring pastoral connotations. Rather, the hinterland beyond the mission boundary emerged from the commission as a place much more threatening than 'the country' as it pertained to non-Aboriginal children. The country beyond the mission featured as populated by its own dissolute and dangerous classes that inhabited shanties; took advantage of prostituted girls and met Aborigines with grog on secluded bends of the river; attempted illicit liaisons any chance they got; exploited the labours of Aborigines, dumping them after droving jobs and so on; or represented plain old misery and starvation – that is, the 'country' beyond the mission station featured as the badlands, full of danger and misery for the young Aborigine. And while some would vouch for

[76] Victoria 1877 (RC): ME 91.

[77] See Victorian Children's Aid Society Records, Box 1/2a: Annual Report of the Presbyterian Society for Neglected and Destitute Children, 1893–94.

the good Christian home run by the good Christian woman as a desirable place for young Aborigines, a good number of others would provide testimony that the respectable Christian homestead, as a destination for Aboriginal children, presented a threat, albeit an unintended one, to the well-being of all:

> [COMMISSION:] Do you think it advisable to board out orphan children? – [REV. KRAMER:] I do not think it advisable at all. We have some children at the station who were brought up in families of white people; one of them is spoilt entirely, both for whites and blacks, and the other has got round since she has got married; she was at first quite unmanageable. It seems with the girls that at a certain age they get unmanageable.[78]

Murdoch MacDonald's Presbyterian Committee indicated that even under the most favourable circumstances there would be 'great danger of the girls going astray; and even in the case of boys, the probability is that they would grow up with the feeling that they were regarded as aliens, if not as inferiors, and thus be tempted to contract pernicious and degrading habits'.[79] MacDonald's committee thought the safest and the best course was to continue the present plan 'of bringing them up in a boarding-house under the superintendence of the missionary and his wife':

> They believe that success would be far more likely to crown the efforts put forth in such circumstances to mould their characters for good, than when exposed, as they would under most circumstances be under the boarding-out system, to the influence of companions whose home-training might be very inferior to that which obtains on the mission station. The presumption also is that the oversight, under that system, would be less vigilant, patient, and judicious.[80]

It appears from the commission's inquiries into boarding out that 'country' itself had become racialised – constructed quite differently in the two discourses of the welfare of Aboriginal and non-Aboriginal children. As illustrated in the testimony of mission superintendents, the country beyond the mission was figured as a threat to the welfare of the Aboriginal girl in particular.

COUNTRY HOME/RACIALISED COUNTRY

The girls at the encampment (Aboriginal station) at Coranderrk, just out of Melbourne, were strictly watched by the matron Mrs Halliday. They were continually under her charge except when they were with the schoolmaster James Deans. When the matron was away, the girls were locked in the mission school and, Deans explained, 'there is no way of their getting out' except when they did domestic duties. When Mrs Halliday took time off on Sundays, the girls were locked in, the fear being that they would 'wander about ... I do not think they should be allowed to wander during the matron's absence – that they should be left at large':

[78] Victoria 1877 (RC): ME 60. [79] Victoria 1877 (RC): ME 74. [80] Victoria 1877 (RC): ME 74.

> [COMMISSION:] Do I understand that the children are always under lock and key? – [HALLIDAY:] Oh, certainly not; I am only talking about when Mrs Halliday is away – it is only in regard to the door that I have the key and that I am speaking of.
>
> [COMMISSION:] They are not kept like prisoners? – [HALLIDAY:] No, decidedly not. I said on certain occasions they were kept like prisoners . . .
>
> [COMMISSION:] From your observation during the time you have been there do you think there is much difficulty in keeping the intruders away from the place, such as idlers and larrikins? – [HALLIDAY:] I hardly understand you; do you mean visitors?
>
> [COMMISSION:] They might pretend to be visitors? – [HALLIDAY:] I never saw any visitors except the most respectable people.
>
> [COMMISSION:] Have you heard any complaints about the young population of Healesville visiting there – young lads about fifteen? – [HALLIDAY:] No, I never heard anything of the kind.[81]

Ogilvie was more forthcoming, arguing that 'plenty of white men' would cohabit with half-caste girls but not so readily would a white woman cohabit with a half-caste man. He thought there had in fact been 'evils' at Coranderrk but would not report on everything he had heard. For example, when the road was being built between Coranderrk and the nearby country town of Healesville, 'the road party would fire so many guns at night as a signal that so many women were required in their camp. That was only hearsay.'[82] The commission heard from others testifying about the problem posed by locating Aboriginal stations near white townships, with the onus of responsibility placed firmly on managing the risk to Aboriginal girls reaching puberty and wanting to get married. It would be better for stations to be located well away from townships, but even more important was 'moral training', 'wholesome discipline administered' and above all 'religious superintendence exercised', as argued by Rev. Hamilton:

> The essential thing to be aimed at in the management of the aboriginal heathen here, the same as in the reclaiming the heathen in other parts of the world, is to make it a fundamental principle to educate them in Scripture truth, to teach them pure morality, to train them to act at all times as responsible and immortal human beings and thereby to furnish them with the power to resist temptation when it is presented and not unnecessarily put themselves in the way of evil.[83]

So perhaps it was not unexpected that the commission recommended that it was premature to think of the Aborigines earning their own living and leaving the stations, and also premature to attempt absorption. Certainly the provision of state schools was supported, along with the continued provision of stations headed by missionaries. The commission also appeared ambivalent about boarding out and hiring out to service and apprenticeships in trade, and it was not able to conclude that any real distinction could be drawn between Aborigines and half-castes on

[81] Victoria 1877 (RC): ME 91. [82] Victoria 1877 (RC): ME 3–4. [83] Victoria 1877 (RC): ME 22.

questions of capability and potential for self-sufficiency, despite popular opinion to the contrary. It sided definitely in favour of state schools and acknowledged there was no evidence to conclude that the half-caste was more easily educated or 'more readily civilized' than the 'Aboriginal native'.[84] Half-castes perhaps might receive instruction more readily, but they were just as liable to temptation 'and yield as easily to it . . . an appearance of civilization is, no doubt, more quickly obtained, but it is only superficial and fails at the moment of trial'. Another apparent difficulty for Aboriginal people was a reluctance 'not unnaturally' of the colonists to 'associate freely with the natives' and an added 'peculiar sensitiveness on their part to any slight or rebuff', resulting in Aboriginal people associating with those who would associate with them 'instead of selecting the most suitable companions'. The commission was acknowledging the effects of colonisation itself:

> It may be supposed that attachments to localities, and hereditary tribal enmities, would militate against any efforts to bring them in: but the existing local attachments are . . . of recent origin; on the breaking up of the tribes consequent upon the seizure of their territories, and on the decrease numerically of each tribe, the love of the land on which they were born, and which they considered therefore as theirs, became lessened. The tribes, as tribes, no longer exist, and the individuals yet remaining have formed associations which are not necessarily connected with former tribal boundaries. In fact they are now most attached to the spot in which they are best treated; their motto seems to be, *ubi bene, ibi patria* [home is where it is good].[85]

So gathering up the so-called remnants of Aborigines had to continue, with no false sentimentality about the hardship that this caused, as to leave them alone would be to abandon them to 'lower and lower stages of degradation'. Almost as an epitaph, the commission asserted that the 'care of the natives who have been dispossessed of their inheritance by colonization is a sacred obligation upon those who have entered upon the land':

> There are those who think it premature to assert that the race must necessarily disappear altogether, and that, though at present they have not the moral force to hold their own in the struggle of life, they may, in future generations, acquire the resolution and provident habits which would enable them to do so.
>
> Whether this be too sanguine a view or not, none can deny that the colony is bound to temper, as best it can, the injurious effects which the occupation of Victoria has produced on the Aboriginal inhabitants.[86]

Notwithstanding all that, the royal commission reported on the increased mortality rates on the missions and mismanagement among the superintendents. Following this, the Aborigines Protection Act of 1886 created a new definition of 'Aborigine' – or rather, 'aboriginal', so that those adults and children described as part Aboriginal

84 Victoria 1877 (RC): Report xi. 85 Victoria 1877 (RC): Report xii.
86 Victoria 1877 (RC): Report xvi–xvii.

or half-caste were officially defined as white and forcibly removed from the missions.[87] The act was administered by the Board for the Protection of Aborigines, which put in place regulations forbidding half-caste people access to the mission stations and their families. The broad plan was to remove these children from their parents on the missions when they were old enough to work, and under the authority of the board they would be sent out to service following a period of training at an industrial school, or made available for adoption with non-Aboriginal families. Older people were given three years from the passing of the act to find work and accommodation. The board's attempts to implement these plans will be discussed in subsequent chapters. It will also be shown in subsequent chapters how a distinction between welfare and justice institutions so clearly articulated by the administrators of the white child actually worked on the ground, as moves were made throughout the administration of the Aboriginal child to 'merge' the child distinguished as the problematic half-caste with the white population.

ABORIGINES ARE A 'FREE PEOPLE'

In 1884 the superintendent at Lake Condah, along with other officials, urged the board to amend the first (1869) Aborigines' Protection Act so that young half-castes growing up on the reserves could be apprenticed to the settlers as soon as they reached the school-leaving age. Policies would continue the practice of drawing on Indigenous people as a source of labour in the young colony, but that had also hastened the breakdown of the economic viability of the mission stations by removing potential labour power from the missions and their families. The policy was in fact expressly designed to have this effect. Station superintendents reported to the board on their success in 'carrying out the policy of the Board by sending out to service, all the young half-castes, thus depriving the station of labour'.[88] 'Merging', in the form of insisting that these children would sever connections with their Aboriginal parents and families and become part of a white Australian population, ensured there would be a ready supply of young cheap labour for the white settlers but it also ensured that the missions were starved of labour for enterprises such as farming and agriculture. In a short period of time, the shortage of labour became one of the reasons to close or amalgamate missions, to save money:

> The giving up of [Ebenezer] station will help to greater economy in management . . . The natives are decreasing in number so fast that it will not be long before the Board will be able to make a further recommendation in the direction of closing another station . . . The wish and intention of the Board was, however, to first close Ebenezer Station, Lake Hindmarsh, on the River Wimmera, in which there are now so few

87 Victoria The Aborigines Protection Act (No. 912) 1886.
88 PROV VPRS 1694 Unit 1: J. Shaw (Coranderrk) to Sec. BPA 29 March 1890.

people left that its continuance as a station is no longer justifiable, and after that place has been finally closed and done with to prepare for the breaking-up of one of the Gippsland stations.[89]

But the board was also aware that its actions were constrained by notions that we would normally associate with liberal forms of governing – it regularly observed, for example, that Aborigines were a 'free people'. And certainly it was clear that the administrators of Aborigines from the 1890s in Victoria needed to use 'inducement' rather than direct coercion in carrying out their policies. Having announced its plan to close a number of stations, the board noted:

> In the meantime, efforts might be made to persuade families living on either of these reserves to move to one of the other stations, Condah or Coranderrk, as vacancies occurred by death. On both those stations there are, at present, a good many old people ... and it cannot be long before they die. The vacancies thus caused could be taken by younger people. It is, however, to be remembered, that the Aborigines are a free people, and not prisoners, who cannot summarily be deported against their will. Some are so attached to their homes that it is almost impossible to move them, and the only means the Board have of enforcing their will is to stop the supply of rations, which has not always the desired effect. In a case where a man has made himself objectionable on a station by quarrelling, drunkenness or immorality, he can be removed by an Order in Council; but this means of removal would not be justifiable when people have done no wrong, and whose only fault is attachment to their homes ... The Aborigines of Victoria are steadily decreasing in numbers, and the expense of managing them also decreases from year to year. In another twenty years they will probably be extinct and, in the meantime, the poor remnant of the original owners of this splendid State of Victoria should be dealt with kindly, wisely and generously.[90]

The board had also recognised that cases of hardship would arise when half-castes were compelled to leave the reserves by 1890, having been given three years grace after the coming into operation of the new 1886 Aborigines Protection Act. It determined, however, that each individual case of hardship would be dealt with on its merits. For this reason and also because of opinion at the time that the act might in fact be flawed and that the board might be acting in an uncertain legal framework, the secretary wrote to the minister of lands suggesting that half-castes turned off the missions could be given preference in obtaining land.[91] This never occurred. It is also worth recording that under the 1948 Geneva Convention on the Punishment of the Crime of Genocide, notwithstanding conditions of war, acts of 'forcibly transferring children of the group to another group' with the 'intent to destroy, in whole or part, a national, ethnical, racial or religious group' are acts of genocide punishable by law, as also are acts of conspiracy to commit genocide.[92]

89 Victoria 1902b (BPA): 5–6. 90 Victoria 1902b (BPA): 6–7. 91 Pepper 1980.

92 United Nations 1948a. General Convention on the Prevention and Punishment of the Crime of Genocide, 9 Dec. 1948, Article 2. In the present Convention, genocide means any of the following acts

Initial attempts at merging the half-caste Aboriginal population were made by trying to amalgamate or close the mission stations that under earlier legislation had housed the Aboriginal population as a whole. This was done on the basis of a belief, held by some, that 'full-blood' Aborigines would eventually die out. Every year the numbers of mixed-blood persons on the stations would reduce. At the turn of the twentieth century the board announced a plan to have half-caste children removed to the care of the Department for Neglected Children for training before being sent out to service. Attempts to implement the plan in any systematic fashion were short-lived, but the intention of the plan was clear, as expressed by the superintendent at Lake Condah mission: 'As the blacks are dying out, and the Board removes the half-caste boys and girls by handing them over to the Industrial Schools Department, finality is greatly facilitated, and will, doubtless, be attained within a few years.'[93]

By 1892, however, the board was already becoming impatient that the separation policies were not working as intended. It is clear from the records of the board that the methods of removal involved covert actions by administrators and mission authorities, usually involving a withholding of material resources such as farm equipment or educational resources from the missions so that people would be forced to move to another mission station. At Framlingham mission in the west of the state, resources were starved, in the face of considerable opposition from residents, as a lever to move people to the Lake Condah mission. The plan to engineer a shift in populations by these means was openly spoken about in the official correspondences between the board's officers:

> As I am authorised to take the bullocks and wagon down from Framlingham to Condah it will be an inducement for these families to get their belongings down here ... If they see the bullocks and wagons as well as all the implements on the station being removed it will induce them to an early start for Condah. I would therefore recommend to send the cattle to Lake Tyers or sell them as soon as possible.[94]

In general, in the late nineteenth and early twentieth centuries, Aboriginal children separated from their parents were sent out to service by the board, and only in

committed with intent to destroy, in whole or in part, a national, ethnical, racial or religious group, as such: (a) Killing members of the group; (b) Causing serious bodily or mental harm to members of the group; (c) Deliberately inflicting on the group conditions of life calculated to bring about its physical destruction in whole or in part; (d) Imposing measures intended to prevent births within the group; (e) Forcibly transferring children of the group to another group. Article 2: In the present Convention, genocide means any of the following acts committed with intent to destroy, in whole or in part, a national, ethnical, racial or religious group, as such: (a) Killing members of the group; (b) Causing serious bodily or mental harm to members of the group; (c) Deliberately inflicting on the group conditions of life calculated to bring about its physical destruction in whole or in part; (d) Imposing measures intended to prevent births within the group; (e) Forcibly transferring children of the group to another group.

93 Pepper 1980: 32; Victoria 1900b (BPA): 6, Appendix II (J. H. Stähle).

94 PROV VPRS 1694 Unit 1: J. H. Stähle to F. A. Hagenauer Gen. Insp. & Sec. BPA 1 July 1890.

exceptional cases did the board send them to children's homes. Among the exceptions were children sent to Bayswater Home outside Melbourne. Here was a boy of fifteen who had been maintained by board funds for five years; although having attended school, he was unable to read and write. The board on advice from the superintendent recommended that the boy be returned to Lake Tyers mission.[95] In other words, the destination for a child unable to learn was back to the mission, where 'the blacks will ere long die out'. Further, while robust health fitted a child well for service, poor health and deprivation among Aboriginal children could be taken as reason enough that they not be removed from their families. For example, in 1890, Rev. Stähle requested that a girl be permitted to remain on Lake Condah mission though she had reached the age at which half-castes were compelled to leave. Her widowed mother required her help, 'but apart from this the girl is consumptive, her brother and three sisters having already succumbed to the disease'.[96]

SUMMARY

Two quite distinct sets of legislative and administrative yardsticks were used for intervening in the lives of white and half-caste children. For the child savers and philanthropists who had in their sights the feeble body of the white child in need, its deprivation, poor health and pitiful circumstances were the signs that justified intervention, and the 1864 act that defined non-Aboriginal neglected children listed signs that set the non-Aboriginal neglected child apart from other non-Aboriginal children. The non-Aboriginal neglected child was 'found begging . . . found wandering'. These children became the object of reform and protection and they were to be held in special homes until strong enough to be sent to a 'good country home', though non-Aboriginal parents' perceived all-too-readiness to shirk their responsibility for the welfare of their children had to be guarded against. In the case of the half-caste Aboriginal population under the gaze of 'protection', quite the opposite occurred. The whole of the Aboriginal population was described as neglected, Aboriginal parents' reluctance to part with their children was understood by white administrators as a problem that had to be overcome; the countryside beyond the mission boundaries was perceived as a threat to Aboriginal children's welfare and deprivation and poor health were used as signals for non-intervention – they were signs that children should be considered exceptions to the rule of intervention and removal and instead be returned to or kept on the mission. If we ponder that question of welfare and justice as it pertains to the Aboriginal population, we are now perhaps open to the possibility of a disparity in the meanings of the terms as they were applied to the Aboriginal and the non-Aboriginal populations respectively, and

95 National Archives of Australia (NAA) B337, 635: J. Bulmer to F. A. Hagenauer 28 Feb. 1903; PROV VPRS 1694 Unit 2: Sec. BPA to Vice Chairman BPA 4 Aug. 1908.

96 PROV VPRS 1694 Unit 1: J. H. Stähle to Vice Chairman BPA 13 Oct. 1890.

indeed that their respective applications were underpinned by quite contrasting aspirations, and administered by quite discrete authorities.

D. N. McLeod, member of the state parliament and vice-chairman of the board, summed up progress on the merging of the half-castes and the gradual closing down of some of the missions and also the depots that were used as temporary holding and assessment facilities:

> After full consideration and careful inquiry, the Board found it advisable to close two more depots in far distant parts of the colony; and feel sure that the remaining blacks will either join the nearest depots, or settle on some of the stations ... In connexion with the merging of the half-castes with the general population, the question of giving the boys and girls a suitable industrial training, in order that they might be enabled to earn their own living, has been well considered by the Board, and, after careful inquiry, the practice of transferring these half-caste children on leaving the station schools to the Department for Neglected children has been adopted; and the system of training the boys on the farm at Bayswater, and the girls at the home for domestic service, has been working remarkably well. All the children already transferred are happy in their new surroundings, and there seems every likelihood of them becoming useful members of the community.[97]

As noted previously, the 'system of training' that McLeod referred to was to be short-lived and evidence contradicting this glowing account will be discussed in Chapter 4. Assurances of this kind provided in government reports – of a happy coincidence of the interests of the bureaucracy and the Aborigines – are contradicted in the routine correspondence among the mission superintendents, and in the continuing high levels of morbidity and mortality reported on a monthly basis by the superintendents to the board, which was charged with providing protection to Aboriginal people. In many ways the board was a self-contained authority, operating at a distance from direct ministerial oversight and, though formally constrained by the law after the 1869 and subsequent acts and by their attendant regulations, it had considerable power to establish its own rules and regulations through which it governed the lives of people on the mission stations. Chapter 6 focusses on how the encampments under its control operated in many respects as correctional institutions, as well as providing protection through, say, material support. But as will become clear, these institutions under the new Australian Federation and its 'White Australia' policy came to serve as a liminal zone, a more or less porous boundary that served to restrict and discipline Aboriginal people's access and ties to their communities at the same time as it restricted access to resources, material and otherwise, afforded the non-Aboriginal population. The functioning of the twentieth-century mission, deployed on the basis of the contingent category 'Aboriginal', allowed law to

97 Victoria 1900b (BPA): 3–4.

take second place to institutional regulation provided by the mission, in matters such as marriage, family, cultural ties and access to country, and core elements of bare life itself. Ultimately, however, a population of Aboriginal children defined as *neglected* would be made formally subject to provisions akin to a system of indeterminate sentencing that had been applied to non-Indigenous *offenders* for many years.

3

Neglected and Criminal Children

The evolving colonial settlement of Australian territories, which authorities sometimes chose to regard as largely vacant and unpopulated, necessitated actions by the central government that were quite novel compared with European contexts of governing. This applied particularly to a settler population with no historical connection with land or community, and which was exploratory in relation to both the discovery and conquest of new territories but also in the fabrication of a social domain that would accord with at least the broad contours of liberal rationalities of governing in the European tradition. Perhaps the most effective responsibilisation programme was that taking place against a backdrop of the promise of land; a recently arrived or emancipated labouring class would be 'guided and disciplined by the expectation that they might in time and with hard work and sober habits ascend to the status of landholders'.[1]

In the case of the white settlers, these powers of incitement to status acquisition through land ownership might be contrasted with the spread of coercive powers into family life following the establishment of the industrial schools and reformatory schools. These institutions were established in Victoria as a consequence of the Neglected and Criminal Children's Act (1864)[2] and reflected the views of English philanthropists such as Mary Carpenter, who believed that the cause of delinquency lay in society's neglect rather than children's innate criminal tendencies. In the procedures under the act, both offenders and non-offenders could be apprehended and brought before a court, which would then exercise discretion based on the age and circumstances of the child; neglected children could be sent to an industrial school for between one and seven years, while a child convicted of an offence might be sentenced to a term of imprisonment followed by a reformatory sentence for the same period. The immediate effect of the 1864 legislation was an eightfold increase in the numbers of young destitute children in industrial schools, which in turn compromised the intended training roles of these institutions.[3] Although the industrial schools idea was later abandoned on the ground that it failed to establish the

1 Hogg and Carrington 2001: 52. 2 Victoria Neglected and Criminal Children's Act (No. 216) 1864.
3 Jaggs 1986; McCallum 1993: 134.

'family principle', one effect was to deliver a system of monetary assessment of parents who were compelled to contribute to their children's support. When parents had been given maintenance orders, the court clerks were instructed to maintain a surveillance of those parents:

> It is particularly required that, in each case where an order for payment of maintenance of a child sent to an Industrial School is made by the bench, and the person against whom it is made is able to comply with it, the Clerk shall take the necessary steps to enforce the order. When such person leaves the district, the Clerk is requested to have him kept in view by the police, and the order enforced so long as he is able to pay the amount awarded.[4]

This kind of monitoring ensured parents' oversight of their children in the disposal of criminal cases – a child's good behaviour bond required a parent to enter a financial commitment, often a significant amount, to keep the child out of prison. The parents themselves could be sent to prison if children offended again and the parents were not in a position to pay the money. The importance of devolved and informal powers of the court administrators was in evidence again in the way maintenance orders were processed. Parents had to plead a case not to a magistrate but to the central administration of the court, regarding their financial capability to support their children. Once compulsory elementary school attendance legislation was enforced after the 1870s, the penalties for truancy placed a further financial threat over the family. And with the coming of children's courts after 1906, extended powers through linkages between courts, police, charity workers and probation officers, in addition to the school, added to the number of families and children under various kinds of supervision. The carving out of each element of this social domain was accompanied by the threat of prison, but the powers to intervene took the form of regulation rather than law and were underpinned by the impulse to 'make up' categories of persons, both adults and children.

In practice, child and family regulation also involved increased centralisation of the counting practices of the new agencies, and more detailed classification of families appearing in central welfare offices and on the palimpsest that was the child's record. A sharper disciplinary gaze was reflected in the standardised record keeping of the information on parents.[5] From the 1890s, a 'Children's Depot' was established in Royal Park immediately north of Melbourne functioning as a clearing house for neglected and offending children; it was used to observe children before they appeared in court or were relocated. Particular categories of children and parents were inserted into reports to the courts which, as required in the 1906 Victorian Children's Court Act, commented on the child's 'habits and mode of living'. Newly appointed voluntary probation officers were placed under the control

4 PROV VPRS 1579: 'Extract from the Police Gazette' attached to corresp. Sec. Law Dept to Police Magistrate 12 Oct. 1865.

5 McCallum 1993: 138.

of Alfred Clarke, who had been brought over from the (adult) Prisoners Aid Society.[6] Clarke brought to the children's jurisdiction the concern to identify and separate the 'habitual criminal' that had preoccupied adult penal administrators and police throughout the second half of the nineteenth century, as well as penal disciplinary techniques, such as indeterminate sentencing, imported from the adult jurisdiction. It is important to observe how these extra-legal powers were drawn from the penal establishment rather than from broader sociological or cultural shifts or the humanising influence of the child savers, as though this were an inevitable historical tendency. Powers of representing and intervening carried with them a direct or indirect threat of imprisonment should the family fail to respond to required changes in behaviours.[7]

POLICE AND JUSTICE ADMINISTRATION

The Victoria Royal Commission into the Police Force was established in 1906. Under its first terms of reference it was to report on 'The Efficiency of the Police Force in Connexion with the Repression of Crime'. This commission reflected the problem of policing the habitual criminal that had existed since at least the mid-nineteenth century – the commissioners claimed: 'There is practically no control of any criminal once he leaves Pentridge [Gaol].'[8] The new technology of fingerprinting had recently been incorporated into procedures for identifying the criminal, supplementing photographs and descriptive records. The chief commissioner of police thought it vastly superior to the tedious and inexact anthropometrics of the Bertillon system. Nevertheless, existing forensic science techniques were inadequate and while centralised accumulation of criminal records was useful for the detective, they were of little use to the ordinary constabulary – 'the one body . . . there to prevent the commission of crime'.[9] The ordinary constable on the beat 'may pass by notorious criminals and be unaware of their character'.[10] Better dissemination of descriptive and photographic records was called for, and every constable 'should be compelled to make himself familiar with them'.[11] But in the mind of the Victorian chief commissioner of police, that was 'an utter impossibility . . . you will see whole volumes in the criminal office, whole rows of large volumes. You could not give them to every man.'[12] What was needed was a different way of knowing the 'habitual offender' – systematic, objective, tractable – but one that emanated from a change in judicial administration rather than policing practices.

In this highly devolved system for assessing child criminality, one signal instance of nineteenth-century adult penal policy flowing directly to the children's

6 Victoria Children's Court Act (No. 2058) 1906 s 9. 7 Hacking 1983, 2004.
8 Victoria 1906c (RC): Report xiii. 9 Victoria 1906c (RC): ME para. 1644.
10 Victoria 1906c (RC): Report xiii. 11 Victoria 1906c (RC): Report xiii.
12 Victoria 1906c (RC): ME para. 1648.

jurisdiction early in the twentieth century was indeterminate sentencing. Modelled on the provisions of the UK Prison Act (1898) and the Prevention of Crime Act (1908), this began as a programme in Victoria for adult prisoners, heralded in the 1906 royal commission into policing as an economical method of keeping trace of the 'habitual criminal'. Locating these offenders was an inefficient use of police resources, dependent on photographic and physical measures of offenders stored in the central police files. The chief commissioner of police laid out a classificatory system which had two notable features. First, it was possible to recognise the habitual (male) criminal in quantifiable terms: 'on his third conviction, you would have fair evidence that he is going to live a life of crime'.[13] Second, it offered a programme of reform in which the criminal came to know, keep trace, and act on his own habit: 'so a man knowing the system as he would from having it put before him while in gaol, and knowing that he was determining his own fate, would naturally get out of the more serious class, and go down to the other'.[14] The chief of prisons lauded the economy of indeterminate sentencing as it had the effect of 'creating the desire on the part of those who may be affected by its provisions to go beyond its reach'.[15] Adult prisoners given an indeterminate sentence were held 'at the Governor's pleasure'. The quantitative measure of the habitual criminal had appeared earlier in the New South Wales Habitual Criminals Act (1905).[16] After two or three convictions for a similar offence, a judge was empowered to declare a person to be a habitual criminal, serving first a definite sentence and then an indeterminate sentence until authorities were satisfied that the person had been sufficiently reformed. The inspector general of penal establishments and gaols in Victoria cited this act with approval. A dual track procedure laid down in the Victorian Indeterminate Sentences Act[17] meant, however, that after serving a sentence of imprisonment for the crime committed, the habitual criminal 'may be detained during the Governor's pleasure in a reformatory prison'.[18]

Between 1905 and 1908, the legislative and administrative machinery of the Children's Court in Victoria was formed, hailed as the budding of a new kind of judicial administration shaped to accommodate the special nature of the child and representing the bifurcation of a system geared to the welfare of its subject, separated from the more punitive aspirations of the adult system. But there was a clear continuum between the adult and juvenile populations in dealing with the problem of the habitual criminal, with provisions akin to the indeterminate sentencing principle having been applied to juvenile offenders for many years. Section 333 of the Victorian Crimes Act (1890) permitted the transfer of young prisoners from gaol to the Department of Reformatory Schools, from where they were placed either in private reformatories or 'in

[13] Victoria, 1906c (RC): ME para. 1253. [14] Victoria 1906c (RC): ME para. 1253.
[15] Victoria 1906b (Penal Est. and Gaols).
[16] New South Wales Habitual Criminals Act (No. 15) 1905.
[17] Victoria Indeterminate Sentences Act (No. 2106) 1907. [18] Pratt 1997: 58.

service'.[19] The transfer operated as a remission of the residue of the sentence of imprisonment unless, under Section 334, the offender was transferred back to gaol for bad behaviour. In the five years following 1900, no cases had been transferred back to gaol.[20] Section 333 was ostensibly applied in the name of 'welfare': the transfer of young offenders out of gaol was seen as providing 'freer and healthier moral surroundings' and the department congratulated itself for its enlightened approach to them.[21] In 1905 for example, there were eleven transfers from gaols to reformatories, and official visitors whose duty it was to recommend transfer were 'deserving of praise for the valuable service they have rendered in promoting the welfare of these lads'.[22]

On the other hand, in a number of instances Section 333 was used to perform a second punishment. Boys who had served their full fixed term of imprisonment, less a day or two, were then transferred to a reformatory to begin a further, indeterminate sentence; as the superintendent of Excelsior Reformatory, Brighton remarked, 'One cannot expect to reform a boy who is punished a second time for the same offence.'[23] Moreover, although there were no transfers from reformatory to gaol under Section 334, there were indeed transfers for bad behaviour – not *to* gaol *from* reformatories but *from* various kinds of placement in foster homes or employment *to* reformatories and training schools. Children under care of the Department of Neglected Children and Reformatory Schools (DNCRS) in foster homes or sent into service – not necessarily offenders but children who were reported to the department as exhibiting 'depraved habits' and 'serious misconduct' – were subject to a *de facto* indeterminate sentencing in the form of a transfer to reformatories, at the discretion of the minister and bypassing a court appearance. The provisions of the act show that sentencing policies incorporated a scheme of indeterminate sentencing as a core element of justice administration, and also that a component of judicial administration instituted for the 'welfare' of the child substituted for a ruling by a court. All children sent to foster homes or placed in service, whether or not they had committed an offence, were subject to the provisions of Section 333. Their behaviour was set against the norms in the foster home.

In such circumstances, positing meaningful distinctions between concepts of 'welfare' and 'justice' is both hazardous and sometimes quite irrelevant. Moreover, there was a strong continuity between adult and juvenile populations in the problem of managing the habitual criminal. So to assume the efficacy of reform in the name of welfare is to overlook these continuities in the kinds of questions that vexed administrators in both systems. Moreover, these conditions that were placed on the practical application of so-called welfare provisions in the justice system reinforced the instability of these two categories as descriptors of its operations.

19 Victoria Crimes Act (No. 1079) 1890 s 333. 20 Victoria 1906b (Penal Est. And Gaols): 6.
21 Victoria 1901a (Dept. Neglected Children and Reformatory Schools [DNCRS]): 5.
22 Victoria 1906a (DNCRS): 3. 23 Victoria 1904a (DNCRS): 11.

POLICE AND PHILANTHROPY

Besides policing, a network of both government and philanthropic agencies was also concerned with juveniles in terms of 'habit'. The role of the charities in these networks is demonstrated in one of the major organisations, the Society (previously Presbyterian Society) for Neglected and Destitute Children. The main principle of categorisation of juveniles was malleability: whether, over time, habit had hardened into the habitual. For the child savers and the superintendents of homes and reform schools, there were those who could still be worked on and those for whom the prospect of reform of bad habits was much less likely. The criterion was age. Selina Sutherland, the society's agent, explained:

> A single boy or girl over fourteen years of age who has lived a street life gives more trouble and worry and is less hopeful than fifty who are under seven or eight . . . Sad as it may be it is nevertheless a fact that the efforts made on behalf of these older boys and girls are seldom rewarded with satisfactory results, in proportion to the labour expended on them, leaving them morally and physically weak, preferring a street life with all its hardships to a home life with work, order and obedience. It is not so with children of tender years, who are largely susceptible to good or evil according as they are taught. If they are removed before bad habits are formed and placed in suitable homes they grow up amenable to domestic rule.[24]

The networks between philanthropy and the police had been established initially through the more general policing of the destitute, disorderly and dissolute adult population, rather than juveniles. Children were sent to the society's home at the rear of the central Melbourne court rather than being locked up with their parents in the nearby police cells. These premises were seen as an annex of police work, such that in 1904 the chief commissioner of police agreed to pay the yearly rent of the society's premises.[25] By 1910, besides foundlings, the home was receiving neglected children removed from a parent or parents, or found wandering, and children whose parents had been locked up. Children were also brought to the home having absconded from various other institutions or having been charged with offences such as loitering, begging, gambling on the streets or theft, with a court hearing pending.

The society's home became in effect a short-term remand centre and a relay point between the police and the court. In the early committals of neglected children, the child's physical presence was required in the court no matter how sick or fragile, in some cases dying babies being hauled before the court.[26] Clearly, a place for the philanthropic agent in court proceedings involving children had been established well before the formal establishment of the children's court. The charity workers

24 Victorian Children's Aid Society Records (VCASR): Box 1/2(a). Annual Report of the Presbyterian Society for Neglected and Destitute Children 1893–94.

25 VCASR: Box 1/2 (b), Report and statement of accounts for year ending 30 June 1903.

26 *Argus* 1908, Jan. 10: 6.

began to relay knowledge of the child, from and between the police and the court. In the form of questions, instructions, advice and information, a formal and informal dialogue began to take place that established a space for special knowledge of the child, which then found its way into the committal procedure. So from the earliest reports of the society in 1893, the agent of the charity associations, in this case Sutherland, became a witness speaking for the child in the court.[27] She bore special knowledge of the child's background, collected from neighbours and other informants, which included knowledge of the father's and mother's character and the state of the house. Sutherland also helped shape decisions about the disposal of children. When it finally appeared, the Children's Court Act (1906) required that these previously informal arrangements for providing specialist knowledge of the child be transferred from philanthropy to the newly appointed probation officers, who henceforth, to cite the terms of the act, were to inquire and furnish the court with information as to the child's 'habits, conduct and mode of living'.[28]

The charities considered the home, particularly the 'good country home', as a kind of ready-made mechanism for the reform of habit. Domestic routine was seen as a kind of processing machine, preventing those with bad habits from becoming 'habitual'. Children placed in country homes away from their 'evil surroundings' and under 'judicious supervision' would be 'treated as members of the family, thus changing their whole course of life, forgetting their old names and taking the names of their foster-parents':

> The children have an opportunity of learning gradually and naturally the laws of right conduct and high principle which are simply a part of the everyday life of the ordinary home ... if left unchecked until they reach the age of fourteen or fifteen the struggle for truth and right is indeed a hard one, and they rebel against the necessary restraint and discipline of a well-ordered home, and long to return to their old life of freedom.[29]

Foster parents were required to have testimony from a clergyman that they were 'in every respect fit and proper persons to be entrusted with the moral training of a child'.[30] But once again, sending a child to a 'good home' in the country as a formal means of disposal need not be read as enlightened compassion; thinking of the home as the context for regimentation, rule, discipline and hard work questions any easy opposition, in practice, between 'welfare' and 'justice'. But at this time the influence of philanthropy was beginning to wane, especially with all the problems of surveilling the 'good country home' – even the tireless Miss Sutherland got into serious trouble for 'mislaying' children sent to families in remote parts of the state. By 1906, despite the existence of a paid agent to visit and report on children sent out to service

27 *Argus* 1894, Jan. 29: 6; VCASR: Box 4/4, Casebook 1893–94.
28 Victoria Children's Court Act (No. 2058) 1906 s 9.
29 VCASR: Box 1/2 (b), Report for year ending 30 Sept. 1900.
30 VCASR: Box 19/4, Application form for foster child, 1894.

or foster care throughout the State of Victoria, questions began to be raised about the society's inadequate records of inspection.[31] Subsequent society visitors reported 'great trouble in tracing many of the children on our books'.[32] By 1909 the role of visiting children in country foster homes was taken over by the DNCRS, whose official visitors continued to report an inability to trace a considerable number of children and families.[33]

So while there was no doubt a degree of judicial innovation connected with the passing of the Children's Court Act (1906), in the sense of requiring hearings separate from those for adults, the main change resulting from the act was the provision of oversight of the probation system, an ever-expanding network of voluntary child supervisors who would more systematically link the activities of courts, police and families. The arrival of the court was significant because it brought philanthropy under the aegis of the court system and set about authorising agents to do the work previously undertaken by the charities but now to be performed by a more regulated group of honorary probation officers appointed under its jurisdiction. Continuity with the adult system was maintained by A. E. Clarke's appointment as chief probation officer. He used church and philanthropic contacts as his recruiting agencies for 'a lady or gentleman' willing to act as honorary probation officers, and who would welcome 'a splendid chance for accomplishing much good work'.[34] Clarke enrolled familiar philanthropic names such as Vida Goldstein and the committee members of organisations such as the Charity Organisation Society, the Victorian Neglected Children's Aid Society, the Society for the Prevention of Cruelty to Children, the National Council of Women of Victoria and the Women's Political Association. He reaffirmed the efficiency of the probation officers' reports in registering the 'habitual': in certain cases 'which on facts before the Court appeared childish or trivial', a preliminary investigation as provided for in the act 'would, if undertaken, have shown that the child was on the way to acquire bad habits and in danger of becoming a habitual criminal'.[35]

Although welfare historiography understands the creation of a children's court in Victoria as the consequence of a struggle between reformer philanthropy and reluctant government,[36] the evidence suggests that a network of relations between police, penal and reform institutions and proto–social workers was established well before the court appeared, that strong continuity existed between adult and juvenile administration of the habitual criminal, and that government and philanthropy (justice administration and child welfare) had clear lines of connection rather than separation. These networks, rather than simply the tentative beginnings of the new children's court jurisdiction, were a significant precondition for the

31 VCASR: Box 1/5, Minute Book for Committee Meeting 1902–8, 3 Dec. 1906.
32 VCASR: Box 21/2 Correspondence re Reports on Children, 14 Nov. 1908.
33 VCASR: Box 18/10, Register of Foster Parents Including Departmental Inspectors' Reports (1909–12).
34 PROV VPRS 266 Unit 630: A. E. Clarke to Sec. Law Dept 6 Sept. 1907.
35 Victoria 1909a (Chief Probation Officer): 3. 36 Jaggs 1986.

collection of social information and the soon-to-appear calculative regime of the pathological family.

Here was an elaboration of penal administration, an actuarial programme and a now familiar 'three strikes' regime growing directly out of the prison system, as well as a system of 'governing at a distance' that posited a solitary penal subject with responsibility for his or her own reform. Indeterminate sentencing provisions were transferred directly into the children's jurisdiction and laid the ground for the growth of further arbitrary powers, or what Garland, referring to the UK system, termed 'administrative modes of regulation'.[37] In Victoria, new powers over the movement of children between gaol and reformatory school, or between foster home and reformatory school, were invested in the relevant minister of state rather than a court, taking advice from charity workers and administrators. Furthermore, a child could be removed towards the end of a gaol sentence and transferred to a reformatory school to begin an indeterminate sentence until age eighteen. And under Section 333 of the Crimes Act (1890),[38] non-offending children who displayed 'serious misconduct' or 'depraved habits' while in foster care could be transferred to a reformatory school for an indefinite period, at the discretion of the minister. This move could be made against both neglected and offending children who had been placed 'in service' or in foster care. In summary, while many of the provisions put in place might be understood as a programme of incitement to self-govern – to choose to regulate one's own conduct according to social norms – they were implemented under the coercive and disciplinary constraints of the prison.

THE 'FAMILY PRINCIPLE'

The family in nineteenth-century Victoria was seen as a solution to the failure of institutional care to solve the problem of wayward children. The Neglected and Criminal Children's Act of 1864 established the institutional system of industrial schools and reformatory schools, backed up by orphanages.[39] The reform movement, synonymous with European developments that established Mettray in France and Rauhe House in Hamburg, considered that children were the key to social improvement and that children in fact had a 'right' to a proper upbringing, if not by their parents, then by public or private institutions instead. The immediate impact of the 1864 legislation was to swell the numbers of children counted as neglected, and the subsequent overcrowding then was thought to compromise whatever moral and educational roles these institutions could serve. But most of the criticism focussed on how larger institutional provision failed to provide children with the experience of how to live in families, and how it led parents to abandon their children and thus encourage

37 Garland 1985: 190. 38 Victoria Crimes Act (No. 1079) 1890.
39 Victoria Neglected and Criminal Children's Act (No. 216) 1864.

family break-up and social dependence.[40] As is already clear, there was a dramatic about-face in policy terms over the next few decades, from large barrack-type accommodation to a policy of 'boarding out' in the form of foster care for younger children and paid service for older ones. Reformatories too were to be reshaped according to the family principle. The state-run Coburg Girls' Reformatory (in reality an annex to Pentridge Gaol), and Ballarat Boys' Reformatory were considered too prison-like and the Department of Industrial and Reformatory Schools (soon to be the Department for Neglected Children and Reformatory Schools) was voicing a preference for smaller cottage-like institutions, preferably in the country and free of some of the regimentations of prison life.[41] In its report for 1892, the department announced the closure of the Coburg and Ballarat reformatories and the transfer of inmates to a number of institutions run by private individuals and charitable organisations and formally gazetted as reformatories as allowed by legislation.[42] The shift was designed to offer children a happy, healthy, secure childhood in 'respectable' homes or, where this was not possible, in more home-like institutions. Women volunteer organisers would enjoy the government's recognition of their recently acquired domestic skills, joint philanthropic support for the unfortunate would be maintained and boarding-out would encourage the working classes to be 'better parents' because the penalty for recalcitrance might be a complete and permanent separation from their children.[43]

In the policy debates that ensued in the following decades, the main point of agreement between reformers supporting industrial schools and those supporting boarding-out rested on the family as the key to producing healthy, well-trained and self-reliant children. Disagreement arose over the management of the children and whether government authorities or private charity could most effectively provide the family-type solution. The public/private distinction in policy debates effectively became subsumed under the predominance of the 'family solution'. The failure of the industrial school movement to institute the 'family principle', in cottage-like surroundings and in a 'wholly patriarchal, homely, and affectionate manner' led reformers to prefer boarding-out as the way forward. Industrial schools were a source of infectious diseases and were regarded by some as an opportunity for parents to abandon responsibility to care for their children. So in the case of neglected and sick children, family supervision and foster care provided a space for disciplining parents about their family duties. The evidence pointing to the intense policing of this space unsettles taken-for-granted assumptions of the modern family as a natural, unchanging or eternal category. The 'ideal' family was held up as a cornerstone of society, constituted by children governed by their biological parents, even though this model

40 Jaggs 1986: 36–38.
41 Victoria 1885 (Department of Industrial and Reformatory Schools [DIRS]): 15.
42 Victoria 1892a (Department for Neglected Children and Reformatory Schools [DNCRS]): 5.
43 McCallum 1982–83.

was as recent as the early twentieth century. Even when institutional settings continued to exist as a fall-back to home-based care, those settings became more cottage-style in their design and again attempted to imitate the ideal of a good country home.[44]

By the turn of the twentieth century, the inward-looking domestic space had become an important site for making investments in health, happiness, personal adjustment and self-reliance. As Jacques Donzelot put it in the European context, the family was to become the source of governance which the state had failed to provide and was considered most probably an inappropriate provider. But to deal with the children of the people 'in a fatherly spirit' required the hardware of coercive instruments (the 'strangle hold'), including the newly invented children's court. Analysis of the role of this kind of court in conflating judicial and welfare functions was a 'nodal point of supervision and control' of the family.[45] In both the UK and Australia, the children's court became 'a visible form of the state-as-family', and by now there were 'brigades of counsellors and guidance officers' spreading out from the court to monitor and manage the family. But the apparatus that sought to police the family of the delinquent intersected with a complexity of institutional forms: health and welfare agencies, the school, and the normalising of family life through the progressive interiorisation of domestic life and the construction of the mother as the moral centre of the home.[46] Even formal judicial authority became de-centred in the face of increasingly pervasive forms of knowledge and expertise that were non-legal. These developments as they were occurring in the UK at the same time have been described as a 'legal complex', a set of elements with diverse histories and logics: 'Regulations, practices, deliberations and techniques of enforcement increasingly required supplementation by the positive knowledge claims of the medical, psychological, psychiatric and criminological sciences, and the legal complex thus enrolled a whole variety of petty judges of the psyche.'[47] In Victoria, the networks between charity and the police had first been established in the late nineteenth century through the more general policing of a destitute, disorderly and dissolute adult population. From early in the twentieth century, these formed vast networks of relations between police, penal and reform institutions and proto–social workers who would oversee the evolving parole system that helped to enforce responsibilisation of the family. Beginning with an informal dialogue between the court and agents of philanthropy, knowledge of the ostensible problem child – a palimpsest of increasingly detailed intersecting relations for each individual child, and then the case file and the profile that followed – was contingent on a pattern of institutional arrangements concerned with the surveillance and discipline of children measured against their performance of the family principle.[48]

44 McCallum 1997. 45 Donzelot 1979. 46 Reiger 1985; Rose 1990.
47 Rose and Valverde 1998: 543. 48 Foucault 1979.

For both middle- and working-class families, an adherence to social norms was attempted through the inculcation of values of order and civility, rather than imposed from above.[49] In the case of poor working-class families whose patterns of existence may have been less likely to spontaneously accord with those of authorities, family life started to be caught up in a governmental sphere of 'supervised freedom'.

From the turn of the century, educational and judicial interventions were targeted at families who failed to subscribe to a set of norms and values. In this latter respect, Donzelot's analysis problematises the contribution of the human sciences and new kinds of expertise that were authorised by such bodies as the children's court and increasingly came to be a source of expert knowledge of the problem child. Donzelot describes a European-style grid of governing techniques as a 'tutelary' or ward-ship complex that could range from 'assistance-under-surveillance' to incarceration. Governing through the family instrumentalised a set of administrative and disciplinary controls that coupled welfare assistance and the penal system with a capacity to call up information from doctors, hospitals, social workers and both public and private welfare agencies to provide social assistance and a more intense scrutiny of families and individuals. When psychiatric and psychological domains of intervention were added to this, the grid extended to scrutiny over a broad range of family health and behaviour deviations. The programme sought to strengthen and promote the family, to correct circumstances that would undermine it from within and to channel through it all the techniques constituting a space called 'the social'.[50]

Drawing on Donzelot's analysis we can conclude on the two distinct legislative and administrative yardsticks used for intervening in the lives of Aboriginal and non-Aboriginal children in Victoria. For the child savers and philanthropists with oversight of the white child, deprivation or poor health were signs justifying family maintenance and intervention. Under the authority of the state, children bearing these signs of neglect were to be held in special homes until strong enough to be sent to a 'good country home'. As shown in the previous chapter, quite the opposite occurred among Aboriginal children under the gaze of so-called protection, and in the care of the 'state as housefather'. On rare occasions where Aboriginal children were sent to children's institutions, perceived constitutional weaknesses saw then sent back to their relatives on the missions, and ill-health was taken as justification for half-caste children to be deemed exceptions to the rule of family intervention and child removal. Comparatively then, this tended to ratify the mission as an institution in which to die. A negative eugenic principle was specifically applied to Aboriginal children within an overall policy of separation and removal of children from their families, as against a positive strategy of improving and consolidating the health and welfare of the white child by means of governing through the family. Finally, it is important to acknowledge the ways in which Donzelot's ideas can be developed

[49] Van Krieken 1992. [50] Hirst 1981.

through an understanding of how 'family' has been and is racialised to manage certain problem populations.

THE MEASURE OF CHILDREN

In the second half of the nineteenth century, the new colony of Victoria was creating institutions for saving vulnerable children from the perils of vice, crime and family breakdown for two supposedly distinct categories of children – the neglected and the criminal. By the end of the century it was not possible to easily distinguish discrete institutional formations reflecting these two categories. This period and the first three decades of the new century were marked by several intersecting phenomena in the administration of welfare and law which made attempts to map neglected and offending children onto two clearly separate institutional sites – industrial schools and reformatories – almost impossible. Three such developments are pointed to here as especially relevant: first, a reduction in the significance of an offence as the main variable in decision making on the disposal of a child, and a corresponding increased focus on the morality of the child; second, decreasing impact of court decisions and a concomitant increased significance of administrative officers' decisions about disposal; and third, the growing influence of an incipient positivist science on procedures involving neglected and offending children. These events took place amid attempts to bring order to the governing of vulnerable children, but, as argued here, they were accompanied by an increased criminalizing of children. As White and Habibis note, criminalizing is highly contingent upon how discretion is used throughout the criminal justice system, and an important element of the present argument is that contingency of this kind also relates to the welfare system and state invention more generally.[51] A secondary aim is to consider the significance of these historical phenomena as conditions of possibility for present-day shaping of institutional responses to governing vulnerable children.[52]

Much Australian and European research over half a century has drawn attention to the criminalizing aspects of 'saving children', influenced in part by a constructionist paradigm of childhood.[53] Critique has been offered from a number of sources of the assertion that providing access to specialist children's legal and welfare apparatus has ameliorated harm to children and improved their overall well-being by access to children's rights through specialist legal regimes.[54] The spaces for intervening in child and family have also been framed in the context of 'legal informalism', a contraction or de-centring of law and legal process in family matters, and greater levels of family regulation.[55] A vast literature on criminalizing children encompasses such modern devices as antisocial behaviour orders to the 'gargantuan'

[51] White and Habibis 2005: 8–10; White and Haines 2008: 190. [52] Bacchi 2009.

[53] Ariès 1965; Platt 1969, 2008–9; Carrington 1993; Scraton 2008–9.

[54] Rorty 1993; Van Krieken 1992; Meuwese et al. 2007; Gadda 2008; cf. Jaggs 1986; Scott and Swain 2002.

[55] Donzelot 1979; Hunt 1992; Van Krieken 2000; McCallum 2009.

criminalizing of Australian Aborigines.[56] Kerry Carrington characterises the Australian welfare administration of the 1980s as a 'complex web of governmental technologies' ostensibly to save children from 'bad families'.[57] She observes that while reforms had tried to separate welfare and criminal cases, a nexus still existed between the two because the daily management of the abused and abusive child relied on similar forms of knowledge and power.[58] This knowledge changes over time: in the case of welfare organisations in New South Wales in the 1980s, quite specific 'deficit discourses' were utilised in the identification of pre-delinquency under the logic of providing preventative intervention.[59] Parton identifies 'grey areas outside the gaze of a court' where assessments made in the UK in the 1970s were designed to identify high-risk children and families and to calculate a child's level of 'risk and dangerousness'.[60] Thorpe's research on Aboriginal families in Western Australia reports on the spread of specific norms of child upbringing by welfare workers, which tried to 'abstract children from the practical realities of their day to day existence'.[61] Historical accounts of child welfare, on the other hand, tend to reaffirm the significance of techniques of child measurement underpinning the direction of child welfare policy over time. Wells, for example, argues that in the latter part of the nineteenth century new demands for rights to health, welfare and life produced resistance and struggles over the child's special capabilities and vulnerabilities, these demands superseding older conceptions of political rights.[62] Michel Foucault's College de France Lectures published as *Abnormal* (1974–75) and *The Birth of Biopolitics* (1978–79),[63] draw attention to the functioning of the measurement of the child, including medical assessments. Indeed, as Armstrong notes, the child became the first target of a range of exploratory techniques in part because of the child's availability – in hospitals, maternal clinics and schools and also in children's welfare departments – to be measured on a number of different scales. All of this measuring produced a new view of the body and health. The medical gaze on illness and abnormality moved out of its corporal confines of body and nature and came to describe a new field – the multi-dimensionality of identity.[64]

The next section examines specific sites of governmental oversight of child populations and the administration of children's movement between sites formally designated as for the 'neglected' and those designated 'reformatory'. It asks how decisions about children were made in these administrative/legal sites; in what institutional and historical contexts did child welfare and criminal assessments emerge in this period; what were the effects of the decision-making apparatus on the disposal of children; and what kinds of shifts occurred in the kind of expertise deployed in these decisions over time? There is evidence of a shifting crosstalk of expertise between law and those who claimed an extra-legal knowledge of the child

[56] Ashford and Morgan 2004; Carrington 2011; Weatherburn and Holmes 2010.
[57] Carrington 1993: 111. [58] Carrington 1993: 3. [59] Carrington 1993: 127.
[60] Parton 1991: 203. [61] Thorpe 1994: 200. [62] Wells 2011: 15. [63] Foucault 2003, 2008.
[64] Armstrong 2002: 99–108.

that came to bear on this administration. It is possible to view the effects of various kinds of know-how on decisions about children as made for the most part by authorities in charge of the institutions themselves. These decision-making processes capture the mundane administrative workings of institutions and the kind of expertise deployed in them to assess, categorise and place children. A brief chronological study of the Royal Park Children's Depot in Melbourne will give the reader an understanding of the effects of administrative know-how and particularly how that know-how affected the management of bodies in spaces. It summarises developments up to the early twentieth century where separate populations of children, initially appearing in institutional settings from the mid-1860s as either 'perfectly innocent' or tainted by crime, became less distinguishable over a period of three decades, creating the conditions for all to become objects of criminal inquiry. It provides an opportunity to test out the tools of inquiry about how the crosstalk of legal and administrative understandings came to bear on the disposal of children – all of this in the name of welfare.

SPACE, KNOWLEDGE, POWER: THE CHILDREN'S DEPOT

The courts were the distribution point for children charged under the 1864 Neglected and Criminal Children's Act. Superintendents of the various institutions were to receive and 'dispose' of children according to the letter of the law:

> Every mandate issued under this Act shall be executed and obeyed by the persons to whom the same is directed and delivered and shall be sufficient authority for the detention of the child therein mentioned according to the exigency of such mandate and the production thereof accompanied by a statement signed by the superintendent or matron of any industrial or reformatory school that the child named in such mandate was duly delivered into and is at the signing thereof detained in such school or has been otherwise disposed of according to law shall in all proceedings whatsoever be sufficient evidence of the facts by this Act required to be stated in such mandate and of the subsequent detention and identity of the child named therein.[65]

Magistrates, however, had to be constantly reminded about the correct means of committal and disposal. Immediately following its introduction, they were reminded by the minister through the Crown Law Offices *not* to send neglected children to reformatory schools or convicted children to industrial schools:

> I am directed by the Minister of Justice to call your attention to the Neglected and Criminal Children Act 1864. You are requested to observe the difference between Industrial Schools, which are for the reception of *neglected* children, and Reformatory Schools, which are for the confinement of *convicted* children. It is reported, that heretofore this distinction has been overlooked, and that it not

[65] Victoria Neglected and Criminal Children's Act (No. 216) 1864 s 21.

> unfrequently [sic] happens, that girls and boys, who are proper objects for Reformatories, are sent to the Industrial schools, where they are generally unmanageable and abscond.[66]

In 1878, in the context of the closure of the state's other industrial schools, Royal Park Industrial School's population grew. Police were to deposit children in a separate receiving house. Although it was officially described as an entry point for the Royal Park Industrial School, the Melbourne *Argus* newspaper described two separate institutions co-existing: the 'Receiving House' situated in the old powder magazine previously used as a gaol for 'male lunatics', and following that, a place to quarantine smallpox cases; and an industrial school – 'the great Royal-park School' – inhabiting a large purpose-built barrack-style building. The receiving house was used as a transit point for new committals before their destination was decided, for children on remand whose legal status as 'Neglected' was pending a court decision, and for girls returned from service, including girls returned for unsatisfactory conduct (but not, it was pointed out, for vice or theft). It also held infants either committed as Neglected or on remand pending a court decision, and an accumulation of older girls and even adults who, for reasons including eye disease and epilepsy, could not be placed out to service, including among them 'a negress'.[67]

The receiving house in the old powder magazine was soon replaced by the Children's Depot, built inside the grounds of the industrial school in Royal Park. The huge industrial school building would be closed almost as soon as it had opened; started in 1875 it was purpose-built to accommodate 500 children, right down to its canny plans for thwarting banister sliding. But the design principles were considered redundant in the light of new boarding-out principles, where the contours of cottage-style rather than gaol-like had become the ideal. Trying to emulate the cottage became a major concern for the designers of new institutions. In 1880 a Special Visiting Committee sounded the death knell on the idea of the industrial school, borrowed from the English model, calling it a 'gigantic evil which has grown in our midst'.[68] The committee recommended abolishing the role of departmental inspector, giving more powers to the superintendents of individual institutions, less regimentation and more 'play' and establishing 'an efficiently managed depot to facilitate the management of boarding out'.[69] New regulations were gazetted distinguishing the management, supervision and conduct of industrial schools from reformatory schools (the regulations now required facilities for play in the former). Three hundred inmates were housed in the dormitories of the Royal Park industrial school in 1879, even though the momentum was gaining towards a policy of boarding-out. News reports tried hard to present the building as 'not goal-like'. The (very large) 'family' of 'little fellows' was to be managed 'wisely' and 'humanely'.

66 PROV VPRS 1579: Sec. Law Dept. to Courts of Petty Sessions 12 Oct. 1865.
67 *Argus* 1878, June 8: 9.
68 Victoria 1880a (Industrial and Reformatory Schools: Reports of Visiting Committee [IRSRVC]): 16.
69 Victoria 1880a (IRSRVC): 13–14, 20.

Invalids were under the care of a 'cheery mother' substitute in a hospital described as cottage-like and the dormitories, decorated, it was noted, with pictures and flowers, were under the immediate supervision of married couples, 'except at night'.[70] As already noted, it was an established principle that the more like a home and the less like an institution the better. But the specific contours of the family home for boarding-out were also being mapped out in precise detail: new regulations defined the numbers and span of age and sex permissible within the foster or service home along with mandatory sleeping arrangements and mandatory routines – a new purportedly non-institutional space was being made available for the child, but one not necessarily *less* arranged or less regulated than the institution.[71]

The granting of new powers to the executive of the children's depot and the creation of a new position of superintendent were done with an eye to its new powers over the inmates – it effectively allowed a superintendent to overrule court mandates and transfer children to and from reformatories and industrial schools. The separation of the roles of executive head, inspector and superintendent set in place some of the conditions for the devolution of authority to judge and dispose of children to the superintendent. Up to this point, the legal power to judge and dispose of children was more or less vested in the courts. Co-terminous with the formation of the Special Visiting Committee was an 1878 amendment to the Neglected and Criminal Children's Act – it was not coincidental, as both were outcomes of the one set of concerns. The Amendment Act provided the executive with the power to send children committed to a reformatory to an industrial school or to send children committed to an industrial school to a reformatory.[72] Young boys, having been found guilty of minor offences punishable by imprisonment and committed to a reformatory by the courts, could be formally reclassified by the executive (in the form of the Department for Industrial and Reformatory Schools [DIRS]) as industrial school children, and hence as candidates for boarding-out, and then sent by the executive to a foster home. Similarly, industrial school children sent to foster or service homes and there having committed an offence or having absconded could have their offence judged serious enough for them to be sent to a reformatory (absconding was serious enough), but by the executive not by the courts. A strong pattern of discrimination based on moral grounds emerged in provisions made specifically for girls who, though having committed no offence punishable by imprisonment, and formally deemed neglected by the courts could, 'on account of the abandoned character of their past conduct or surroundings' be rerouted to the reformatory.

Why this 1878 amendment? The Special Visiting Committee in its 1880 report provided a retrospective explanation, under the stern heading 'Morals', to the chief secretary (the government had given the committee temporary charge of the department):

[70] *Argus* 1879, Oct. 14: 7.
[71] See Victoria 1880c (Regulations): Schedule 1, Conditions relating to the boarding out of children.
[72] Victoria Neglected and Criminal Children's Amendment Act (No. 626) 1878.

> In the later session of 1878 an Act was passed which, amongst other things, allowed children to be transferred from the reformatory to the industrial schools, and vice versa. The object of this change, which had been indicated in two official reports (Professor Pearson's Report on Education, p. 156; Report of Jika Committee, p. 6), though Mr. Neal [Inspector, DIRS] has claimed the credit of it, was to allow of magistrates' sentences being revised, so that young thieves might not be kept among the orphans of the industrial school, or children guilty of no worse offence than mounting a horse without leave kept in the reformatory.[73]

The aspiration of the amendment was a clearer bifurcation of the population administered under the Neglected and Criminal Children's Act – to protect the orphan from the thief, the not-so-bad from the reformatory case proper, and to counter the mandates of a judiciary too focussed on the letter of the law and on the offence, and unpractised or unwilling to apply the necessary kind of judgement (of morality) necessary in dealing with children. This *administrative* responsibility for *separation* of categories of children (as distinct from the *merging* of categories that had resulted from *judicial* decision making) was encapsulated in the duties according to the newly defined position of superintendent in the industrial schools adopted in 1880:

> [Regulation No.] 35. It shall be the duty of every officer in charge of an Industrial School to carry out a scheme for the classification of the inmates of the school under his charge, with regard, so far as circumstances will permit, to the physical and moral characteristics of such inmates, and take steps to ascertain the views of his Committee respecting such classification.[74]

The relevant powers in the regulations in 1873, compared to 1880, on the transfer of children between industrial and reformatory schools underline the point.

16. [1873] Children presented for admission with mandates must not be refused admission to the school to which such mandates are directed; provided that children under sentence to a Reformatory shall not be received into an Industrial School, or *vice versa*; nor children of one sex into a school directed to be set apart from children of the opposite sex, unless by written direction of the Inspector.[75]	16. [1880] Children presented for admission with mandates must not be refused admission to the school to which such mandates are directed, subject, however, to any special direction in any Act relating to Neglected and Criminal Children being complied with in such mandate; provided that children under sentence to a Reformatory shall not be received into an Industrial School, nor children of one sex into a school directed to be set apart from children of the opposite sex, unless by written direction of the Inspector.[76]

73 *Argus* 1880, Sept. 23: 7 (Published Report of Industrial Schools Committee to Chief Secretary).

74 Victoria 1880b (Industrial Schools Regulations): 1944–54.

75 Victoria 1873 (IRS General Regulations).

76 Victoria 1880b (Industrial Schools Regulations).

The intention remained that industrial school and reformatory children be accommodated separately, but moral grounds now sat over and above grounds of an offence committed in determining who were reformatory and who were industrial school candidates. The judgement of the executive now sat over and above that of the judiciary – the 'special direction' clause added to the 1880 regulations allowed for transfer between industrial and reformatory schools 'by written direction of the Inspector'. The act conferred such power of transfer on the executive. By the early 1880s the department was receiving children deemed candidates for an industrial school and reclassifying them as cases for the reformatory, and vice versa.

The amendment to the act in 1878 and the addition to the regulations in 1880, testify to a recognition of the unwieldiness of the classification practices at this time. But up to the mid-1880s, classification practices continued to prove troublesome. By then, the legal categories Neglected/Convicted inscribed in the act and the administrative categories Industrial/Reformatory applied by the department were proving increasingly difficult to reconcile. In its statistical returns, the Department of Industrial and Reformatory Schools sorted the children received at the depot according to the two latter categories and they served as headings for discussion in its annual reports – children in its care were either industrial school children or reformatory cases. They were sent to the depot by the courts as either deemed legally Neglected or on remand having been charged with being a neglected child. The depot was also receiving children who had been sentenced by the courts to a reformatory and were awaiting placement therein or who were on remand having been charged with a criminal offence. But, as discussed previously, with the new powers conferred on the executive, one could be sent out to service as a Neglected child and, having failed at that, be returned and re-categorised Reformatory. Nor were categories of Convicted and Reformatory child co-terminous. Those charged with an offence, punishable by imprisonment but too young for a reformatory, could be sent to an industrial school. Those charged with a minor offence could be boarded-out. Those not charged with an offence at all could, after suitable inquiry, be understood as better belonging in a reformatory. There was general agreement that the spirit of the 1864 act was to be preserved – the non-offending child should be separated from those who displayed criminal tendencies. Acknowledging that there was no clear distinction, the government set about drafting new legislation. On the eve of its introduction a Visiting Committee for the Ballarat Reformatory congratulated the government of the day in 1886 for recognising the necessity for committing the 'purely unfortunate' and 'perfectly innocent' on the one hand, and those who had been convicted of a crime on the other via separate acts, protecting the former from the taint of criminality:

> We are very strongly impressed with the desirability of dealing with the criminal and the purely unfortunate children in separate Acts of Parliament. The fact of perfectly innocent, or even neglected, children being committed to the care of the State in

> the same Act as those who have been convicted of crime leaves a stigma which is never wiped out, and appears to us unjust, and quite opposed to the spirit of modern legislation in this direction, and to the evident desire of the Government to foster every effort having for its object the intellectual and moral improvement of our rising generation.[77]

The year 1887 saw the passing of the two separate acts anticipated by the Visiting Committee – the Juvenile Offenders Act and the Neglected Children's Act. The acts provided for a nominal separation – a Department for Reformatory Schools and a Department for Neglected children – but the two branches continued to operate under a single secretary. The Department of Industrial and Reformatory Schools had become the Department for Neglected Children and Reformatory Schools.[78]

DIVIDING PRACTICES

Under the administration of the Department for Neglected Children and Reformatory Schools (DNCRS), the bifurcation industrial/reformatory had disappeared. Populations entered the depot at the turn of the twentieth century as, ostensibly, either neglected or reformatory children. But in the very separation of the acts, it becomes abundantly clear (yet again) that these two categories by no means mapped onto the two categories inscribed in the legislation – 'Neglected' and 'Juvenile Offenders'. Nor, with the new nominal separation of the administration into a Department for Reformatory Schools and a Department for Neglected Children, did juvenile offenders and neglected children find themselves neatly assigned to one or the other branch, the one headed for the reformatory, the other boarded out to a private home. Rather, the law allowed for a series of further caveats and crossings over, some certainly at the discretion of the courts but others at the discretion of superintendents of institutions.

Under the new legislation, some of the crossings over were the result of judicial determinations. Children who committed a crime punishable by imprisonment could be committed to a reformatory. But children who had committed no offence could also be committed to a reformatory if in the opinion of the judges they had been leading an immoral or depraved life. If they had committed an offence punishable by imprisonment, they could still be sent to the Department for Neglected Children at the discretion of the judges. Aside from judicial discretion, provision existed at the discretion of the officer in charge of the depot, with the approval of the minister, for the reassignment of children from reformatory to neglected and vice versa. Judgements as to immoral and depraved applied especially to girls. Special care was to be taken regarding their separation even in the reformatory. Though they had not committed an offence punishable by imprisonment, they

77 Victoria 1887 (DIRS): 18.

78 Victoria Neglected Children's Act (No. 941) 1887; Victoria Juvenile Offenders Act (No. 951) 1887.

were to be all but excluded from the possibility of transfer to the Neglected Children's Department, and then only after very careful consideration. So offenders could find their way into the administrative space responsible for the neglected; non-offenders could find their way into the administrative space responsible for the reformatory population. New regulations specific to the management of the depot were gazetted in 1890 which set out the powers and authority of the matron or superintendent in charge – that officer had enormous discretion handling the child on remand, pending committal as neglected. She could isolate the child or send the child to a reformatory, and she could segregate the immoral and depraved. The depot also had a space for the isolation of the refractory girls, but this was not simply a space for the segregation of the reformatory girl per se. It doubled as a space for the segregation of 'contagion' and misconduct, though at the time it was taken for granted that the conduct of the morally depraved *was* contagious.

A departmental report from 1890 noted that the 'Girls' and Infants' Receiving Depot' had left the old powder magazine and come to occupy new premises directly opposite the existing depot.[79] DNCRS Secretary George Guillaume confirmed in 1891 that the matron/superintendent then had the material resources – the space – to classify and to segregate and isolate refractory inmates, which was interesting given that the regulations specifically excluded the superintendent of the *depot* from the role of classification. But there was formal classification and also the informal, pragmatic kind operating at the depot:

> The Matron, Miss Wilson, has now the much needed facilities for due classification, as well as for the isolation of refractory children, or those taken with contagious disorders. Advantage was taken of the now close proximity of the two Depots to utilize the large experience of Miss Wilson by investing her with the responsible charge and superintendence of the boys also.[80]

In 1892 and early 1893, at the same time as the government was congratulating itself on the closure of its state-run reformatories, sections of both the Boys' and the Girls' Depots were officially gazetted as reformatories, though no specific reference to the fact was made in departmental reports. With the gazetting of these reformatory spaces along with her official appointment as officer in charge, the matron's formal authority extended to that of other reformatory school superintendents, namely, to classify as she 'thinks fit' with regard to 'conduct, age, moral and physical characteristics'.[81]

The depot had acquired a space for the segregation and isolation of refractory boys and girls – a small section of it was now an official reformatory – and given the new set of regulations the matron or superintendent had the power to manage that space and the coming and going of its inmates. Children could be sent in and out of the reformatory section at the discretion of these officers. There was now a material arrangement for the

79 Victoria 1891 (DNCRS): 11. 80 Victoria 1891 (DNCRS): 11.

81 Victoria 1891 (DNCRS): 11; Victoria 1892c (Government Gazette): 2168; Victoria 1893b (Government Gazette): 1893.

segregation of some inmates, received as neglected but legally yet informally recognised as more *akin* to reformatory inmates, more criminal than the rest.

The problem of accommodating the reformatory child who arrived at the depot in 1900 was not considered a particularly urgent one. There were problems accommodating this group along with all the others. Outdated and run-down buildings were the main issue for both reformatory and non-reformatory children. And there were no more than one or two transitory reformatory cases as such, with which the depot had to deal at any given time. Spaces for the boys' and girls' reformatories at Royal Park revealed themselves as basically distinguished by no more than the sometime presence of locks and bars. For boys, the reformatory was a dormitory with bars on the window, compared to a non-reformatory dormitory without bars. For girls, it was a separate lock-up that accommodated only one or two at a time. By the middle of the second decade of the twentieth century, however, there was increasing focus on the inadequacy (in terms of the amount and the nature) of reformatory accommodation at the depot. There were not enough beds, and not enough means of properly segregating the reformatory inmates from the rest. By 1917 accommodation was overflowing to the extent that 'at times beds have to be made up in the room used for meals'. Curiously though, the number of cases of children sent to the depot by the courts as sentenced to a reformatory and awaiting placement, or returned by a reformatory for one reason or other and requiring temporary accommodation at the depot, had not increased. The statistical returns in the department's annual reports show that numbers of officially recognised reformatory cases at the end of the year were two boys in 1913 and two boys in 1917, one girl in 1913 and no girls in 1917. So, a decade and a half into the twentieth century, the depot was accommodating only one or two, and a handful at most, of formally designated reformatory cases, and yet adequate accommodation and segregation within a defined reformatory space had become a matter of urgency. Clearly, by the middle of the second decade there was a mismatch between those held at the depot who had been legally and formally sentenced to a reformatory and those deemed by the *depot* to be proper inmates for reformatory-style accommodation and administration. Evidence further suggests that this mismatch had been operating for some time: those deemed proper inmates for the depot's reformatory section were much more inclusive than those deemed reformatory cases by the courts.

The catalyst for a new urgency around the accommodation and segregation of a group of inmates in the depot's reformatory was an influx of remand cases, from 1908 onwards, from the newly inaugurated children's courts. Common sense might characterise the establishment of a dedicated children's court as an unequivocal step in the direction of welfarism – perhaps the final step that completes the picture of a separate 'justice' system for children. The child had already largely been removed from the prison. As noted previously, the 'too prison-like' large state-run reformatories had closed their doors, replaced by smaller, privately run reformatories refashioned as home-like cottages to accommodate the child *as* child. So, finally, that child would now have a special court with a special ear to the circumstances of the child *as* child, and one which would increasingly seek to know and, in that knowledge, to better dispose of that child. In the interim, children on remand were sent to the depot, within which they were locked in a reformatory space, which, ironically, was the antithesis of all the principles which saw the dismantling of the old prison-like accommodation in the name of the child and which served as the very foundations upon which the depot was established. Basically, that reformatory space in the depot was a prison. As we will see in a later chapter, it was a prison in 1900 and became more prison-like, more punitive over the first three decades of the twentieth century.

SUMMARY

The authorities in charge of implementing the foundational legislation in mid-nineteenth-century Victoria were charged with establishing two sets of institutions for children, designated neglected and criminal, that sought to mark out lines of separation between the neglected, orphans and destitute children on the one hand, and children who had been convicted of an offence on the other. The evidence presented thus far shows that the actual workings of these institutions and the systems of knowledge underpinning them were much less clearly differentiated than their formal designation suggested. The Royal Park Children's Depot serves as a case study of the conditions and the practices whereby administrative knowledge and know-how began to replace formal legal process, establishing itself at the centre of decision making affecting children in the care of the state. Despite claims that child welfare was progressively improving their life chances, vulnerable children were candidates for a series of criminalizing practices in a welfare system that was formally set up to protect them.

In the last two decades of the twentieth century the categories of neglected child and reformatory child show themselves to be inherently unstable such that, by the early years of the twentieth century it made little sense to refer to the neglected child as dissociated from those with criminal tendencies. The instability is reflected in the various changes to the title of the department, from the Department of Industrial and Reformatory Schools to the Department for Neglected Children and Reformatory Schools. In 1923 the department underwent another name change. The full title – Children's Welfare Department and Reformatory Schools – was rarely used and by the mid-twentieth century it had become simply the Children's Welfare Department. As we shall see in Chapter 5, into the twentieth century, despite the absence of any allusion to criminality in the new title, the association between neglected and offending children was further forged in such a way that criminality came to enfold the whole of the population of children in state care, to the extent that those who did not bear the signs of actual criminality had to be scrutinised for the possibility of their bearing its potential.

4

Science, Race and Separations

Immediately following its constitution in 1860, the Central Board to watch over the interests of the Aborigines in the Colony of Victoria announced an intention to found a school for 'neglected black and half-caste children' and an asylum for 'infirm blacks'.[1] As noted in Chapter 2, the board operated for nearly a decade without any legislative powers and during this period it certainly had no formal authority to take children from their parents. After the passing of the first 1869 protection act, it operated with little direct contact or first-hand knowledge of Aboriginal people. It met for only a few hours each month and with little ministerial oversight and was free to make determinations on virtually all aspects of the lives of Aborigines on the reserves and mission stations during the latter half of the nineteenth century.[2] Following its early determination to establish a school for children and an asylum for the infirm, the board decided that a suitable place could be found on the north side of the River Yarra but it came up against the objections of a powerful local squatter. The plan collapsed when, in the words of the board, 'the site interfered injuriously with the rights of a neighboring [sic] settler'.[3] The board established Coranderrk (taken from the name given by the local Woiwurrung people for a flowering shrub indigenous to the area) as an official encampment for Aborigines. It was situated next to the Coranderrk Creek and the River Yarra, in the hills close to Melbourne. A 2300-acre parcel of land was temporarily reserved in 1863 which in 1866 was extended to 4850 acres.[4]

Initially Coranderrk was hailed by the board as a model for Aboriginal settlements and described in idyllic terms:

> The Central Board stated, in their last Report, that they had commenced the erection of a school-house for the use of the blacks at Coranderrk ... They are happy to say that it is now completed, and that it is in every way suitable for the purpose intended. The large school-room is airy and well lighted, and the three bedrooms adjacent are properly placed and well built.[5]

[1] Victoria 1862 (BPA): 5. [2] Barwick, Barwick and Barwick 1998; Nanni and James 2013: 12.
[3] Victoria 1864a (BPA): 6. [4] Massola 1973; Nanni and James 2013: 8–9.
[5] Victoria 1864b (BPA): 5–6.

But sickness among residents quickly emerged as a problem. In the three years from 1865 to 1867, there were sixteen deaths on the station and six births and six marriages. In May 1867 a 'low fever' was prevalent and five people died. Causes of death were listed as inflammation of the lungs, the effects of 'over indulgence in spirituous liquors', St Vitus' dance, old age and consumption. But the annual report for 1869 simply pronounced that 'on the whole the health of the Aborigines has been good'.[6] By the end of the 1860s even though the board continued to hold up Coranderrk as a model, many correspondences including the medical inspector's reports were casting a critical eye, painting quite a different picture from the one presented by the board. Coranderrk was first constituted and then regularly spoken about as a settlement for the reception and residence of 'orphan and destitute [and] neglected' children. Later, it was replaced by a less overtly stated aspiration – to gather half-caste children there, particularly girls. By the end of the decade, a practice was established of recording numbers of half-castes and Aborigines across all settlements in the colony, including Coranderrk. But the reports no longer differentiated between so-called neglected, orphan or destitute children. They show evidence of attempts to collect, retain or relocate children and the gradual formation, *de facto* if not *de jure*, of a programme of child removal through inducement, persuasion and suggestions of coercion through the manipulation of the provision of rations. It is possible also to discern another administrator's problem – the impediment of Aboriginal parents refusing to give up their children.[7] As shown in Chapter 2, Aboriginal parents' strong attachment to their children emerged from the 1877 Royal Commission into Aborigines as a problem confronting white administrators.

By the early 1870s there were 567 Aborigines recorded settled on all the stations under the direct control of the board. This was thought a promising development:

> [T]he natives will not only be guarded and usefully employed, but the cost of their maintenance will be largely reduced. Though exertions are made to gather together the children and young persons on several reserves set apart for their use, inducements are held out at the same time to the young men to engage in useful labors on the sheep stations.[8]

These themes were reiterated frequently throughout the decade. A clearly concentrated effort was made to remove all so-called orphan children to either Lake Condah or Coranderrk stations. Younger half-caste boys, and all girls were regarded as amenable to removal. Of one girl, the board noted it was 'very desirable that she should be removed before she gets contaminated'. It noted a case of a 'black boy about two years of age, but of course he could not be taken unless his mother came with him'.[9] Mr Green reported from the Murray River region that there had been a decrease in numbers of Aborigines of about 131 though 'the actual decrease due to

6 Victoria 1869 (BPA): 3. 7 McCallum 2006. 8 Victoria 1872 (BPA): 3.
9 Victoria 1872 (BPA): 8.

deaths is not so great as these figures would make it appear'. But seventy-eight of that number were children under fifteen years, and the majority, it was noted, were half-castes:

> All the guardians consider that these should be removed to some school, as they are growing up in ignorance and vice; the girls if not removed at once, will become common prostitutes; in fact many of them are already . . . I would urge on the Board the necessity of at once taking steps to have all the children collected, especially the girls, over six years of age, and brought to Coranderrk. It is a fact that many of the girls are contaminated before they are 10 years of age, and that by white men – their parents give them for money or drink – the consequence is that very few of them live to womanhood.[10]

Green's report urged the board to 'do more to prevent the race becoming extinct' by collecting and looking after the girls: 'I consider it is the duty of the Government to do all that can be done to save these girls from a life of infamy and misery.'[11] New buildings 'for orphans' were going up at the Lake Condah mission, and there was optimism about the progress made in reading and writing on the Ebenezer Mission on the Wimmera River. Keeping the young people on the mission was improving their education, but it was difficult to keep those referred to as 'the old ones' who preferred a 'wandering life . . . as a rule they like hunting, and indulge in it to a great extent'.[12]

By 1875 it had become standard practice to separate children from their families within the mission grounds. Inspection reports for that year note that at Lake Hindmarsh 'the house occupied by the children (20) was clean, and the air in the bedrooms sweet and pure', at Lake Tyers, '[t]he house occupied by the children was clean and tidy', at Coranderrk, '[t]he schoolroom is well kept and so is the girls' dormitory attached to it . . . I also inspected the children living with the superintendent apart from their parents.'[13] In summary then, via the emphasis on special supervision of children in accommodation away from their parents, along with remarks about inducing young adults to seek paid work off the station, an initial policy of separation emerged which may not have been be forced removal from parents *per se*. The board appeared at pains to point out that it could not and would not separate a mother and infant. However, in its reports from this era there is little mention of 'destitute' and no mention of 'neglected' children. What seemed to emerge was a policy of separation of all children: a generational separation, rather than a focus on the neglected and destitute as was the stated aspiration of the board when it was first constituted. The next two sections focus attention on one mission in particular, Coranderrk, with a view to pursuing an understanding of the relations between children, health and administration at the closer range of an individual mission station.

10 Victoria 1872 (BPA): 9. 11 Victoria 1872 (BPA): 9. 12 Victoria 1872 (BPA): 23.
13 Victoria 1875 (BPA): 5, 9, 16.

DISEASE, MEDICINE AND RACE

From optimistic beginnings, Coranderrk station was increasingly presented as a failure, despite plans to make it self-sufficient, free of cost to the public purse. It was plagued by illness and overall reckoned as an unhealthy situation, economically, morally and physically. By 1879, far from a model for others to emulate, Coranderrk compared unfavourably with other stations, and the board had recommended its closure.[14] In 1874 a local medical practitioner named Gibson reported on increased cases of serious chest infections which he claimed resulted from 'the thoughtless exposure the blacks submit themselves to while hunting or fishing, by camping out in all weathers' and also 'the shoeless condition of the younger portion of the community during the winter months'.[15] Consistent with the reasoning that Aboriginal people were responsible for their own ill health, the doctor thought that less camping out in bad weather and wearing proper footwear in the winter months would prevent much of the suffering and sickness. The following year Gibson claimed that an 'eruptive disease' had taken hold at Coranderrk, a species of *papulae siccae* 'almost peculiar to the Aborigines . . . there is no danger from it but it sometimes continues long, and causes great inconvenience. Among Europeans it is not reckoned contagious, but I have more than once seen it spread over nearly all the young persons on this station.'[16] The doctor claimed the diseases posed 'no danger' but the death rates were steadily increasing. The new manager Heinrich Stähle reported two births and four deaths, and much sickness including fever and 'native-pocks'.[17]

The sickness and death at the station had come to the attention of the state's Chief Medical Officer McCrea, who claimed that excessive mortality was largely the result of the position and the condition of Coranderrk: 'no less than fourteen deaths have occurred at Coranderrk from pneumonia, the best preventive for which might have been the removal of the people to a more genial climate'.[18] Coranderrk was described by the board's officers as sour rangy country, not suitable for rearing either sheep or cattle. Even the sheep had become 'flukey' and it was too cold for cattle. McRae made explicit that the climate was too cold and wet for Aborigines to remain all year round, and it was also too near the white population for the Aborigines to be 'kept clear of the vices incidental to the two races being in such contiguity' – the vices being drunkenness and prostitution. However, McCrea did not mince words about the medical causes of the illness and death. The people, he noted, had complained greatly of the cold and wet in the winter, 'and I have no doubt that the situation of the establishment contributes not a little to the development of chest diseases'. The slope was gradual and well adapted for drainage purposes, 'but the natives' huts are built . . . across the face of

14 Victoria 1879b (BPA): 13. 15 Victoria 1875 (BPA): 8.
16 Victoria 1875 (BPA): 9, Appendix II (Dr Gibson's report on Coranderrk).
17 Victoria 1875 (BPA): 16, Appendix VI Coranderrk, 4 Jan. 1875. 18 Victoria 1876 (BPA): 3.

the slope ... the natural advantage of the fall of the ground for drainage being thus lost':

> In wretched hovels like these it is no wonder the mortality is excessive. It appears by Mr. Ogilvie's report that in 1875, with a population of about 150 people, 31 deaths took place – one out of every five human beings in one year perishing from disease. This awful mortality was doubtless exceptional, an epidemic of measles having been prevalent in the early part of the year; but this epidemic prevailed all over the colony, about 17 per 1,000, is compared with that of Coranderrk, the discrepancy is appalling, the latter amounting to 193 per 1,000, or, in other words, for every person out of the general population who died, 11 deaths occurred at Coranderrk.[19]

Two out of the thirty-one deaths in 1897 were caused by measles directly and four others from colds caught after measles. The highest number of deaths was fourteen reported cases of pleuro-pneumonia and chest disease which McRae claimed resulted from draughty walls and roofs and to the damp floors of the huts. McCrea's conclusion was that anybody attacked by such diseases had little chance of surviving in such 'hovels':

> Were an epidemic of scarlatina to invade the settlement, and they are liable to it at any moment, the remaining natives would be in danger of being swept away altogether. A very erroneous impression is generally prevalent regarding the power of natives to withstand the vicissitudes of the weather; it is assumed, because in their aboriginal condition they were able, with little clothing, and under the mere shelter of a mia-mia, to resist the influence of severe cold and wet, that their dwellings should be very open. This is a great mistake; the altered conditions in which a comparative civilization places them render them much more obnoxious to changes of temperature than when they led a savage life; the circumstances of wearing clothing causes them to perspire more freely in exertion, and the exposure to draughts under these conditions renders them unusually liable to diseases consequent on suppressed perspiration, and particularly to diseases of the lungs.[20]

McRae wrote that Aborigines themselves complained bitterly about the effects of cold air especially in wintertime, 'rushing through the crevices of their ill-constructed huts'. Their sleeping accommodation was cramped, from four to ten persons in some cases occupying a single hut, where there was scarcely space to accommodate two people. Their bedsteads were 'untidy constructions of sticks and bark likely to engender vermin, and to inculcate want of cleanliness and habits of self-respect in the occupants'.[21]

But a later medical report from the local doctor (Gibson) contained no references whatsoever to illness – health was simply 'good' – and pointed instead to the need for a school master: 'At my visit the girls under your matron, Miss Robertson, were busily

[19] Victoria 1876 (BPA): 21–22, Appendix XII Coranderrk (W. McCrea, Chief Med. Officer). Reprinted in Victoria 1879a (Report and Correspondences Relative to ... Mortality [Mortality Report]).

[20] Victoria 1879a (Mortality Report).

[21] Victoria 1879a (Mortality Report).

engaged in sewing, but there is a very urgent want of a school master, as the juvenile part of the community, except those few girls, are at present receiving no attention.'[22] New station superintendent Halliday reported that general health at the station had picked up, which he attributed to improved condition of the huts – five new huts were put up during the year – and to warm clothing supplied by the board. Having said that, he noted that there had been ten births and ten deaths during the year, seven of which were child deaths, now attributed to the 'coldness of the climate'. Halliday reassured the board (incorrectly) that two doctors from the local town of Healesville (Drs Gibson and Elmes) attended the station once or twice a week, or more often as occasion required.[23]

Initially, given the evident problems at Coranderrk, and in light of the fact that the people had expressed a 'very decided and natural objection' to leaving the station, the board decided that the wisest course would be to 'replace about twenty of the worst huts' and to establish a sanatorium for 'any Coranderrk invalids'.[24] But by the end of the decade the board offered this summary:

> The general health on three of the stations has been good, but the death rate on the whole has been larger than last year. Lung disease is the chief cause of death among the Aborigines, who, once affected, very seldom recover . . . The Board has recently called the attention of the Government to the serious mortality among the natives, and it also contemplates calling in the aid of Dr W Thompson, of South Yarra, who has devoted much attention to this branch of disease . . . Messrs Le Souef and Curr were deputed in May to visit and report on the two Gippsland stations . . . In [the report] reference is made to the Coranderrk station near Healesville, which they consider should be broken up, and the blacks distributed among the other stations. The Board fully coincides with Messrs Le Souef and Curr, and has since brought the matter under the notice of Sir Bryan O'Loghen when Acting Chief Secretary.[25]

Clearly two quite conflicting views on the reasons for the high death rate were circulating through the colony, including opposing medical assessments of the death rates and their causes. In one account, Chief Medical Officer McRae submitted that the station was dangerous to health because it was poorly built and drained, the residents especially children became sick with chest infections and often never recovered, and everyone had insufficient clothing and footwear to withstand the heavy winters. In another account, officials of the BPA along with local medical practitioners reported that the Coranderrk Aborigines suffered from a disease unique to Aboriginal people which, combined with the physical and moral climate, meant they were never likely to recover. The Reverend Strickland expressed it thus:

22 Victoria 1876 (BPA): 28, Appendix XVI 19 Feb. 1876 Coranderrk (J. Gibson).

23 Victoria 1878 (BPA): 5, Appendix 1 Coranderrk 24 July 1878.

24 Victoria 1876 (BPA): 3.

25 Victoria 1879b (BPA): 3–4.

> The health of the Aborigines is, I fear, much affected by the cold and damp climate; scarcely any of them are sound, as they are the subjects of phthisis, which is much promoted by their *innate indifference* to exposure to all kinds of weather. Proximity to a township, with its adjuncts, militates against the moral culture of the people.[26]

Henry Jennings, vice-president of the BPA, wrote to the Victorian government chief secretary about the health of 'the unfortunate remnant of the tribes under their care'. Jennings claimed that the board had made attempts to 'arrest the terrible death rate' on the stations but this had proved 'completely futile'.[27]

It was then becoming apparent that the reduction in the numbers of the tribes was not attributable to the intoxication and debauchery that had been the favoured explanation thus far, but rather the facts seemed to show that the 'sober and moral' had fared nearly as ill as the drunkard. Individuals age 30–35 taking up residence on the stations preserved their health, worked hard and often lived to age 60 or 70. It was the children who were most vulnerable:

> [T]hose who are born or enter our establishment in childhood, on attaining a suitable age are unable to work for any time without inducing spitting of blood, and for the most part die between their twelfth and twenty-fifth years, and seem in few cases likely to reach 30. From this it happens that instances are daily becoming more frequent of parents who have buried two, four, or six children, and occasionally been left childless. We have further the honor to bring under your notice the very important fact that death in most cases is the result of a disease of *the lung peculiar to the natives*, which ends fatally in every case – that no cure has ever been known, nor, as far as we can judge, does medical attendance seen to have ever retarded the fatal catastrophe. In view of these facts it seems to us that there is strong reason for concluding that the cause of death, whatever it may be, is intimately connected with the daily life of these people, and it has been stated at one of our meetings that a similar mortality has prevailed on an establishment in Queensland. In that case it was successfully met by making a great reduction in the clothing used, and keeping the children (there are no adults in the establishment) as much as possible in the open air, day and night.[28]

Two members of board, Curr and Le Souef, agreed that the station should be disbanded and moved elsewhere:

> We consulted Messrs. Hagenauer and Bulmer with reference to Coranderrk, and both unequivocally condemn it as an Aboriginal reserve, Mr. Hagenauer stating that he considered it utterly impossible for any one to manage it satisfactorily. As we have always held the same opinion, we recommend the Board to request permission from the Chief Secretary to disband and break up both it and the Framlingham

[26] Victoria 1879b (BPA): 5, Appendix 1 Coranderrk (F. P. Strickland, Superintendent), emphasis added.

[27] Victoria 1879b (BPA): 13.

[28] Victoria 1879b (BPA): 13, Appendix XIII, 12 June 1879 (Henry Jennings, Vice President, Board), emphases added. Reprinted in Victoria 1879a (Mortality Report).

> Station, and distribute the natives now living on them among the other four stations.[29]

The following year Strickland reported constant sickness and further losses of life on the station, now claiming that the climate was 'too humid' for the Aborigines.[30]

ABORIGINAL RESISTANCE

Led by William Barak, the Coranderrk Aborigines mounted a campaign supported by some influential citizens of Melbourne including the chief secretary and succeeded in holding onto the land. Aboriginal people achieved a partial victory and also the conditions on the mission improved a little, but the appalling rates of mortality and morbidity continued. The lead-up to these events had been provoked by a programme of medical management peculiar to the sick Aboriginal child – less clothing and less shelter for those suffering from that mysterious form of lung disease purportedly peculiar to Aborigines. McCrae had in 1876 attributed a good deal of the illness at Coranderrk to 'appalling sanitary conditions'.[31] He wrote again directly to the chief secretary in 1879 reiterating that 'sanitary defects . . . were the cause of the excessive misconception that Aborigines are constitutionally unique in their ability to resist the influence of severe cold and wet' – a misconception that led to the conclusion that they did not need the same warmth and shelter as the non-Aborigine. Nor was he in much doubt that the illness afflicting the population was the same pleuro-pneumonia as afflicted any white population subject to bad sanitation, lack of warmth and shelter, bad climate and overcrowding. The board simply disagreed with the chief medical officer. Vice-chairman Henry Jennings repeated that it was 'a disease of the lung peculiar to the natives', that the 'cause of death, whatever it may be, is intimately connected with the daily life of these people' and that a Queensland example had shown less clothing and shelter was the solution.[32] Le Souef (philanthropist and director of the Melbourne zoo) in his role as BPA vice-chairman, responded in correspondence to the government that the good doctor McCrae

> seemed to have overlooked the fact that this fatal lung disease exists on all the other stations, though some of them are under entirely different conditions with regard to climate, drainage, etc . . . Experience has led the Board to think that it is not well to make the native cottages so air-tight as he suggests, and it is of the opinion that there are causes other than those referred to in his report which occasion the development of the peculiar form of chest disease which carries off so many of the natives, especially among the young.[33]

29 Victoria 1879b (BPA): 10, Appendix VII, 21 May.
30 Victoria 1880c (BPA): 5, Appendix 1, Coranderrk July 1880 (F. P. Strickland).
31 Victoria 1876 (BPA): 21–22, Appendix XII, Coranderrk (W. McRea, Chief Medical Officer).
32 Victoria 1879b (BPA): 13.
33 Victoria 1879a (Mortality Report): 6 (Vice Chairman A. le Souef to Chief Secretary, 7 July 1879).

The historians Barwick and Nanni and James document the political background to these events, including an attempted land-grab by local residents close to the Coranderrk site, a plot by locals to sell the land to finance an extension of the Melbourne railway network to the nearby town of Healesville, and the extraordinary lengths taken by the local doctors and government appointees to the Board for the Protection of Aborigines to 'invent' a disease peculiar to Aboriginal people that would necessitate their departure from Coranderrk.[34] At the government inquiry instigated because of the treatment of Aborigines and the high rates of morbidity and mortality, including the death through tuberculosis of David Barak, the son of William Barak, a 'slew of medical experts' provided evidence on the unsuitability of Coranderrk's climate, using the latest theories of germ contagion gaining favour in Europe, and attributing the high mortality rate instead to the 'neglected' manner and 'carelessness of dealing with the sick and their discharges'. A specialist hired by the board, William Thomson, informed the inquiry that the 'mysterious' disease was tuberculosis, which occurred in all the other stations 'no matter whether the climate was high or dry, or low and marshy'. All the medical witnesses recommended that a local hospital be built where the sick could be quarantined to prevent contagion and where they could be treated locally instead of having to travel into Melbourne.[35] This was a crushing blow to the ambitions of locals with their eyes on the valuable Coranderrk estate and to the BPA, whose attempts to bring the Aborigines of Coranderrk into line had failed dismally. Work on fixing the condition of the station commenced shortly afterwards.

SCIENCE, RACE AND SEPARATIONS

In the 1860s the Board for the Protection of Aborigines constituted the Aborigine or the 'pure Australian' as an anthropological entity, viewed through an anthropological or quasi-anthropological lens. Issues about the *moral* constitution of the Aborigine were often couched in these terms – in the context of where they were to be positioned on a racialised scale. In the following decade, however, there was little comment along these lines and little of the anthropological curiosity that the board was expressing in its first decade of operations. In the light of vital statistics on mortality resulting from sickness, new questions and disagreements occurred around the *physical* constitution of the Aborigine. Medical science finally was called upon to answer questions about the high mortality rate. It was given new questions of the physical rather than moral constitution – the answers to which were used to shape management practices differently.

The move to physicality also brought with it issues about the complexion and colour of Aborigines that had appeared only rarely in the previous decade. Statistical charts prepared in 1871, on Aborigines provided with certificates which allowed them

[34] Barwick et al. 1998; Nanni and James 2013. [35] Nanni and James 2013: 94.

to be employed off the station, included a column listing 'peculiarities', including 'half-caste' or 'very dark complexion', along with scars and other distinguishing factors of appearance. Here half-caste features appeared as a visual sign that could be read off from the appearance of the individual for the first time officially: J. D. is age 23, height 5 foot 11 inches, 'has a piece out of his upper lip . . . is a half-caste'; T. K. is 40, 5 foot 8 inches, 'very dark complexion, speaks English tolerably well'. By the mid-1870s, on statistical charts, half-caste or black became the central distinguishing features.[36] The following year provided information signed by board members Curr and Ogilvie focussing on married couples, the status of each (black or half-caste) and the number and status of sons and daughters. Sometimes children of the same couple might be listed as black *or* half-caste, suggesting again that the authority was applying some judgement on the ground of complexion. In the following year, colour was first used as a category in Ogilvie's report to the BPA on Coranderrk 'in accordance with the wish expressed in your letter of 17th December 1875' in relation to educational attainment. Under the heading 'Color' [sic] residents were documented as either 'B' or 'HC'.[37] An appendix to Ogilvie's report included the following:

> I have now only to add a few remarks on what I conceive ought to be the general management of the Aborigines, and I think in reference to this they should be divided into classes:
>
> 1st Class – all full-blooded Aborigines, partially or wholly ignorant of the laws of civilization, and all the infirm and aged; all of whom should be managed in a purely paternal manner.
>
> 2nd Class – all others above a certain age, on being admitted to the station, should be required to sign an agreement with the superintendent to obey all his lawful orders, &c., and that on any breach of this agreement the superintendent should be authorized to administer such mild punishment as might be thought adequate to the offence (stopping tobacco &c.); but that for any flagrant breach of discipline they should be summoned before a bench, and treated exactly as a white man would be under similar circumstances, for which purposes it would be necessary that their accounts with the station should be so kept that there should always be a small balance to their credit to meet any probable fine imposed. Of course the superintendent would also be instructed that the less he felt it necessary to call in the aid of a magistrate to assist him in the management of the Aborigines the better the Board would be pleased.
>
> 3rd Class – which may be called the Educational Class, would of course be composed of the youths of both sexes. I think this class should be so educated that as they arrive at a sufficient age they could be sent into the world to compete for employment with the white population, the station never being closed against them in periods of distress or sickness.
>
> Under some such system as I have sketched, I do not think it would be too much to anticipate, and that at no very remove period that the necessity for a Board might

36 Victoria 1872 (BPA): 3, Appendix XIV; Victoria 1875 (BPA): 24.
37 Victoria 1876 (BPA): 18–19, Appendix XI.

> cease; but I do fear that unless the grown-up half-castes are made to feel their personal responsibility to a greater extent than I think they do at present, and unless the young are taught that they will have to battle for their living the same as white people, some future Board for the Protection of Aborigines will have to deal with a vagabond race only distinguishable from the whites in that they will be lower sunk in depravity than the basest of those whites.[38]

Then in 1878 the term 'quadroons' made an entry. Among further suggestions for the separation of 'classes' of Aborigines and absorption into the white community from Coranderrk's new superintendent Halliday was his note that quadroons would 'pass as such':

> I think before long the Board will have to consider the advisability of giving the half-caste Aboriginals of the colony a station to themselves apart from the blacks, a proceeding which I am strongly in favour of, as I believe it would lead to their further moral and social improvement; they do not agree too well together on the same station, and when any dispute arises the ill feeling shows itself, and requires to be firmly and speedily checked. The quadroons, when they arrive at a certain age, might be licensed out as whites, *and would pass as such*. I think these people might become absorbed in the general community quicker in this way, as I presume it is not intended to keep these kinds of stations longer than can be possibly helped.[39]

By 1880 colour had become a standard form of categorisation in tables of population statistics, including vital statistics, and terms such as 'quadroon' had well and truly entered the lexicon: 'I have married 2 couples; there have been 7 births; at the present time we have 34 pure blacks, 59 half-castes, and 9 quadroons, making in the whole 102.'[40] More commonly, though, 'aborigines' or, less frequently, 'Aborigines' had become the generic term, sometimes 'natives', and there was no use of the phrase 'blacks including half-castes', common a decade earlier. More commonly, numbers of Aborigines included numbers of half-castes, as in the body of the report for 1881: 'There are about 300 Aborigines supplied by the Board away from the stations, principally located in the Swan Hill District and about the junction of the Goulburn and the Murray. Of this number about 60 are half-castes.'[41]

The terms 'black' and 'half-caste' had become unstable and often required further definition. New qualifying terms such as '3/4 black' and 'full-black' were used as descriptors under the heading 'Colour'. Colour had become a quantification – a calculation as to an amount of Aboriginality – a 'science' of the quantification of Aboriginality. Given that Aboriginality was what was to be managed, a science of colour formed the basis for management practices. When mixed with talk of 'blood', as had begun to appear over the previous few years – 'mixed blood', 'full-blooded' – the descriptions gained a kind of quasi-physiological legitimacy.

38 Victoria 1876 (BPA): 6, Appendix II. 39 Victoria 1878 (BPA): 5, Appendix I, emphasis added.

40 Victoria 1880d (BPA): 5, Appendix I, Coranderrk, July 1880 (F. P. Strickland).

41 Victoria 1882 (BPA): 3.

A WELFARE *AND* JUSTICE SYSTEM?

As noted in Chapter 2, evidence suggests that those terms 'welfare' and 'justice' as applied by administrators of the non-Aboriginal population were applied quite differently by the administrators of the Aboriginal population; they were underpinned by quite different logics and geared towards contrasting aspirations. The stations and reserves under the control of the BPA may indeed have provided protection of sorts, including material support, but that support also functioned as a leverage for imposing discipline. The second half of the nineteenth century was a period that affirmed that the specifics of an Aboriginal child's personhood were not produced in the same way that the white child was being produced as a specific object of government. Indeed, in the fashioning of personhood, no less than 'the child' should 'the Aborigine' be considered an achievement – an entity fashioned as knowable so as to be governable given the toing and froing of legislative definitions of Aboriginality. So this exploration of how welfare and justice pertain to the Aboriginal child as the subject of governing practices has to explore how welfare and justice pertain to 'the Aborigine' in *its* make-up as an entity fashioned by white administrators in a knowable and hence governable form – how is this 'Aborigine' known as the subject of welfare and justice? The approach to that question needs to take into account broader imperatives to do with managing Aborigines, rather than simply searching for the Aboriginal child and comparing how that child was treated by the welfare system or the justice system, as compared to the white child. The previous chapter explored the practices of welfare and justice as they pertained to the non-Aboriginal population, and in particular the non-Aboriginal child, in the second half of the nineteenth century. It looked to such institutions as the various tiers of the justice system: the police, the courts, the penal system and particularly the Department of Industrial and Reformatory Schools/Department for Neglected Children and Reformatory Schools, and the correctional and welfare institutions and practices under its administration and explored the means by which children under state care began to be criminalized. But the argument presented there was not dependent on evidence that persons were placed in formally designated institutions for the offenders or delinquents *whereupon* they took on (or achieved) the persona of the 'criminal type'. This underestimates the processes that in a European context have been well described by Michel Foucault as those of a 'disciplinary society'[42] and might usefully be borne in mind in exploring the criminalization of young Aboriginal people.

The young Aboriginal trouble-maker was thrown into relief as a consequence of the government's particular aspirations regarding Aborigines as a whole, and as a consequence of the BPA's actions in carrying out government policy. In short, the problem for the BPA as reported by the mission managers was the trouble caused by young half-castes hanging around the missions when they were supposed to be

[42] Minson 1985; Foucault 2007.

'merging', and drawing on the rations of their relatives on the mission stations. Under the 1886 protection act, and in the terms inscribed in that act, half-castes were defined as distinct from the 'aboriginal' and lost entitlement to remain on the missions, which included the entitlement to receive rations. Half-caste children on the mission lost that entitlement once they were deemed old enough to earn their own living. This was reiterated in the 1890 consolidation act which formalised an added offence of sharing rations by making it an offence for any person to 'take whether by purchase or otherwise any goods or chattels issued or distributed to any aborigine (as defined under the act)', with a penalty or conviction not exceeding twenty pounds, or, in default, imprisonment for not less than one month nor more than three months.[43] Further, regulations pertaining to the 1890 act gave the board authority to have 'any half-caste or child of half-castes ... dismissed and removed from any station for misconduct on advice from the manager of such station or the general inspector'.[44] As a certificate was required to enter the mission, being on the mission without the correct papers was an offence under the act. From 1886 'misconduct' on the part of young half-castes was construed as behaviour which thwarted the board's (and the government's) aim of reducing the size and number of missions. The board had reported the ongoing problem of the young half-caste men 'ready to take advantage' of anyone receiving rations.[45] In 1894, H. P. Bogisch, manager of Lake Hindmarsh station, reported to the Board that the 'half-castes who are under the operation of the Act have not quite left the station, especially the boys still hang about the place'. The following year: 'A good many half-castes have left the station, a few boys, however, are spending too much time with all kinds of sports and should be stopped.' Reports in the same vein were received from other stations: 'I am sorry to say that there is a general tendency among the young people to be lazy, disobedient, and careless, which, if not stopped in due time, will become very troublesome to the Board and dangerous to the white population as well as for themselves.'[46]

The trouble making involved in wilful sharing of resources and wilful maintenance of family ties demonstrates a disparity in welfare and justice policies as they pertained to Aboriginal and non-Aboriginal populations. Compared with the white welfarist policies of building support for the norms of family life, the 1886 and 1890 acts, their attendant regulations and the practices that followed in their wake demonstrate a racialised disparity with young white law breakers inasmuch as it was made an offence for family to share rations and resources with youths deemed non-Aboriginal and who refused to leave their homes. With these legislative and administrative arrangements in place, the mission stations took on more and more of

43 Victoria Aborigines Act (No. 1059) 1890 s 13.

44 Victoria 1890b (BPA): 23, Appendix XXII, reg. 23.

45 PROV VPRS 1694 Unit 1: J. Shaw (Coranderrk) to Rev. F. A. Hagenauer, Gen. Insp. Aborigines 16 July 1890.

46 Victoria 1894 (BPA): 10; Victoria 1895 (BPA): 9; Victoria 1899 (BPA): 8, Appendix III, Mission Station, Ramahyuck, Gippsland.

the operations of a correctional institution, a shift that is discussed in greater detail in Chapter 6.

While government in Australia in the second half of the nineteenth century seemed intent on making the services of supposedly discrete institutions for neglected and criminal children available also to Aboriginal children, there is little evidence that in Victoria there was any large-scale formal transfer of eligible Aboriginal children from the missions into these institutions once the legislation and regulations were up and running. Nevertheless, some Aboriginal children, orphans and otherwise, were recorded as received by the DNCRS in the late nineteenth century and at the turn of the twentieth century, a plan was hatched for all half-caste orphans to be transferred to the care of the Department for Neglected Children and Reformatory Schools, and from there, after appropriate training, placed in service. (By this stage, it is possible to argue that the category 'orphan' in department documents may be a euphemism for children separated from their parents under the earlier mission legislation.) Under these circumstances Aboriginal children transferred to the DNCRS would have been made subject to the *de facto* indeterminate sentencing discussed in the previous chapter. As noted in Chapter 3, both offending and neglected children reported to the department as exhibiting 'depraved habits' and 'serious misconduct' were subject to transfer to a reformatory for an indeterminate period, usually until age 18. Children sent out to foster care or into service could be transferred to a reformatory on the basis of reports about their behaviour by their guardians, in a system administered by the DNCRS and by the 1890s transfer to a reformatory was largely at the discretion of the executive, bypassing any court appearance. A little later it was announced that the plan to send mission children to the DNCRS was to be extended to 'all suitable Aboriginal children whether orphans or otherwise ... in order that they may have the advantages of being dealt with in the same way as other wards of the State'.[47] The next section examines in more detail both the late-nineteenth-century transfers of children and the extent to which the early-twentieth-century plan to transfer children was implemented.

THE FUNCTIONING OF LIMINAL ZONES

The legislation passed in the 1886 Aborigines Protection Act gave the Board for the Protection of Aborigines power to send an Aboriginal child, or a child of an Aborigine almost anywhere it liked – which would, under the act include children of half-caste parents living under licence on the station, given that those under licence were deemed Aboriginal. By 1890 the newly consolidated Aborigines Act (Section 5, Regulation 13 under the title 'Custody of Children') authorised the BPA to remove any children neglected by their parents 'to any of the places of residence

[47] Victoria 1901a (DNCRS): 7.

specified in Regulation 1, or to an industrial school or reformatory school'.[48] The practice of transferring children from the board to the DNCRS was not, strictly speaking, confined to the transfer of orphans, and in general it was the board itself, not the department, that had responsibility for placing mission children into service. In 1890 Secretary Guillaume of the DNCRS reported that 'seven little orphan half-caste aboriginals' were received into the care of the department, and also three whose mother was dead and father unknown, their ages averaging six and a half years. A statistical chart noted this event by describing the BPA as a 'Bench', alongside those courts throughout the state that heard cases for disposal of children into the 'Care of the Department' or 'Reformatory Schools'.[49] There was no further mention in the department's reports in the last decade of the century of reception of children transferred from the BPA. Nor was there any mention in the reports of the BPA of Aboriginal children in the care of the department until the turn of the century. A later reference in the correspondences of the BPA suggests it was less than meticulous in its own recording of pre-1900 transfers of children. In early 1920 J N, unemployed and residing in Melbourne, was making application to reside at Lake Tyers:

> Mr [JN] finds it impossible to obtain work in Melbourne and is willing, if allowed, to go to Lake Tyers Aboriginal Station. Will refund cost of ticket. Mr [JN] alleges that he was born at Corryong about 40 years ago and resided at Coranderrk but was transferred to the Middle Brighton Orphanage Asylum. No record in Books, but Mr Ditchburn has previously verified fact that [JN] is a Victorian.[50]

JN was granted a pass to Lake Tyers on condition that the fare was refunded from his wages. Given his age, JN would have been around five or six at the passing of the 1886 protection act. Forty years on, his situation in the city of Melbourne was deemed 'impossible', and it was deemed proper that he reside at an Aboriginal station. So much for the 'merging' of JN.

In 1900, in the context of the planned transfer of 'all suitable Aboriginal children' from the control of the BPA to the DNCRS, Secretary Millar presented the rationale for aiding the board in intervening when 'paternal claims conflict with the higher welfare and interests of their children':

> I feel sure that it is a step in the right direction, seeing that it practically places at their disposal for the benefit of their wards the machinery of this Department, which has for so many years been in successful operation in dealing with and disposing of the ordinary wards of the State. And here I should like to add how pleased we are at being called upon to aid the Board in trying to solve what, I feel sure, they must have long felt to be an anxious and difficult problem, viz., how best to dispose of their young wards when paternal claims conflict with the higher welfare and interests of

48 Victoria 1890b (BPA): 21–25, Appendix II; Victoria 1891 (DNCRS): 44.

49 Victoria 1891 (DNCRS): 44.

50 PROV VPRS 1694, Unit 8: Sec. BPA to Vice Chairman BPA 5 Feb. 1920.

their children. While the mere fact of the transfer of these children to the Department constitutes them wards of the Secretary, I propose in dealing with them to largely avail myself of the expert knowledge of them possessed by the Board and its officers; and with a view to satisfying them that the children in whom they are so deeply interested are being well and kindly treated, I have thought it well to invite them and any of the respectable parents of the children to visit and satisfy themselves on this point. Some of the parents and officers have already done so, and have expressed themselves as being greatly pleased, which I felt sure they would be. In the Appendix will be found a very gratifying and interesting letter from the Vice-Chairman of the Aborigines Board, giving a result of a visit to some of the children.[51]

The board reported that the boys undergoing training at the Bayswater farm, and girls at the home for domestic service, were doing 'remarkably well':

> In connection with the merging of the half-castes with the general population, the question of giving the boys and girls a suitable industrial training, in order that they may be able to earn their own living, has been well considered by the Board, and, after careful inquiry, the practice of transferring these half-caste children on leaving the station schools to the Department for Neglected Children has been adopted.[52]

The board envisaged a period of 'institutional training' before these children were put out to service. However, we might note that by 1900, with the system of boarding-out in full swing, it was not the case that, to use DNCRS Secretary Millar's phrase, 'ordinary wards of the State' were sent to institutions for training. The demise of the old industrial school system had already occurred. While some vestiges of that old system remained – the Girl's Training School at Albion still operated under the old nomenclature of industrial school – there was by 1900 the depot at Royal Park for receiving and disposing of children, and a number of institutions operating under the auspices of the DNCRS as private reformatories. The model referred to in the report of the BPA harks back to a system already deemed redundant for the so-called ordinary white child. Under boarding-out as many as possible children, as soon as possible, were to find their way into private homes, the younger ones as foster children and the older ones in service. Moreover, part of the so-called machinery at the disposal of the 'ordinary ward of the State' was a system that allowed many children committed as neglected to be fostered to their own mothers, who received a foster payment for their support. In 1900 of the 874 children received into the care of the DNCRS, 328 were boarded-out to their own mothers. The proportion continued to grow, such that by 1901 half the non-Aboriginal children received by the state were boarded to their own mothers.

The BPA named Bayswater as the destination of the boys sent from the missions to the department. By 1900 the Salvation Army operated two children's homes at Bayswater: one formally gazetted as a reformatory and also a home for younger boys opened in 1899. Although not gazetted as a reformatory, in reality it was understood as

[51] Victoria 1901a (DNCRS): 7–8. [52] Victoria 1900b (BPA): 4.

a place to send the young offender or the particularly 'depraved', who were too young for the reformatory proper. It was, in effect, a reformatory in everything but name for younger boys, as borne out by Secretary Millar's remarks on the opening of that establishment. Millar noted that the Salvation Army Bayswater Home for Young Boys 'has already proved a success, and certainly was much required by the Department in dealing with the very young but wayward and, in some instances, already depraved boys'.[53] On its establishment, the superintendent reported of his charges that it was 'very distressing to find so much depravity among small children'.[54] And in 1901 Bray wrote on the Bayswater Intermediate Home that the 'majority of cases are younger than the lads in the Reformatory, some of them are very depraved . . . [T]hey have in numerous cases been guilty for years of conduct that shows them to be vicious, and undesirable companions for children of tender years.'[55] While the sight of so much depravity was cause for remark by the superintendent of the Bayswater institution, in that very same report members of the BPA on visiting the Aboriginal boys sent there, were nothing but delighted with the sight that met their eyes. Their letter of gratitude is printed in the DNCRS's annual report:

> Commandant Booth
> Salvation Army, Bourke – street, Melbourne
>
> Dear Sir,
>
> On Friday last I visited your two farms near Bayswater, accompanied by the Rev. F. A. Hagenauer, the General Inspector and Secretary for the protection of Aborigines, and Mr Le Souef, one of its members. Our primary reason for the visit was our wish to see some half-caste boys, who have lately been sent to the farms. Brigadier Kyle accompanied us from Melbourne, and we were courteously received on our arrival by Major Bray, the superintendent, who kindly showed us over the whole establishment.
>
> All the arrangements seemed to us most complete, and the perfect cleanliness and comfort of the dormitories elicited our warmest eulogisms. The numerous scripture texts in the rooms, and other evidence of the value to be attached to the higher life, must have an elevating effect on the young people brought up under Christian influences . . . The boys we were more particularly interested in, and they appeared to be happy and contented. The training they are now undergoing is well calculated to make them upright and intelligent members of the community.
>
> We spent a very pleasant and instructive afternoon, and were much impressed with our visit, and wish you every success in your good work.[56]

First then, while Millar claimed that the proposed system of transfer would allow these half-caste Aboriginal children the same 'machinery' afforded 'ordinary' (non-Aboriginal) wards of the state, what was in fact extended to the board was a system of institutional industrial training already deemed redundant and most unsuitable for

53 Victoria 1900a (DNCRS): 5. 54 Victoria 1901a (DNCRS): 12 (Supt Bray).
55 Victoria 1902a (DNCRS): 10–11 (Supt Bray).
56 Victoria 1901a (DNCRS): 18 (D. N. McLeod, Vice Chairman BPA).

the majority of the state's wards. Second, the boys were placed in an institution openly acknowledged as a reformatory in everything but name. Third, whatever the advantages this system was foreseen to bestow on these children, it was understood to be, and embraced as serving the broader agenda of facilitating the white aspiration of Aboriginal population decrease, contributing to the 'extinction by statistics' of the category of 'Aborigine', via merging. J. H. Stähle, manager of Lake Condah, openly acknowledged this: 'As the blacks are dying out, and the Board removes the half-caste boys and girls by handing them over to the Industrial Schools department, finality is greatly facilitated, and will, doubtless, be attained within a few years.'[57]

Finally, there is little evidence that the BPA or the DNCRS actively pursued the scheme of transferring any children to the department beyond the first couple of years of the twentieth century. In 1901 twelve children were registered by the BPA in a table as in 'Industrial Schools and Orphanages' – that is, the number there at the time, not the number transferred that year. There remained twelve in 1902, the number rose to thirteen in 1903, was nine in 1904 and only four in 1905.[58] The BPA's 42nd report (1906) made no mention of children in orphanages or industrial schools, and there was no further mention of them between 1907 and 1912, at which stage publication of reports ceased until 1922. It is clear that none of these sources can be trusted as indicators of a complete picture. It is not possible to be absolutely sure about the numbers of those who, denied any recognition of their Aboriginality, found their way by other means into these institutions. What is apparent is that in the first decade of the twentieth century little more than a dozen Aboriginal children, formally transferred by the BPA, were in the DNCRS institutions at any one time, and that after that initial intake, transferring half-caste children to the DNCRS to train for service positions was not pursued as a matter of course and fell fairly quickly by the wayside.

Evidence further shows that children sent to institutions by the board were removed from the missions for reasons quite contrary to those expressed in the reports and communications of the BPA and DNCRS regarding a plan for training half-caste children, that they were often explicitly referred to as full-blood, that the BPA sometimes by-passed any involvement with the DNCRS and that children were often sent to institutions as a matter of expediency, rather than in the name of their welfare. Here are some examples to demonstrate how these removals were accomplished. In 1903 the manager Bulmer at Lake Tyers recommended MR (Born 22 April 1893, Lake Tyers, half-caste) be removed to the industrial schools and away from the influence of his grandparents who 'take him away in all their wanderings and wholly neglect his moral training'. He was transferred as an orphan to the DNCRS in April 1903. His grandfather protested. MR was in Bayswater for the next five years, reported as unable to read or write though well behaved, and his return to Lake Tyers was recommended. He was discharged from the care of the

57 Victoria 1900b (BPA): 6, Appendix II (J. H. Stähle).

58 Victoria 1901b (BPA): 3; Victoria 1903b (BPA): 3; Victoria 1904b (BPA): 3; Victoria 1905 (BPA): 3.

DNCRS in 1908 (age fifteen) and was escorted to Lake Tyers by the Secretary of the BPA in 1910, age seventeen. There he became the subject of complaints (acting aggressively to white children), named by management as having 'criminal instincts', subject to medical examination as to the state of his mind (there was no evidence that he was other than sane) and brought up on two separate charges (indecent language and assault). While he was serving time, arrangements were made to have him transferred to Lake Condah, where from 1913 to 1916 he was the subject of constant complaints by management, given further medical examination, 'absconded' and then returned. In 1916 an Order in Council was achieved, on account of his 'weak intellect' and need for constant supervision and control, prescribing Bayswater as his place of residence. Meanwhile, MR enlisted in the army but was discharged soon after and was returned to Bayswater where he remained until he absconded in 1918 and then again enlisted, only to be discharged again as unfit and incorrigible. Bayswater refused to take him back so he served some time in military prison before making his way to Victoria's Warrnambool district and then interstate for a time before returning to Victoria. He was in Antwerp in 1922 and from then on continued to fall foul of station managers, local authorities and the law. He was last recorded when he made application for an old-age pension in 1955.[59]

AS, half-caste, born around 1890, was committed via a court to Bayswater in 1905. In 1905 Hagenauer advised that given AS's reported dishonesty, disobedience and a case of theft at Lake Tyers, 'the only good thing' was to have him charged by police 'so that he may get committed by the Court to the Reformatory of the Industrial Schools Department as soon as possible'.[60] He was convicted of larceny and at around age fourteen committed to Bayswater 'for some years'. How long is unknown, but by 1911 he was back in the district of Lake Tyers, though being an adult half-caste he was not allowed on the station. In 1911 the Lake Tyers manager alleged 'immoral intercourse' with an Aboriginal girl EB, a minor and described in correspondences as a full-blood. AS was charged, pled guilty and was sentenced to three months imprisonment. On his release he returned to the district and resumed his relationship with EB, then pregnant with his child. Attempts to remove him and others camped near the station were to no avail – he was charged with trespass; the board urged further charges of vagrancy but the police were reluctant, suggesting it was stretching the law. His presence and that of others were considered by the police to be a sign of general lack of control at Lake Tyers Station. Given the unlikelihood of successfully removing AS from the district, it was decided instead to remove EB, who was transferred to the care of a Salvation Army Home in 1914.[61]

EB was born in Gippsland to parents who moved on and off Lake Tyers. A white publican shot her father HB.[62] EB was the niece of RF. In July 1910, R. W. Howe, then manager at Lake Tyers, wrote to the Secretary of the BPA:

59 NAA B337, 635.

60 PROV VPRS 10309 P0001, 17: F. A. Hagenauer, Gen. Insp. and Sec. BPA, 25 July 1905.

61 NAA B337, 689. 62 Pepper 1985: 222; Attwood 1986: 21; Horton 2010: 4.

> [RF] crossed the Lake this afternoon without permission, taking with her, two girls, [EB] and [AJ] aged 13 and 15 years respectively. Her object in taking them across the Lake, was to prostitute them with some white men who are cutting wood & to whom I believe [RF] herself has paid numerous visits. I have never had any trouble of the girls until [RF] came here & I am afraid that if she remains here long her evil influence will have such an effect on both of those girls more especially her niece [EB] aged 13 that eventually they will get into serious trouble. Both Mrs Howe & myself are always warning the girls never to cross the Lake unless with some reliable person.
>
> I cannot punish them except stopping their rations but that is really no punishment as the other blacks will always provide them with food.[63]

Horton notes that in 1911 EB began a relationship with AS at age fourteen (he, twenty-one, an off-station half-caste). As noted earlier, a charge of carnal knowledge was brought against AS and he was sentenced to three months imprisonment. On his return he continued to see EB who was pregnant by him in 1912, at which time Howe, station manager at Lake Tyers, pressed for her removal. In August 1912 Howe reported to the Secretary of the BPA that EB 'is in an interesting? [sic] condition':

> This of course was inevitable after her intercourse with [AS]. I do not think it would be advisable to keep [EB] on the Station among the other girls in her present condition & would recommend that she be removed to some home, until after the child is born at any rate. It would probably be unnecessary to have an Order in Council to remove her, her removal might possibly have a salutary effect upon some of the other girls who are now growing up.[64]

A later retrospective summary of AS's case by the police inspector at Bairnsdale noted:

> From the information supplied by Const Ryan it will be seen that . . . the offences which culminated in his AS's] conviction viz: – Larceny, Carnally Knowing and Trespass were all attended by circumstances which were of a mitigating nature . . . The Carnally Knowing was committed at Cunninghame (Lakes Entrance) the girl being [EB] . . . who with other aborigines were for days wandering about the bush . . . Dr Tuthill who examined the girl stated that though under the age of 16 years was physically a fully developed woman and the evidence disclosed the fact that she was in the habit of wandering about the bush with [AS] and others.[65]

It is worth noting that the point regarding EB's physical maturity – 'a fully developed woman' – was made by the same Dr Tuthill with regard to another girl, IJ, a minor also implicated in a case of 'immorality'. There, Dr Tuthill noted IJ at age eleven, was physically 'practically an adult'.[66]

63 NAA B337, 253: R. W. Howe (Lake Tyers) to Sec. BPA 17 July 1910.
64 NAA B337, 56: R. Howe (Lake Tyers) to Sec. BPA 26 Aug. 1912.
65 NAA B337, 689: Police Insp. Hewitt, In the Matter of Complaint &c Re Conduct of Aboriginals at Lake Tyers, 15 July 1913.
66 PROV VPRS 1694 Unit 5: Victoria Police: Statement of Dr J. Tuthill 9 Nov. 1911.

With regard to EB's reported condition, the secretary replied that arrangements had been made for her accommodation: 'If there is any circumstance or condition in connection with the girl which should be brought under the notice of the authorities at the Home, you will please let me have all the particulars essential.'[67] Howe noted that EB was due around November, and that he had allowed her to go camping at Orbost meanwhile with relatives but had sent word to the police to bring her back immediately.[68] A week later a police telegram from Orbost requested permission for a doctor to attend EB urgently for her confinement.[69] Howe reported that 'instead of coming back when ordered to do so the parents took her down to some island near the mouth of the Snowy River' where the police had relocated her, but that she was in a 'bad way'.[70] A police report gave an account of the birth. She was camped on 'the Island' with her parents, but apparently could not give birth to her child without medical assistance':

> I immediately procured the services of Dr Kerr who at once attended to her, and after him performing some operation the child was born ... As she was very neglected, and was lying on the banks of the River without the necessary food and assistance I had her removed to Orbost and procured a room for her and also for her grandmother Mrs [C] ... the doctor is still attending and she and her child (female) are progressing favourably.[71]

In late September the board informed a Miss Morton of the Salvation Army's Women's Social Department that given that EB had given birth 'your good offices will not be required'.[72] A further police report had EB and her grandmother removed from the hotel to a tent 'as [EB] became very discontented and wished to be taken away from the hotel'.[73]

EB's baby did not survive and she returned to Lake Tyers and continued her relationship with AS and in February 1913 the board considered Howe's suggestion that AS – an off-station half-caste be removed to another district:

> The Board is unwilling to send the girl to another station as that course may be undesirable. It is essential that [AS] be kept away from L. Tyers Station and the Board trusts you to use every reasonable means within your power to prevent him having access to the station or obtaining any help from the natives.
>
> With regard to the girl [EB] the matron might have a quiet talk with her, as to her conduct and offer some encouragement to lead a better life. If a little gentle persuasion were frequently used it may help to achieve good results.[74]

67 NAA B337, 56: Sec. BPA to R. W. Howe 21 Aug. 1912.
68 NAA B 337, 56: R. W. Howe to Sec. BPA 5 Sept. 1912.
69 NAA B337, 56: Const. Simpson to Sec. BPA 16 Sept. 1912.
70 NAA B337, 56: R. W. Howe to Sec. BPA 16 Sept. 1912.
71 NAA B337, 56: Victoria Police Report of Const. Simpson 19 Sept. 1912.
72 NAA B337, 56: Sec. BPA to Miss Morton 25 Sept. 1912.
73 NAA B337, 56: Victoria Police Report of Const. Simpson 29 Sept. 1912.
74 NAA B337, 56: Sec. BPA to Manager Lake Tyers 12 Feb. 1913.

Howe replied that he and matron 'have made every effort in our power to persuade [EB] to lead a better life' but to no avail. He noted that he once had AS arrested having caught he and EB together in a room in one of the residents' houses and that he did not 'trouble the Board with any of these matters, until I find that all my efforts are unavailing'.[75] The secretary suggested their marriage given 'there appears little likelihood of [EB] and [AS] being separated, as [AS] has apparently formed a strong attachment to the girl':

> In view of the recent history of these people and the scandal caused by such flagrant disregard for morality, it seems desirable that action should be taken in the direction suggested, at the earliest opportunity. This would remove from [AS] the liberty – as a half caste – of obtaining drink whenever he desired, as he would then be brought under the provision of the Act No 2255, and regarded as an aboriginal.[76]

The secretary invited Howe's views. Howe did not agree: he had 'been told' that [AS] did not in fact have great fondness for the girl but merely wanted, once married, to prostitute her or 'failing this his idea is to make application to the Board to sanction his marriage with [EB]; he would then under licence be enabled to lead a life of ease on one of the stations'.[77] For months, Howe continued to complain about the unwelcome presence of AS on the station: he had him before the court for trespass but to little avail, the case being adjourned and AS told to leave and find work: 'This sort of thing is very disorganising to the Station & I would suggest as a solution to the difficulty, if [AS] does not leave, that [EB] be removed from the Station. I may mention that [EB] passed the age of 16 on 20th June last.'[78] The secretary of the BPA made inquiries of the DNCRS and reported that 'the Secretary of the Neglected Children's Department has informed me that the only Institution to which a case of this kind could be sent is the Salvation Army Home at Riddell. There are already two half-caste girls at that place and it would be inadvisable to send [EB] to mix with them.'[79]

It was decided instead to send her to Lake Condah and inquiries were made of the manager (Captain Crawford) there: 'It is felt that if the girl were removed from her present surroundings and placed in a cottage where she would be under the Matron's personal control and different conditions, some good may be effected.'[80] Crawford agreed and would 'place her where she will be under the Matron's personal control. The Matron will set a room apart for her at the Station House.' He also alerted the board to the fact that Mrs S, mother of AS and resident at Lake Condah, had recently requested that her son be allowed on the station on account of her ill health and that the police should warn AS that if found at Lake Condah he

75 NAA B337, 56: R. W. Howe to Sec. BPA 24 Feb. 1913.
76 NAA B337, 56: Sec. BPA to Manager Lake Tyers 10 March 1913.
77 NAA B337, 56: R. W. Howe to Sec. BPA 13 March 1913.
78 NAA B337, 56: R. W. Howe to Sec. BPA 18 Sept. 1913.
79 NAA B337, 56: Sec. BPA to Vice Chairman BPA 22 Sept.1913.
80 NAA B 337, 56: Sec. BPA to Manager Lake Condah 23 Sept. 1913.

would be immediately arrested.[81] Whether this was a deciding factor or not, EB was not sent to Lake Condah but remained until June 1914 at Lake Tyers, at which point Howe again raised the subject of her conduct. Both she, and another girl, AH

> have been acting very badly over the past week, taking a boat upon two occasions at night time, and crossing the Lake to some white men who are camped about two miles away at the landing where they work . . . I think the only thing to do now is to have them removed from here. I would therefore recommend that [AH] be sent to Condah & [EB] who is just 17 years of age – to some home for 12 months . . . I think the removal of these two girls would be a moral lesson to the other girls who are growing up & I do not think it is advisable to be always cautioning them without some punishment being awarded to them.[82]

The BPA was informed by the secretary that the matron at the Salvation Army Home Brunswick would take EB 'on payment of 7/- per week' and recommended that she be placed there by Order in Council.[83] An Order in Council was sought and obtained.[84] EB was escorted to the Salvation Army home (The Harbour) by the police.[85] Howe informed the board in September of 1914: '[IJ] & his wife are always bothering me to suggest how long their daughter [EB] will be in the S.A. Home & whether she would be allowed to communicate with them at least fortnightly.'[86] The secretary of the BPA noted that he had interviewed the matron of the Home who had no objection to their corresponding once a fortnight, that she was reportedly 'quite happy and contented': 'With regard to the period the girl may be detained in the Home, I think it is rather too soon to consider the matter in view of her history, but should be glad to have your opinion on the question.'[87] R. W. Howe replied: 'as long as possible'.[88]

It is important to note that, to date, there had been no involvement of the DNCRS. The Order in Council had the Salvation Army Home in Brunswick as her prescribed place of residence – she was not transferred to the care of the department. This was an arrangement directly between the board and the Salvation Army. But in May 1921, with EB now age twenty-five and confined to the home for eight years, the BPA sought the help of the DNCRS to help find a service position for her away from the city. In May 1921 the secretary wrote to the matron: 'At the last meeting of the Board it was decided to request the Secretary of the Neglected Children Department [sic] to find a suitable home to which EB could go to Service. Steps are being taken accordingly and I have to request that EB be notified.'[89] And from the secretary of the BPA to the Neglected Children's Department secretary:

81 NAA B 337, 56: Manager Lake Condah to Sec. BPA 20 Sept. 1913.
82 NAA B 337, 56: R. W. Howe to Sec. BPA June 1914.
83 NAA B 337, 56: Sec. BPA to Vice Chairman BPA 20 June 1914.
84 Victoria 1914a (Government Gazette): 2628.
85 NAA B 337, 56: Victoria Police Form for payment of expenses incurred 3–6 July 1914.
86 NAA B337, 56: R. W. Howe to Sec. BPA 28 Sept. 1914.
87 NAA B 337, 56: Sec. BPA to Manger Lake Tyers 1 Oct. 1914.
88 NAA B 337, 56: R. W. Howe to Sec. BPA 3 March 1914.
89 NAA B337, 56: Sec. BPA to Matron SA Home Brunswick 11 May 1921.

> There is a full blood Aborigine woman named [EB] who has been for the past eight years in the Salvation Army Home West Brunswick. She is now 25 years of age and although her history prior to being placed in that Home was not a happy one the Matron speaks highly of her and reports that she would make a first class domestic servant having been well trained at that Home. As the girl is desirous of entering service I have by direction to request that a suitable place be found for her if possible some distance from Melbourne.[90]

EB was notified, and it seemed that despite all the assurances of contentment and reluctance to leave the home, according to the matron, on hearing the news, EB became uncontrollable. It was also reported that she had absconded in the past 'on several occasions' – the EB of this report was revealed as much more troublesome an 'inmate' over the years than previous reports had indicated:

> [EB] who for a number of years has been an inmate of our Home, and from time to time have [sic] had turns of discontentedness and on several occasions have [sic] absconded and been brought back again; has lately been very troublesome. Some weeks ago members of the Board paid her a visit and promised to let her go out to a situation, and since then we have not been able to do anything with her.

The matron outlined a series of events – her absconding, her being brought back, her 'subsequent fit of temper', her kicking one of the officers, the police being called in, her refusing food on being told she would have to come to the table at an appointed time, their having to prevent her attempts to 'get away again', her being locked in a bathroom but forcing a door and window in an attempt to escape: 'I am therefore writing to ask the Board to relieve us of her as soon as possible.'[91]

That same day, a recommendation for a new Order in Council was made (and approved) prescribing Lake Tyers as EB's place of residence.[92] She was quickly found a service position – in Parkville as a 'nurse' involved in 'house duties' for a Mrs S of 'The Corso' which took in 'patients' but was also Mrs S's private residence and she explained that EB would have a room with her own daughter. The form required a list of ages of the male members of the household and included a 'Clergyman's Certificate'.[93] EB lasted just a little over a week. An account of that week was sent by Mrs S to the BPA: 'Her work was unsatisfactory and she left on her own accord. She returned to the SA Home in Brunswick.'[94] EB was found a second position, this time in response to a request from a Miss D who wrote 'to know if you know of any half caste Chinese maids you can recommend':

> My cousin has two nice Christian girls she heard of through the Army, they are such a comfort to her, one a very good cook and the other a house parlour maid. I would

90 NAA B337, 56: Sec. BPA to Sec. 'Neglected Children Department' 11 May 1921.

91 NAA B337, 56: E. Johansen, Matron 'The Harbour', Brunswick to Sec. BPA 20 May 1921.

92 NAA B 337, 56: Chief Secretary to Governor in Council 20 May 1921.

93 NAA B 337, 56: Application for an Apprentice or Servant.

94 NAA B 337, 56: L. N. S. (Nurse) to Sec. BPA.

> very much like to get a half caste maid if possible . . . If you have a half caste Chinese of good character would you ring Mrs Walters . . . I prefer protestants.[95]

EB's services were offered via the Salvation Army and Miss D was delighted: 'She seems just what I want . . . I had an aborigine before for two years. She was a splendid servant and a girl of good Christian character and was very happy with me. I like her to have neat dresses and aprons for working.'[96] EB went to service there. Six days later Miss D wrote to Adj. Mary Anderson of the Salvation Army's Lonsdale Street women's shelter, where EB was staying. She complained of EB – she was not well trained, was an inexperienced cook and was 'only suitable for a rough house, not a house like mine.' She would only keep her until she could find a replacement.[97]

On June 18 the secretary of the BPA received a (four-page) letter from EB at Miss D's house expressing her unhappiness there, her homesickness for Lake Tyers, her mother's displeasure at her going out to service, her own sense of her failure and requesting a pass to return to Lake Tyers.[98] That same day EB was reported as having 'absconded' from Miss D and that arrangements had been made for her return to Lake Tyers.[99] In July 1921 Bruce Ferguson, manager at Lake Tyers, reported that EB and a man, CC, wished to get married, but her parents objected 'principally on account of his having been born in New South Wales and the possibility of his taking [EB] to another State'. Ferguson noted there was 'nothing unusual' about this kind of family upset and expected the matter to be resolved.[100] Horton notes that EB's death at Lake Tyers was registered as a result of typhoid in 1923 (age around twenty-five), at which stage she was noted as having 'never married'.[101]

In Chapter 2 it was suggested that the mission functioned as a liminal zone: its boundaries were porous and Aboriginal people were moved in and out of the missions according to a logic designed to restrict their access to their families and communities but also to restrict their access to resources provided to the white community. At the turn of the twentieth century, the BPA claimed that a plan to send Aboriginal children from the missions to children's institutions was underpinned by a desire to afford them the opportunities afforded their non-Aboriginal peers. But as shown in the examples documented here, children were shunted between mission and institution according to the explicit aim of severing their connections with friends and relatives and in a way that provided them with little chance of establishing a life for themselves beyond the station boundary.

95 NAA B 337, 56: Miss L. M. D. 'Darraweit' Darlington (addressee unknown) 30 May 1921.
96 NAA B 337, 56: Miss D to 'Matron' 7 June 1921.
97 NAA B 337, 56: Miss D to Adjt Anderson 16 June 1921.
98 NAA B 337, 56: EB to Sec. BPA (no date: received 18 June 1921).
99 NAA B 337, 56: Chief Secretary's Department, 'EB' (no date).
100 NAA B 337, 56: B. Ferguson to Sec. BPA 9 July 1921.
101 Horton 2010: 12.

5

Unstable Categories: Children in Welfare and Justice in the Early Twentieth Century

The authorities in charge of implementing the foundational Neglected and Criminal Children's Act (1864) initially established two sets of institutions – industrial schools and reformatories. But an examination of the practices of these institutions presented in Chapter 3 showed that industrial school children, reformatory children, neglected and offending children and the systems of knowledge underpinning the constitution of these administrative categories were much less clearly differentiated than their formal designation suggested. Using the state's central clearing house, the Royal Park Children's Depot, as a case study, evidence presented in Chapter 3 showed that the authority to decide which child belonged in which category and in what kind of institutional space shifted in incremental fashion from the courts to the executive and its officers. By the end of the nineteenth century administrative knowledge and know-how, rather than formal legal process, lay at the centre of decision making affecting the children who passed through the depot's gates. This chapter returns to the Royal Park depot and traces the entry of new forms of scientific expertise from the beginning of the twentieth century, namely, laboratory medicine, psychiatry and an emergent child psychology. It examines the effects of their presence on the practices of the depot. It will show how, within the depot, what began as quite a small space for the accommodation of the infant – initially the epitome of innocence and misfortune – expanded to accommodate a newly morphed class whose contours would acquire enough definition over three decades for it to constitute a 'species' distinguished by mental and moral deficiencies and criminal instincts which cried out for segregation and containment. Elsewhere within the confines of the depot, a small reformatory space ostensibly set aside to accommodate the (few) transient reformatory cases that passed through the depot would also open up to accommodate an expanded class of delinquents. They too were marked by their mental and moral characteristics the nature of which called for their complete and remote separation. Two cohorts of children, ostensibly distinguished thirty years earlier, would come to share the same profile of mental and moral misfit. The first part of this chapter traces the conditions within and beyond the depot which made possible the final collapse of the distinction between offending and neglected children within the depot and the drawing of a new line of separation between the normal and the mentally-and-morally defective child.

Early in the twentieth century medical science began to determine the shape and practices of the depot, its new authority made possible by a growing public anxiety over the threat of contagion, and the threat of syphilis in particular. A decade later, the threat of physical and moral contagion would usher in a specifically psychological medicine. A decade from that, the depot would serve as a psychological laboratory accommodating a range of experts. The proliferation of expertise within the depot was concurrent with a proliferation of new clinical sites beyond its walls, operating independently from the Department for Neglected Children and Reformatory Schools (DNCRS)/ Children's Welfare Department and Reformatory Schools (CWDRS). After 1930 child psychiatric and psychological clinics were constituted under a number of authorities and organisations and their work was geared to a variety of outcomes – educational, legal, vocational and general mental health. The emergence of these clinical sites and the often contradictory and competing knowledge claims underpinning them are the focus of the second part of this chapter. Discussion focusses on two clinical sites in particular, the Children's Court Clinic and Travancore which operated under the direction of the Mental Hygiene Department (MHD). Within the crosstalk of psychological and psychiatric expertise emanating from these and other clinical sites with which they intersected, established ways of knowing children as the subjects of justice begin to exhibit instability. Emergent psychiatric knowledge claims would eventually feed directly into a reshaping of juvenile justice in Victoria. That eventuation is discussed in Chapter 9. The second part of this chapter focusses primarily on the processes by which psychiatric and psychological expertise (the psy-sciences) achieved an authoritative position between both the child welfare administration and child, and the Children's Court and child. The argument here is in support of the proposition that the naming of the institutions, and the stated intentions of their administrations, was overridden in significance by their shared function in the formation of categories of persons – to 'know' particular sections of a population in order to 'govern' them.[1] These functions reflect an ever-proliferating variety of disciplinary aims and governance procedures, which insinuate themselves between institutions of government and the governed, and between law and populace. It is in this sense that the disciplines might be thought of as infra-legal mechanisms 'which attempt to reduce an ungovernable *populace* to a multiply differentiated *population*'.[2]

THE DEPOT BECOMES A HOSPITAL

During the first decade, the old guard that had seen the DNCRS's Royal Park Children's Depot into the twentieth century left. Prior to their departure, the high

[1] Rose 2005; Dean 2007. [2] Minson, 1985: 24; see also Armstrong 2002.

levels of infant mortality at the depot were regularly remarked upon in annual reports as nothing more than routine. In 1901 the DNCRS secretary reported there was 'nothing worthy of note' regarding the depot. Statistical returns recorded that twelve infants died from marasmus and congenital disease, another from pneumonia.[3] But shortly thereafter a new urgency was attached to the need for resources for sick, white infants. The note of urgency corresponded to Victorian government statistician W. McLean's harnessing of the problem of infant mortality to the population question. McLean did not agree with his New South Wales counterpart that addressing the problem of a falling birthrate alone was the key to the problem of increasing Australia's (white) population, as articulated by the New South Wales government statistician:

> Large as is the area of the Australian continent, it is impossible that its people will ever become truly great under the conditions affecting the increase of population which now obtain. Immigration has practically ceased to be an important factor, the maintenance and increase of population depending upon the birth-rate alone – a rate seriously diminished, and still diminishing. No people has ever become great under such conditions, or having attained greatness, has remained great for any lengthened period. The problem of the fall in the birth-rate is therefore a national one of overwhelming importance to the Australian people, perhaps more than any other people, and on its satisfactory solution will depend whether this country is ever to take a place amongst the great nations of the world.[4]

In short, McLean argued that the fundamental problem was not that too few children were being born but that too many were dying: the problem of infant mortality had hitherto been 'almost entirely overlooked'.[5] Infant mortality was constituted from that time as a new kind of problem, and by 1906 there was a marked change of tone with reference to the numbers of infants dying at the depot:

> The improvement under the able management of the Acting Matron Miss M. Johnson has been very marked ... We find that the over-crowding of inmates is at times excessive, and exceeds the accommodation. For the health of the children, this should be avoided as much as possible. The necessity of providing isolated accommodation for infectious cases in connexion with the nursery is urgent.[6]

A new Infant Life Protection Act (1907) came into operation in January 1908 and an immediate effect was an influx of infants received at the depot, making the already recognised problem of accommodating infants, and particularly sickly and infectious infants, even more urgent.[7] Mandatory medical supervision of children was required for children received under the authority of this act which contributed to the increased presence of the medical officer at the depot and to medicine's direct

3 Victoria 1901a (DNCRS): 5, 11; see also Victoria 1902a (DNCRS): 10; Victoria 1903a (DNCRS): 4.
4 McLean 1904: 110 (quoting NSW govt. statistician). 5 McLean 1904: 110.
6 Victoria 1906a (DNCRS): 10 (Report of Visiting Committee Royal Park).
7 Victoria Infant Life Protection Act (No. 2102) 1907.

input into the management of bodies in space – this group here, that group there – the medical officer calling the tune to such arrangements with new authority. In 1910 then medical officer Clarence Godfrey noted that Royal Park was no longer simply a depot but was becoming a hospital.[8] The management of space dealt with a different kind of population, requiring new rules and personnel:

> With the present buildings and structures it is impossible to do justice even to the healthy babies, much less to the great number of sick and congenitally enfeebled . . . and I consider that to maintain efficiency in nursing, there should always be on duty, two or more trained nurses in the day time, and one at night. A great strengthening of the nursery staff all round would be advisable.[9]

Among the congenitally enfeebled, the child with congenital syphilis was a particularly charged entity in the context of public anxiety around a possible epidemic of syphilis, an anxiety generated in part by the fact that prior to the introduction of the Wassermann test syphilis was notoriously difficult to diagnose. Uncertainty lingered within and beyond the medical profession regarding the threat the 'syphilitic child' posed to others and indeed to future generations.[10] By 1911 the Wassermann test had made more certain diagnosis of syphilis possible. Along with testing of suspected syphilis cases among infants, Godfrey introduced new practices of segregation and isolation, as much, it seems, to dampen public anxiety as to control infection:

> It has been recognised that a definite proportion of the infants are doomed before admission, either by reason of certain inherited diseases, defects, or malformations; or from their assimilative powers being destroyed by previous ill-feeding or starvation. They do not thrive in foster homes and institutional treatment does not appear to mend matters . . . It should be pointed out that only a small proportion of children, the subject of congenital syphilis, are capable of infecting others; nevertheless, as a precautionary measure, every proved or suspected case of this disease is, on admission isolated, and segregated with other similar cases, in a large tent; and directions are given as regards quarantine and personal hygiene, that should make hetero-infection impossible.[11]

Sandison Yule was the next doctor installed at the depot and under his medical superintendence every infant on arrival was tested for syphilis. Segregation and isolation tents were being replaced by permanent physical structures to allow those infected and suspect cases of syphilis to be 'railed off securely'.[12] Sandison Yule was an active campaigner and lobbyist for the care and control of the 'feeble-minded'. He was a central figure of a movement inaugurated at the 1911 Medical Congress at Sydney and was appointed honorary secretary of a committee

[8] Victoria 1911a (DNCRS): 18 (Reports of Schools – Royal Park Depot).
[9] Victoria 1912a (DNCRS): 18 (Report of Medical Officer Clarence Godfrey).
[10] *Argus* 1911, July 11: 5.
[11] Victoria 1912a (DNCRS): 17–18 (Report of Medical Officer Clarence Godfrey).
[12] Victoria 1914b (DNCRS): 7.

(composed of himself, Ernest Jones, Beattie-Smith and Harvey Sutton) to push for the concern around the 'quality of the population' in the newly federated Australia. In that role Sandison Yule alluded to, and aligned himself with, the growing respectability of eugenics.[13] When the results of a national census of the feeble-minded were reported, revealing that medical practitioners and private schools had shown exceedingly poor engagement with the survey, Sandison Yule said the results showed 'deplorable apathy' but that the figures 'must vastly understate the actual number of defectives ... a very conservative estimate must at least demand multiplication by ten'.[14] But poor returns of the survey from the medical profession also underscored the fact that by no means did they think as one on the problem of feeble-mindedness.

Not surprisingly, Sandison Yule soon called attention to the appearance of the feeble-minded at the depot:

> Several cases of mentally defective children appear from time to time in the depot. In many cases, such have to be sent to an asylum, from the want of a special institution for the care of the feeble-minded. It is, indeed, eminently desirable that such a home may be soon provided for this class of child.[15]

The following year the new (acting) Medical Officer Gerald Sheahan failed to make any mention of mental defectives at the depot in his annual report. Rather, he underscored and echoed the theme of proper feeding, of restoring the neglected but otherwise healthy infant to vigour, and for this he was castigated in the pages of the *Medical Journal of Australia* (MJA):

> The report of the Department for Neglected Children and Reformatory Schools in Victoria, covering the period 1916, is a short document containing a large amount of information compressed, as far as possible, into tables ... As the Secretary and Inspector did not assume office until April 1, 1917, he refrains from making general remarks having reference to the period before he was in charge of the Department ...
>
> From the information contained in the Secretary's report it would seem as if the whole problem were regarded from the point of view of the neglect to which these children are subjected. The department has control of 10,780 children, of a class peculiarly fertile in mental deficients. Not a single word is published concerning the mental condition of the 7,357 children who had reached their sixth year. The facts that the more able of these children are pressed into high schools and technical colleges, and that as many as possible are placed in service from the training homes, indicate that those responsible are not seized with the necessity of discriminating between normal-minded children and mental defectives. It is relatively easy to prevent children in homes or institutions from committing ethical offences. Training may keep these children safe as long as

13 McCallum 1990. 14 Sandison Yule 1914: 722.

15 Victoria 1914b (DNCRS): 18 (Report of Medical Officer Sandison Yule).

> the skilled supervision lasts. But when they are allowed to go out into the world and to fill positions as free men and women, the danger to themselves and to their neighbours manifests itself. We would urge that these children, committed under the Neglected Children's Act or the Crimes Act, should be carefully watched by an expert psychiatrist, and that all those found to have a mental development behind the average age, be guarded by the State for the rest of their lives. In this way, crimes will be avoided, girls will be saved from a life of shame, venereal infections will be checked to some extent, and the propagation of the mental defect would be prevented.[16]

Subsequent annual reports reaffirmed the existence of the problem which Sandison Yule had 'discovered' during his time as medical officer. Department Secretary Molloy noted the problem of defective children in 1917 (his note is dated after the publication of the MJA article):

> There is, unfortunately, a number of mentally deficient or otherwise defective children in foster homes and institutions. The question of how to deal with some of them on attaining manhood and womanhood is a matter of grave consideration. It is gratifying to know that public interest has been aroused on this important matter, and that definite action is likely to be taken to treat such cases.[17]

In the same year, Sheahan, the medical officer at the depot, recanted:

> There came under my notice a number of children below the average in mental efficiency, who will not be able to compete with their fellow men later on in the stress of life. These mental defectives have not sufficient will control, and may develop abnormal instincts. They should be under the guidance of a skilled psychiatrist, who would observe their criminal or moral tendencies, and if necessary they should be kept under the control of the State for the rest of their lives, and thus prevent the propagation of their species.[18]

It is worth noting the knowledge 'achievements' captured by these statements: the fudging of a distinction between the department's neglected and reformatory populations, the shared (criminal) characteristics bestowed upon them, the making of a whole population suspected of mental defect (the status of their mentality, defective-or-not, just added a further dimension to their being), and the gesturing to a new form of specifically psychological medical expertise at the depot now required to assess that status.

During the second decade of the twentieth century, there were increasing indications in the annual reports that all was not well at the depot, particularly in the part of the depot given over to the accommodation of reformatory boys. References to trouble tended to be oblique – the dismissal of an attendant on the grounds of unsatisfactory conduct, the fact that it did not measure up to the discipline achieved

16 *Medical Journal of Australia* 1918: 381.
17 Victoria 1918 (DNCRS): 6.
18 Victoria 1918 (DNCRS): 4 (Report of Medical Officer).

at the girls' depot, the need for separating older and younger inmates, especially at night. Increasing references to trouble were coincidental with increasing references to troublemakers among its inmates, whose protagonists came to be understood as remand cases regardless of whether they were officially on remand from the courts. A separate Remand Centre 'wholly remote from the other inmates' was called for and eventually opened in 1927, but no sooner had it opened than it became clear that it accommodated inmates other than those on remand: it had come to provide the means of 'separation of boys on remand *and* delinquent boys of various ages *and* mental *and* moral characteristics'.[19]

The end of the first decade of the twentieth century saw a hardening of the association between the congenital syphilitic and the mentally defective child. Both were difficult to detect and both were understood to pose a threat to those around them and to future generations. The science of bacteriology in the form of the Wassermann test had made it possible to know syphilis was here, but not there, and to 'rail off' and practice upon an identified syphilitic population. As syphilis was once, mental defect remained deceptive, elusive and everywhere 'in our midst'. Conditions were ripe for the embrace of new laboratory tools which would do for mental defect what the Wassermann test did for syphilis – provide a practical means of giving certainty and visibility to its presence. If control of mental deficiency was going to be achieved, mental deficiency too was going to have to go into the laboratory and come out of it in a 'practicable form'.[20] In the early 1920s a new kind of medical expert equipped with specifically psycho-medical tools which offered a practical method for the recognition of mental deficiency was invited into the depot. In 1923 the depot's Medical Officer A. P. Derham was appointed superintendent of the whole establishment. Derham invited R. J. A. Berry, 'mentalist' and professor of anatomy at Melbourne University, to extend the depot's testing regime; Berry arrived with an additional set of laboratory tests with which to subject, know and manage the depot's inmates:

> Miss Barling, of Professor Berry's staff, has carried out a series of mental tests on the more defective inmates. She has been assisted in this by Mr. Keddie and Miss Clark, school teachers, and her work has been checked and diagnoses made by Professor Berry who visits the depot at intervals in an honorary capacity ... Of the mental defectives tested by the Wassermann test about one half were found to be congenital syphilitics, and many more were probably syphilitic.[21]

The arrival of psychological medicine saw a further achievement – a calculation of the percentage of the depot population who were defective, mentally, morally or physically:

19 Victoria 1928 (Children's Welfare Department and Reformatory Schools [CWDRS]): 6, emphasis added.

20 Latour 1988: 43–49.

21 Victoria 1924 (DNCRS): 6 (Thomas, quoting from Medical Superintendent Derham's report).

> *Neglected Children's Depot, Royal Park*: The functions of the Depot are varied and numerous. It serves as a depot and clearing house for all children committed to the care of the State. The ages of these range from one day to 17 years, and the number in residence seldom falls below 300. On arrival at the Depot approximately 60 per cent. are definitely defective, mentally, morally, or physically, and over 20 per cent are congenital syphilitics.[22]

By the end of the decade and under a new medical officer the testing regime at the depot had been taken over by psychologists from the education department and 'a system of routine mental testing was initiated at the Depot in February 1930. Among 100 children submitted to the Binet and Porteus tests, approximately 30% were found to be subnormal.'[23] Later reports shed light on the practice; only school-age children manifesting problems were tested. Nevertheless, the selection process – to test or not – brought the whole population under the gaze of psychology. A small space that opened up for the segregation of the contagious infant had expanded – first through an urgent call for a proper isolation ward to segregate the danger of physical contagion, among whom a particular urgency was given to the segregation of the syphilitic, and then by the attachment of the threat of moral contagion to this group in particular. By 1930 the whole population at the depot became subject to tests for physical, mental and moral defects. All inmates were tested for venereal disease and, excluding infants, all inmates were eyed as potential candidates for mental testing. With a testing regime in place, the whole population was treated as 'suspect' on their entry, there were now no 'purely unfortunate' or 'perfectly innocent' among them. By this stage, the psy-sciences had gained an informal role of superintendence at the depot which in turn had become a laboratory for identifying the social misfit, the delinquent and the latent criminal. As shown in the following section, it was soon practising as a recognised clinic.

PSY-SCIENCES AND THE LEGAL COMPLEX

By 1930 there had been calls from a number of stakeholders for a clinic to work in association with the work of the Children's Court. W. Ernest Jones, longtime head of what was, until the mid-nineteen thirties, the Victorian Lunacy Department, produced a 1929 Commonwealth Report on Mental Deficiency. His report recommended a psychological clinic in each state for the examination of all mentally defective children and young adults, composed of a medical practitioner experienced in childhood diseases, an educationalist with psychological training, a practitioner

[22] Victoria 1923a (DNCRS): 3.

[23] PROV VPRS 5694 Unit 1: 'Children's Welfare Department. Report of Medical Officer D. M. Embelton, Royal Park Depots', in Report: Children's Welfare Department and Reformatory Schools (for the year 1929, unpublished).

with experience in psychiatry as well as social workers – 'the best way to make the clinic efficient is to attach it to a Children's Court'.[24]

In 1929 Edith Onians was a special magistrate of the Children's Court operating out of North Melbourne (children's courts then operated out of several metropolitan courts). A Dr Booth was chairman of the court at North Melbourne. That year's report on the Children's Court, penned by the officer in charge (F. P. Morris), quoted Onians who had returned from a recent study tour abroad. Among her recommendations were the following:

> A Clinic which should be a separate branch of the Court for study of the child. Personnel required for Clinic includes a physician, trained in psychiatry, a psychologist, and one or more social investigators.
>
> All through the States and in English Courts the Magistrate has these particulars placed in his hand which he reads over and thus knows better how to deal with each child – so, he should have when the child comes before him –
>
> 1. Social report
> 2. Medical Officer's report
> 3. Psychologist's report;
> 4. Social Worker's report of Home.

Morris also quoted Booth:

> [O]ur judicial authorities have been slow to realize that research work by psychologists in the field of juvenile delinquency is capable of providing more accurate data … crime is the greatest social disease, and as humanitarian efforts gradually leaven through Society, the findings of science come to be taken more and more into consideration by those who must grapple with crime.[25]

With the Children's Court firmly established, Morris argued for a 'wide study and dissemination of knowledge of the relationship between mental deficiency to juvenile delinquency'. Indeed, interesting facts could be learned from such a study in the 'summary of the first hundred young delinquents recently tested under the supervision of the North Melbourne Children's Court … made at the request of the Court magistrates supported by Professor Berry' and made possible financially by the Edward Wilson (of the *Argus* newspaper) Fund. Miss Lucy Barling assisted as psychologist:

> The test combines three methods – the Stamford [sic] modification of the Binet and Simon test, the percentile test of Professor Berry and the maze test of Professor Porteus (formerly of Melbourne but now working at Vineland, New Jersey). A combination of these methods made our results more reliable and made possible a comparison with results previously obtained by Professor Berry in other investigations. The Binet and Simon test depends to a great extent on educational

24 Australia (W. Ernest Jones) 1929: 16.

25 Victoria 1930 (Report on the Children's Court [RCC]): 8–9.

attainments; the percentile test is a standardisation of anatomical and psychological data; the Porteus test registers the innate capacity of the individual. None of these tests took place at the Court; most of them were conducted at the University or at the Hospital. Usually one parent, at least, attended with the child, and thus our psychologist's observations were more complete. Of course, visits were also paid to the child's home. Environmental influences were studied as far as possible.

	Mental capacity rating
Children above normal	4
Upper grade defectives	24
Lower grade defectives	4
Doubtful but suggesting deficiency	16
Normal children	52[a]

[a] Victoria 1930 (RCC): 8–9.

Morris wanted to 'adopt some system in all of the Courts whereby such examinations can be made'. Meanwhile he noted 'we continue to send some cases to Royal Park for such examinations'.[26] Morris did not consider mental deficiency the sole cause of juvenile delinquency; he also cited parental neglect, the abandonment of the traditions of home life and the disregard for religion, but mental deficiency headed the list and clearly the proposal for clinical testing was associated specifically with testing delinquents for mental deficiency.

In his 1930 report, Morris suggested the court use the proposed Child Guidance Clinic. This was a short-lived fee-for-service clinic set up under the patronage of the Council for Mental Hygiene and supported by educational psychologist K. S. Cunningham.[27] This proposed clinic might serve an important preventative role and would not preclude the necessity for a Children's Court Clinic, 'a necessary adjunct, if Children's Court work is to be carried out successfully'.[28] The following year Morris called for the appointment of trained special magistrates who could 'be kept abreast with modern psychological movements' and for trained stipendiary probation officers, noting that 'many of our probation officers are beginning to realize the value of mental tests and psychological examinations'. He noted that such examinations were included in all sexual cases, and in reports provided to the courts and indeed to the probation officers. The relationship between mental deficiency and crime was reiterated, but it was now cited as but one of multiple factors causing juvenile delinquency: 'Our experience is that unfit parents, lack of parental control, disregard for religion, mental insufficiency and adverse social conditions are the main factors that cause child delinquency.'[29]

The general discussion in the 1932 CWDRS report was full of discussion of the problem of the mental defective. Children 'who manifest mental backwardness or

[26] Victoria 1930 (RCC): 8–9. [27] Wright 2012: 10–12. [28] Victoria 1931 (RCC): 8–9.
[29] Victoria 1932 (RCC): 2, 11.

behaviour problems' underwent tests for 'Mental Efficiency', the implication being that intelligence testing would shed light on behaviour problems. Of the children who had been at the depot for more than a year (some of them for more than six) seventy-eight could be accounted for by reason of mental and/or physical defect, nine as a result of other causes.[30] It would be another ten years before personality tests were introduced in any of the clinics.[31] But once children were tested for intelligence *because* of their problem behaviour, and once those children were shown to have normal intelligence, a new question arose: what, then, led to the problem behaviour if not mental deficiency, sub-normality, mental weakness? And in attempts to answer that question, a psychology of the normal child began to be activated. A fuller account of that activation is discussed in Chapter 7 but some beginnings of that process appeared in 1932. The court had two clinical sites at its disposal: the CWDRS's depot, and the newly established Child Guidance Clinic. At the former mental testing was performed by a teacher overseen by education department psychologists and under the authority of the depot's medical superintendent. The latter was headed by a psychologist but with a psychiatrist working under him![32] The court published examples of case reports from both clinics: 'John Blank' and 'William Blank' were both children named as 'mentally backward' after intelligence testing.[33] The case studies give an insight, at the 'capillary' level, as Foucault would describe it, of psychological medicine wielding its tools and producing its knowledge.[34] Albiston, the psychiatrist from the Child Guidance Clinic, deemed the boy John Blank incapable of judging right from wrong 'by complex ethical and social standards', one proof being the boy's admission that 'he felt no resentment, rather pity when a tramp once stole his overcoat'. So the boy failed to apply right and wrong as, according to the psychiatrist, he should have. Of course, one could argue that from the psychiatrist's own account, the child employed quite complex arguments and indeed quite complex mathematical calculations. John (wrongly) applied 'such factors as the value of the goods stolen and the relative needs of the thief and the loser'. What contemporary eye could read this account of John and *not* think 'now there's a *smart* lad living on his wits in a hostile environment'? But the question here is: how has it become possible for such a contemporary eye to develop? In both accounts – that of psychiatrist Albiston and of Embleton, medical superintendent at the depot – the children were willed into the category of the mentally-deficient-due-to-constitutional-heredity as the over-determining factor producing their delinquency, more overtly so in Embleton's classification of William Blank as a 'high grade moron'. Except for the fact that the case against William Blank failed at court Embleton would have

30 PROV VPRS 5694 Unit 1: Children's Welfare Department and Reformatory Schools. Report of the Secretary and Inspector for the year 1932 (unpublished), 29–31.

31 See Victoria 1950a (Mental Hygiene Department [MHD]): 35.

32 Wright 2012: 11.

33 Victoria 1933 (RCC): 9–11.

34 Foucault 2003: 94.

had this child locked up in a reformatory 'during the King's Pleasure' for stealing a pair of braces. We might also reflect that despite the sophisticated tools of analysis – the Binet, the Porteus, the Healy, the Kohs – and despite the aid of psychological expertise from the education department, Medical Superintendent Embleton's decision making was not so different from that of her predecessor, the matron of the 1890s, whose 'opinion' – bad or not – decided the fate of the depot child.[35] What the tests did provide was an element of scientism, lending dubious but also increased authority to the opinion that the boy William Blank was bad through and through, and fated to become a criminal:

> This boy is a high grade Moron, on the high road to becoming a very effective 'Criminal'. He will probably be unable to rise beyond the morality of a clever criminal code. Incarceration in a Reformatory during the King's Pleasure is suggested. It is quite probable that after his release he will revert to his former ways.[36]

In one sense, and through these clinical reports, the relationship between mental deficiency and delinquency and the differentiation between normal and mentally deficient children would seem to be reinforced. As noted, they were published in a report for the Children's Court. But in other parts of this same report, a different kind of knowledge was contending otherwise. The court, in that same year 1932, under the heading 'Psychological Examinations and Reports' called again for a magistrate open to 'modern methods of examination' and quoted extensively from a paper by Dr James Kent W. Bruce, in charge of the clinic operating in relation to the Children's Court in Sydney, to reinforce the importance of the Victorian Children's Court drawing on psychological know-how. Bruce included a definitive statement about the multi-factorial nature of the cause of delinquency:

> There is no single cause of delinquency. Certain factors are predominate – physical, environmental, intellectual, heredity, mental conflicts. Each in turn may be the major factor in delinquency, but this major factor is always combined with one or more of the above causes acting as minor factors.[37]

Bruce's paper downplayed the link between mental deficiency and delinquency, with mental deficiency sitting as but one factor among multiple causal factors, among them 'non-adjustment to social conditions'. In other words, in the early 1930s there was a destabilising of what had been a stable causal given and the appearance of a new term 'non-adjustment' heralded the formation of a new entity, or a new administrative category of being. The terminology associated with this new entity would soon steady and edge itself into the standard nomenclature – 'the maladjusted child' – and maladjustment would emerge as the primary factor and primary focus of psychological medicine, such that it would soon not be the case that mental deficiency could be held up as 'one of supreme national importance'[38] and it

[35] Victoria 1890a: Part II, Receiving Depot, Regulation 7. [36] Victoria 1933 (RCC): 11.
[37] Victoria 1933 (RCC): 9. [38] Australia (W. Ernest Jones) 1929: 3.

would not be possible to claim that 'there is no more urgent problem that presents itself to-day than that of the mentally defective members of the community'.[39] Although the statistical returns for that year showed that of the 1019 cases before the courts only 36 were recorded as 'Dull and Subnormal', this result received no attention. But by the end of the decade, the fact, drawn from statistics, that most delinquents were of normal intelligence would be very much brought to the fore.

In his 1933 Children's Court report, Morris noted that the court was still using both the depot and the Child Guidance Clinic for referral of cases. He included a quite lengthy section on the work of mental testing carried out at the depot. Again there was a gesture to multiple factors of which mental deficiency was now but one, and it was becoming standard to refer to the multi-factorial nature of the causes of delinquency.

PROBLEMATISING THE 'NORMAL' CHILD

A mental test is often found helpful in reaching conclusions with respect to a case, although the defined mental capacity can, of course, only be considered as one of the factors and may not necessarily be the dominant one.

Mr Vick, the Head teacher at Royal Park, has had exceptional opportunities of testing a large number of children. Although many of them are non-delinquent, in the Children's Court sense, they are practically all from the environment from which most of the delinquents come.[40]

In his 1933 report on the Children's Court, Morris devoted a substantial section to the work of the headmaster of the state school in the depot's grounds, Mr Vick, and quoted from Vick's own comments on 'the mental factor' of the children returned as boarding-out 'failures' for reasons of 'petty thieving, telling lies, out of control, etc. . . . and thus the mental tests were taken as a guide to whether a child should be boarded out or retained in an institution to keep him away from outside temptations'. Morris quoted Vick on the fact that of the 680 tested at the depot, '74% are below normal in intelligence, and . . . 27% are feeble-minded'.[41] Morris included in this same report a separate section on the court's approach to treating the sex offender. Curiously, the emphasis in the later section was on keeping children charged with sex offences out of institutions – 'to ensure some treatment at home rather than in an Institution, following the success of Saturday morning sex instruction – the results are most gratifying'. In one section of this report, informed by one clinical site (the depot) petty thieving and telling lies were underscored as indicators by which to assess the need to retain a child in an institution. In another emerging site (the Children's Court itself) sex offending was regarded as no good indicator of

39 PROV VPRS 5694 Unit 1: Report. Children's Welfare Department and Reformatory Schools for the year ending 30 Dec. 1929 (unpublished): 10.

40 Victoria 1934 (RCC): 8.

41 Victoria 1934 (RCC): 8.

the need for institutionalising a child. Morris offered (another) pertinent case study, this one from the Child Guidance Clinic – the child charged with a sex offence was found to be 'much below the average in natural intellectual ability'.[42] This case study confirmed the relationship between mental deficiency and delinquency, and in particular, mental deficiency and juvenile sex offending. The 1933 report from the Children's Court testifies to the instability of what had hitherto established itself as a fact: mental deficiency led to delinquency. Before the decade was out, statistics emanating from the Children's Court would be used to firm up a new relationship between the normal child and delinquency, and a little later, specifically, the normal child and sex offending. These later developments will be traced in Chapter 7.

The year 1933 also saw an amendment to the 1928 Children's Welfare Act to expand the category of 'neglect' to include children who were 'lapsing or likely to lapse into a career of vice or crime', and a clause was added pertaining to unfit guardianship. It had been long called for. Such an amendment forged anew the enmeshment of child welfare and juvenile justice practices, since it served to bring before the court a cohort of children deemed within law to be likely to become criminals. The neglected child could now be legally known in these terms. In the 1934 Children's Court report, reference was made to an increase in the number of cases coming before the court in that year – 3322 compared to 2993 the previous year, that were explicitly linked to this 1933 amendment.[43] Morris noted a decrease in the number of cases involving girls brought before the court that year – the 'increase in the number of boys is 353, but the girls have decreased from 249 in 1933 to 223 in 1934'.[44] But note that there was now a new discretionary element, or imperative on the part of those bringing charges of neglect before the court. The complaint that gave rise to the amendment in the first place, as expressed by Special Magistrate Rapke in 1931, was that as long as it could be shown that the child had means of subsistence and 'that there is a home of sorts' no matter how undesirable that abode, the court could not legally intervene.[45] Now 'likely to lapse' and 'unfit guardianship' required a different kind of judgement based on a different kind of evidence. Any old 'abode' would no longer do. The amendment would seem to make room for a trained eye, expert in scrutinising home and parents. Morris alluded to the over-zealous social worker and perhaps he used the term loosely – professionally trained social workers were at this stage few and far between.[46] But it would seem that from this point on, the law required new measures of home and parents beyond the simply material, and upon which to base decisions regarding the identification and disposal of neglected children. It was now those deemed under unfit guardianship who figured as potential delinquents in the amended legislation, along with those deemed 'likely to lapse'. Undoubtedly, the amendment also helped produce the

[42] Victoria 1934 (RCC): 9–13. [43] Victoria 1935 (RCC): 1–2. [44] Victoria 1935 (RCC): 1–2.
[45] Victoria 1932 (RCC): 8–9. [46] Victoria 1935 (RCC): 1–2.

conditions making possible a shift in emphasis regarding the cause of juvenile delinquency, away from the long-held understanding of its relationship to mental deficiency or sub-normality of one form or another, and towards the 'home environment'.

Certainly the amendment coincided with such a shift in emphasis. In 1935, in the context of a noted increase in the number of cases brought before the court, 'unsuitable homes' were given unprecedented prominence as a causal factor in delinquency as shown in research conducted in association with the Children's Court by the influential social housing reformer F. Oswald Barnett and presented in Morris's report for that year:

> Without any attempt to over-state his case or to attribute child-delinquency to any one particular cause (indeed, he deals with the other contributing factors) Mr Barnett proves most conclusively that slum-homes and the slum-minded are prolific in their production and their re-production of the delinquent and the recidivist.[47]

Notwithstanding that change of emphasis, Morris did not leave behind the 'great social problem' of mental deficiency, noting for instance the problem of 'the Court committing the fifth child of a weak-minded unmarried mother to the Department' and the 'fact' that 'most of the cases of indecent assault on little girls are committed by subnormal boys'.[48] But the importance of the psychological sciences, and the legitimacy of the expansion of their field of operation well beyond just testing for mental deficiency, were emphasised from this point by the Children's Welfare Department: 'The key to the treatment may be *within*, just as much as *outside* the person concerned, and the solutions invariably require careful recognition of moral, temperamental and personal considerations.'[49]

CWDRS Secretary Henry carried out his own research, surveying reformatory school superintendents on their opinions as to the causes of delinquency (they reportedly classed 50 per cent of their inmates as mentally deficient). Although the means by which Henry established his findings might be spurious, his research, along with that of figures such as F. Oswald Barnett, helped establish the fact that, by the second half of the 1930s, the assumption that the mentally and morally deficient were the predominant cohort from which future criminals would be drawn did not have the purchase that it once did. 'Pernicious environment' was right up there, and although a large number of the reformatory population was deemed mentally deficient, heredity was the least attributed cause. An assumed deficit on the part of the parent was beginning to take precedence over any assumed deficit in the child's 'mental equipment'. Secretary Henry concluded that for 94 per cent of juveniles 'the chief causes of crime among them are largely due to their parents'.[50] At the same time, Henry nevertheless reiterated 'the menace that exists in permitting the mentally deficient or feeble-minded to be at large without protection or guidance'.[51] And

47 Victoria 1936 (RCC): 1–4. 48 Victoria 1936 (RCC): 4–5.
49 Victoria 1937a (CWDRS): 3, emphasis added. 50 Victoria 1937a (CWDRS): 7.
51 Victoria 1937a (CWDRS): 8.

in that same report, the depot's medical superintendent noted that mental testing at the depot had to cease by order of the Education Department.

One can perhaps overemphasise these small shifts, but oft-used phrases such as 'mental and psychological' would tend to evince an understanding of psychological examination as something more than simply testing for intelligence. As did the secretary of the CWDRS, the Children's Court published research on opinions as to the cause of delinquency, this time through the police, and emanating from the officers handling the cases. And as in the Children's Court own research, the findings pointed to the parents:

> Although there are many contributory factors that cause child delinquency, such as truancy, lack of playgrounds, unemployment, &c., it will be seen that the main factor as shown by this return is 'lack of parental control coupled with bad company'. My own experience has shown that this is undoubtedly so.[52]

The following year's (1938) report from the court likewise emphasised the multiple causes of juvenile delinquency: 'mental deficiency, backwardness, truancy, environment, heredity, lack of parental control, &c are all mentioned as the main or contributory cause, and they all exert more or less influence', and the research on the causes of delinquency also included the opinion of the officer in charge of the Children's Court, L. R. Ripper, that 'one important remedial measure is an all-round improvement in our social conditions'.[53] The report coincided with the opening of yet another clinic, Travancore which operated under the authority of the Mental Hygiene Department (MHD). Ripper anticipated its involvement in examining children referred by the court: 'Magistrates have expressed their gratification of the appointment of a Psychiatrist, a Psychologist, and a Pediatrist [sic] at the clinic at "Travencore"[sic], who will be available to furnish, as occasion arises, reports upon the mental condition of persons accused of crimes.'[54]

The work of Cyril Burt was drawn on as to the causes of delinquency. In order of importance, Burt placed 'Defective discipline' at no. 1, 'Intellectual disabilities such as backwardness or dullness' at no. 6, and 'Poverty and its concomitants' at no. 14. Following Burt's list, Ripper commented: 'To my mind parental neglect, which arises so often because of a "broken home", together with the lack of moral and religious training, is the chief cause of juvenile delinquency.' The mental defective remained 'a distinct problem' for the courts, but was no longer regarded as, to use Ripper's words, the chief cause of delinquency.[55] The suggestion from the previous year that the MHD's Travancore Clinic be available to furnish the court with reports, was by 1938 one of its established functions. Here Ripper referred to the valuable work of Prosecuting Officer Loftus, who, in addition to his other duties 'also makes special investigations at the homes of problem children to assist the Psychiatrist and Psychologist at the Travancore Clinic, in cases referred to them

52 Victoria 1937b (RCC): 8 (L. R. Ripper). 53 Victoria 1938b (RCC): 4.
54 Victoria 1938b (RCC): 4. 55 Victoria 1939b (RCC): 5.

by the Courts for special examination'.[56] V. P. Johnson, psychiatrist-superintendent at Travancore Clinic, drew a firm distinction between mental deficiency and problem conduct, and between the kinds of delinquent problem conduct likely to be exhibited by those he termed normal children and the kind of non-delinquent problem conduct likely to be exhibited by children with mental defects. It is worth bearing in mind that once Travancore Clinic began to accept referrals from the Children's Court, this way of knowing the delinquent and the mentally deficient child had a direct feed into that agency.

In summary then, the amendments in the 1933 Children's Welfare Act might be the cause of a new cohort of those 'likely to lapse' appearing before the court, but the conditions for this legislative decision were drawn together by the contributions of a fast-developing science of delinquency which was increasingly asserting the effects of the home environment on its make-up.[57]

THE PSYCHOLOGICAL EXAMINATION

Beginning in 1939 a number of Children's Court positions shifted from honorary to stipendiary. This was the first year a stipendiary special magistrate had been appointed, with L. R. Ripper, formerly officer in charge of the Children's Courts, assuming that role. Two stipendiary probation officers were also appointed – Mrs B. Trigellis-Smith and Mr A. W. Meadows. Meadows immediately established connections between the court and the psychologists at the Education Department's Teachers' Training College in setting up what was, in all but name, a fully functioning investigatory and advisory clinic at the court – but devoid of any direct psychiatric or medical input or oversight – though it is worth noting that some cases were referred to Travancore Clinic for consultation.[58]

Take the example of case studies of Leslie Blank and John X carried out by the two probation officers and published in the court's report for 1939. The first (Leslie Blank), was simply headed 'Psychological Examination' and was written by Trigellis-Smith. The report on John X consisted of a magistrate's summary and Meadows's 'General Report'. The tests ('Kohs Block, ACER Non-Verbal test for mental age and Binet') were but one aspect of these examinations, and in both probation officers' reports the emphasis was very much on familial relations. Both were peppered with psychological diagnoses of relationships. The father of Leslie Blank suffered from 'war strain and a feeling of personal inferiority'; John X was 'slightly introverted', and so on. The follow-up report of Leslie Blank noted that 'home adjustment has been very satisfactory'. Topping the list of recommendations was the advice that the father should be worked upon to improve his relationship with the boy. In the second boy, John X was pronounced as having 'a low level of mental ability' with an IQ of around 54–55 and

[56] Victoria 1939b (RCC): 10. [57] Victoria Children's Welfare Act (No. 4152) 1933.
[58] Victoria 1940b (RCC).

a mental age of around eight or nine years (he was sixteen). But by 1939, that was understood as but one dimension of his being. Given what was at this point pretty much an accepted orthodoxy – that mental deficiency was but one of multiple factors causing delinquency – so, it seems, the mentally deficient delinquent had by this time been furnished with multiple dimensions of his delinquent personhood. In particular, with a deficient social/familial environment looming increasingly as the primary cause of delinquency, and as a site for professional intervention and adjustment, the mentally deficient delinquent too had acquired a social/familial environment to which adjustments had to be made. Like his so-called normal counterparts, he had acquired 'maladjustment' as a dimension of his being and as a primary focus of causal investigation.[59] At the end of the 1930s, in the thick of a kind of normalisation of the mentally retarded child, the normal, hitherto other-than-mentally-defective child was becoming increasingly problematised. Of these two psychological reports emanating from the two new stipendiary probation officers at the Children's Court, one was a child of normal intelligence (Leslie Blank: IQ 105), one was not (John X IQ 55). But there was little difference in the orientation of the two case reports. Both children were investigated for, and found to have, problematic familial relations, especially problematic father-child relations, and both reports recommended the father's relationship with the boy as a primary target for professional intervention. So with Leslie Blank: 'A skilled worker [is required] to induce father of boy to understand his needs better.' On John X: 'the father be directed to give the boy help and sympathy'.[60]

There is further evidence pointing to the increasing problematisation of the normal child. Meadows was not only active in psychological testing, investigating the home environment and producing reports for the court. As Ripper explained, Meadows was also busy refining his own group test with the aspirations of, first (1) standardising an intelligence test especially for the use of the Victorian Children's Court, and second, extending psychological testing to *all* offenders coming before the court, as a means of sifting out those warranting closer examination and treatment. He was doing this in co-operation with Education Department psychologists.[61] That year the court also carried out a 'Delinquency Survey' in association with the Board of Social Studies. Meadows's involvement was not named in this account of the survey, but subsequent Children's Court reports reveal that he was the principal researcher. The home addresses of delinquents were used to produce a 'delinquency map', the density per unit area calculated, thus revealing the relative densities of juvenile delinquency in the various areas, hence revealing 'areas that merit the attention of social workers' identified as both the social environment surrounding the home, which required for example, 'provision of more playgrounds with supervisors and clubs that offer activities for every night in the week' plus the homes themselves:

> Careful study of the home conditions of delinquents show [sic] them to be for the most part average or below average. It is these areas that merit the attention of social

59 Victoria 1940b (RCC): 3–7. 60 Victoria 1940b (RCC): 5–6. 61 Victoria 1940b (RCC): 7.

workers ... It is felt that added to economic improvements some form of Parent Education is vitally necessary. It is not sufficient to blame economic conditions alone. Problem parents make problem children.[62]

These were the first of a series of substantial research papers on delinquency emanating from the Children's Court and published between 1939 and 1944 in its yearly reports, all largely driven by Meadows. The court was setting itself up, not just as a centre for examination, reports and recommendations on the delinquent child but also for research and education. Among activities reported in that year, Ripper noted a training programme for honorary personnel, the syllabus including descriptions and demonstrations of psychological tests. Lectures 'on the psychological approach to the problem of child delinquency' were delivered to police recruits and trainee detectives. Trainee probation officers joined 'representatives of other bodies which were concerned with Social Work and Child Welfare' in post-lecture conferences. Ripper expressed a keenness to establish connections between the court and the various agencies and stakeholders, including the Children's Welfare Department. To overcome a perceived lack of co-ordination between the Children's Court and the CWDRS, conferences were to be held between the two bodies.[63]

In 1940 the Mental Hygiene Department advised that the work of its Travancore clinic 'has many potentialities in the prevention and treatment of many and varied types of emotional mal-adjustment, which are frequently the forerunners of delinquency, crime, nervous and mental disorder and social inefficiency'.[64] Clearly the maladjusted child had come to be associated with both delinquency and social inefficiency – once the provinces of the mentally defective. Of the 273 cases referred to the clinic, only 7 were listed as referred from the Crown Law department, that is, the courts. This was perhaps not surprising given that the report from the Children's Court for 1940 showed that the court had been busy establishing its own testing regime and investigation of cases, such that its officers were beginning to function in a manner similar to that of a fully fledged child guidance clinic. The court had now established a procedure of follow-up in which children were found positions by the officer in charge, and remained under the court's supervision for 'guidance and advice'.[65] The two stipendiary probation officers, Meadows and Trigellis-Smith, were continuing their psychological testing, home visits, reports and recommendations and follow-up work in the home. By then, however, most of the preliminary psychological testing had been delegated to Meadows with Tregellis-Smith doing the follow-up work. And Meadows was pursuing statistical research on delinquents. As well as a detailed account of the process of investigation and testing carried out by the stipendiary probation officers, it was noted that the Children's Court Intelligence Test, developed by Meadows, had been completed and was ready to provide 'valid and reliable results with the cases'.[66] Meadows added to the research

62 Victoria 1940b (RCC): 9–11. 63 Victoria 1940b (RCC): 8. 64 Victoria 1941a (MHD): 18.
65 Victoria 1941b (RCC): 3. 66 Victoria 1941b (RCC): 4.

reported from the previous year, this year adding 'Truancy' to the survey of delinquency areas, indicating an exploration of the relations between delinquency and truancy. Meadows was much other than naïve when it came to statistics. In contrast to the CWDRS secretary's survey of opinions as to the causes of delinquency and similar research carried out by the police, Meadows's research showed a high level of sophistication:

> The figures were collected from case studies for the years 1939 and 1940 and must be regarded as indicative only for the group under examination. An unselected group may or may not show deviations from the results obtained from this group. A comparison of the incidence in this special group with that of an unselected group would add to the importance of the results whether confirmatory or otherwise. Full tabulation of the figures is omitted and the percentages only are given of those categories that are of general interest.[67]

Two of Meadows's conclusions are particularly noteworthy. He found that 65 per cent of delinquents tested fell within the 'normal' range of intelligence which Meadows himself noted 'seems to be in keeping with the more conservative statements of authorities in the field of mental testing of delinquents and also serves to reiterate the statement that generally speaking delinquents should be treated as a normal and not a sub-normal group'. Further, Meadows concluded that the backwardness of the truant needed to be distinguished from mental deficiency:

> The percentage of children who are one or more grades retarded is to be regarded as highly significant when it is compared with the intellectual level of the group which is normal. This backwardness is therefore largely the result of temperamental and environmental factors and not lack of ability.[68]

In 1941 it was announced that a formal Children's Court Clinic was to be established. The events which precipitated its formal constitution require some explanation. The MHD's Travancore premises were to be taken over by the US Army and the staff of Travancore clinic was to be relocated to Carlow House in Flinders Lane, Melbourne to share premises with the Children's Court staff, though the two authorities give different accounts of the move. From the Mental Hygiene Department:

> *Travancore Clinic* – The Clinic has worked under various handicaps. The psychiatric part of the work is now done by Dr Troup on three days per week, and by Dr Bailey on two afternoons per week. Dr. Bailey deals with cases referred to the Clinic by the Children's Court. The Clinic is now established in Carlow House, Flinders-lane. The total number of cases examined during the year was 212.[69]

And from the 1942 Children's Court report:

[67] Victoria 1941b (RCC): 4. [68] Victoria 1941b (RCC): 6. [69] Victoria 1943a (MHD): 15.

> In June last, owing to the war, it became necessary to find fresh accommodation for Dr Bachelard and Sister Purcell (the Clinic's nurse) who were formerly engaged at 'Travancore' Clinic. They were accommodated in the Children's Court Clinic and the services of Dr Bachelard and Sister Purcell have been available to assist in all cases referred by the Children's Court.[70]

According to the court it was *their* clinic and the Travancore personnel had been accommodated and would help *them*. The MHD regarded the court-related activities as merely an extension of the functions of Travancore. State psychiatrist H. K. Bailey would head the clinic, though wartime shortages delayed his full-time appointment and other staffing arrangements and it was stipulated that the stipendiary probation officers would serve them until such time as a psychologist was appointed. The 'psychological' expertise that was beginning to flourish independently at the Children's Court was now subsumed under psychiatric authority and placed under the jurisdiction of the Mental Hygiene Department.

The gap between perceptions about this clinic may well betray deeper territorial tensions between psychological medicine and a lay psychology, over the right to stake their knowledge claim over the problem child. In fact, these tensions were on the eve of bubbling over. With the war drawing to a close, the Travancore Clinic personnel vacated the premises and returned to their original Flemington premises by early 1944, leaving the Children's Court once again bereft of any formal clinical facilities, although they would still have Meadows until the clinic was re-established at war's end.[71] Meadows's activities at the Children's Court during the war, and in the context of the increasing influence of psychiatry, will be examined in Chapter 7.

70 Victoria 1943b (RCC): 3.
71 PROV VPRS 6345 Unit 95 Item 82: Dr H. Featonby, Maternal and Child Health Hygiene Branch, Dept Health to Sec. Dept Health 9 July 1945.

6

The Mission Station as a Correctional Institution

By the turn of the twentieth century, it was a truism in government policy circles that non-Aboriginal children did not belong in institutions. By the early 1880s, for the non-Aboriginal child, home and institution were thoroughly understood as contrasting parameters, defining and articulating the trajectories of neglected and reformatory children alike. The non-Aboriginal child might, by necessity and also in the name of welfare and/or justice, be compelled to move from home to institution. But that home life was better than institutional life for children had become an entrenched principle, through which were articulated the ideals of welfare and justice practices. The Department for Neglected Children and Reformatory Schools (DNCRS) had established its policy of boarding-out on that principle. Evidence presented in Chapter 3 showed how, in the era of the industrial school, non-Aboriginal children were formally categorised in the department's various statistical returns as industrial or reformatory children: they were counted, known and acted upon as rightly belonging to this or that institution. Hand in hand with the demise of the industrial school went, of course, a process of administrative recategorisation. Children could no longer be known and acted upon as industrial school children and from the early 1890s the department's statistical returns show them newly grouped under the heading 'Neglected'. But this was more than a simple change in nomenclature. As a newspaper remarked at the time: 'The place [Royal Park Industrial School] is not a home to which *young natures* might reasonably be expected to attach themselves, but rather an asylum, hospital, or barrack';[1] and 'some of the great barrack schools have been swept away. Two-thirds of the waifs of the state are living *natural lives* in healthy homes.'[2] Or note Department of Industrial and Reformatory Schools Secretary Guillaume's 'contrast of this free *natural home life* with that of children confined within the four walls of an institution, however well conducted'.[3] The home and the institution had come to be defined each as the negative of the other: the home was what the institution was not, and vice versa, and unlike the institution, the home catered to the nature of the child. It may be

1 *Argus* 1878, June 8: 9, emphasis added. 2 *Argus* 1880a, June 19: 6, emphasis added.
3 Victoria 1883 (DIRS): 3–4, emphasis added.

questionable whether in actuality the contrast stood up to scrutiny, but it nevertheless became a fundamental principle and the underpinning logic through which the 1887 Neglected Children's Act and Juvenile Offenders' Act and attendant policies and practices were articulated.[4] Moreover, although there were still a few non-government institutions classified as industrial schools, given the principle that children *by their very nature* did not belong in institutions, the term 'industrial school children' became something of an oxymoron and certainly stood in contradiction to the new logic. The new administrative category of neglected child allowed the department to bestowed (in principle if not in practice) the nature of childhood upon its charges. At one and the same time the nature of childhood had to be figured into the department's practices. Institutions had to become more home-like, styled as much as possible on the cottage. As we shall see, the nature of Aboriginal children was conceptualised quite differently by the authority responsible for their governance.

There is some evidence of a contemporaneous investment in the 'cottage principle' on the Aboriginal stations. Certainly by the turn of the century, children's dormitories if they still stood were regarded as relics of a past administrative ideal. J. H. Stähle for example made reference in 1911 to the old dormitory at Lake Condah mission as empty and in a state of ill repair.[5] On the stations, once common references to 'the natives' living in 'huts' were replaced by reports of adults and children living in cottages or houses, as part of a family. But however else home life and family were understood, lived and felt by the mission station Aboriginal residents, the Aboriginal home and Aboriginal family were understood by managers and by the Board for the Protection of Aborigines (BPA) as integral to, rather than in contrast to institutional life, and unquestionably subject to administrative scrutiny and administrative authority. The minutia and habits of daily life – every aspect of conduct – were thought by the administration (but not by the residents) as properly open to inspection and subject to regulation, to reporting and to correction.

This distinction is important in the argument put forward in this chapter. Those parameters 'home' and 'institution' within which an administration came to shape justice and welfare practices for the non-Aboriginal child were not the parameters which held and gave shape to the Aboriginal child. There was no 'home' for Aboriginal children that was not thought of as, in essence, a correctional institution for parents and children alike. The evidence presented in this chapter documents the way in which the BPA administered *a* justice-welfare system, if not *the* justice-welfare system, according to which conduct was tightly controlled via a disciplinary regime that bore a strong resemblance to the disciplinary regimes of correctional institutions, including reformatories. In Chapter 4 discussion turned to the specific subject of the transfer of Aboriginal children to the DNCRS in the first two decades of the twentieth century – how many, under what circumstances, and for what

[4] Victoria The Neglected Children's Act (No. 941) 1887; Victoria The Juvenile Offenders Act (No. 951) 1887.

[5] PROV VPRS 1694 Unit 4: J. H. Stähle (manager, Lake Condah) to Sec. BPA 18 Dec. 1911.

purpose. The implementation of a plan to systematically transfer so-named half-caste children from stations under the control of the BPA to the control of the DNCRS, purportedly for training and with the express purpose of 'merging' them with the white population, was short-lived. Some children were sent from stations to children's institutions but evidence showed that first, children deemed full-blood were sent to institutions, second, children were sent from the missions to institutions for reasons other than training, and finally arrangements with institutions were not necessarily dependent on formal DNCRS involvement. So the fact that, for the most part, Aboriginal children were *not* formally transferred by the BPA to institutions under control of the DNCRS does not mean they avoided placement in an institution. In this chapter, examples of the BPA choosing not to involve the DNCRS in forced child removals will be encountered. But these examples will show that the BPA was ready and willing to invoke the threat of DNCRS involvement as a strategy for managing station residents and that the choice not to involve the DNCRS by no means represented a *less* coercive, less violent action upon Aboriginal families. A question more sensibly asked in the circumstances just described is the following: why *would* the board resort, as a matter of course, to transferring its wards to the DNCRS when it had its own little archipelago of correctional institutions?

A distinction needs to be emphasised here between, on the one hand, the aspirations of an administration regarding the scrutiny and control of every aspect of conduct of Aborigines and, on the other, the experience and understandings of Aborigines themselves on and off the stations. There is a difference of course between the aspirations of an administration to know and to govern Aborigines and the outcomes of their attempts to discipline and control a people who thwarted imposed categories, rules and regulations and who refused to live as 'aboriginal' *or not*, under the meaning of the 1886 protection act and the amendments and consolidations in the years that followed. As some of the evidence testifies, although the board and its station managers regarded the Aboriginal home as an institutional space rightfully open for scrutiny and subjection to its authority their perspective was not necessarily shared by its inhabitants.

HABITS AND 'HABITUS'

The daily and weekly routine on the Aboriginal stations was punctuated and regulated by 'work bells', 'meat bells' and 'prayer bells' through which residents could be mustered, accounted for and reported on. The interiors of houses were regularly inspected by the matron (more often than not the wife of the station manager) for order and cleanliness but also for signs of immorality or ineffective parenthood. Permission was needed for everything from absence from the station, to medical treatment, to marriage, all of which were subject to approval and arrangement by station management operating under the direction of the board. Every aspect of conduct was understood as legitimately open to scrutiny and subject to written reports to the board by station management, including and especially the conduct of station residents' personal relationships. Stähle, manager at Lake Condah Station until 1915, made the point succinctly enough in a correspondence with the BPA regarding 'misconduct' on the part of problematic half-caste families relocated onto Lake Condah from the outskirts of the Framlingham reserve, where their presence was proving problematic: 'these men will have to learn that the Board Pro. Aborigines is their proper Authority, who will *protect as well as correct* them if they find it necessary to do so'.[6]

The arrangements that constituted the administration of station life are already familiar enough, and we have seen some of the same kinds of practices in other institutions. The station had multiple roots in multiple institutional forms, from the adult penitentiary and juvenile reformatory (we could probably add the religious order and the poor house, even the slave plantation). This is not to suggest that the Aboriginal station was simply modelled on this rather than that kind of institution – the term 'modelled' implies a well-thought-out construction based on a plan and belies the messiness inherent in the relations between individual board members, between the board and the government of the day, between the board and its own executive and managers, between church and state – and those relations would change over the first few decades of the twentieth century. By 1910 the mission at Ramahyuck had closed and by 1915 government appointees had taken over management of Lake Tyers and Lake Condah from longtime missionary managers, Reverends Bulmer and Stähle, much to the chagrin of longtime board member and staunch advocate for church-run mission stations Mrs Bon. The constitution of the board changed with the death or resignation of older longtime board members and with the installation, in 1916, of members of Parliament, themselves often with pastoral interests in areas accommodating Aboriginal populations. What we do not see is any evidence, in the context of these changes, of the development of a more 'liberal', more 'enlightened', less coercive approach to the management of the Aboriginal population. Indeed we will see, from the time that a long proposed programme of 'concentration' finally got off the ground, a chosen site – Lake Tyers station – was redrawn along *more* overtly correctional lines; that is, there was a consolidation of understanding at that time that containment and correction were the primary functions of the Aboriginal station, and that a station 'in the bush' was the proper place for the 'native'.

There may well be a different logic regarding the application of 'welfare' and 'justice' to Aborigines, applied in the name of quite different aspirations and administered by quite a different authority. In many ways the Board for the Protection of Aborigines was a law unto itself, with a self-contained authority to mete out welfare and justice according to *its* rules and regulations, shaped by *its*

6 PROV VPRS 1694 Unit 4: J. H. Stähle (manager Lake Condah) to Sec. BPA 10 Oct. 1912, emphasis added.

aspirations. The Aboriginal stations and reserves under its control operated, in many respects, as correctional institutions as well as providing 'protection' through, say, material support. On bells and musters and regimented daily routines, for example, dotted throughout the reports are accounts of some men arising too late from the ringing of the morning bell to collect their meat rations and therefore being punished by doing without. Greene reported on this from Lake Tyers in 1917:

> Of course it is necessary to have a fixed time for giving out meat and to stick closely to that time or some of the natives would be wanting to get their supply at all hours through the day. It is also necessary to make a daily distribution because they invariably eat all they have at one meal & they would do exactly the same if they got it weekly or bi-weekly.[7]

There are a multitude of accounts of the inspection of the houses, with one at Lake Tyers complaining it was occupied by the 'dirtiest family on the station and the matron has the greatest difficulty in making them keep their cottage even decently clean'.[8] The interiors of houses were scrutinised for signs of ineffective parenthood: 'I went to [K] and told her quietly to send her children to bed and get them up in proper time in the mornings, as the others did. Upon this she flew into a rage asking "how I dared to come into her house and tell her what to do about her children".'[9] Interiors of houses were also scrutinised for signs of immorality:

> There being three young girls in that home, and parents frequently out rabbiting, for the safety of the girls in general and the suppressing of jealousies among them, I have instructed all outside half castes to visit their own relations only, and not the homes where there are young girls. When [matron] Mrs Robarts entered the house on Friday, she found a young half caste in company with [ML] and [LL]. She quietly asked the young man what he was doing there and asked him to leave the room, which he did at once. [ML] flew into a temper calling Mrs Robarts a demon. Her mother soon joined in ... Neither of these women have made any apology or expressed any regret ... I have put up with the above family a very great deal and now asked that they be removed to another station.[10]

The station was effectively a marriage bureau, which used the threat of expulsion from the mission (and hence exposure to further poverty and racism) to maintain the colour bar of marriages between full-bloods and half-castes.[11]

There was also a range of punishments for misconduct. Among them were withdrawal of material necessities such as food, forced public apologies, presentation before the board for a formal dressing down, imposed separation from family and friends via forced relocations to other stations, and finally banishment from all

7 PROV VPRS 1694 Unit 4: C. L. Greene (manager Lake Tyers) to Sec. BPA 15 May 1917.
8 PROV VPRS 1694 Unit 4: C. L. Greene to Sec. BPA 29 Feb. 1917.
9 PROV VPRS 1694 Unit 3: Matron Mary Stähle (Lake Condah) to Sec. BPA 25 Nov. 1910.
10 PROV VPRS 1694 Unit 4: C. A. Robarts (manager Coranderrk) to Sec. BPA 30 June 1916.
11 Ewald 1990; Ellinghaus 2001.

stations, depending on the deemed seriousness of the misdemeanour and the required severity of the response. These were meted out largely at the discretion of individual station managers. The board's formal approval was required for relocations and banishments, but it rarely acted against the advice of the manager. Likewise, the board was legally required to obtain an Order of the Governor in Council in instances of forced relocation or banishment, but this was little more than a formality as it was rarely refused. Managers very frequently reported that they had stopped the rations of this or that miscreant. Managers, on occasion, actively sought such Orders in Council to have a troublesome individual better 'bound down'. Manager Robarts wrote to the secretary of the board about a persistent troublemaker M:

> He is getting worse instead of better and should not be allowed any liberty, he should be placed under an Order in Council or other measures restricting him from going off the station. This I strongly recommend should be done as soon as possible as the Holidays are nearing and some of the young men & youths are following his example which should be put down. If [M] be put under an Order in Council it will have a salutary effect on the other men.[12]

The C family at the Lake Condah Station for some time had caused the management trouble by defying authority. DC, banished from the station, had been recently permitted to return on condition that he behaved and worked to the satisfaction of the manager. However, a report by the manager indicated that DC had without permission taken twenty bundles of wattle bark from the reserve 'with the intention of disposing of them'. When spoken to by Captain Crawford, he had become abusive and left the station but subsequently returned. On advice from station management, the board sought the necessary order from the government: 'In order that proper discipline might be maintained it is desired that [DC] be transferred to Lake Tyers Station.'[13] The manager of Lake Condah received official confirmation from the board that the necessary order had been received:

> I have to inform you that an Order in Council has been issued prescribing Lake Tyers as the place of residence of [DC] and his family. The Police Department having been requested to remove them to Gippsland, it is probable you will be interviewed by the local Constable in the course of a few days.[14]

It was common for the police to be called to carry out official orders for forced relocations but managers were expected to manage the day-to-day discipline and order of the station without, if at all avoidable, resorting to police involvement, and managers could be chastised for calling in the police unnecessarily. In response to a question from the manager at Coranderrk as to the circumstances in which he might

12 PROV VPRS 1694 Unit 5: C. A. Robarts (Coranderrk) to Sec. BPA 15 Dec. 1913.
13 PROV VPRS 1694 Unit 4: Sec. BPA to Chief Secretary 27 April 1915.
14 PROV VPRS 1694 Unit 4: Sec. BPA to Acting Manager, Lake Condah 17 May 1915; Victoria 1915 (Government Gazette): 1703.

be justified 'calling in the Police', the board responded: 'While every effort should be made to maintain order on the station, it is advisable that the aid of the Police be asked only when there is grave danger of a disturbance.'[15] In most cases the forms of misconduct subject to punishment at the hands of a station manager did not constitute the kind of act that would be punishable by law in a non-Aboriginal non-institutional setting. Evidence of an adult having an affair with another adult might result in a report and punishment for 'immoral conduct'. But forms of conduct that may well in another context result in a formal charge might be kept in-house, so to speak, with the board preferring to mete out its own form of punishment rather than resorting to police involvement. DC's alleged stealing of wattle bark from Lake Tyers was a case in point: an Order in Council was sought rather than a charge of theft. In early 1916, Robarts, manager at Coranderrk station reported to the board that a half-caste boy stole a cheque from the station mailbag and attempted to cash it to buy a bicycle. The police were informed and the boy confessed, but Robarts noted that he would 'hesitate to recommend that he be sent to a reformatory ... He however deserves a severe punishment.' The board informed Robarts that he was to 'discharge him from the station without delay'. When the boy subsequently turned up at another station, the manager was instructed to turn him away.[16]

As already observed, just because Aboriginal children were not transferred to state institutions of the Department of Neglected and Reformatory Schools as was originally planned this did not mean they avoided placement in an institution. Inasmuch as the early-twentieth-century Aboriginal station was home, there was no 'home' for Aboriginal children on a station that was not thought by an administration as in essence a 'reformatory' institution, the understood function of which, as noted, was to 'protect as well as correct', and this for parents and children alike.[17]

SEPARATIONS: HALF-CASTES FROM REMNANT OLDER FULL-BLOODS

What was once a mission station at Framlingham in 1889 had been reduced to a 500-acre 'Aboriginal reserve', a large part of the original lands being sold off to the Department of Agriculture for an agricultural college and from the 1890s the board was keen for the reserve to close. Some of the early efforts to close Framlingham have already been noted in Chapter 2, efforts which included placing impediments in the way of Framlingham residents to induce families to move elsewhere. In the 1890s several obstacles were thrown in the way of Aboriginal people remaining in the Framlingham district, including removal of stock and resources, making it more

15 PROV VPRS 1694 Unit 3: C. A. Robarts (Coranderrk) to Sec. BPA 2 April 1912; Sec BPA to C. A. Robarts 4 April 1912.

16 PROV VPRS 1694 Unit 4: C. A. Robarts (Coranderrk) to Sec. BPA 19 Feb. 1916; Sec. BPA to Manager, Coranderrk 23 Feb. 1916.

17 PROV VPRS 1694 Unit 4: J. H. Stähle (Lake Condah) to Sec. BPA 10 Oct. 1912.

difficult for Aborigines to receive rations, and enforcing fencing off by Aborigines of the remaining reserve lands. Stähle and Hagenauer, then BPA secretary and inspector, conspired to get people to move on by closing the local school and the A and A families featured largely in the board's machinations:

> As I am authorized to take the bullocks & wagon down from Framlingham to Condah it will be an inducement for these families to get their belongings down here and after these two families have left Miss Powell will only have three pupils left, provided the [A family] can be kept at Lake Tyers. But if they return she will have five children still attending school. I think the closing of the school would bring about an early solution of the question at issue at Framlingham.[18]

Stähle reiterated the strategy in closing the school: 'I desire to say again that I believe the closing of the school at an early date will lessen to a great extent to opposition now carried on at Framlingham with regard to the breaking up of that Station.'[19] But despite the board's aspirations and machinations, Framlingham was not emptied of its residents. Most resisted its closure, refusing inducements to leave, and sending their children to the local Purnim state school despite opposition from the local white community. And neither, as shall be seen, were the A and A families to be successfully 'kept' at Lake Tyers.

It was customary for a local guardian to be appointed in districts not served by a working station, and hence had no need of a station manager or in areas where smaller numbers of Aborigines resided. It was also customary for the local guardian to be sought from among the local police constabulary, under whose guardianship protection and correction, welfare and justice merged so as to be indistinguishable. On the closure of the station, a local guardian was appointed to oversee the Aboriginal residents of Framlingham.[20]

Into the twentieth century, an arrangement with the local police constable to serve as local guardian remained in place, as was an ongoing concerted effort to empty the area surrounding the reserve of their half-caste children, and of their children's children. Police officers appointed local guardians assumed that role along with their regular policing duties. The practices at Framlingham show that, in whatever other role the police officer as local guardian was acting, he acted in the name of law and order for the local white community. Again, in the early years of the twentieth century the A and A families featured largely in yet another effort by the board to confect schooling as a reason for moving Aborigines on.

The local guardian for the Framlingham Reserve and surrounding area including Purnim in 1911 was Constable Gleeson of Woodford. Among his duties Gleeson, like the station managers before him, was to submit summary reports to the board to be

18 PROV VPRS 1694 Unit 1: J. H. Stähle (Lake Condah) to F. A. Hagenauer; Gen Insp. & Sec. BPA 1 July 1890.

19 PROV VPRS 1694 Unit 1: J. H. Stähle (Lake Condah) to F. A. Hagenauer, 7 July 1890.

20 PROV VPRS 1694 Unit 1: Sec. BPA to Chief Secretary, undated draft reply to corresp. Chief Secretary to Sec. BPA 3 March 1890.

included in appendices of their published reports, including reports of schooling. The topic had been highly animated around the time of the 1877 Royal Commission and up to the 1886 Half Caste legislation as this protection act was commonly known. Leading up to this legislation, the board and the stations invested quite heavily in schooling on the stations with managers reporting with some pride on the state school inspectors' 'very pleasing testimony of the progress made ... Several children have again passed the standard of education fixed by the law of the land.'[21] With the new act on the horizon and a policy of 'merging' already underway if half-caste children were to be sent from the station on completion of their schooling, then station schooling had to be seen to be doing its job of making half-caste children knowable as on a par with non-Aboriginal children in terms of educability, and hence having the capacity to 'do for themselves'. But by the beginning of the twentieth century the BPA was showing little interest in Aboriginal schooling. The reports of the BPA included little other than desultory one-liners about the state of education at individual stations, and information concerning the state of education at Framlingham was no exception. From 1902 to 1907, schooling for Framlingham children was described in a single sentence as 'satisfactory'. From 1908 to 1910 Constable Gleeson, as local guardian, reported in the same single sentence, no more than the fact that children attended Purnim state school. In 1911, the situation was suddenly revealed as unsatisfactory: 'For secular education the children attend the Purnim State school, about two miles away. In winter the roads are very bad (almost impassable), and the children then attend school very irregularly.'[22] Then in 1912, Gleeson reverted to his standard single sentence: no mention of bad roads or irregular attendance.[23] Given what follows, there can be little doubt that the 'blip' in the 1911 report represented an attempt by an administration to fashion legitimate grounds for bringing a perceived out-of-control half-caste population under control – to use schooling at Framlingham, and through schooling the children, as an instrument for control.

In August 1911 a memo was sent to Constable Gleeson as local guardian from the secretary of the BPA: 'Re children of [A], [A] and [R] families ... Please suspend action in connection with this matter until further advised.' Gleeson returned the memo, with a note: 'Memo returned as both [A] families have now gone to Lake Condah.'[24] (Separate arrangements had been made for the R family.) The action referred to was a planned transfer of the children of three families, A, A and R, to the DNCRS, a plan that was hatched at a time coincidental with Gleeson's atypical report on the schooling situation for Framlingham children. CA, JA and HR were adult half-caste men living with their families on the outskirts of the Framlingham

21 Victoria 1884 (BPA): 10 (F. A. Hagenauer, Ramahyuck).

22 Victoria 1911b (BPA): 9 (M. J. Gleeson, Local Guardian).

23 Victoria 1912b (BPA): 9 (M. J. Gleeson, Local Guardian).

24 PROV VPRS 1694 Unit 4: Sec. BPA to Local Guardian, Woodford 10 Aug. 1911; M. J. Gleeson to Sec. BPA 10 June 1912.

reserve. Of the three families, one was noted as having seven children in 1911, with ages ranging from 15 years to 19 months. Another had, at that time, four children ranging from 10 years to 16 months; and the third, six children ranging from 12 to 2 years[25] – seventeen children in total, of which at least ten were of school age. Among the correspondences concerning the families was a pencilled unsigned note:

> W. John Bell Wangoom [near Warrnambool]
> States that [CA's] boys and other half castes at Framlingham are a source of annoyance to the neighbours.[26]

And a police report to the BPA by Constable Gleeson two days later:

> I have to report . . . that in my opinion it is advisable to have the Half castes families viz. [A, A and R] brought under the Aborigines act. Each of these people have large families and are living in Huts of one or two rooms and leading a depraved sort of life. The fathers in each case are drunkards and [CA] & [JA] are convicted thieves.
>
> Although assisted by the Board with rations and clothing, they are no better off than when they were not in receipt of these supplys [sic], they will make no attempt to help themselves and what little they do earn wood collecting they spend on drink. They are really under no Control and roam about the district at will. Their children receive no training worth speaking of, 'of a moral or secular kind', and brought up as they are in such bad surroundings, it is almost certain that the girls will get into trouble and the boys follow the footsteps of their fathers.
>
> I would therefore respectfully and strongly urge that these families be brought under the application of the Aborigines act so as to give the Board better and fuller power over them.
>
> It would also be advisable to remove [CA] & his family to a Mission Station where he would be constantly under strict supervision and I believe this would have a good effect on the other Halfcastes as they would be afraid if they did not conduct themselves properly, they would also have to go.[27]

Shortly thereafter Walter Synnot Manifold, a prominent member of the Legislative Council and grazier in the Warrnambool area interviewed the secretary of the BPA. Following that interview the secretary sought advice in a memo (though from whom it is not clear). The minister quoted from the 1910 Aborigines Act, a short act that extended the powers of the BPA with respect to 'half-castes' living beyond the stations, and who had been declared non-Aboriginal in the 1886 protection act and hence beyond the remit of the board. It seems this was to be something of a test case:

> In an interview the Honorable W. Manifold M.L.C. had with me to-day with reference to the half caste families [A, A, R] and others, at Purnim it was suggested that these people should be brought under the Aborigines Act, in order that more effective supervision might be exercised with regard to them.

25 PROV VPRS 1694 Unit 6: M. J. Gleeson to Sec. BPA 20 Oct. 1911.
26 PROV VPRS 1694 Unit 6: unsigned note 25 July 1911.
27 PROV VPRS 1694 Unit 6: Report of Constable Gleeson 27 July 1911.

The Act-No 2255, passed last year provides – 'the Board in addition to any powers conferred upon it with regard to half castes may if it thinks fit and subject to the approval of the Minister exercise in the case of any half caste all or any of the powers conferred on the Board with regard to aboriginals by the said Act or any regulation thereunder'. It is therefore incumbent that the circumstances of each case be clearly stated in order that the Board may be able to determine the action to be taken in connection with any representations made by these families or on their behalf with a view to applying the Act.

Will you be good enough to let me have a full report as to the proposal that the families referred to be taken under the care of the Board, as well as in regard to any additional supervision etc, that may be required, if such a course be adopted.[28]

In response to that interview the secretary of the BPA sent the following letter to Manifold (as MLC, Parlt. House):

With reference to your interview regarding the half castes at Framlingham, I have now to inform you that the Board have [sic] given consideration to the conditions under which the people in question are living at Purnim, and have decided that the children should be transferred to the neglected [sic] Children's Department for their better care and education. It is considered that the immoral atmosphere in which the little ones live will have a most debasing effect upon them and they should be removed without delay. Steps will be taken as soon as possible to have them transferred to the department.

In connection with the suggestion that cottages be erected for the three families [at Framlingham] – [A, A and R] – I am to point out that the proposal would be practically a reversal of the Board's policy with regard to that settlement and that the Board cannot sanction such a course.

The removal of the people named to the aboriginal stations would not be conducive to the best interests of those establishments and was therefore considered undesirable.[29]

A revealing letter, serving as it does to underscore the options available to the BPA and the logic by which it decided on a course of action. The board could have bettered the conditions for half-caste families at Framlingham – but such would have countered its aspirations to empty the area of all but, in its terms, 'remnant' older full-bloods whom it maintained on what was once a station but now a 'reserve' much reduced in area. The board could have sent the families to other stations but that would of course have subjected those stations to an 'influx … of undesirable half-castes'. Instead it invoked a phrase, 'care, custody and education of children of aboriginals', inscribed since 1890 in the Aborigines Act,[30] to legitimise the reason for the decision. The correspondences show quite clearly that the welfare of children

[28] PROV VPRS 1694 Unit 6: Memo, Sec. BPA 21 July 1911; Victoria Aborigines Act (No. 2255) 1910.

[29] PROV VPRS 1694 Unit 6: Sec. BPA to W. Manifold MLC, State Parlt House 7 Aug. 1911.

[30] Victoria Aborigines Act (No. 1059) 1890 s 6: 'It shall be lawful for the Governor … to make regulations and orders … [for] the care custody and education of the children of aboriginals.'

was not the primary objective of the board, or 'the children' the primary object upon which it acted. Rather the children became the means to the end objective of bringing the half-caste under control. The board acted through the children to achieve the desired outcome: removal of half-castes from Framlingham.

On 10 October 1911 plans were still ostensibly afoot to remove the children to the DNCRS, and Gleeson was requested to provide their names and ages.[31] On 25 October the secretary of the BPA informed the manager at Lake Condah, in confidential correspondence, that the chief secretary had approved the removal of CA, JA, HR and their families to Lake Condah, and that he was to furnish particulars as to available accommodation.[32] With official approval in place, the families were to be offered a choice: Gleeson was directed to 'visit the three families mentioned to ascertain whether they are prepared to remove to one of the Aboriginal stations, provided the children are allowed to remain with them'.[33] Shortly thereafter, Gleeson informed the secretary:

> These people have consented to go to the Mission Stations rather than have their children taken from them as they put it . . . I believe these people may use influence yet to be allowed to remain but I would respectfully suggest that Mr Ditchburn [secretary, BPA] write direct to each family pointing the advantage [sic] of going & also that if they refuse their children will be taken from them. They seem now quite satisfied to go but a little advice from you would help considerably.[34]

Correspondences back and forth reveal that Lake Condah was ill equipped to provide for an intake of large families; it was eventually decided to make hurried repairs to its 'dormitory', by then redundant and in a state of dilapidation, to accommodate the families.[35] In April 1912, Constable Gleeson, impatient with delays, urged the board to hurry on with the planned relocations:

> With reference to the removal of Halfcastes [CA] and[JA] & families to Condah: I respectfully beg to point out that it would be a good thing if these people could be removed at an early date as they are roaming about the district to all Race and Sports Meetings and are rarely at Home. They get drunk and cause annoyance and inconvenience to white people and it is useless to bring them before the Court, they have no sense of shame and Police generally simply turn them away.
>
> [JA] when returning from Panmure Races recently called at [EE's] late at night and commenced pulling her about probably with a view to assaulting her. [JA] denies this, but old [EE] is certain it was him.
>
> Mounted Const. McQuillan of Panmure can bear me out as to the nuisance these two men are to him.

31 PROV VPRS 1694 Unit 6: Sec. BPA to M. J. Gleeson 10 Oct. 1911.

32 PROV VPRS 1694 Unit 6: Sec. BPA to Manager Lake Condah 25 Oct. 1911.

33 PROV VPRS 1694 Unit 6: Sec. BPA to Local Guardian, Woodford, 6 Nov. 1911.

34 PROV VPRS 1694 Unit 4: M. J. Gleeson to Sec. BPA 14 Nov. 1911.

35 PROV VPRS 1694 Unit 4: Correspondences between J. H. Stähle and Sec. BPA 18 Dec. 1911; 21 Feb. 1912; 7 March 1912.

> If they were on a Mission Station they would be under constant supervision and could not roam about at will.
>
> As it has already been decided to move these people I would be pleased if the matter could be attended to at an early date.[36]

To the BPA secretary's reassurance that accommodation would probably be ready in a fortnight, Gleeson responded with a reiteration of these families' need for 'constant supervision': 'I am pleased that they will soon be going to a place where they will be under constant supervision, as they are continually roaming about the district and it is hard to find them at their Homes.'

CA, JA and families were eventually bundled off to Condah (HR had expressed a preference for Coranderrk, though after a short stay there he and his family would also arrive at Lake Condah). Gleeson reported their departure in mid-June.[37] And Stähle reported their arrival, though he was shocked to find that they had come with no provisions other than 'a poor supply of threadbare clothes & four single blankets which are the worse for wear & a very few old dishes – not enough for doing any cooking nor even eating their dinners decently'. Gleeson had assured the families, though without the authority of the board, that they would be provided for once at Lake Condah.[38] Once there CA and JA and their families continued to cause trouble. In early July 1912, Stähle penned a long 'Urgent' letter to the board outlining 'certain developments' since the arrival of the families at Condah and listed numerous instances of their insubordination. In particular, it was the administration's attempts to assert its authority over JA's children that, in Stähle's account, apparently threw JA into a wild temper:

> When the question about the children had to be considered I told them that in accordance with the rule of the Board, they would have to learn habits of usefulness. He evidently not understanding me got again into a temper & declared wildly, that he would not allow his children to be tampered with, & Miss Bagnall whom I had as a witness as well as my daughter (my son the assistant manager being absent & engaged with the men at the time) tried to explain to [JA] what I meant by them becoming useful – when he rose again in a temper & ordered Miss Bagnall in a raging tone to be quiet – he would not allow her to say anything in the matter while he spoke to me. Miss Bagnall was so overcome with surprise about his rudeness, that she turned pale & never opened her lips again. I asked him what he meant by tampering with his children. He said he meant that he would not allow his children to be sent out in the world when they came of age, to go into service. I said that time was a long way off & that when it came, it rested not with me, but with the Board as to what should be done with them.[39]

Numerous reports and telegrams ensued in which Stähle described the men's united attempts to cause disturbance on the station. He was authorised to stop the men's

36 PROV VPRS 1694 Unit 4: M. J. Gleeson to Sec. BPA 10 April 1912.
37 PROV VPRS 1694 Unit 4: M. J. Gleeson to Sec. BPA 15 June 1912.
38 PROV VPRS 1694 Unit 4: J. H. Stähle to BPA 18 June 1912.
39 PROV VPRS 1694 Unit 4: J. H. Stähle to Sec. BPA 3 July 1912.

rations but to no effect. Finally, Stähle threatened to resign if CA and JA were not removed. At this point the vice-chairman gave the following directions to the secretary of the BPA: 'If [CA] & [JA] are utterly impracticable I think that they with their wives should be removed from the Station but that the children should if possible be retained. Ask Mr Stähle if he can arrange for the custody of the children in the event of their residence at Condah being ordered.'[40]

Once again the suggestion of separation from children had the desired effect. Stähle responded rapidly in yet another telegram: 'Defer proceedings [CA] and [JA] apologise letter following.'[41] Stähle forwarded a letter from the men apologising and promising obedience in future. Notwithstanding, the board wanted a contingency plan: 'Send replies to [CA] & [JA] that on this occasion their apology is accepted but that should the manager have any further occasion to complain of their behaviour they will be removed from the station. Ask manager as to providing for children.'[42] CA and JA were each written an identical official letter from the board notifying them that their apology was accepted: 'Should the Manager however have cause again to complain of your conduct, you will be removed from the station.'[43] Meanwhile, Stähle formalised the contingency plan to retain the children and send JA away should there be further insubordination:

> In the event of [JA] again breaking out (which of course it is hoped will not occur), the question of sending him and his wife away from the station and retaining the children may be taken into consideration. The Board would therefore be glad to learn as soon as convenient, whether you can arrange for the care and custody of the children of both families should their residence at Lake Condah be ordered.[44]

But the peace was short lived. Stähle made further reports to the board regarding CA's behaviour. CA, having been refused permission from the board to seek outside work shearing, declared his intentions to go anyway. Now armed with the authorised contingency plan of retaining the children and hence forcing a separation of parent and child, Stähle was able to deploy the threat as a means of bringing him into line:

> This morning [CA] came to me & said . . . he was going. I told him that he knew that he could not go . . . As he . . . did not seem to regard the Board's authority, I told him that I had a letter in my possession intimating that if they defied the Board's decision their children only would be kept here.[45]

Matters did not end there. As Stähle made clear in the same correspondence, the last thing he wanted was to be left in charge of CA's wife and now seven children. CA continued to make trouble at Lake Condah, outlasting Stähle's period of management

40 PROV VPRS 1694 Unit 4: BPA to Sec. BPA 12 July 1912.
41 PROV VPRS 1694 Unit 4: J. H. Stähle to Sec. BPA 12 July 1912.
42 PROV VPRS 1694 Unit 4: Vice Chairman, BPA to Sec. BPA 12 July 1912.
43 PROV VPRS 1694 Unit 4: Sec. BPA to CA and JA 15 July 1912.
44 PROV VPRS 1694 Unit 4: Sec. BPA to J. H. Stähle, 15 July 1912.
45 PROV VPRS 1694 Unit 4: J. H. Stähle to Sec. BPA 19 Sept. 1912.

and indeed that of Captain Crawford who followed Stähle.[46] CA was eventually dismissed from the station in December 1913. His wife and children remained there, but over the next three years CA 'returns from time to time and causes endless annoyance'. In 1916 the board advised the manager:

> As the maintenance of discipline is of primary importance, I am directed to request that you will inform [CA] that unless he at once, conforms to the regulations of the Board, he and his family will be removed from the station. It would be as well if you were to also notify Mrs [A] of this determination in order that she may understand and realise her position.[47]

In the context of a final attempt to discipline CA, the threat was now that all material support would be withdrawn from his wife and children.

Soon after, CA and his wife worked to have themselves and their children freed, one by one, from station life and from the control of the board. By 1917, against the wishes and the machinations of the board, CA, his wife and children were once more living on the outskirts of Framlingham.[48] CA's family is most interesting because it demonstrates again the surprising reluctance on the part of the board to force a separation of parents and children via the latter's transfer to the Department for Neglected Children and Reformatory Schools – which is not at all the same thing as a reluctance to force a separation of parents from children. But the strategy was precisely one of avoiding a formal legal process that would expose the board to the accusation that it had undermined a central tenant of liberal governance – and oft-repeated aspect of the ethical demeanour of the board – that the Aborigines were a 'free people'. Separation of children from parents could be achieved without involvement of the police or the courts and, importantly, without engagement with the department. As long as the board remained responsible for its wards, it had in its hands a powerful tool, in the form of the threat of forced separation, with which to achieve 'correction of conduct'.

THE ABORIGINAL POPULATION – A 'NATURAL' DECLINE

> It is most likely that Lake Tyers will be selected as the future home of all the blacks. There they can live with all their natural surroundings, such as game, fish and hunting . . . To either lease or sell the various reserves would find more than sufficient funds to keep the blacks in comfort for the rest of their natural lives . . . The climate is mild and contamination with whites could be prevented, and the blacks also kept free from drink . . . As regards Coranderrk: . . . With the services of a first class engineer, I think a scheme could be made for draining the flat lands, thus rendering it of more value, and the estate would then be cut

46 PROV VPRS 1694 Unit 4: S. Crawford (manager Lake Condah) to Sec. BPA 29 Nov. 1913.

47 PROV VPRS 1694 Unit 4: Sec. BPA to W. Galbraith (manager Lake Condah) 12 Aug. 1916.

48 PROV VPRS 1694 Unit 4: W. Galbraith (Lake Condah) to Sec. BPA 6 Nov. 1916; Sec. BPA to W. W. Johnstone, Bushfield 13 Nov. 1916; W. Galbraith to Sec. BPA 25 Nov. 1916; MA to Sec. BPA 18 July 1917.

> up into suitable agricultural or dairy farms. It must be remembered that this property . . . is a most valuable property.[49]

In the early decades, the overarching purpose of the administration of Aborigines, and the logic by which it was to be achieved, was nicely illustrated in a press clipping from the local *Guardian* newspaper from 1917 that sits among the correspondences of the Board for the Protection of Aborigines. The article quoted parliamentarian J. Rought MLA, who was responding to rumours that the station at Coranderrk was to be closed. It usefully encapsulates a settled logic through which the Victorian government of the day presented to its (non-Aboriginal) constituency its aspiration of concentrating and confining the Aboriginal population on a single reserve as just and proper, and serving both the Aboriginal and the non-Aboriginal populations' well-being. A knowable, identifiable entity – 'the blacks' – would be peaceably, not forcibly enclaved in a reserve, free to do what 'blacks' do (hunting and fishing) and in which nature, not government, would inevitably take its certain course. Here we have black and white, the natural and the engineered, the pre-historic or ahistorical and the liberal progressive, co-existing, but each contained, albeit one much more tightly bound than the other. Note too that the plan for this future reserve came with a built-in obsolescence – it would last 'for the rest of their natural lives'. Here the *Guardian* article shows itself as representative of a broader taken-for-granted belief: the Aboriginal population was subject to natural forces – its decline in numbers was a 'natural' decline.

It should be noted, in passing, the great distance between the Eden that was Lake Tyers as represented in the *Guardian* and both the reality that was Lake Tyers in 1917 and the way it was envisaged in plans that circulated within government circles. For instance, earlier statements from station managers noted that hunting-and-fishing, as a way of life, was largely a thing of the past among station residents. John Bulmer, manager at Lake Tyers, noted a decade earlier: 'The natives do not hunt native game. Each year they rely more and more on the resources of the station';[50] restrictions on Aborigines fishing at Lake Tyers had long been imposed to prevent their interfering with commercial enterprises.[51] Members of the board sent out in 1917 to inspect and report on conditions at stations and plans to concentrate the Aboriginal population there advocated sweeping away 'sickly, mawkish sentimentalism' and replacing it with a philosophy of 'practicable hard-headed common-sense' in which the 'mental, social and spiritual welfare' of a newly concentrated population lay in the dictum: 'If man work not, neither shall he eat', although it was conceded that all work and no play 'makes "Black" a dull boy'.[52] But to the main point: it was upon the achievement of the 'fact' of a naturally, peaceably declining population that by the turn of the twentieth century, the Victorian government had

[49] PROV VPRS 1694 Unit 4: press clipping, *Healesville & Yarra Glen Guardian* 28 July 1917.
[50] Victoria 1907 (BPA): 10. [51] Victoria 1912b (BPA): 9.
[52] PROV VPRS 1694 Unit 4: 'Remarks of Mr [James] Menzies, with reference to proposed Amendment of the Present Management of the Aborigines of Victoria', 5 June 1917.

presented its rationale for governing Aborigines, according to which the Board for the Protection of Aborigines took its *raison d'etre*, its moral authority and shaped its practices.

A commonly held expression to describe these arrangements is 'smoothing the dying pillow'. But what is being underscored in this part of the study is the hand-in-hand coming into being of the 'fact' of a naturally declining population with the engineering of that decline. It is important to observe that in the article in the *Guardian* the 'natural' enclave to be afforded 'the blacks' was offset largely by means of the rhetorical exclusion of science and technology: it was the absence of anything engineered, an absence presented in the newspaper as just and proper, which distinguished the world of the 'blacks' from the white world beyond. Of interest is the arrival – the achievement – of a fact that nature, not government, was doing the work of producing a decline in population numbers; how that achievement served to justify the exclusion of the application of science and technology (including, as we shall observe, medical science and sanitary engineering); and how that exclusion helped, in turn to engineer a reduction in population. It is on the basis of that understanding that we arrive at a fundamental disparity – contrasting logics – according to which the 'child' and the 'Aboriginal child' differentially become the subjects of administration.

The argument that the decrease in the Aboriginal population, though declared natural was in fact engineered, is to a degree self-evident given that the unit of population inherited by the new century's administration, that is, 'the aboriginal', was largely an invention of the 1886 Aborigines Protection Act – an instance of what has been called 'extinction by statistics'.[53] Prior to that act the half-caste was counted as 'aboriginal'. After the 1886 legislation those deemed half-caste were excluded from the category. But what more effective way to engineer a reduction in numbers than to change the criterion according to which one counts? How the administration of the mission stations arrived at the fact of a natural decline in the Aboriginal population has already been alluded to in Chapter 4 and became accepted as the indisputable ground on which an administration would proceed. One way involved the wilful exclusion of the application of science and technology to the problem of a decline in the numbers of Aborigines. Let us briefly revisit this evidence so as to establish a starting point from which to explore the new century's practices.

In the late 1870s, board members Albert Le Souef and Edward Curr reported on their visit to Ramahyuck and Lake Tyers stations:

> We think well of the management of both stations; the natives appeared happy and contented, and the discipline, education, and routine work is satisfactory.
>
> We observed, however, with deep regret, that consumption, or lung disease, here as elsewhere, was very prevalent, and the natives are rapidly decreasing in numbers; few of those born on the stations seem likely to attain the age of thirty years. The

[53] McGregor 1997.

> disease is always, sooner or later, fatal, and it has been for many years a terrible scourge among the blacks, thousands having no doubt died from its effects in the last thirty years. The complaint was most likely engendered in the first instance by an entire change of life, consequent on coming into contact with the whites. We recommend that the Government be asked to appoint a board of the best medical talent procurable, to investigate the disease, and, if possible, point out how it may be mitigated or prevented in the future. From inquiries we made it seems to us a form of lung disease peculiar to the blacks.[54]

The policy of 'concentration' was first officially communicated by BPA Vice-Chairman Henry Jennings to the chief secretary in the 1879 Report and Correspondences Relative to the Mortality amongst the Residents of the Aboriginal Stations of Victoria, Etc. (Mortality Report), produced shortly after Le Soeuf and Curr's report was sent to the board, and in the context of the 'painful fact' of a rapid decrease in the population of 'aborigines . . . including half-castes':

> I have the honour to inform you that the Board for the Protection of Aborigines has recently had under its serious consideration the advisability of concentrating the natives on fewer stations than at present. It is a painful fact that the aborigines throughout Victoria are rapidly decreasing in number, the total numbers being now probably not more than 800, including half-castes.

This correspondence was one of two from Jennings included in the Mortality Report, and having asserted this 'painful fact' the rest of this first correspondence, he outlined the details of the envisaged plan of concentration.[55] A separate correspondence from Jennings to the chief secretary, on the same date, devoted itself to the cause of mortality among Aborigines, wherein he argued that the deaths could no longer be put down to 'intoxication and debauchery' because the 'sober and the drunkard' seemed to share the same fate. Rather, the cause was put down to a disease that though it manifested itself via symptoms similar to consumption – spitting blood among them – it was 'a disease of the lung peculiar to natives'. Further medical opinion was sought. Chief Medical Officer McCrea responded almost immediately. It was no great mystery. In 1879 as three years earlier when McCrea first reported on the matter, 'gross sanitary defects' on the stations were the cause of the lung infections and the high mortality rates:

> The Aborigines Board allege as an excuse for these necessary changes not having been carried out that they have not been provided with funds for the purpose. Under these circumstances it is not surprising that the health of the aborigines does not improve; but if the recommendations in my report were carried out in their entirety, I have no doubt but that their influence on the health of the natives will be very great and beneficial.[56]

54 Victoria 1879b (BPA): 10.
55 Victoria 1879a (Mortality Report): 3 (H. Jennings, Vice Chairman BPA to Chief Secretary 12 June 1879).
56 Victoria 1879a (Mortality Report): 5 (W. McCrea CMO to Chief Secretary 26 June 1879).

Albert Le Souef, newly appointed vice-chairman of the BPA, sent the chief secretary a rejoinder to McCrea's correspondence, stating that the board 'differs with Dr McCrea'. Le Soeuf, director of the Melbourne Zoo, reiterated the board's opinion that the cause of death was a 'peculiar form of chest disease' – peculiar to the natives. Chief Medical Officer McCrae saw the problem of a decline in the numbers of Aborigines as of the administration's making. It was bad drainage, poor accommodations, lack of adequate dietary, hygiene and medical resources, and he provided quite detailed advice regarding better drainage and ventilation and sanitary facilities. He also advised on the specifics regarding dietary improvements and resources for isolating contagious cases and for providing basic medical services and equipment. The solution lay in the application of existing sanitary engineering and medical scientific know-how. The board rejected this solution: instead it located the cause in a disease peculiar to this population and situated the cause beyond any known medical scientific or sanitary engineering solution. The status of the Aboriginal population was achieved – made up – as subject to nature rather than the product of bad administration. Scientific and technological solutions would have no effect on vital statistics – so there was no reason to apply them.

The 1879 Mortality Report showed something of the willing into existence of what by the early twentieth century had become a given fact: that is, the affiliation of the Aborigine with nature, and the decline of the Aboriginal population as a product of natural forces. We can see something of the conditions by which the planned preservation of Lake Tyers as the single natural enclave, excluded from interference, could be heralded as just and proper. There is evidence from the second half of the 1870s of the transmutation of rapid population shift from being a problem (i.e. something that begs a solution) into an immutable fact of nature. As such, it offered the ground from which to launch new administrative responses, including the policy of concentration. By the beginning of the twentieth century, what was previously voiced as a problem solidified into an immutable fact, to the extent that the inevitable decline in the Aboriginal population was beginning to sound very much like a fortuitous solution to the problem of the cost of administering a population. Let us recall the voice of the BPA's vice-chairman C. M. Officer in 1902, first encountered in Chapter 2 and offered in the context of the board's decision to close the Moravian Mission Station, Ebenezer, with others to follow:

> The natives are decreasing in number so fast that it will not be long before the Board will be able to make a further recommendation in the direction of closing another station ... In the meantime, efforts might be made to persuade families living on either of these reserves to move to one of the other stations, Condah or Coranderrk, as vacancies occurred by death. On both those stations there are, at present, a good many old people ... and it cannot be long before they die. The vacancies thus caused could be taken by younger people. It is, however, to be remembered, that the Aborigines are a free people, and not prisoners, who cannot summarily be deported against their will. The Aborigines of Victoria are steadily decreasing in numbers,

> and the expense of managing them also decreases from year to year. In another twenty years they will probably be extinct and, in the meantime, the poor remnant of the original owners of this splendid State of Victoria should be dealt with kindly, wisely and generously.[57]

In short, into the twentieth century managing the Aboriginal population meant managing a declining population which simply involved letting nature take its course – a course that also happened to turn out favourably to the government's purse. As in this extract, there was not to be any indication that an administration was hurrying that decline – just waiting it out.

INVESTMENTS IN THE DEMISE

An overarching investment in a declining Indigenous population left the managers of stations in a peculiar position. They had to oversee a working station as a viable economic entity. They had to see to it that the population within its boundaries was fed and clothed and kept fit enough to work to keep the station a temporarily viable economic entity. But the overall investment was in that population's demise. In 1904 J. H. Stähle, manager at Lake Condah, alluded to something of the difficulty of maintaining a viable station and investing in the health of its population, according to the contradictory imperative of achieving a non-viable population:

> The men were employed in the same manner as in former years, viz., in gardening, clearing ground, fencing, haymaking, shearing sheep, &c. As the number of men and women gets less, and those left become advanced in age, the work done by them decreases every year. Our object must be more to keep them usefully employed, so as to maintain them in good health, rather than to make their efforts a commercial or paying success.[58]

In the first few years of the twentieth century, managers reported dutifully to the board, and the board reported dutifully to government, on the latest figures of population decline (it was now standard to present the mortality rates as the first item of substance in the body of these reports, immediately following the board's reporting on the number of meetings it held and also, quite appropriately of course, on its 'deep regret' for deaths of board members). In 1901 the board reported that 'the number of Aborigines and half-castes under certificates who have resided, or are belonging to, the stations and different depots, has considerably decreased, as shown by the reports of managers'.[59] A table followed. Similar statements and tables were made in each year onwards. In the 1905 report, numbers were 'exactly the same'. The 1906 to 1912 reports, while including a table of numbers, made no statement about a decrease. In fact between these years the numbers of people supported by the board

57 Victoria 1902b (BPA): 5–7.

58 Victoria 1904b (BPA): 9, Appendix II (Mission Station Lake Condah).

59 Victoria 1901b (BPA): 3.

appeared to remain reasonably steady, a reported 275 in 1906 and 269 in 1912 – there was certainly no 'considerable decrease'. In the 1910 report, the numbers were for the first time divided into 'Blacks' and 'Half-castes', with the following statement: 'The number on the 30th June, 1909, were 173 aborigines and 80 half-castes.'[60] By the 1912 report '136 aborigines and 116 half-castes' were reported as under the board's administration.

Unsurprisingly there was no articulation of the 'problem' of population decline in these reports. A decrease in numbers of persons administered by the board could be achieved in two ways: first, by clearing those it deemed half-castes out of the station once thought able to earn their own living – this was an achievement reported with satisfaction. Joseph Shaw, manager at Coranderrk in the first few years of the new century, noted in 1905: 'We have still a few half-castes to be merged into the general population, but up to the present we have got over 60 away.'[61] And second, by death, including death by disease. And that too was not articulated as a problem, but again came close to being articulated as a solution. In 1902 Johannes Hagenauer, acting manager of the soon-to-be-closed Ramahyuck Aboriginal Mission Station, articulated the subject, but not the *problem* of high mortality rates through disease, thus:

> The health of the people has not been very good, and signs of their old disease of consumption are to be found among a good many of them, although the best medical attention is paid to them. There is a constant decrease amongst them which 'ere long will close their earthly pilgrimage.[62]

Now, there are two things to note here, pertaining to earlier remarks about the achievement of the 'fact' of a natural decline in the population – most pointedly the decision by the board in 1879 to differ with the medical officer in recognising consumption as the cause of high mortality rates and lack of dietary, hygiene, sanitary and medical resources as the cause of consumption. In several respects Hagenauer echoed the sentiments expressed by Le Soeuf and others nearly three decades on, not the least that this disease was peculiar to the 'natives': it was '*their* old disease', not *the* disease of consumption. It was certainly not, as articulated by Hagenauer, something owned by an administration and for which an administration should have taken responsibility. Hagenauer noted that 'the best medical attention is paid them' but the message was that they were fated to die regardless – because of *their* disease. Perhaps the medical superintendent of the DNCRS's Royal Park Depot in the early 1920s, A. P. Derham could serve as an example of the 'best medical advice' from the public medicine point of view. In a prior role as captain in the Army Medical Corps (prior to that he was a public health vaccination officer), Derham wrote of the peculiar susceptibility of the 'coloured races' to chest infections. He drew on his observations 'while I was convalescent in Quarantine, Sydney in 1918':

60 Victoria 1910 (BPA): 3. 61 Victoria 1905 (BPA): 7, Appendix I (Coranderrk Aboriginal Station).
62 Victoria 1902b (BPA): 9, Appendix III (Ramahyuck Aboriginal Mission Station).

> The coloured races are markedly susceptible, and the mortality among them is very high. Though exact figures are not available, the mortality in some areas is said to be approaching 50% among natives. The mortality is usually not more than about 5% among Europeans. Again, the psychical element comes in, as the native gives up hope at once, expects to die, and often dies.[63]

So although into the twentieth century it was plainly understood that large numbers of Aborigines suffered not from some TB-like disease but from tuberculosis proper, the racial peculiarity was preserved but shifted to 'the susceptibility of the natives to tubercular & various chest troubles'.[64] It was at Le Soeuf's and the board's insistence following the 1879 Mortality Report, of the peculiarity of the natives' lung disease, that there was a de-problematisation of mortality rates and a justification for an administration's disinvestment in the application of medical science and sanitary engineering. In the new century, lung disease among Aborigines had now been named for what it was – tuberculosis: one Louisa Russell had 'Tuberculosis' recorded as 'Cause of Death'.[65] Nevertheless, the perpetuation of a peculiar native susceptibility to disease as a causal explanation continued to contribute to a normalisation of the presence of illness on stations, the substantiation of the equation of Aboriginality with a diseased state, and a justification for a nihilistic attitude on the part of an administration to the presence of disease among the Aboriginal population. Is there evidence of such? Let us start with TB.

Coranderrk in particular experienced a number of epidemics over the first two decades of the century, and TB was a constant presence. It was noted in 1910 that 'owing to the prevalence of tuberculosis at Coranderrk, the Board requested the Chairman of the Board of Public Health to have the station inspected by an officer of his Department. Dr Robertson accordingly made the desired inspection, and submitted a report, which is under consideration.'[66] And that same year, station manager C. A. Robarts reported from Coranderrk: 'There has been a deal of sickness among natives since January, which has resulted in a heavy death rate. The existence of tuberculosis is much to be feared.'[67] It continued in the following year, with Robarts reporting: 'The amount of sickness and many deaths that have occurred have been a heavy strain on us, especially on my wife, who attends to the sick and provides many comforts so much needed in that slow and lingering disease.'[68] But if we turn to the correspondences around the topic of TB and its management at Coranderrk that year, we see a much less edifying picture of the context in which public health and medical knowledge was sought, and what was done with it – that is, ultimately nothing. The BPA notified the medical officer in the Shire of Healesville that in connection with

63 Derham 1919: 65.
64 PROV VPRS 1694 Unit 4: Dr Parker to Manager Coranderrk, 24 March 1917.
65 Victoria 1906d (BPA): 5, Appendix I Coranderrk Aboriginal Station (J. Shaw).
66 Victoria 1910 (BPA): 5. 67 Victoria 1910 (BPA): 6, Appendix I.
68 Victoria 1911b (BPA): 6, Appendix I.

the recent death of a woman from tuberculosis at Coranderrk, the manager had informed them

> that a number of deaths from various causes have occurred in the house in which she died and during the last 12 months, three were from tuberculosis. In these circumstances the Board desires that the house be thoroughly fumigated and disinfected, and would be glad if you will kindly advise as to the most effective measures to be adopted towards that end.[69]

Further correspondence some years later reveals that numerous deaths in the house from typhoid were among the 'various causes' alluded to in the previous notification.[70] The shire's medical officer did not think that 'any measure of disinfection would be really effective' and advised its destruction, 'preferably the burning on the ground where it stands'. He went on to describe the difficulty he had in attempting to adequately treat the 'native phthisical [sic] patients' at Coranderrk, given the conditions of accommodation there and hoped 'your Department will not think I am taking a liberty when I say that for some time I have felt the need of isolation for the phthisical native'.[71] Shaw was asked to 'kindly favour the Board with your views as to what you consider a rationally constructed house for the purpose ... in order that proper consideration might be given such an important question'.[72] Shaw obliged, forwarding a list including an isolation settlement on one of the stations with control over the to-and-fro of healthy relatives; accommodation inclusive of wide verandas; separate accommodation for attendants inclusive of 'a large copper for boiling infected things'; washable furniture, no drapes, adequate floor ventilation, walls of 'smooth, hard, impervious material, with no ledges, and all the corners rounded'. Shaw recommended sending a doctor to Coranderrk in company with 'an architect experienced in hospital building'.[73] The board promptly thanked Shaw 'for the information afforded'. There was no further discussion or follow-through of the plan. Meanwhile, on Shaw's advice that the cottage should be condemned, the BPA's Vice-Chairman Callaway asked for a second opinion from the Public Health Department as to whether 'this course is absolutely necessary'.[74] The secretary of the Board of Public Health having received a second report from one of its officers, advised Callaway 'that building in its present condition is insanitary and considerably out of repair, and it is strongly advised that Dr Shaw's recommendation that the building be destroyed be carried out'. But contrary to the advice of the Public Health Department, the BPA decided that rather 'the house should be made habitable', listed the work that would need to be done, and asked the manager to submit particulars of the materials needed to

69 PROV VPRS 1694 Unit 4: Sec. BPA to Medical Officer, Shire of Healesville 4 March 1911.
70 PROV VPRS 1694 Unit 4: Sec. BPA to Manager, Coranderrk 26 March 1917.
71 PROV VPRS 1694 Unit 4: Dr Shaw to Sec. BPA 9 March 1911.
72 PROV VPRS 1694 Unit 4: Sec. BPA to Dr Shaw 14 Nov. 1911.
73 PROV VPRS 1694 Unit 4: Dr Shaw to Sec. BPA 18 March 1911.
74 PROV VPRS 1694 Unit 4: Vice Chairman BPA to Chairman, Board of Public Health 4 April 1911.

carry out the work.[75] Robarts, then manager at Coranderrk, replied to the board that given that the house had been disinfected, and given that there were other empty cottages available for accommodation, it would be a waste to apply any further resources to the house:

> The costs for the necessary works on this station having been so great, I, in the interest of my duties and responsibilities here, would like to see whatever funds might be available, spent in the purchase of one or two good brood mares which would be a productive asset to the station. The holding over of the above repairs means a saving of at least £20.[76]

In 1917 the house that the board refused to condemn in 1911 was still standing. That year the board wrote to the manager: 'It has been alleged that the old house at Coranderrk from which so many deaths occurred is still standing and is a menace to the health of the natives. Will Mr Robarts be good enough to report re this matter.'[77] Shortly after, the board noted its intentions 'to destroy the same by demolish the house and burning the old materials'.[78] It is not known from the records whether this actually happened.

The previous example provides an indication of governmental practices at the level of population. Practices at the level of the individual also tell us, among other things, something of the relations between station management and medical expertise. More specifically they reveal reluctance on the part of the board to prioritise the authority of medical expertise. This is in part because of the way illness and infirmity were inscribed into the very means by which Aboriginality was constituted as a legal category. In actuality, being ill or infirm or, using the terminology of the time, being other than able-bodied, could constitute the grounds upon which one's legal status as Aboriginal or half-caste was determined within the meaning of the act. It needs to be remembered that in the fashioning of the 1886 Aborigines Protection Act, able-bodiedness featured prominently in the logic of re-figuring the two categories:

> During the year [1884] the Board agreed that able-bodied half-castes capable of earning a living should be merged as soon as practicable into the general population of the colony. The following are the proposals of the Board, and the Government has been requested to pass the necessary legislation in order to carry out the policy herein enunciated:–
>
> The Board for The Protection of Aborigines are unanimously of the opinion that all able-bodied half-castes capable of earning their living should be merged as soon as practicable in the general population of the colony. Inasmuch, however, as the State, by Act of Parliament [1869] (No. 349) declared that 'half-castes and their children' should be 'deemed Aboriginals', the Board faithfully carried out the

75 PROV VPRS 1694 Unit 4: Sec. BPA to Manager, Coranderrk 10 Aug. 1911.
76 PROV VPRS 1694 Unit 4: C. A. Robarts (Coranderrk) to Sec. BPA 4 Sept. 1911.
77 PROV VPRS 1694 Unit 4: Sec. BPA to Manager, Coranderrk 26 March 1917.
78 PROV VPRS 1694 Unit 4: Sec. BPA to Mrs Bon 13 April 1917.

> provision of the Act; and inasmuch as the State has for years supported these half-castes, and induced many of them to come to the stations, thereby to a considerable extent destroying their self-reliance, it would be hard and unjust to cast them adrift without due notice and preparation. The Board, in framing these resolutions, have kept these considerations in view, and believe that the policy proposed to be adopted is for the best interests of the half-castes themselves. The object aimed at is that the process of merging should be completed as soon as possible, after which all responsibility of the Government as regards them would cease – finality being thus attained.
>
> The following are the proposals of the Board:– 1)That from 1st January, 1885, all able-bodied half-castes now on the station under the age of 35 years should be told to look out for employment, or seek settlement elsewhere.[79]

Those half-castes deemed not to be Aboriginal and having attained school-leaving age, forced to leave the station to 'make it on their own', could under certain circumstances be reincorporated into station life as Aborigines. Regulations pertaining to the consolidated 1890 Aborigines Act denote 'illness, infirmity, or other necessitous circumstances' as the grounds upon which, at the discretion of the board and, on 'the recommendation of the general inspector or the manager of a prescribed station', any 'half-caste or child of half-caste' could, under licence, come to reside on stations 'for a period of three months . . . and the Board may renew such licence for a like period as often as it may think fit, and may at any time cancel such licence'. According to the 1886 act onwards, those under such licence were indeed 'deemed to be aboriginals'.[80]

The point for the moment is that, at the discretion of the board, individuals could be shifted in and out of the category of 'aboriginal': one of the grounds for being deemed an Aborigine was 'illness or infirmity', along with 'necessitous circumstances'. Movements into the category meant an increase in a population, and that meant an increase in expenditure in the form of rations on a dependent population which, in the case of illness or infirmity, could not work to increase productivity. In daily dealings with individual cases, the BPA and station managers showed themselves most unwilling to re-categorise and incorporate individuals and their dependents on the grounds of illness and infirmity. They were less reluctant to re-categorise and incorporate the less infirm, or those suffering necessitous circumstances, if it meant acquiring a decent labourer. In 1917 W. Galbraith, manager at Lake Condah, complained to the board: 'This station for years past has evidently been more of a convalescent home than anything else & in my opinion should have been self-supporting long ago, if the management had been more strict.'[81] Into the twentieth century, being other than able-bodied remained one of the criteria according to which

79 Victoria 1884 (BPA): 4.

80 Victoria 1890b (BPA): 23, Appendix XXXII: Aborigines Act 1890 Regulations – VII: Half-castes (para. 21); Victoria The Aborigines Protection Act (No. 912) 1886 s 4 (5).

81 PROV VPRS 1694 Unit 4: W. Galbraith (Lake Condah) to Sec. BPA 11 June 1917.

one was to be judged an Aborigine under the meaning of the act. So in 1909, in response to a query from the board as to why a particular half-caste was still included in the requisition for rations, and whether or not this individual was earning wages, Stähle at Lake Condah explained:

> Yes, he earns wages, but being a cripple he does not earn as much as a strong man. Therefore the Board has supplied him with his clothing ever since he went off the Station. Being exempt from the Half-Caste Act owing to his infirmity he has been counted as one of those belonging to this station in respect to the above.[82]

The board and management continued to think of illness and infirmity in terms of being able-bodied or not. Acting effectively on health and illness, whatever else it meant, included guarding the boundaries between the truly able-bodied and those deemed not so – which is quite different from measuring effectiveness in terms of restoring health.

A doctor's diagnosis continued to carry little weight with the board. It was ultimately the call of the manager or the local guardian of a district to give his 'opinion' as to whether an individual was sick enough or well enough to be granted or refused support from the board. One such case follows:

> Would you kindly ask the members of the Board if they would allow me two months rations for myself & wife as I am not well having a touch of dry pleurisy. I am an out-door patient & at present not able to work, so if you would kindly ask my request to be granted, you will oblige me very much.[83]

The secretary of the BPA referred the matter to the police officer in charge in Hamilton in the Western District for a report. A constable Mahoney noted on this correspondence: 'I do not think this request should be granted. There is plenty of work obtainable about here at the present time, and this man is not that unwell but what he could go and do some work enough to keep him and his wife in food.'[84] It was also up to management rather than any medical authority to direct the board's attention to cases where support for an individual as a result of illness was required. Station managers dispensed medicines themselves, and Galbraith noted that he regularly set broken bones.When Bulmer was in charge of Lake Tyers he used to handle inoculations himself. Among those receiving support off-station, the authority of the local guardian or a member of the police force (as noted earlier, they were often one and the same) was required before the board would assume responsibility for payment. The board itself kept a constant eye on costs of medical attendance. Managers, local guardians and local police also acted as the moral gate keepers to medical care; it was on their advice that the board judged the deservedness of a would-be recipient of their support for medical services. There is also evidence in

82 PROV VPRS 1694 Unit 3: J. H. Stähle (Lake Condah) to Sec. BPA 20 March 1909.
83 PROV VPRS 1694 Unit 3: A. S. to Sec. BPA 7 Nov. 1917.
84 PROV VPRS 1694 Unit 3: Report of Const. Mahoney 12 Nov. 1917.

these correspondences that Aborigines were not welcome in some hospitals, receiving differential, segregated and grudging treatment. One gets the distinct sense that the public health authorities did not want to venture too far into the territory of the consumptive Aborigine. In 1918 under pressure from Mrs Bon, the secretary wrote to hospital management at Bairnsdale:

> One of the Members of the above Board has stated that aborigines going from Lake Tyers Aboriginal Station to the Hospital for treatment are placed in tents away from the main Hospital Buildings and that as a consequence aborigines are loth [sic] to enter the Institution when sick. I have by direction therefore to request that you will inform me whether aborigines are treated differently to other cases and if so, state the reasons of your Management discriminating thus.[85]

It was a misunderstanding, according to the manager at Lake Tyers Bruce Ferguson, who made his own enquiries:

> The matron was good enough to grant me an interview ... Some patients are admitted to the inside wards, others are on the verandahs, or in tents, according to the nature of the illness, the accommodation available etc. This applies to all ... After careful enquiries I am of the opinion that the Hospital Authorities have done all and will continue to do their best for the Aborigines.[86]

But an account of the treatment of a child, a case in which Mrs Bon had also taken a special interest, substantiates evidence of first, complacency, and then prejudice and differential treatment. The boy, a doctor reported, suffered from recurring attacks of inflammation resulting from a 'perforating wound of one of his ears some years ago'. The doctor suggested hospital treatment.[87] Mrs Bon visited the boy in the Eye and Ear Hospital in Melbourne and reported as follows:

> I visited [FD] in the Eye and Ear Hospital where he was receiving every attention. From want of proper training his habits were perfectly filthy, he rebelled against the nurses and would not use a commode but did everything in his cot. They could not ask their servants to wash the bedding, but gathered them daily for his mother, who was provided with soap &c and sent to the laundry to wash them, which is the only instance of the kind I have ever known in any hospital.[88]

This last example was drawn from a time when the board had made a firm decision to implement its policy of concentration of all Aboriginal people in Victoria located on Lake Tyers station, a decision that required, for the first time in many years, first-hand scrutiny by the board in its various fact-finding and inspection missions. It had already begun to put the population, including the health of the population, under new scrutiny. By 1920 in the context of the policy

85 PROV VPRS 1694 Unit 5: Sec. BPA to Sec. Bairnsdale Hospital 28 May 1918.
86 PROV VPRS 1694 Unit 5: B. Ferguson (Lake Tyers) to Sec. BPA 1 June 1918.
87 PROV VPRS 1694 Unit 6: Medical certificate 18 July 1918.
88 PROV VPRS 1694 Unit 5: Mrs Bon, Report on D family (to BPA), undated, received 27 Sept. 1918.

of concentration, medical treatment, medical inspection and reporting on the health of the population at Lake Tyers was given a formal structure, with a medical officer appointed on an honorarium and with regular reporting to the board a condition of the appointment.

GOVERNING THE POLICY OF CONCENTRATION

The consolidation of the station as an institution for correction and containment went hand-in-hand with the closure of existing mission stations and the secularisation of the management of the remaining ones and the replacement of members of the BPA with parliamentarians. The board was advocating concentrating the natives on fewer stations as early as 1879 – it was a long-term and enduring ambition.[89] A firm decision to adopt the policy of concentration was noted in 1917 following which the board decided to ascertain what land was available for cultivation, inspect additional sites which might be obtained and to decide for what purpose land could be utilised.[90] So a three-day visit to the station was arranged, a most unusual event. By that stage a new board had been constituted, made up largely of members of parliament, themselves with pastoral interests, who articulated the need for a more 'hard-headed' approach to replace older 'sentimentalism'.

The decision to concentrate the Aboriginal population on Lake Tyers station emerged in the context of an increasing frustration on the part of the board and management over the Aboriginal population's refusal to acquiesce to the imposed administrative categories Aborigine/half-caste – and its refusal to 'merge' and 'disappear'. In an attempt to shore up its administrative authority and to fortify the boundaries of the territory over which it administered, both conceptual and geographic, the board began to rethink categories, to count anew and indeed to change the standard by which individuals would count as falling under their administrative control. Importantly, the process of the actual concentration of a people at Lake Tyers – the physical and material processes of rounding up and removing and accommodating – went hand-in-hand with a concentration (in the more cerebral sense of the word) on just who was and who was not to be removed to Lake Tyers, to what purpose and to what effect. So it was to be a concentration on, as well as of the Aborigine. This would involve a redrawing the Aborigine/half-caste distinction. Again.

The stations at Condah and Framlingham had been effectively closed and remained as reserves under the supervision of local guardian/constables. Lake Tyers and Coranderrk still had managers. At Lake Tyers 'where it is proposed to finally concentrate the whole of the aborigines' twenty-five additional cottages were to be built, ten of which had been built by 1923, and all 'natives and their descendants' at

89 Victoria 1879a (Mortality Report): 3 (H. Jennings, Vice Chairman BPA to Chief Secretary 12 June 1879).

90 PROV VPRS 1694 Unit 4: Sec. BPA to BPA 5 June 1917.

Coranderrk, Framlingham, Condah and Antwerp were to be moved there.[91] The phrase 'natives and their descendants' indicates the shift that had taken place on the ground, in the criteria by which persons were understood to fall legitimately under the remit of the board under what was then the current act. The half-caste descendant of the Aborigine was an entity which, in 1886, had been made up as *not* 'aboriginal'. The purpose had been that descendants of the Aborigine would be made progressively 'not aboriginal', progressively sent beyond the remit of the board and beyond the station boundary, to 'do for themselves' and to merge until they disappeared. So the phrase 'natives and their descendants' indicates a rethinking of who belonged within the bounds of board management and within the geographic bounds of the station and natives *and their descendants* had now been governmentalised.

Following the 1886 legislation, the instability of categories defining Aboriginality and non-Aboriginality provided both an advantage and a bugbear for an administration. A person's status as Aborigine or half-caste could and did shift from one category to the other over the course of an Aboriginal person's life. Moreover, following the 1886 legislation the status of children born onto the station and deemed other than full-blood shifted from Aboriginal to half-caste as a matter of course, on the child's attainment of an age whence he or she was deemed capable of earning a living.[92] The instability of the categories was deliberately advantageous for the administration: inasmuch as a half-caste residing on a station under licence and hence in receipt of material support in the form of rations, accommodation, material domestic necessities and whatever medical services existed, as well as the social support of living with family and friends, could, on advice from the station manager to the BPA, have his or her licence and legal status as Aboriginal and attendant rights to material and social support withdrawn. Those individuals would then be put off the station to fend for themselves. Alternatively, the board could (and regularly did) exercise its power to confer the status of Aborigine on, say, a troublesome half-caste who refused to respect the conceptual boundaries of Aborigine/non-Aborigine and the geographical boundaries of inside and outside designated Aboriginal stations or reserves. Such troublemakers could be reincorporated as Aboriginal on the grounds of necessitous circumstances through the granting of a licence to reside on stations or reserves, and hence made subject to the rules and regulations and confinements of station life.

On the other hand, the inherent instability of the categories also meant that the categories lent themselves to manipulation by Aboriginal people who could, and frequently did bypass the standard chain of bureaucratic advice and authority whereby a station manager advised the secretary of the BPA, who advised the vice-chairman, who brought matters to the attention of a board under the nominal chair of the chief secretary of the state. Aborigines often put their case directly, either in person or by letter, to those known as likely to provide a sympathetic ear – an individual sympathetic

[91] Victoria, 1923b (BPA): 3. [92] Victoria The Aborigines Protection Act (No. 912) 1886 s 4.

board member such as Mrs Bon, the vice-chairman of the board, or chief secretary and sometime premier John Murray, or his sister who was known to have a sympathetic ear. In articulating their grievances and appeals in writing, Aborigines showed themselves to be adroit at 'playing' an administration, often succeeding in turning the inherent instability of confected and imposed racial categories against an administration's attempt at control. So persons could shift in and out of the category of half-caste and Aborigine over the course of their lifetime.

The detail required to show how this problem was actually dealt with by the BPA in this early part of the twentieth century cannot rely on its published reports, as these ceased from 1912 until 1922. However, plenty of evidence shows that the instability of the category of 'Aborigine' continued through this period and that the usual ploys to remove half-caste troublemakers were used. A particular favourite was the one used at Framlingham in 1890 and again in 1911 when the board used an apparent inability to provide satisfactory schooling in the area to legitimate the removal of troublesome half-caste families from the vicinity of the Framlingham reserve. Similar ploys were repeated elsewhere.[93] Overall, the increasingly desultory attitude towards the education of Aboriginal children displayed in the annual reports after the 1886 half-caste act was perpetuated over the first two decades of the twentieth century. Education was not seen as a matter of immediate concern of station management or of the board unless concern for education could be deployed as a means of bringing those adults who threaten the authority of an administration into line. A succinct indication of the degree to which the board had distanced itself from educating the population it administered was in its response in 1918 to a request from the commonwealth statistician for information regarding the Aborigines of Victoria. The scant, one-page report offered to the statistician by the secretary of the BPA concluded: 'I regret that I am unable to give a report on the aboriginal schools which are under the control of the Education Department. An inquiry to that Department might be of value to you.'[94]

THE FAILURE OF GOVERNMENT

A brief legislative shift announced in the Aborigines Act (1910) brought the so-called half-caste once again under the control of the Aborigines Protection Board, but this was subsequently repealed in the 1915 consolidation act. One of the regulations stipulated: 'All quadroon, octoroon, and half-caste lads on the Board's stations and reserves of or above the age of eighteen years shall leave same on notification from the Board, and shall not again be allowed upon a station or reserve except for a brief visit to relatives, at the discretion of Managers of stations.'[95] An effect of the 1910

93 See PROV VPRS Unit 3: C. A. Robarts to Sec. BPA 10 Feb. 1910; R. W. Howe to Sec. BPA 7 April 1911; Sec. BPA to Dir. Ed. Dept 19 April 1911, 5 Oct. 1911.

94 PROV VPRS 1694 Unit 5: Sec. BPA to Commonwealth Statistician 9 Aug. 1918.

95 Victoria Aborigines Act (No. 2255) 1910; Victoria Aborigines Act (No. 2610) 1915; Victoria 1916 (Government Gazette): 4257, Regulation 56.

legislation was that it allowed the board to exert its newly extended powers to control troublesome half-castes by removing them from the fringes. Again, in this case it was off the Framlingham reserve, where they were deemed a law-and-order problem. The preferred destination for troublemakers requiring increased supervision was Lake Condah. But once on the mission – lawfully, but without licence, and as half-castes – were they Aborigine or not? Were they subject to the rules and regulations that others deemed 'Aborigine' were subject to, or not?

In the board's attempt to apply this legislation, the ambiguity and instability of that term 'half-caste' came to the fore. The board and its proponents would on occasions make perfectly explicit the rationale underpinning these 'making up' of categories of persons and the reasons to persist:

> The half castes are stronger, more intelligent and more capable of work than an aboriginal. For the future welfare of the more capable race and also the material advantage of the station I would say a classification is necessary. The question is an important one and deserving of consideration.[96]

But by the time the board made its decision to implement its policy of concentration, the problem had shifted to one of how to draw a line of distinction between those who were deemed 'half caste and up to full blood' and those deemed 'less than half caste standard'.[97] By 1917 any meaningful geographic distinction between half-castes dwelling beyond the station boundary and full-bloods within the station boundary had collapsed. Various attempts at census taking showed that half-castes outnumbered so-called blacks on some of the depots and reserves and were fast approaching the number of blacks at Condah and Lake Tyers. On the eve of the execution of the policy of concentration, the 'native' population had been refigured according to the now primary distinction between those who were half-caste and up to full-blood, and those who were less than half-caste. The former have come to be known by an administration as constitutive of the 'native' population, to be contained within new conceptual and administrative boundaries, and newly differentiated from the less than half-caste standard. One can observe a reversal in the direction of the board's exertions from working very hard for decades to keep the half-caste out of the station to working very hard to get the half-caste in.

Once publications of BPA reports resumed in 1922, the board reflected on its operations over the past five years or so, particularly with regards to concentration. In the first of those resumed reports the board was careful to articulate the process of concentration as having adhered to the existing policy of maintaining 'all blacks and half-castes *needing assistance*'; 'blacks and such half-castes *as are unable to maintain themselves*'.[98] In its 1923–24 report, the board explained its aspirations more bluntly,

[96] PROV VPRS 1694 Unit 3: C. A. Robarts, Report on Coranderrk 14 Aug. 1916.
[97] PROV VPRS 1694 Unit 3: C. A. Robarts, Report on Coranderrk 14 Aug. 1916.
[98] Victoria 1922 (BPA): 4, emphasis added.

without the needs-based qualification regarding the inclusion of half-castes as the target for concentration:

> After the personnel of the Board was re-arranged in 1916, it was decided that the general policy should be to gradually concentrate the aboriginals and half-castes on one Station . . . Natives and their descendants . . . were transferred from Coranderrk, Framlingham, Condah, and Antwerp.[99]

The biopolitics to emerge from that resolution – that there would be no compulsion in moving this specific population to a concentrated encampment of 'approved' Aborigines – was that the choice made available to this population was either to relocate or to 'forego [sic] any future assistance of any kind from the Board'.[100] From an official point of view, the two categories of persons eligible to be free to choose encampment at Lake Tyers was a compromise, one which did not necessarily sit easily with all of the officials; Coranderrk's enthusiastic manager Robarts criticised the concentrating of 'the two classes on the same settlement':

> A new scheme having been introduced, the half castes and quarter castes should not be encouraged to live lives of aborigines by concentrating the two classes on the same settlement. The black race is a dying race, the half castes are on the increase and unless they are separated the increase will go on and will become a problem in the future. Half castes should be encouraged to live independent lives, helping them by so doing to merge into the white race. In the case of large families having to leave the station, the Board could grant a little help where needed but that should be done with the utmost care with the help of an Inspector, who knows each family and who understands the characteristics of a coloured race, the generosity of the Department having been much abused in the past by half castes also aboriginals.[101]

SUMMARY

The contents of this last statement were available to be uttered more than half a century earlier, at Coranderrk in 1864: the blacks will die out; the half-castes will merge; Aboriginality will be extinct. The chain of events show evidence of a wilful blindness to the systematic repression of children that formed around their removal from family and community and the continuing death of children as well as adults. A statement written by a civil engineer employed to pursue the concentration of Aboriginal people at the Lake Tyers station was an address to the architects of these powers showing how people at the time clearly perceived these policies and their implications, besides those who were actually subject to them:

99 Victoria 1923b (BPA): 3.
100 PROV VPRS 1694 Unit 5: Sec. BPA to Local Guardian of Aborigines Swan Hill 7 Feb. 1918.
101 PROV VPRS 1694 Unit 6: C. A. Robarts (Coranderrk) to Sec. BPA 25 Jan. 1918.

I cannot conclude without remarking on the emaciated appearance of some of the children and youths in the existing settlement evidently suffering from tuberculosis. I believe the exposed position of the houses and the sea air is injurious to them in Winter and they seem in need of a change to the hills. In fact a change to the hills would in my opinion be beneficial even for adults and a home for some of the suffering should be retained elsewhere, but this would be a matter for your medical adviser.[102]

[102] PROV VPRS 1694 Unit 2: Report of Carlo Catani (undated). Report requested Jan. 1918. See Unit 6: Sub-committee visit of inspection, Lake Tyers, 18–21 Jan. 1918.

7

From Mental Defectives to the Psychology of the Family

In discussion to date, one stream of research into the 'making up' of categories of children in institutional spaces in Victoria has followed the constitution of and practices upon the neglected and the reformatory child in white populations to the end of the 1930s. Another quite separate stream followed the logic and aspirations underpinning governmental actions upon the Aboriginal child. By the late 1930s the whole population at the Royal Park Children's Depot was characterised according to the twin problems of crime and social inefficiency. In Chapter 5 an account was provided of how a close association of the neglected and reformatory population with the mentally and morally defective was achieved over time. It was more or less a given – a truth – that the future criminal was born and not made, and constitutional mental and moral defects were understood as the root cause. Although there was general acceptance across administrative agencies that the means for identifying the mentally and morally defective lay primarily in the intelligence test, the question as to whether the job belonged to the educationist or the doctor was in dispute. We saw tensions exhibited over this question in the late 1920s and across the 1930s.

By the late 1930s established truths about the mentally and morally defective were beginning to show signs of instability. Evidence for this was discussed in Chapter 5. This chapter takes the inquiry to a next stage and towards another arrival point in the mid-1950s upon which the ground will be staked out to draw some conclusions. It traces the emergence of tensions and contestations between and within administrative bodies and sites of scientific expertise, the growing influence of psychiatry as an authoritative voice in the establishment of a new set of truths and the effects of these new claims to truth on the shape and practices of child welfare-justice.

Prior to the mid-1950s, throughout the archival material reviewed for this section, in all the administrative decisions and discussions of governing personnel responsible for overseeing the child welfare and justice systems, no mention was made whatsoever of the Aboriginal child. However, as will be indicated in the final section of this chapter, the Aboriginal child would surface abruptly in the mid-twentieth century as a recognised concern for these administrators. That concern was articulated in such a way as to underscore a new core problem in relation to Aboriginal welfare – the problematic 'psychology' of the Aboriginal family. The final section traces the conditions which allowed the problem of the Aboriginal family to sit over and against understandings of the problem of 'biological disability' that circulated earlier in the twentieth century. In the second half of the twentieth century those understandings would be declared old-hat although, as will be shown, confected theories of biological destiny were never really ever abandoned.

REFIGURING MENTAL DEFICIENCY: ITS DISSOCIATION FROM DELINQUENCY

In 1927 Secretary Lewis of the Children's Welfare Department and Reformatory Schools (CWDRS) declared the problem of the mentally defective 'the most pressing one at present'. The Education Department had been testing children at the CWDRS's Royal Park depot and Lewis included the findings of educational psychologist K. S. Cunningham who concluded that up to 85 per cent of the whole of the depot's population were mentally sub-normal, with up to 50 per cent requiring permanent institutionalisation. Lewis declared himself in full agreement 'with criticism which condemns the mixing of mental defectives with more normal children – and mixing is *harmful in the extreme*, not only to the normal child, but even more to the mental defectives themselves'. Discharging them at adulthood often meant 'immediate drift, especially in the case of girls, and more or less serious delinquency in the case of boys'.[1] Ernest Jones's 1929 Commonwealth Report on Mental Deficiency named the problem of mental deficiency 'one of supreme national importance, inasmuch as it involves the physical and mental health of the whole population of Australia, as well as its economic prosperity and efficiency'. F. P. Morris, officer in charge of the Children's Court noted that 'mental deficiency and the lack of any satisfactory method of dealing with such cases . . . help to swell the ranks of child delinquent'.[2] The solution was understood to lie in segregation.

Even into the mid-thirties the CWDRS was urging some way of relieving the depot of its mental defectives, who should 'unquestionably be placed in a separate or distinct institution and be segregated from the normal members of the community, as they are in many instances a menace'; such segregation 'would most assuredly reflect itself in a diminution of crime, disease, immorality, illegitimacy, as well as definitely place a check on the prevalent dangerous increase of subnormals'.[3] And in his report for 1936, Secretary Henry of the CWDRS reiterated the relationship between mental deficiency and criminality, underscoring 'the menace that exists in permitting the mentally deficient or feeble-minded to be at large without protection or guidance', their mental weakness rendering them 'suitable and plastic

[1] Victoria 1928 (CWDRS): 12–14. [2] Australia (W. Ernest Jones) 1929: 3; Victoria 1930 (RCC): 10.

[3] PROV VPRS 5694 Unit 1: Report – Children's Welfare Department & Reformatory Schools (unpublished), Melbourne, 20 June 11 1933.

material in the hands of master criminals'. He called for laws permitting control and segregation.[4]

Well into the 1930s the problem of the mentally and morally deficient was understood across the range of stakeholders as the primary problem facing the administration of child welfare and justice and was thoroughly enmeshed in the problem of delinquency. But it was around this time that the hitherto strong association of mental deficiency with problematic moral conduct in general, and with delinquency in particular, began to weaken. This moment occurred unevenly, but as shown in Chapter 5 it was in part an effect of the proliferation of the clinical sites that were annexed to various institutions for children – the CWDRS's depot, the Children's Court, and the state schools. This-or-that cohort of children associated with these sites underwent intelligence testing. Each of these became sites for dedicated clinical activity, which was established initially to identify and act upon the mental defective in the name of addressing the twin problems of crime and social inefficiency. The evidence suggests that once under a dedicated clinical eye (at first, but not exclusively psychiatric), the mental defective began to be refigured. Certainly by the late 1930s, the mentally defective's supposed contribution to crime and social inefficiency was no longer, always and everywhere, the ineluctable fact it once was. New vocabularies would gradually replace the old: 'mentally handicapped', 'mentally retarded'. At the same time, the normal child began to be refigured. The normal child first appeared as a by-product of intelligence testing in these same sites: that is, as the unproblematic remainder of the problematic mentally deficient. From the late 1930s the normal child gradually became a positive category of being in its own right rather than simply defined (in the negative) as that which the mental defective was not. The normal child would move from the periphery to the centre of psy-scientific attention so that, by the early 1950s 'the normal child' and children 'who are of normal intelligence' would be named explicitly by the psychiatrist heading a newly constituted Mental Hygiene Authority as the cohort from which most delinquents were drawn. Segregation of mental defectives would be declared an illogical response to the problem of delinquency and the normality of the delinquent would serve as a new truth upon which the government would base its moves to overhaul the Victorian juvenile justice system. The specifics of these pronouncements will be discussed in the next section. It was, nevertheless, attempts by the CWDRS to disburden itself of the problem of the mental defective that created the conditions for psychiatry to begin to assert itself as an authoritative voice in the government's administration of child welfare, and, increasingly, in matters pertaining to juvenile justice.

By 1930 under arrangement with the Education Department, children were being tested for intelligence at the depot as a matter of routine, and the next year the CWDRS noted that decisions on disposal of its wards were made 'after medical and

[4] Victoria 1937a (CWDRS): 8, 12.

mental examination and tests'. A residential institution (Travancore) was finally established in the early 1930s, followed by Pleasant Creek at Stawell (1937) and Janefield (1942), all under the auspices of the Mental Hygiene Department (MHD) and with the express purpose of relieving the CWDRS of the problem of the number of mentally defective children 'accumulating' at the depot who because of their purported mental and moral characteristics were deemed most unsuitable for boarding out. A clinic was established at the Travancore residential school a few years later, under psychiatric oversight, and again under the jurisdiction of the MHD, 'primarily to assess the mental equipment of those patients who were accumulating at Travancore, Stawell and Janefield, and to deal with matters involved in their control and development'.[5] Under the new clinical psychiatric eye the *apparently* mentally defective children examined at Travancore Clinic came to be known in quite different terms. First, many of the initial cohort were, when tested, found to be of normal intelligence:

> It was soon found that a great amount of misapprehension was prevalent, even among school teachers, regarding what constituted mental deficiency, so that problem children, retarded children and children whose condition had a purely medical background were all being regarded as being mentally deficient. Of the children examined in the first year of the Travancore clinic's existence 25% were found to possess normal intelligence.[6]

Second, many of them came to be considered capable of employment in the community. V. P. Johnson, from the start, and a bit out of line with predominant segregationist thinking, aimed to establish Travancore as a training centre for those capable 'of becoming wage earning and socially useful', and to establish 'facilities for the social training of the older children as a stepping stone for their return to the community'.[7] By the late 1930s, even plans for Janefield, long held in mind as a colony for segregating adult mental defectives, began to be articulated by MHD director J. Catarinich according to the aspiration of eventually returning its inmates to the community, even as he urged the passing of a mental defectives bill:

> It is becoming increasingly evident that a Mental Defective Bill is necessary to enable the Department to assume control and guidance of those children, who, in addition to a mental defect are handicapped by a vicious environment and possibly by unsatisfactory home conditions. The opportunity for placing such patients as self-supporting members of Society is increasing as a result of the mechanical repetition of simple procedures in manufacturing. It has been shown that the mentally defective person can carry out with efficiency, simple monotonous tasks which would endanger the mental integrity of a sane individual. In addition, such

5 Victoria 1939a (MHD): 19–20.
6 PROV VPRS 6345 Unit 72 Item 236: J. Catarinich, Director of Mental Hygiene, to Minister of Health 23 June 1949.
7 Victoria 1939a (MHD): 3.

patients are very suitable for certain phases of farm work and female defectives can be educated to become excellent household workers.[8]

Third, it was also discovered through mental testing that those exhibiting problem conduct were not necessarily of sub-normal intelligence. Returning inmates of special schools to the community had become a mark of success of these institutions, and a mark of achievement of the children themselves. It seemed it was now possible for the mentally defective to fail *or to succeed* in tests of conduct and worthiness of citizenship. So at least some of those deemed mentally defective and exhibiting problematic conduct came to be understood as not necessarily acting because of mental deficiency: 'Dr Johnson points out that the mental defect or retardation is not the root cause of behaviour problems which are often grounded on failure and maladjustment in school, employment or community life.' And fourth, under V. P. Johnson's clinical eye, the problem conduct exhibited by the mentally retarded was deemed less likely to be delinquent than the problem conduct exhibited by the child of normal intelligence: 'The figures suggest that anxiety and fear reactions as opposed to delinquency ... [are] the outstanding type of mal-adjustment in the feeble-minded and mentally-retarded children, whereas the reverse is true of the intellectually normal.'[9] Bearing all four points in mind, we can see that from 1940, at least at one clinical site, what had been the singular problem of mental deficiency and delinquency was emerging as two separate and distinct problems. By 1946 the MHD suggested that both Travancore Residential School and Travancore Clinic should be given over to children with 'severe conduct disorders', moving the 'stable mentally retarded' to a new and larger special school under its auspices.[10] Moreover, by the late 1940s the MHD began returning some children from its special schools to the CWDRS. Children were returned from the MHD to the Royal Park depot on grounds of their 'persistent behaviour problems' which posed a danger to its other students. This prompted the ire of both the depot's superintendent and CWDRS Secretary Pittard: if the MHD could not cope with these children 'the hopelessness of this Department's task in disposing of them can well be imagined'.[11]

So we arrive at an interesting historical moment. The special schools were set up under the jurisdiction of the MHD under pressure from the CWDRS first and foremost to take mental defectives accumulating at the CWDRS because mental defectives were considered *en masse* a cohort to be properly segregated from the rest of society as posing a danger 'to themselves and others'.[12] The children being *returned* to the CWDRS from the Mental Hygiene Department's special schools were now marked out as unsuitable for those institutions on the very grounds for which those institutions were established in the first place. One thing this showed

[8] Victoria 1938a (MHD): 30. [9] Victoria 1940a (MHD): 23. [10] Victoria 1947 (MHD): 20.

[11] Victoria 1949 (MHD): 31; PROV VPRS 6345 Unit 2: Sec. CWDRS to Under Secretary 1 Aug. 1949.

[12] Victoria 1928 (CWDRS); PROV VPRS 5694 Unit 1: Report – Children's Welfare Department and Reformatory Schools (unpublished), Melbourne 30 June 1930; Report – Children's Welfare Department and Reformatory Schools 30 June 1934 (unpublished); Victoria 1937a (CWDRS).

was that those deemed mentally defective were no longer considered dangerous per se. There were, among them, *some* who were dangerous, but these children had no place in an institution for the mentally defective. Once, the mentally and morally defective was a catch-all category; now a distinction could be drawn between the 'straight-out' mental defective or 'ordinary cases of mental deficiency' and those among them who, like their counterparts with normal intelligence, might exhibit maladjustment and delinquent tendencies. So, in a sense the 'ordinary mental defective', though not considered normal was nevertheless normalised and dissociated from delinquent behaviour. The point was borne out in the MHD's response to the CWDRS's fury at having these children returned:

> At present a clinical team under the control of Dr R. G. McLean is investigating the mental and intellectual equipment of a number of the inmates of the Children's Welfare Department. This work will not be concluded for some time. It is, however, already apparent that only a part of the problem of what is required in the way of housing conditions would be met by dealing with mental deficiency alone. The delinquent defective, those with emotional problems and the straight out cases of mental deficiency all react unfavourably on one another. Apart from such considerations, there are at the Depot cases of maladjustment and some of early psycho-neurosis. Both these classes require special attention. It would seem, therefore, that specially designed and separate units would be required, quite apart from any accommodation which may be provided for the ordinary cases of mental deficiency.[13]

Under a psychiatric clinical gaze, children who were accumulating at the depot and for whom placement could not be found were no longer characterised according to the catch-all of mentally and morally defective. Rather, they emerged as distinct groups, among which the so-named ordinary mental defective was the least administratively problematic, at least according to the MHD, given that an administrative solution existed at the time in the form of special schooling, even if there were not enough of them and they were poorly resourced.

On that point, reference was made repeatedly to the prospect of Janefield developing into the kind of institution envisaged when first the Lunacy Department/MHD acquired it – a 1000-bed farm colony for adult mental defectives. It had, in the meantime, been used as a special school for a hundred or so mentally defective children – children deemed more defective than those at Pleasant Creek, and mainly girls. For a time it was also used to house depot children during an epidemic. The proposal for its large-scale development was first mooted at a time when segregation of the mental defective was still generally seen as the solution to the care and control of a cohort deemed dangerous, on the grounds of both their potential for criminality and their promiscuity – the latter leading to an increase in their numbers and hence a decline in social efficiency. The various moves towards meeting the needs of the mentally

[13] PROV VPRS 6345 Unit 102: J. Catarinich, Director, Mental Hygiene Branch, Health Dept to Sec. Health Dept 1 Sept. 1949.

defective child *as a child* would not have been possible three or even two decades earlier. Then the mental defective was a social pariah whose management seemed to consist mostly of segregation and indeed banishment to the outposts of the likes of Stawell and Janefield. But between 1930 and 1950 the 'social menace' that was the mentally defective child at the beginning of this period, and a category of person that had come to characterise the whole of the CWDRS's depot population, had morphed, largely under a psychiatric clinical eye, into a new category of person, more often than not referred to by this stage as the 'mentally retarded' or 'mentally handicapped' child. This new category, now dissociated to a large degree from the once inherent characteristics of delinquency and social inefficiency, and hence *made safe* so to speak, emerged as something of a *cause célèbre* with various philanthropic and service groups and MPs scrambling over one another to get a piece of it.

MAKING UP THE 'NORMAL CHILD'

If discussion in the previous section paints the Mental Hygiene Department in a rather hagiographic light, there is a counterpoint to this process. At the same time as the mental defective was made safe and less administratively problematic, the so-named normal child was made dangerous and more problematic, largely as an effect of the same processes and the same technologies introduced under the increasing influence of psychiatric know-how. Despite the increasing dissociation of the mental defective from delinquency and social inefficiency, particularly within the MHD administration, the CWDRS persevered with the practical problem of disposing of children at the depot for whom alternative accommodation could not be found. The secretary of the CWDRS wrote in 1952:

> While this establishment is intended to function merely as an observation, classification and treatment centre for new committals prior to transfer elsewhere, and also as a place of remand for the retention of children pending their appearance in Children's Courts, it has for many children become a permanent residence . . . In the special circumstances under which the Depot must necessarily operate, mentally handicapped children do not progress during a long-term retention there.[14]

The CWDRS had all but abandoned the older nomenclature 'mentally deficient' and replaced it with newer terms such as 'mentally retarded' or 'mentally handicapped', and it was also articulating the problem in a different way compared with, say, its 1933 association of mental deficiency with 'crime, disease, immorality, illegitimacy . . . dangerous increase'.[15] By the 1950s, although the superintendent at Royal Park was still confronted with growing numbers of children at the depot who were deemed not suitable for boarding out, the problem was articulated as one of meeting the needs of

14 Victoria 1954a (CWDRS): 55.

15 PROV VPRS 5694 Unit 1: Report – Children's Welfare Department and Reformatory Schools (unpublished), Melbourne 30 June 1934.

the mentally retarded rather than the danger the mentally defective posed to others. Nevertheless, into the early 1950s this remained, according to the CWDRS, its primary and most difficult problem. But Dr Cunningham Dax, the newly appointed chair of the newly constituted Mental Hygiene Authority (of which the MHD was a branch), disagreed.

Dax was by then the state's leading psychiatric authority, and his understanding of the problem is very telling. Dax explained that the Mental Hygiene Authority (MHA) had been seriously concerned with problems within the CWDRS, visiting its buildings, consulting files and discussing matters with clinic staff. There were difficulties making improvements. Indeed according to Dax the professed difficulties the MHA's clinical teams had in working with the CWDRS sprang from that department's insistence that it was merely 'a matter of removing the intellectually sub-normal children'. Dax begged to differ: 'The solution to the C.W.D. problem is not the removal of the mental defectives but an overall policy in keeping with modern thought.' From the outlook of the MHA, the shortcomings of the whole CWDRS warranted serious reconsideration, and Dax laid out a proposal for an overhaul. First, Dax provided his own breakdown of the population for which the CWDRS had responsibility:

> The [Children's] Welfare Department covers, mainly, three different types of children: (1) the normal children who have come from broken homes or need State care temporarily or indefinitely and who are of normal intelligence, (2) the intellectually sub-normal children, and (3) those who have been through the courts and are remanded or committed to State care.

Dax argued that each group needed to be dealt with in different ways. Those he termed intellectually sub-normal should be absorbed into the MHD, but accommodation was insufficient. According to Dax, the CWDRS had no 'low grade mental defectives', only those 'of the upper grades of subnormality' which gradually merged into the 'dull and backward' group and through them to 'the normal'. No hard and fast line was to be drawn in dealing with these cases: 'Selection would thus in many cases depend upon conduct rather than intelligence.' For the third group, whom Dax termed the 'frankly delinquent', a state-sponsored Borstal training system was needed, in which proper care could be given to those children who were 'often psychopathic personalities and need prolonged residential socialisation' – for them, 'the present system seems quite inadequate'. The state would be required to draw the necessary legislation and to make proper arrangements for the institutional training of this group. But it was the first group – the group Dax called normal children – who required particular and close psychiatric oversight because, he claimed, it was from this group that most delinquents would come:

> These children produce a considerable proportion of the behaviour problems and the adult nervous disorders. It has been shown beyond doubt that family disruption,

> separation and institutional upbringing are major factors in the production of delinquency, conduct disorders and the neuroses. It is strongly urged on grounds of preventive psychiatry, that these children should have the benefit of psychiatric guidance and council [sic]. Additionally and for similar reasons it is recommended that a psychiatric relationship be established to the various church homes and other institutions and the foster homes in which such children are placed.

Dax noted that there were no adequate facilities for this group within the CWDRS: 'The rapid turnover mainly to places (however good they may be) without proper liaison with the Children's Welfare Department, or psychiatric supervision of the children is, in principle, wrong.' Given this, and given all he had laid out, Dax asserted that 'a psychiatrist is the only person who can be properly in charge' and that with the state playing its part and with appropriate interdepartmental co-operation in place, 'the MHA would gladly take over the administration, staffing and care responsibilities of the CWD forthwith'![16] Much of what Dax said here would be echoed in the conclusions of a government inquiry (headed by one of his senior officers) a few years later. How did psychiatry achieve the ear of government over other agencies and how did 'normal children' displace the mentally defective as the primary focus of psychiatry and as the cohort from which the delinquent was most likely to emerge?

The first section of this chapter traced the effort that went into identifying the mental defective with an eye to separating and segregating a cohort most closely associated with delinquency from the normal child. But once that cohort was segregated and under psychiatric scrutiny the association of mental defect with delinquency began to dissolve. From where then did delinquency emerge? Recall the discussion in Chapter 5 of F. Oswald Barnett's 1935 research on the relationship of the 'slum' to delinquency, cited extensively in the Children's Court report at the time. Recall too Stipendiary Probation Officer Meadows's production of a 'delinquency map' some five years later, again cited extensively in the Children's Court report. The measure of the delinquent had extended beyond individual psychology to that of home and environment. And, from a broader historical perspective, no longer was the 'good home' simply a good home or otherwise at the say-so of the philanthropist, the clergyman, the honorary or lay inspector as it was in the late nineteenth and early twentieth centuries. The child's home as a subject and object of welfare and justice was beginning to appear – to be 'pictured'. The picture of the home, produced, for example, in Meadows's 'delinquency map' was drawn out of an application of the science of statistics and its measure was fast becoming the province of professional expertise.

16 PROV VPRS 6345 Unit 102: E. Cunningham Dax, Chairman, Mental Hygiene Authority to Minister of Health 10 Oct. 1952.

THE 'DANGEROUSNESS' OF THE NORMAL CHILD

Stipendiary Probation Officer Meadows, meanwhile, continued to produce research findings conducted in the Children's Court. The second part of his study was first recorded in 1940 and given more elaborate coverage in the court's report for 1942. These findings underscored the need to differentiate backwardness at school among delinquents from mental retardation and repeated his earlier findings: among delinquents 'backwardness is largely the result of temperamental and environmental factors and not lack of ability'. The resultant backwardness led to high levels of truancy. So truancy and delinquency emerged as symptoms of 'a psychological disposition to anti-social acts', and Meadows concluded that 'delinquents should be treated as a normal and not a sub-normal group'.[17] This further weakened the once assumed strong relationship between mental deficiency and delinquency and inasmuch as the work situated the problem of delinquency among those of 'normal intelligence', it served also to problematise the normal child. This was a significant point of arrival.

In the Children's Court report for 1943 yet another substantial piece of research by Meadows was published titled 'Preventing the Increase of Delinquency'.[18] It was in two parts, a statistical survey of trends in delinquency from 1911 to 1943 and a survey of preventive agencies in the field of delinquency. He addressed a series of questions: Was delinquency increasing? Had the war made a difference to juvenile delinquency figures? Was it possible to treat or cure delinquents? And were there any methods of preventing children from becoming delinquent? Meadows claimed that delinquency included the following events: housebreaking and larceny, assault, wilful damage, neglected children, traffic offences, offences against railway by-laws and trivial offences such as kicking footballs in the vicinity of electric wires: 'The *trend* indicates that we are likely to find higher figures for juvenile delinquency over the next few years unless conditions change.'[19] Most interesting here was Meadows's inclusion of neglected children as a category or type of delinquency. How so? Meadows reiterated a point made already: that up to 1919 neglect was in reality a label that more often than not signalled destitution: women would have their children 'charged' with being neglected and the state would pay mothers an amount to foster their own children.[20] A change in legislation allowed women to apply for relief without application to a court, and the figures dropped. And the 1933 Children's Welfare Amendment Act, made operative in 1934, expanded the category of neglect to include children 'lapsing or likely to lapse' into vice or crime, one effect of which was to bring the categories of neglect and delinquency closer together.[21] Meadows noted that there could be no legitimate comparison of rates of delinquency for World Wars I and II, given, among

[17] Victoria 1943b (RCC): 17.
[18] Victoria 1944 (RCC). 15–24 (A. Meadows, 'Preventing the Increase of Delinquency').
[19] Victoria 1944 (RCC): 17.
[20] Victoria 1944 (RCC): 18; Victoria. Children's Maintenance Act (No. 3001) 1919.
[21] Victoria Children's Welfare Act (No. 4152) 1933.

other factors, the pre-1919 use of the category of neglect and the use of the category following the amendment to the act in 1933:

> Since the 1914–18 war period included the applications of destitute families as stated, no comparisons are possible between the two war periods. It is of some significance, however, that the cases have increased considerably during the war years 1939–43. And this, in the main, is due to that fact that it is under the neglected child section that young girls 14 to 16 years of age, who are living promiscuously, are charged. Such cases of females increased from 47 in 1939 to 156 in 1943.[22]

So Meadows was virtually arguing that the courts used the category of neglect as a charge of female delinquency.

In the second part of the study, Meadows addressed the questions: 'Is it possible to treat or cure delinquents? . . . Are there any methods of preventing children from becoming delinquent?' He had nothing to say about the role of psychological medicine in relation to treatment or cure, or indeed about the relationship of mental deficiency to delinquency, but rather advocated pragmatic structural changes which in effect meant changing a child's conduct. If a boy was 'busily and happily engaged in club work or sports' during his leisure hours, since he could not be in two places at once, it was impossible for him to be engaged in mischief. Since the greatest amount of crime took place in leisure hours, the greatest amount of crime could be eliminated. But not all delinquency could be eliminated. Meadows figured that if the majority, instead of 3 per cent to 20 per cent of youth were in some club or scout work, 'then it would not be too much to anticipate that the delinquency would drop from the present 9 per cent. It is not too much to anticipate that if those conditions obtained then crime would be reduced to a third of its present level.'[23] The picture of (primarily male) delinquency that emerged from Meadows's research certainly firmed up the idea that the delinquent was made, not born. Furthermore, it also firmed up the emergent relationship of the 'normal' child with delinquency: it helped to bestow upon *any child* the potential for delinquency. The sense a reader is left with is that whether or not a boy would become delinquent was to a goodly degree dependent upon the contingencies of environmental factors.

The final piece of research in this series by Meadows was on the sex offender. Consider, for the moment, that this was published just prior to the establishment of a new full-time, officially recognised Children's Court Clinic. At the time of its publication no clinic was operating, and it seems that Meadows, a stipendiary probation officer, was once again examining children in lieu of the presence of a psychiatrist or psychologist. From 1939 to 1945, a total of 107 cases of male sex offenders were referred by the courts for special investigation and report – 56 cases by the clinic while it was functioning between August 1941 and April 1944, and 51 cases by Meadows: 'subsequent to these reports being obtained two of the offenders were committed by the Court to the care of the Children's Welfare Department and

[22] Victoria 1944 (RCC): 18. [23] Victoria 1944 (RCC): 23.

the other 105 were placed under the care of Mr Meadows for supervision and re-education'.[24] That was a big number. We observed in Chapter 5 that the court appeared to have a *laissez-faire* attitude to the juvenile sex offender at the time approaching mid-twentieth century (Saturday morning sex education in preference to institutionalisation), a curious approach given the current focus on child sex offences and an approach in stark contrast to previous configurations. A turn-of-the-century conclusion from Royal Park depot reported that discharging 'abnormal children . . . committed chiefly for reformatory discipline and frequently described as vicious from childhood, with precocious sexual habits . . . at the age of 20 years is a positive danger to the community'.[25] And just ten years prior to Meadows's research the Children's Court stated that 'most of the cases of indecent assault on little girls are committed by subnormal boys . . . The mating of subnormal people and the problems created by their many children should surely force the community to take action.'[26]

It may be now that we get a better purchase on what was occurring. Meadows subjected sex-offending children to intelligence tests, noting that 'the intelligence of sex offenders is, on the whole, normally distributed'.[27] This was in line with his earlier findings, which, we recall, he noted were in line with contemporary international understandings 'that generally speaking delinquents should be treated as a normal and not a sub-normal group'.[28] Meadows noted that he steered a course relatively independent of the prevailing popular understanding (perpetuated, he noted, in literature) 'that the sex offender is "more sinned against that sinning" and secondly that a short course of psycho-therapy taken like a bottle of medicine will clear the matter up', and that 'the sex offender should be regarded as a psychological problem'. He concluded:

> The persons referred therefore are regarded not as mere psychological cases. The attitude taken up is that they will be required to respect society, and endeavour to comply with its demands, as well as seeking its help in reform. Juvenile sex offenders are taken to be sociological and not purely psychological cases.[29]

So, rather than simply having the effect of de-emphasising the danger of the juvenile sex offender, this particular figuring served to bestow upon *all* juveniles the potential for aberrant sexual proclivities once associated in particular with the menace of the sub-normal.

DE-PROBLEMATISING THE SLUM

But what of this emphasis on environment displayed in Meadows's work? There are moments in this material where it may strike the reader that knowledge of the delinquent might have taken a different direction than that pursued. Meadows's

[24] Victoria 1945 (RCC): 5 (A. W. Meadows, 'The Problem of Sex Offenders').
[25] Victoria 1903a (DNCRS): 4. [26] Victoria 1936 (RCC): 5. [27] Victoria 1945 (RCC): 4.
[28] Victoria 1943b (RCC): 7. [29] Victoria 1945 (RCC): 8.

research reports constituted, together, one such moment. His delinquency map revealed high rates of delinquency in 'Industrial and slum areas', areas with the highest rate were also areas 'least provided with recreational facilities',[30] a relationship which would seem to point the finger at poverty. Stipendiary magistrate L. R. Ripper's court report for 1939 included the following commentary, penned, it may be assumed, by Ripper himself, on the conclusions that could be drawn from the delinquency survey:

> It is these areas that merit the attention of social workers. Provision of more playgrounds with supervisors and clubs that offer activities for every night in the week are needed ... Careful study of the home conditions of delinquents show them to be for the most part average or below average. It is felt that added to economic improvements some form of Parent Education is vitally necessary. It is not sufficient to blame economic conditions alone. Problem parents make problem children. Young people preparatory to marriage and parents who find difficulty in maintaining normal family relationships or parents who are experiencing trouble with their children should be able to seek skilled advice.[31]

There is something quite perverse about the direction in which this conclusion headed. While economic conditions were not totally dismissed, the problem parent and the other-than-normal family were made to take precedence as the determining causes of delinquency. In this commentary the delinquency map was made, in effect, to locate the problem family – which, just perchance it seems, was situated in the poorest areas of the city. That is, the conclusions drawn from the delinquency map pulled away from any sense that poverty *per se* might seriously have needed to be addressed. Rather, the poor family needed simply to be made to operate as a normal one. On this point it is worth recalling that in his previous report, and in the context of an 'alarming' increase in cases before the court, Ripper cited Cyril Burt, with approval, on the causes of delinquency. Burt's list of fifteen contributing factors, in order of importance had 'defective discipline' at No. 1 and 'poverty and its concomitants' at No. 14 – that is, second to last in importance.[32]

Another moment that the pursuit of causes of, and solutions to, delinquency could have taken a different direction was that at which F. Oswald Barnett's work came into play. In his 1935 Report on the Children's Courts, then Officer in Charge F. P. Morris cited Barnett's findings of 'the close relation that exists between the slum-area problem and the problem of the delinquent child':

> Whether in slum- or semi-slum areas, or in 'pockets' in various suburbs, there are many so-called homes that are a menace to the children. Even granted that many parents are slum-minded and that any house would become a hovel through their occupancy, the fact remains that children living under shockingly adverse home conditions have a slender chance of becoming decent citizens; while these

30 Victoria 1940b (RCC): 9–11. 31 Victoria 1940b (RCC): 9–11. 32 Victoria 1939b (RCC): 4–5.

> conditions exist we are simply preparing children for the Children's Court ... Over one-fourth of the boys came from homes where the parents are classified as 'slum-minded'. Three-fifths come from homes that are on the border line, but have been given the benefit of the doubt, and are therefore classified as 'indifferent'. It will thus be seen that only one-eighth come from homes that can be called good.[33]

Whether or not true to Barnett's original work, the court's account of Barnett's research suggested that the root cause of delinquency was situated less in the slum per se than in the mind of the slum dweller, such that, in similar fashion to the 1939 survey on delinquency, what could possibly have been conceived of as primarily an *economic* problem was instead reshaped into a predominantly *psychological* one.

More than a decade later, Barnett's work was put to use again, this time by Children's Court magistrate F. E. Williams, and once more despite evidence of the relations between delinquency and economic conditions, Barnett's work was used to serve an argument that the root cause of delinquency lay not in poverty but rather in problematic familial relations, in this case as a product of mothers' absence:

> A situation akin to that existing during the period commonly known as the depression years is arising. In the depression the father [sic: upper case elsewhere] of the family often could not obtain employment. Work of some kind for women was more available and the Mother of the family perforce had to take up some position to provide for the family. At present the Father of a family is almost always in employment but notwithstanding the fact that he gets higher wages, living costs have risen to such an extent, that in many homes, the Mother takes outside employment to help in maintaining the family.
>
> Mr F. Oswald Barnett in his book 'The Making of a Criminal' commenting on the economic problem facing families at that time said 'The fact that so many Mothers are forced to go out to work, would probably tend to make the home less attractive and accentuate the drift to the streets.'
>
> Obviously a Mother tired from a day's work outside her home, cannot run her home as efficiently as the Mother who is able to devote the whole of her time to her household duties nor can she cope as effectively with the problems of her children. Social workers view the situation with some alarm, as it is thought the absence of the Mother from the home – either daily or at less frequent but regular intervals – must inevitably result in an increase in juvenile delinquency.[34]

There may well have been contending voices that constituted the problem of delinquency in quite different ways. However, across the period from the 1930s to the mid-1950s the mantra that although 'slum ... areas do produce an unduly high proportion of delinquents ... *it should be remembered that* ... it is not poverty which gives rise to delinquency' would become the line taken in the subsequent and

[33] Victoria 1936 (RCC): 1–4. [34] Victoria 1950b (RCC): 4.

influential 1956 Report of the Advisory Committee on Juvenile Delinquency, produced under Justice John Barry as chair (Barry Report).[35] It was surely a palatable message for government to receive. Before turning to the report and the role psychiatry played in its production, it will be necessary to investigate that process by which psychiatry consolidated its authority and in particular the means by which psychiatry began to lay claim to the normal child. By the mid-twentieth century 'normal' no longer meant what it meant little more than a decade before. By the early 1950s, any and potentially all children could deviate from the norm, so that conditions were fast being put in place that would make it possible for psychiatry to inform government, as the state's senior psychiatrist Cunningham Dax so informed the government of the day, that it was the normal child who served as the base material for 'the production of delinquency, conduct disorders and the neuroses'.[36]

CONSOLIDATING THE AUTHORITY OF PSYCHIATRY

In 1950 Professor Alexander produced a report for the minister for health which was highly critical of the state's psychiatric institutions and of then-Director Catarinich's oversight of an outmoded Mental Hygiene Department.[37] In the wake of this report E. Cunningham Dax would replace Catarinich as the head of a new Mental Hygiene Authority. On the release of the Kennedy Report, MHD psychiatrist V. P. Johnson mounted a vigorous defence of the work of the Collins Street and Observatory Clinics which specialised in child psychiatry. He noted the MHD's intentions to expand services to the 'now well-furnished and equipped' clinic at the Royal Park depot, so that it could operate on a full-time basis allowing the clinical team to undertake 'psychiatric treatment of maladjusted children in urgent need of direct psychiatric help' in addition to simply examining children and reporting to the CWDRS. He also noted that this clinic proposed to expand services to state wards in foster homes. The depot clinic under the authority of the MHD Collins Street and Observatory Clinics was relatively short lived, however; one could speculate that this was a fall-out from the Kennedy Report. In the 1950 MHD Report, psychiatrist V. P. Johnson noted the loss of a number of experienced staff. The clinic at the depot carried on as a regular but reduced service in the form of a clinical team visiting the depot on three and half days of each week until it pretty much ran out of staff:

> It would seem that the most the [Mental Hygiene] Department can do to help the Children's Welfare Depot at the present time is to provide psychiatric investigation and advice for the more urgent problems of delinquency, predelinquency and mental deficiency through the departmental clinics specializing in these matters.

35 Victoria (J. Barry) 1956c: 29, emphasis added.

36 PROV VPRS 6345 Unit 102: E. Cunningham Dax, Chairman, Mental Hygiene Authority to Minister of Health 10 Oct. 1952.

37 Victoria (A. Kennedy) 1950c.

> To this end one of the assistant psychiatrists appointed to this clinic could be made available to assist the other clinics with this work.[38]

At the same time, however, A. R. Phillips, psychiatrist in charge of the MHD's Travancore Clinic, made the suggestion in his department's annual report that *its* services be extended to serve the depot and beyond – into other children's institutions: 'Children's Homes catering for the needs of normal children are apt to accumulate groups of children who are suspected of being retarded, and we are finding that it is more efficient to send a team from the clinic to deal with the whole group of children than to have these children brought to the clinic separately.'[39] And in that same MHD report, the Children's Court Clinic reported that it was also extending its activities at the depot. That year Bailey, psychiatrist in charge of the Children's Court Clinic, noted that of the new referrals 112 were referred by the courts and 66 from 'other agencies, including the Children's Welfare Department'.[40] The Children's Court Clinic had reached its maximum caseload under the existing conditions of staff and accommodation. Bailey emphasised that the psychiatric investigation and treatment of juvenile delinquents took a considerable time: 'Our aim has been to thoroughly investigate and treat a limited number of cases rather than to deal with greater numbers in a more superficial manner, as the former method is likely to give the best results.' Bailey noted that the Children's Court Clinic needed at that stage to provide more adequate provision for therapy and follow-up work and to extend the facilities to 'all delinquents passing through the Children's Welfare Receiving Depot at Royal Park. It has been shown that most of the children in the latter group are in urgent need of psychiatric help.' Hence, the plan was to appoint assistants to the psychiatrist and the psychologist including an additional two social workers: 'The time has now come for psychiatry to make a much greater contribution towards the prevention and treatment of juvenile delinquency in this State.'[41]

With Collins Street Clinic withdrawing its services from the depot, the Children's Court Clinic now stepped into that role. Importantly, in describing the needs of the inmates at the depot, Bailey's commentary did not differentiate between those children with cases before the court and those referred from elsewhere, including the CWDRS. He reported to his department that the clinic was seeing children deemed 'delinquent' but not necessarily just those cases before the Children's Court. He also included a report from the clinic psychologist R. G. Andry. Andry rehearsed the now orthodox distinction between mental retardation and school progress and his statistics reinforced the now orthodox position which affirmed the

38 Victoria 1951 (MHD): 34 (V. P. Johnson, Psychiatrist, Psychiatric and Observatory Clinics, Mental Defectives and Prevention Branch).

39 Victoria 1951 (MHD): 28 (A. R. Phillips, Psychiatrist in Charge, Annual Report for Travancore Clinic, Mental Defectives and Prevention Branch).

40 Victoria 1951 (MHD): 36 (H. Bailey, Psychiatrist in Charge, Children's Court Clinic).

41 Victoria 1951 (MHD): 36.

normal intelligence of most delinquents.[42] One could conclude that whereas by the late 1920s the depot population, neglected and reformatory alike, were all suspected syphilis carriers and then all suspected of mental deficiency, one of the achievements of psychiatry by the mid-twentieth century was the association of the whole of the depot population with juvenile delinquency. This shift was aided and abetted by the fact that of the MHD's psychiatric clinics under the new Mental Hygiene Authority, it would be the Children's Court Clinic which came primarily to serve all the depot's inmates.

WHO IS IN CHARGE? THE SCRAMBLE FOR LEGITIMACY

It has already been made clear that by 1952 the tensions between the CWDRS and the Mental Hygiene Authority had increased. Note again the MHA's director Cunningham Dax's response to the CWDRS's insistence that it take those inmates at the depot that it deemed mentally deficient: it was not the disposal of mental defectives that constituted the CWDRS's major problem but those Dax named normal children, a cohort requiring psychiatric guidance, as it was from this type that the maladjusted child – understood as the harbinger of the delinquent – would emerge unless subject to psychiatric intervention. Under Dax, the MHA's general outline of its four existing clinics and the demarcation of their territories were presented and it was officially noted that the Children's Court Clinic was now the primary service provider of the CWDRS's depot at Royal park:

> Through the particular interest of their senior psychiatrists, the clinics appear to be developing secondary functions which should be encouraged so that a wider field of preventive psychiatry can be covered. Thus the Collins-street Clinic is concentrating on the social adjustment of the child as a fundamental method of guarding against adult ill health. The Children's Court Clinic is extending its relationship with the Children's Welfare Department. The Observatory Clinic is developing its work in several fields of adult psychiatry and expanding its teaching. At Travancore, there has been a movement towards some out-patient and short-term in-patient stabilization and guidance in a few disturbed but intellectually normal children.[43]

In that same report, the Children's Court Clinic noted its sources of cases:

> The majority of cases (124) were referred to the Clinic by the Court or the Court Officer in Charge of Children's Court; 19 children with delinquent tendencies by the Senior School Medical Officer; 17 by the Children's Welfare Department; 3 were examined at Pentridge [Gaol] and the remaining 21 were referred by various

42 Victoria 1951 (MHD): 36–37.

43 Victoria 1953 (Mental Hygiene Authority [MHA]): 5. In 1953 the MHD fell under the MHA which published subsequent reports.

> agencies. The reasons for referrals have always included delinquent tendencies although many of the children have never appeared before the Court.[44]

Again, in the body of its report for 1953 the MHA noted:

> Besides its original function of dealing with cases referred by the Children's Court, the Children's Court Clinic is extending its activities to cases referred by the Children's Welfare Department, and also to privately-referred cases of delinquency, who have not as yet been actually charged with any particular offence.[45]

In the section specifically on the Children's Court Clinic, the psychiatrist now in charge (T. G. C. Retallick) noted that of the 288 cases, 48 were referrals from the CWDRS and a number of 'screen examinations' were carried out on children from that department. Retallick underscored the clinic's policy of encouraging referrals of children 'who have not yet been charged with an offence, but who shows [sic] a delinquent trend'.[46]

Although the Children's Court Clinic had become the principal clinic connected to the depot, from time to time other MHD clinics had their continued involvement confirmed. For example, in 1953 the CWDRS requested that cases be seen at the Observatory Clinic, Collins-street Clinic, or at the depot and that these clinics accept new referrals from the depot and from foster homes for assessment or treatment.[47] Besides children from foster homes the MHD's clinics began to extend their activities to include examination of children in a private institution – one of the many to which the CWDRS sent state wards. The Observatory Clinic surveyed the child population at the Methodist Peace Memorial Home at Cheltenham. Dax, we recall, had recommended a couple of years earlier that a psychiatric relationship be established with the various children's homes and foster homes, recommendations that had clearly come to fruition. Further, psychological surveys of the Janefield population were carried out for its medical superintendent.[48] Prior to 1953, Janefield and Pleasant Creek had been under the supervision of a medical officer, but after that date each was appointed a psychiatrist-superintendent of its own.[49] In 1955 at Travancore Clinic, 35 of its 382 cases were CWDRS referrals, and it was involved in surveying children from various institutions, mainly day centres for so-called retarded children and also the CWDRS's depot at Royal Park.[50] Meanwhile, the influence of the MHA in CWDRS matters continued to increase through the Children's Court Clinic, such that by 1955 (on the eve of the Barry Report), the clinic was involved in testing and advising on the disposal of children from the depot and from foster homes and institutions at the behest of the CWDRS and the courts.

44 Victoria 1953 (MHA): 37–38 (J. V. Ashburner, Psychiatrist, Children's Court Clinic).
45 Victoria 1954c (MHA): 8.
46 Victoria 1954c (MHA): 40 (T. Retallick, Psychiatrist-Supt Children's Court Clinic).
47 Victoria 1954c (MHA): 41.
48 Victoria 1954c (MHA): 41.
49 Victoria 1953 (MHA): 33, 35; Victoria 1954c (MHA): 45.
50 Victoria 1956d (MHA): 70.

But it was also having a direct influence on the shaping and the running of the depot itself – its material shape and its practices upon its inmates. Of the activities of the Children's Court Clinic, the 1955 MHA report noted:

> One Psychologist was seconded to the Children's Welfare Department and did much work on the various Wards of the State there ... the Psychology Staff was supplemented when the Principal Psychologist, who previously had worked on special cases only, returned to the Clinic full time in August. A special psychological survey was carried out by him on children for likely placement in the Cottage system at the Children's Welfare Depot. Further 'follow-up' was continued on these children to observe whether they progressed, and help given to the special staff placed in charge of them.[51]

To explain the reference to the 'Cottage system' operating there, we need to take a small step backwards. Since its inception there had been sporadic press reports expressing concern about conditions at the depot. One such moment was in 1954 with a cluster of articles and correspondences on that subject instigated by a Melbourne University criminologist, Norval Morris. It was Morris's drawing attention to the plight of delinquent girls in Pentridge Prison that had caused a stir a couple of years earlier. It had become clear that by the mid-twentieth century the boarding-out system had all but collapsed with only a few hundred children left in foster homes – 391 of 2980 wards in 1954, 1425 in institutions.[52] We might compare those figures to the thousands in foster care at the height of the boarding-out policy. Norval Morris in an article 'The sink of human decency is also blocked' cast the problem at the depot in the same terms that the CWDRS has been using for years – as one primarily of the accumulation of mentally defective children.[53] Up until 1952 the CWDRS had been pleading with the government for the MHD to do more to take those it designated mentally defective, sub-normal and later, retarded and Dax had refuted their claims that this cohort was the CWDRS's major problem – it was, we recall, those Dax named 'the normal children' who most required the depot's and psychiatry's attention.[54] Now, the government's immediate response to Morris's article was to stress the number of normal children at the depot, with the chief secretary reported as stating: 'Of the 168 children at Royal Park, 120 were normal', though the under-secretary 'said last night the Children's Welfare Department and other institutions would welcome action by the Mental Hygiene Authority to provide accommodation for sub-normal children'.[55] From the point in 1952 when the MHA (Dax) made its position clear, a curious thing happened.

The CWDRS was still confronted with the problem of disposing of children from the depot, whatever the terms in which they came to be named and articulated. But

51 Victoria 1956d (MHA): 64 (Psychiatrist-Superintendent T. Retallick, Children's Court Clinic).

52 Victoria 1956c (CWD): 5. 53 *Argus* 1954a, July 19: 4.

54 PROV VPRS 6345 Unit 102: E. Cunningham Dax, Chairman, MHA to Minister of Health 10 Oct. 1952.

55 *Argus* 1954b, July 21: 11.

from 1952 onwards, within the CWDRS the depot population began to be named and articulated differently. A large number might be 'normal' but they were *all* more or less 'disturbed'. It was as if problems with the administration of the 'disturbed' child were much more likely to reach the ear of government than those of the mentally defective child. For example, its 1953 report the CWDRS made no mention of the problem of accommodating the so-named mentally retarded children at the depot, though the previous year it had complained that this cohort represented its primary problem. Perhaps the department, now under a new secretary, J. V. Nelson, had finally decided it was flogging a dead horse. There was instead much discussion of the problem of the disposal both of children with mild behaviour problems and of delinquent children. The CWDRS noted that the numbers of delinquent children arriving at the depot had increased (which the CWDRS suggested was a result of increased policing of delinquency):

> There are very many children for whom foster-home placement is impracticable for one reason or another, but nevertheless, there is a substantial number, mostly of school age and naturally a number with minor behaviour or emotional problems, who are in need of individual fostering in a private home.[56]

The CWDRS had started to articulate its population, offender and non-offender alike, in terms of the primary problem of delinquency and the presence of the delinquent, and the problem of disposal and accommodation of the delinquent permeated discussion. Moreover, the problem of delinquency was now couched in terms that were in line with that solidified in the psychiatric clinic: that is, the source of the problem of the delinquent lay in the problem family. It is also worth noting that in 1955 the Children's Welfare Department and Department for Reformatory Schools underwent another name change. In all but official reports it had, for some years, simply been known as the Children's Welfare Department (CWD). In 1955 this became its official title.

The Barry Report (1956) shows how influential the psy-sciences generally and psychiatry in particular had become in matters pertaining to child welfare and, as that report would have it, its 'morbid aspect juvenile delinquency'. Allen Stoller, one of the three-member committee headed by Magistrate Barry, joined the MHA staff in 1954 as chief clinical officer to head research, training of medical officers and co-ordination of psychiatric treatment. Stoller was formerly of the Commonwealth Repatriation Department. The other committee member was Daphne Barrett, principal of the first non-private MacRobertson Girls' High School in Melbourne. At this stage psychological and psychiatric expertise had situated itself firmly on top of the hierarchy in relation to the educationist.[57] A psychologist from the MHA had carried out much of the research – which consisted of interviewing 'representatives of various governmental departments and of private institutions for the purpose of

[56] Victoria 1954b (CWDRS): 4. [57] McCallum 1990.

obtaining answers to questionnaires we compiled'.[58] By 1956, the year of the completion of the report, there was something circular about this, given that the MHD/MHA had already achieved a position in which other departments and agencies had largely succumbed to a logic emanating from psychiatric know-how in framing their problems with and practices upon children. So the Barry Report may well have recommended close working relations between the Children's Court and the Children's Court Clinic and may well have conferred upon psychiatry and psychology a leading role in the disposal of children in the justice-welfare system, but those recommendations had already largely been achieved. The Barry Report based its recommendations on a number of truths, the establishment of which has been the subject of this chapter. Its inquiries 'found nothing to support the theory, once held, that criminal tendencies are passed on ... as an inborn characteristic'. Rather, 'broken or inadequate homes [were] presumed to be potent factors in bringing about juvenile delinquency'. And although '[s]lum or deteriorated areas do produce an unduly high proportion of delinquents ... it should be remembered that it is not poverty which gives rise to delinquency but the lowered moral standards which poverty tends to produce.'[59] The report's means of conceptualising a population and its recommendations echoed those that Dax had presented a few years earlier. It used the terms pre-delinquent and delinquent in much the same way as Dax had referred to 'normal children who have come from broken homes' and those he called 'frankly delinquent'. The report was critical of the state's reliance on a system of non-government reformatories and recommended, as had Dax, that the state resume responsibility for an institution 'for the most difficult and hardened types'. As had Dax, the report called for the means 'to identify potential delinquents at an early stage ... [for] proper medical, psychiatric and social treatment'. For this group, intervention was to begin in the home: 'State recognition and support should be given to properly-qualified and constituted agencies which give assistance, advice and guidance to parents who, for various reasons, have proved inadequate to meet the needs of their children.'[60] Deficiency, long used to characterise the child in state care, had come to characterise the parent.

THE PSYCHIATRIC FRAMING OF THE PROBLEM FAMILY

At 31st December, 1954, there were 2,980 wards of the Children's Welfare Department and 141 wards of the Department of Reformatory Schools – a total of 3,121 children.

Of the former, 1,425 children were in institutions – a decrease of 131 from 1953. At 31st December, 1954, there were 718 wards on probation in one form or another with relatives and others, as against 571 at 31st December, 1953. Such children include not only those who have had institutional training on account of delinquency lapse and are themselves on probation, but also children whose parents are in effect on probation – having failed in their duty to their children to

[58] Victoria (J. Barry) 1956c: 7. [59] Victoria (J. Barry) 1956c: 29, 54, 90.
[60] Victoria (J. Barry) 1956c: 16, 33, 58, 67.

such an extent that the children had to be sent by a children's court to the care and protection of the Department but to whom, after some rehabilitation and provision of a reasonable home set-up for the children, the children are returned by the Department to their care 'on probation'.

> The Department regards the matter of rehabilitation of the family as one of utmost importance. Whilst a great deal is now being done in positive action to counsel, guide and help parents to get into a position where the Department can return their children to them, there should be intensification of this work. For this, additional trained field staff is necessary. Re-establishing the family after disintegration is of course a most difficult matter at that stage. In very many cases the factors leading to family break-up should have been tackled when drift was first apparent. In other words, the emphasis should be on more preventive work.[61]

In its discussion of children in foster homes, the CWDRS made it quite clear that the system of boarding-out was in decline in the mid-1950s, and the swing back to institutional care was clearly evident. Of the 2980 wards of the Children's Welfare Department at the end of the year, only 391 were boarded-out in private foster homes. This number was notably small in relation to the 1425 wards boarded-out in institutions. For the healthy baby or toddler with consent to legal adoption, the course was clear and apparently satisfactory – 'many arms are stretched out eager to enfold him'. On the other hand, there were all the other wards 'who were not attractive babies and toddlers without brothers and sisters', and who were not available for legal adoption and in relation to whom, therefore, permanent and undisturbed custody could not be assured. Who were these other children who came to the care of the department? They were of all ages, 'from babies to teenagers, delinquent and non-delinquent, normal and sub-normal physically and mentally in varying degrees – in family groups'. Many of them would be only temporarily under the care of the department – their parents 'will get on their feet again and re-establish a home'. Adolescents who had 'gone off the rails and had been through the Children's Court responded to rehabilitative guidance and training and return to community life':

> Inevitably there must be institutional care, rather than care in private foster homes, for many of these youngsters. But at the same time there are many wards placed in institutions who the Department feels should have the advantages, the security, and warmth of family life – that is, if private foster homes not insistent on permanent custody are available.[62]

That year the depot was renamed 'Turana' – which was, according to the department, an Aboriginal word for 'Rainbow'.[63]

Two decades before, the depot population had come to be figured according to 'mental deficiency' as the overarching frame of reference. Now, that population had

[61] Victoria 1956a (CWDRS): 5. [62] Victoria 1956a (CWDRS): 5.
[63] Victoria 1956b (CWD): 4–5.

come to be figured in terms of greater or lesser degrees of disturbance. The connection between a disturbed childhood and delinquency had by now been well and truly forged. The disturbed child if not yet delinquent soon would be without intervention. And the whole of the depot population had now come to be characterised as 'disturbed'. The Royal Park Receiving Depot, or Turana as it was now called, was described by CWDRS in the following terms:

> This establishment, now known as Turana, is a reception, remand, and transit centre, conducted by the Department. As well as being multi-purpose, it is required to accommodate a heterogeneous collection of children – generally from 200 to 250 children, from babies a few days old to late teen-agers – both sexes – all of them disturbed to a lesser or greater degree – delinquent and non-delinquent – some mentally and physically handicapped – some staying a few days, some a few months and some longer. To Turana, come the children for care and custody pending decisions by the Children's Courts, as well as the children whom the Courts have ordered to be wards of the department. Medical and dental treatment is given; psychiatrist, psychologist, and trained social workers are brought into action where necessary; investigation, observation, and classification is [sic] made and the appropriate placement from Turana is decided upon.[64]

Experimental cottages were also established at the depot in 1954, for some children described as disturbed and handicapped and who were 'unacceptable' in foster homes and institutions. So, again, there is evidence that the CWDRS was busy reframing the problems of administering its charges in psychiatry's terms and in terms dictated by the MHA prior to the appearance of the Barry Report. The very subject of the Barry Report – the 'juvenile delinquent' – had in one sense already been born out of psychiatric practice.

THE PSYCHIATRY EFFECT

As with juvenile delinquency neglect was also refigured according to psychiatry's frame of reference, and in such a way as to draw the condition of being a neglected child much closer to the condition of being a delinquent. First we may recall the changes to the Children's Welfare Act that came into force in 1933, as discussed briefly in this chapter and in more detail in Chapter 5. Those changes saw the expansion of the legal category of 'Neglect' to include 'lapsing or likely to lapse' into crime, and 'unfit guardianship'. Prior to this amendment the complaint was that as long as means of subsistence and 'a home of sorts' could be shown, the child could escape 'arrest'. The amendment created a legal imperative to scrutinise the *type* of home and the *types* of guardianship in other than material terms. The legislative change made it possible for 'neglect' to shift to something other than a measure of material circumstances such as adequate sustenance and shelter.

[64] Victoria 1956a (CWDRS): 6.

By the mid-twentieth century, under the increasingly authoritative gaze of a state-sanctioned psychiatry, there was once again an active enmeshment of the 'neglected' child with criminality, as in the following extract from Bailey's report on the Children's Court Clinic in 1950. Here, 'neglect' was no longer a sign of the child's material state of being, but of the parents' psychological make-up. The clinic produced a chart with statistical data underpinning the psychiatrist's conclusions on the causes of delinquency:

Psychiatric classification of new cases was calculated as follows:

Character defect	66
Intellectual defect	38
Psychoneurosis	55
Organic	1
Psychopathic personality	2
Psychosis	3
Diagnosis incomplete	13
	178

Conclusions were drawn along the following parameters:

> From the clinical standpoint the most striking contributory factor elicited in our cases was the presence in many of them of parental rejection by either one or both parents. The importance of this factor in juvenile delinquency is becoming increasingly apparent to us, though it is not always obvious at first sight. Nevertheless, it is a fact that many of our juvenile delinquents are unwanted and neglected by their parents. The delinquency in such cases is the outcome of a lack of parental affection and guidance from infancy. The readjustment of these children is greatly complicated by their behaviour problems being closely related to the emotional difficulties of the parents themselves.[65]

With the introduction of the 1954 Children's Welfare Act, the term 'neglected child' disappeared from the legislation and was replaced by 'child or young person in need of care and protection'. The term 'neglect' still featured in the legislation but in such a way as to produce a marked shift in focus from the neglected child to the neglectful parent: 'Every person who . . .without reasonable excuse neglects to provide adequate and proper food nursing clothing medical aid or lodging for any child in his or her care or custody . . . shall if such neglect . . . has resulted or appears likely to result in causing bodily suffering . . . be liable to a penalty . . . .'[66] Much was made at the time of the new act's decriminalizing effects in that it was no longer necessary for the child to be formally charged with being neglected and to be burdened with that stigma. But given that the act made its appearance after the establishment of what Bailey termed the 'fact that many of our juvenile delinquents are unwanted and

65 Victoria 1951 (MHD): 36 (H. Bailey, Psychiatrist in Charge, Children's Court Clinic).
66 Victoria 1954 Children's Welfare Act (No. 5817) s 4c Part IX 70 (1).

neglected by their parents', its overall effect was surely to nudge all 'children in need of care and protection' into the frame of potential criminality.

SUMMARY

In 1956 the Barry Report certainly emphasised changing the social environment (mostly in the form of providing playgrounds and clubs) and the report certainly maintained that institutional life was 'thoroughly undesirable for young children, and every effort should be made to keep children, particularly those under ten, out of institutions. Adoption and upbringing in approved foster homes, are courses which should be followed wherever possible.'[67] But the report also called for an extension of institutions (under psychiatric oversight) – it bemoaned 'the grave lack in Victoria of proper institutions for children and juveniles', particularly for 'those children and juveniles whose delinquent conduct is such that they require discipline and training'.[68] At the time of the release of the report, the state was already moving to re-establish institutions for delinquents. Meanwhile, in this period fewer children were being boarded-out and more and more children sent to charity- and church-based institutions. In summary, there is clear evidence that by the mid-1950s child welfare and justice administrations began to fashion themselves as governmental responses to the maladjusted way the poor family thought and acted. The solution lay in adjusting familial relations rather than dedicating any direct effort to alleviating poverty.

The conclusions from the period leading up to the Barry Report can be reduced to the achievement of a series of truths that emerged in the policy-related machinations of government and the human sciences. By 1955 the primary problem facing the child welfare-justice system was no longer the mental defective but the juvenile delinquent. Unlike the mental defective, the juvenile delinquent was made, not born. The problem was no longer one of distinguishing the problematic mental defective from the largely unproblematic child of normal intelligence; rather, the problem was now one of distinguishing the pre-delinquent from among a group of children of mainly normal intelligence and preventing that pre-delinquent from becoming a delinquent. The private family home, by and large referred to up to 1930 as a key solution to the problem of child welfare was now, more often than not, spoken of as the source of the problem – the primary site for the production of maladjustment and delinquency.

Where once the large-scale institutional separation of the mentally and morally defective was proposed as the necessary cornerstone of an effective child welfare system and as a means of preventing crime, now the solution to the problem of waylaying the development of delinquency lay in expert intervention at the level of the family. By the second half of the twentieth century it had become an established

67 Victoria (J. Barry) 1956c: 34. 68 Victoria (J. Barry) 1956c: 87.

truth that the psychology of the family contributed more to delinquency than any other cause, including poverty, heredity and pathology.

As noted at the beginning of this chapter, in all the pages of policy and of institutional, departmental and government reports reviewed for this chapter there was not a word emanating from the courts, from Mental Hygiene, or from the CWD on Aboriginal children. Between 1930 and 1950 Aboriginal children were, it seems, beyond the margins of the various departmental concerns with welfare, with governing, educating and policing children. In practice, Aboriginal people were literally living a marginalised existence – many who were not living on Lake Tyers station were subsisting on the fringe of country towns where they were largely ignored, or tolerated as a source of cheap seasonal labour. But by the mid-1950s the Aboriginal child was registered with new urgency as the subject of governmental concern.

Charles McLean's 1957 Report on the Operation of the Aborigines Act and the Regulations and Orders made thereunder (McLean Report) made its appearance shortly after the publication of the Barry Report.[69] The circumstances, details and effects of that report will be discussed in Chapters 8 and 9, but one effect of the report was to draw mainstream political and administrative attention to the specific problem of Aboriginal child welfare. The problem, however, was figured in a very particular and now familiar way. Slum dwelling became a known characteristic of Aboriginality. And as slum dwellers Aborigines became known as exhibiting the aberrant psychology and aberrant familial relations of the slum dweller. The solution lay in intervention at the level of the family to teach them to live like normal (white) families, a role delegated to an army of professional welfare workers of one ilk or another. Subjected to the scrutiny and conjecture of this flood of expertise, Aborigines either measured up to the norm or failed. If they failed, well it was their failure and the consequences included such actions as child removal. This chapter has presented an argument that by the mid-1950s the influence of the psy-sciences in figuring the relations between poverty, the family, child welfare and juvenile delinquency underpinned the logic of administering *sections* of a non-Aboriginal population. In Chapters 8 and 9 an argument will be presented that those same influences helped produce the administrative logic and the tools and techniques according to which the Aboriginal population *as a whole* came to be acted upon.

69 Victoria (C. McLean) 1957b.

8

The Discovery of the Aboriginal Child

Between 1930 and 1950, the Board for the Protection of Aborigines (BPA) operated under the authority of the chief secretary. The secretary to the BPA operated out of his office, as did the under secretary – a permanent public service position, and perhaps the most senior public service position. The under secretary was also a member of the BPA. For most of this period the post of under secretary was held by L. L. Chapman who also acted as vice-chairman of the BPA (often chairing board meetings in the absence of the chief secretary). The chief secretary had a large and diverse portfolio – cause for comment on the floor of Parliament on more than one occasion. The chief secretary's office had 'multifarious duties and interests in matters from A to Z – Aborigines to Zoos'.[1] One can imagine, perhaps, a gentle guffaw following the comment. Another version, again from the floor of Parliament and from the same period made much the same point, and raised a laugh: 'Only a little while ago the honorable member for Mornington was Chief Secretary, in which capacity he handled matters ranging from gaols to zoos, including such diverse matters as aborigines, children's welfare, fire brigades, and the aquarium.'[2]

Member of the Legislative Assembly (MLA) Mr Barry made the remark to Mr Leggatt, former chief secretary, then in opposition. The context was a debate regarding the Mental Hygiene Authority Bill – should it have its own minister or fall under the Health Department? The bill was to usher in that new entity under Dr Cunningham Dax which, as discussed in Chapter 7, saw the increasing influence of the voice of psychiatry in the administration of children's welfare and juvenile justice. The comment made – 'such diverse matters as aborigines, children's welfare' – is striking. Would it be possible in the present for a politician to speak of Aborigines and child welfare as 'diverse administrative matters' – at least without being put right? But it would be unlikely that such would be said, because at present, as indicated in Chapter 1, it is well-nigh impossible to think any matter pertaining to the administration of matters Aboriginal without thinking in terms of child welfare.

1 Victoria Parliamentary Debates (VPD) Session 1950–51 Vol 232 Legislative Assembly (LA) 9 Aug. 1950: 279.

2 VPD Session 1950–51 Vol 234 LA 14 Nov. 1950: 2169.

That white children and Aboriginal children were figured differently, administered according to different logics, underpinned by different aspirations has been an ongoing focus of this study. The way in which the allusion to the gap between 'child welfare' and matters 'aboriginal' was offered here, in 1950, on the floor of the Lower House in the Victorian Parliament, speaks to the general acceptance of such a perception up to this time. As noted in Chapter 5, from 1930 to 1955, in all the crosstalk between the Children's Court, the Mental Hygiene Authority (MHD/MHA) and the Children's Welfare Department (CWDRS/CWD), which saw a fundamental refiguring of the problem of child welfare-justice, there was no mention of the Aboriginal child. But only a few years on from the parliamentarian's casual remark, a government inquiry into the administration of Aborigines was launched. On the basis of retired stipendiary magistrate Charles McLean's 1957 'Report upon the Operation of the Aborigines Act 1928 and the Regulations and Orders made thereunder' (McLean Report) a new administrative body would be ushered in – a board with 'welfare' rather than 'protection' in its title, and the report recommended the application of that same intellectual, professional and institutional machinery built over the previous couple of decades with the white child exclusively in mind, to the (newly configured) Aboriginal population. That is to say, in the McLean Report, we begin to see the configuration of the Aboriginal *child* in terms of child welfare, as it had by then come to be understood. It is the point at which it was no longer possible for government to recognise the administration of Aborigines and the administration of child welfare as 'diverse matters'.

In the period preceding the McLean Report, the Aboriginal child was known and acted upon, first and foremost as Aboriginal and governed via a set of practices quite distinct from those by which the white child was administered. The Aboriginal person, irrespective of age, was understood to embody a set of inherent racial deficits, moral and intellectual – childishness, laziness, untruthfulness, untrustworthiness, dirtiness, shiftlessness, animal cunning, inability to persevere, sexual promiscuity coupled with an animal fecundity and so on. These capacities and conducts were articulated by the various officers, government and administrative figures, responsible for their oversight and control, as the reason for a whole people's 'failure' to achieve the necessary 'ordinary standards' of productive citizenship and served to justify increasingly desperate and draconian attempts to control and discipline the Victorian 'native' population. This chapter documents the demise of that logic, and the conditions which made possible the entry of a new way of knowing the Aborigine. The new logic was still underpinned by a recognition of failure to achieve the necessary standards of the so-called 'ordinary' white citizen, but that failure now came to be understood, in terms informed by a psychological science, as largely the product of the immediate social and familial environment. Approaching the mid-century, the environment of the Aborigines was voiced by the critics of the BPA as the product of its own administrative ineptitude.

In the 1930s the problematic Aboriginal child was known and acted upon as an entity quite distinct from the problematic white child. As shown in Chapter 7, by 1955 the problematic white child sat firmly within the frame of the psy-sciences. By 1955 it had become possible to know and to begin to gear action upon the problematic Aboriginal child as also a psychological entity, made not born, and also the proper subject of the existing machinery of (white) child welfare. The effects of that shift were an unprecedented surveillance by multiple professional welfare officers – new state-run institutions for problem young folk quickly filling up with Aboriginal children. This set the circumstances and the conditions of possibility of present-day government administration of children.

THE BOARD AND ITS CRITICS

Much has been made in the previous chapters of the way the Board for the Protection of Aborigines operated as a law unto itself. In the second decade of the twentieth century it had to defend itself from the critical gaze of the non-Aboriginal outsider, particularly during the concentration period when the very gathering and movement of people and things to Lake Tyers, often via Melbourne, made the condition of Aborigines much more visible, and the board had to open up to some scrutiny of more outsiders as it implemented plans for the expansion of Lake Tyers station. The board might have been tardy in doing its job, but up to the 1920s there was little sustained criticism of the legality or legitimacy of the job the board was doing – other than, of course, from the Aborigines themselves who had maintained a sustained protest through their various correspondences of the illegitimacy of the board's attempts at coercion and control.

By the late 1920s there was more criticism from white authorities and stakeholders of some of the fundamental practices of the board. The board was anxious to place beyond its remit anyone it deemed less than half-caste, on the grounds that these people were legally white, and it insisted that any problems regarding their welfare or their conduct were the responsibility of agencies other than the board. Local police, magistrates, shire authorities and concerned citizens protested that the board was merely producing a new problem. Sometimes accusations of lack of sympathy and compassion for Aborigines might be directed at the board. Sometimes criticism was more self-serving – those newly constituted as beyond the remit of the board represented, in one way or another, a threat to the white population. For example, the following came from a concerned citizen in 1930, in response to a complaint from an Aboriginal resident of Lake Tyers station over his banishment. The Member for Gippsland forwarded it to the board:

> Considerable danger to white women may result from this drastic treatment of a native with his mind poisoned through a sense of injustice and deprived wrongfully

> of his conjugal rights & practically made a pariah and an outcast from the home which the people of Victoria are taxed to maintain for him.[3]

Whatever the motivation, most of the criticism that ensued at this time was urging an *extension* of the board's powers: the board's remit should include all people of 'aboriginal blood', liquor laws which exempted half-castes from prohibition should be extended to all, and *all* belonged properly on the station where the board should itself attend more aggressively to their confinement, discipline and control and so on. By the late 1920s criticism of the board was growing louder and reaching a wider public audience.

Changes were also made to the composition of the board. In 1916, just prior to the decision to implement its policy of concentration, the BPA was made up of members of Parliament who were also landholders in districts with Aboriginal inhabitants.[4] Mrs Bon continued to serve on the board from 1904 through to her death in 1936 at age ninety-eight. By the 1920s any distinction between the board, the public service, Parliament and the government of the day became increasingly fudged. For example, in 1927 it was noted that in more than one instance a minister might act as chair of this or that board – the chief secretary's position as chair of the BPA was cited as an example. However, the chief secretary rarely officiated in this capacity, the task usually falling to the under secretary, a permanent public service position. The following year, in response to arguments for the reconstitution of the BPA, the then chief secretary claimed that it represented all sides of politics and consisted of a sort of Select Committee of the House, which should just be left to do its job. The chief secretary was accused of unduly interfering in matters properly left to the public service, and it was suggested that something along those lines had occurred in the BPA. As time passed, the board met spasmodically. Sometimes it would have a rush of meetings – several a year. At other times more than a year would pass without a meeting. Chapman was under secretary from 1932 to 1955 and held the official position of vice-chairman of the BPA until his retirement. To Chapman, then, fell the job of carrying on the day-to-day business of the board between meetings – often very long intervals. Chapman was a constant presence and significant figure in shaping the deliberations of the board. Given all of this, the term 'the administration' is used in the following discussion to signify the enmeshment of government, the BPA and the executive. Reference to these specific entities is made only when it is possible or appropriate to do so.

In the period under review the BPA had to defend itself against two waves of criticism. The first extended from the late 1920s through to the mid-1930s. Its principal spokesperson was Gordon Sprigg, a senior office-bearer of the Baptist Union. The second wave of criticism began in the mid-1930s and operated through

3 PROV VPRS 1694 Unit 11: Geo B. Merrifield (Melbourne) to the State Member for Gippsland 24 April 1930.

4 Victoria 1922 (BPA): 3.

to the mid-1950s. It became a chorus of Aboriginal and non-Aboriginal voices affiliated with a range of political organisations. But from beginning to end of this second wave, the administration itself was particularly attuned to the critique emanating from a group of white political activists associated with the New Education arm of the Victorian Aboriginal Group and the Women's International League for Peace and Freedom (WILPF). First, it was in response to these two waves of criticism that the government of the day, the board, station management and the various attendant officers and stakeholders (the chaplain, the schoolteacher, the local designated doctor, adjacent landholders) laid bare the knowledge base from which they operated, and something of the practices at the coalface. The message to critics from the administration was along the lines of the following: 'You do not *know* aborigines (natives, half-castes, blacks . . .). Those of us who work with them *really* know them, and they are like this . . . and because of the fact that they are like this, it has been necessary to do this or that.' So, the material in the defence is very valuable to the present discussion. Second, the marked contrast between these two waves of criticism represents a shift in ways of knowing Aborigines. In short, across that first wave of criticism, 1927–36, Sprigg was most concerned with an alleged state of moral laxity at Lake Tyers which the board had failed to address. The solution lay in the imposition of even stricter discipline. The board, while publicly denying the extent of the problem, pursued an agenda behind closed doors similar to Sprigg's proposals. As far as the way Aborigines were problematised, there was very little disparity between the board and its critics. If anything, the criticism served to reinforce rather than disturb the knowledge base from which the administration operated, although a lasting legacy of Sprigg's criticisms was that they served to prise open administrative practices for greater public scrutiny.

From 1937 onwards, a different kind of critique began to emerge – one that challenged at a fundamental level the way the administration problematised Aborigines. Issues such as petty criminality and promiscuity among the young were still very much to the fore. But against the administration's defence that these problems stemmed from an inherent racial deficit of moral character, these critics argued that the problem facing the administration was in fact the product of illegitimate coercive practices of the board itself. The Aboriginal child for the first time came to be understood as 'formative', as child-like, rather than simply as a little Aborigine. The young Aboriginal 'delinquent' – a term rarely applied to Aboriginal youth prior to this time – was made, not born, fashioned out of a problematic home environment, itself the legacy of maladministration. The tenets of this critique eventually became the basis of the McLean Report which will be discussed in the next chapter.

THE FIRST WAVE OF CRITICISM

It is clear that Sprigg's criticisms had their basis in information supplied by residents from Lake Tyers. His criticisms represented a continuation of that most troublesome practice by Aborigines of bypassing official channels of complaint to bring their concerns to the fore. Sprigg first went public with his concerns at a moment when there was considerable unrest at Lake Tyers – there had been a 'strike' at Lake Tyers in September 1927,[5] understood by some as a result of a resentful, recently dismissed sub-manager stirring up trouble among some of the men. The bishop of Gippsland described that same sub-manager's fundamental sin: 'he . . . placed himself on terms of equality with the natives, and became very familiar with them – thus he had no control'.[6] The moral and spiritual well-being of the Lake Tyers population had by this stage been delegated to the Anglican bishop of Gippsland, who oversaw the chaplain, Rev. A. R. Raymond. The latter, following previous negotiations between the board and the church was responsible for Sunday school and church services but, at the board's insistence, he was not permitted to reside on the station. In the fairly recent past, the board had experienced trouble controlling outbursts of 'excess religiosity' following station visits by Pentecostal revivalist Miss Hetherington. Further back, the continuing presence of old guard missionaries such as the Bulmers were sometimes a thorn in the side of a new secular management.[7] These past experiences might explain the board's reluctance to have a chaplain in residence. The official arrangement with the church served as a mechanism whereby the board could ward off those it characterised as interfering do-gooders. It could reply to requests for involvement in 'social work' of various kinds, that the moral and spiritual well-being of the population was in the capable hands of the bishop, at the same time keeping the church's involvement at Lake Tyers at a distance.

The September 1927 strike saw a number of people put off the station – banished. Sprigg deemed the practice of banishment unjust, inhumane and heavy handed; for the next decade or so, banishment was 'the sore point' for Sprigg. His response to the strike suggests he did not see it as unreasonable: 'The natives unhesitatingly affirm that they struck for more tucker and more freedom.'[8] And he was not averse to the idea of some kind of Aboriginal representation in administrative matters. But he was *not* arguing for any recognition of the rights of Aborigines according to any liberal understandings of freedom and equality. The board certainly showed itself to be inhumane and neglectful of both the physical and material conditions of its charges. Sprigg began in late 1927 with accusations of not enough milk for infants; a badly managed rations system often leaving residents with not enough food, the food itself of varying consistency and quality; and crowded accommodation and dilapidated bathing facilities – the common bathhouse had been in a state of disrepair for years. Later, he would add inadequate medical care especially for maternity cases – rumour had it

5 NAA B356, 93: F. McMahon (Rep., Associated Press) to Chief Secretary 6 Sept. 1927.
6 NAA B356, 93: Bishop of Gippsland 10 Sept. 1928.
7 See Grimshaw 2008; PROV VPRS 1694 Unit 4: C. A. Robarts to Sec. BPA 17 July 1916.
8 NAA B356, 93: G. Sprigg 'Lake Tyers Aboriginal Station. Report by Mr Gordon Sprigg, setting forth results of Investigation of affairs', 22 Dec. 1927.

that the manager himself 'sees the women through', and in 1935 he got word of an alleged 'flogging' of two youths by the station manager and added outright brutality to his set of concerns.[9] But Sprigg's main concern was the board's failure to successfully oversee the moral well-being of its charges. That 'immorality is rife' on Lake Tyers remained his chief concern, and that the board had failed to 'lessen breaches of morality' remained his chief criticism. Sprigg's specific criticisms in 1927 included claims that girls 'who got into trouble are being forced to marry by the management'; that there was 'utter absence of control of the young people on the station during the evening hours' – in particular – 'there is practically no check on the movements of girls at night' and that accommodation did not adequately provide for separate sleeping quarters for girls and boys.[10]

As an alternative to the inhumane punishment of banishment, Sprigg proposed a 'house of detention' on the station. To control the immorality of the young he proposed a curfew bell and/or night watchman. So his argument, in the name of welfare and justice for Aborigines, was about an *extension* of the coercive powers of the board.[11] The administration sought responses from its various officers and office-bearers – station management, the bishop, the local medical practitioner delegated to serve the station. In their responses and in the responses of the board itself and those of the chief secretary as representative of the government of the day are revealed a shared and distinct set of understood inherent racial characteristics upon which they justified their practices. For example, the medical officer disputed Sprigg's criticisms:

> In his nearly two years' work at the station he had had no serious cases of illness amongst the adult natives ... and he had only seen a very few cases due to malnutrition. All of these were in the young baby, and were due in almost every case to ignorance or stupidity of the parents as regards dietary.[12]

The chief secretary noted: 'I find that the care of these people under our protection presents many problems, as it is evident that they cannot be made to live up to the standard of our civilization, but I hope to do something to improve the conditions under which they live.'[13] Under Secretary Chapman added: 'The fact should be borne in mind that the Board has a peculiar problem to deal with, in that the natives are of a very low moral and intellectual order, and the standards which apply to the white population cannot be applied fairly to the aborigines.'[14] Others on the floor of the House revealed a set of taken-for-granted understandings that they were happy to articulate:

9 NAA B356, 93: G. Sprigg to Chief Secretary T. Tunnecliffe 2 July 1930; *Argus* 1935.

10 NAA B356, 94: 'Notes of deputation from Baptist Union of Victoria which waited on the Chief Secretary ...', 11 Feb. 1936.

11 NAA B356, 93: G. Sprigg, 'Lake Tyers Aboriginal Station. Report by Mr Gordon Sprigg, setting forth results of Investigation of affairs', 22 Dec. 1927.

12 NAA B356, 93: Press clipping: *Bairnsdale Advertiser* 4 Nov. 1927: 2.

13 NAA B356, 93: Chief Secretary to G. Sprigg 26 April 1928.

14 NAA B356, 93: (No author) Response to Report of Bishop of Gippsland re Lake Tyers 10 Sept. 1928.

MR GRAY:	Anybody who understands the psychology of the Australian native –
DR ARGYLE:	Do you think that many people understand that psychology?
MR GRAY:	Honorable members will know that a native has to be treated with the greatest amount of firmness and yet with the greatest amount of kindness . . . There is no one more susceptible to yarns and more receptive than the Australian aborigines. If outsiders whisper into the natives' ears that they should do this and that, and undermine the authority of the manager, the administration cannot be successful . . . The morals of the aborigines are not of the same standard as the morals of the white races. They are easily led and need firm supervision.[15]

And this from a Rev. Dobbinson in a press report of discussion of the Council of Churches: 'We preyed on their lands, we preyed on their labor and we preyed on their weak morals. It was a deplorable thing that the most childish and most simple of all the races should have been made a puppet of by the white men, simply because of its weakness.'[16] The secretary of the BPA had some advice in response to an assertion from Sprigg that the board should take responsibility for half-castes:

> It is a peculiar fact that where a person has an admixture of aboriginal blood, however small, his inclination tends towards the aboriginal method of living rather than that of the white, but surely that should not be accepted as a reason for admitting such people to aboriginal Reserves.[17]

In the wash-up, the nature and sciences of Aboriginality were stretched over a fairly broad canvas. The board's vice-chairman warned that it was 'a common error to judge the local conditions by the standards pertaining to the white community'. Allowances had to be made 'for the lower standards that, despite constant striving, appertain to the aborigine'. The morality of the Aborigine in sex matters was 'very low, despite all efforts by the authorities to improve their outlook in this respect'. And the laziness and lack of concentration of the Aborigines had to be constantly combated.[18] And this from the Lake Tyers chaplain in response to Sprigg's (1935) criticisms and allegations of 'flogging':

> Of course there is immorality: if you place 250 people of low-class heredity in one community, where there is very little need to work, what will you get? You can't enforce a school discipline – there are thousands of acres to roam about – the blacks don't know as much about contraceptives as the whites do – above all, they are non-moral and have

15 VPD Session 1928 Vol 177 LA 11 Oct. 1928: 2213–16.
16 NAA B356, 93: Press cutting: *Herald* 26 Oct. 1928.
17 NAA B356, 93: Sec. BPA to W. H. Edgar MLC 29 Feb. 1932.
18 NAA B356, 93: L. L. Chapman, Vice Chairman BPA 're: Visit of Mr Gordon Sprigg to Lake Tyers Aboriginal Station', 8 March 1935.

been so for generations: they esteem sexual contacts as almost a lawful pastime, noting the habits of bulls and rams as proper justification.[19]

But in-house, in meetings and discussions of and between the board, the executive and the ministry, a serious problem of discipline and control was acknowledged. There was virtually no acknowledgement of less than satisfactory material or physical conditions. Various schemes through which the problem might be addressed were entertained. The private reformatories (at this stage there were *only* private reformatories) were voicing their reluctance to admit any of the board's charges. From 1927 onwards, that reluctance remained firmly in place, leaving the board with the particularly vexing problem of how to punish women in general, and how to discipline young women in particular.

In 1928 the bishop of Gippsland, in response to Sprigg's criticisms, defended the current manager (Baldwin), noting he could not remove girls 'giving trouble' to 'homes', 'even though they have been the chief source of most of the troubles (immorality and quarrels) on the Station'. In response to the bishop's concerns a report was produced, most likely penned by Under Secretary/BPA vice-chairman Chapman for the chief secretary:

PUNISHMENT OF WOMEN
This is one of the difficult problems which the Board has to solve. How to punish women. Under existing conditions punishment can only be meted out to women by stopping their rations or expelling them from the Station. It is not wise to adopt such severe measures for minor offences, but it must be admitted that bickering and quarrelling, while trifling in themselves, impair the harmony of the Station seriously if they are indulged in extensively. Before the days of concentration when we had other Stations under control we could transfer malcontents and offenders as a punishment. The plan is closed to us now.

REMOVAL OF IMMORAL GIRLS
Recommendations were received from Mr Baldwin that this should be done. Apart from the question of whether the Board had power to transfer in the way suggested it was ascertained that there was not a home to which they could be transferred nor anyone willing to take charge of them. Moreover it must be remembered that these girls are free and unless they had broken the law they could not be placed under restraint. The only alternative was to dismiss them from the Station, a course which obviously could not be taken.[20]

The CWDRS's reluctance to accept, in particular, young female charges from the BPA first emerged around 1916 with the Salvation Army's Riddell's Creek first to openly declare its opposition to the presence of four girls sent some years earlier from

19 NAA B356, 94: 'Report by the Chaplain, The Rev. G. A. Hancock, at Lake Tyers Aboriginal Station', undated, attachment to corresp. Archdeacon Weir, Administrator of Diocese of Gippsland to Sec. BPA 7 Nov. 1935.

20 NAA B356, 93: (No author) Response to Report of Bishop of Gippsland re Lake Tyers 10 Sept. 1928.

Lake Tyers. The matron urged the secretary of what was then the Department for Neglected Children and Reformatory Schools to have them immediately removed on account of their ostensible depravity and the objectionable necessity of 'having them mixed up with the white girls ...sleeping in the same dormitories ... and bathing in the same baths as the white girls'.[21] The reluctance would persist into the mid-century. Thirty years later a BPA meeting in February 1947 noted a communication from the secretary of the CWDRS 'pointing out the difficulty of affording supervision to wayward girls under the Children's Welfare Act and expressing the view that it was preferable to deal with such cases at the Lake Tyers Station, where the girls were the least public menace'.[22] In the late 1920s and early 1930s, at the height of Sprigg's criticisms, the board was having the usual difficulty gaining the co-operation of the CWDRS. The board seemed to recognise the possibility of some success in placing miscreant youths via the CWDRS into private reformatories at the same time as it recognised the CWDRS's strong objections to receiving any of its female charges. The board resolved at its May 1930 meeting that certain problem cases at Lake Tyers should be transferred to the Salvation Army's Bayswater reformatory, and inquiries were also to be made 'as to whether any Institution would be prepared to accept aboriginal girls'. By the board's next meeting the CWDRS had conveyed its view that it was averse to the transfer of Aboriginal boys to Bayswater.[23] The board had been more successful in past years in transferring a few of its younger charges to the department but on their attaining adulthood the board was reluctant to have them returned despite protestations from the girls' relatives and from the CWDRS. Longtime board member Mrs Bon did not favour their return to Lake Tyers for fear of moral contamination. Clearly an alternative to departmental transfers of young miscreants at Lake Tyers was needed. Mr Everand 'desired it recorded that he had pressed the foundation of a reformatory Station at Tortoise Head Island to which the undesirable male population could be transferred' and was informed by the chief secretary that the matter was under investigation.[24] A fairly newly established reformatory prison for young adult male offenders had been established by the Penal Department on French Island, along the lines of a working forestry camp – probably why Tortoise Head, just off the coast of French Island, came to mind. The board continued to have difficulty finding practical means of bringing its young female charges under its control. In 1933 the board was dealing with persistent complaints from parents that girls should be returned from a reformatory. Mrs Bon opposed the board's attempt to transfer a young girl to Riddell's Creek, taking the view that as the bishop of Gippsland had undertaken the spiritual control of the natives at Lake Tyers, 'he be asked to make provision for her reception

21 PROV VPRS 1694 Unit 4: Matron A. Young, Riddell's Creek Reformatory for Protestant Girls to Sec. DNCRS 5 Dec. 1916.

22 NAA B314, 8: Minutes of Meeting of BPA 9 Feb. 1947.

23 NAA B314, 7: Minutes of Meeting of BPA 7 May 1930; 4 June 1930.

24 NAA B314, 7: Minutes of Meeting of BPA 4 June 1930.

in a suitable Church of England Home'.[25] The information contained in the board's files at this time is piecemeal but there is enough evidence to be able to assert that up to the mid-1930s the relations between the BPA and the CWDRS were less than comfortable. The CWDRS was responsible for overseeing the entry of children into reformatories, all of which were at that stage non-state institutions. It was reluctant to accept any of the board's recalcitrant charges. And the board was equally reluctant to have any children in the hands of the CWD returned to the station. So in the 1930s, what to do with the recalcitrant young under the board's authority, and indeed, what to do with all children at Lake Tyers? In 1935, Chapman noted that, regarding the future of children at Lake Tyers:

> Whilst probably it would be in the best interests of the children if they were removed as infants to ordinary institutions or to white foster homes, where they could benefit by their environment, and so merge into the ordinary life of the community, such a policy would be so inhuman from the point of view of the parents that it cannot be contemplated.[26]

In May 1931 the secretary of the BPA visited Lake Tyers to install Acting Manager J. F. Edwards who had been seconded from the Penal Department where he had served as senior warder, reaffirming the penal orientation of the station. Meanwhile the BPA pursued the possibility of establishing some form of Aboriginal reformatory under its control. In March 1935 in response to a new wave of criticism from Sprigg, Under Secretary/BPA Vice-Chairman Chapman reported to the board that although limited punishments for men were available on the station, followed by expulsion if necessary, 'with the women the position is more difficult. A woman cannot well be expelled and left to roam at large. On rare occasions an institution will accept her, but there is no real form of punishment beyond verbal reproof.' To deal with miscreants and 'to provide a complete system of punishment, a second station would be necessary, with an ample staff, where there would be compulsory labour without pay, and a restriction of both liberty and rations. Provision would have to be made for both males and females', although 'a penal settlement on any part of Lake Tyers would not be practicable'.[27]

In January 1936 there was a request from Major Glen, manager at Lake Tyers, to the secretary of the BPA for a visit from board representatives 'as soon as possible, and to get them here with the gloves off', given that in the context of publicity of Sprigg's latest criticisms, 'the idea is spreading that I am on the carpet'.[28] Secretary Parker, Vice-Chairman Chapman and Hon. Everand MLA made their way down to Tyers to address the residents. The spectre of a reformatory station at Tortoise Head was

25 NAA B 314, 7: Minutes of Meeting of BPA 11 April 1933.

26 NAA B356, 93: L. L. Chapman, Vice Chairman BPA, 're Visit of Mr Gordon Sprigg to Lake Tyers Aboriginal Station', 8 March 1935.

27 NAA B356, 93: L. L. Chapman, Vice Chairman BPA, 're Visit of Mr Gordon Sprigg to Lake Tyers Aboriginal Station', 8 March 1935.

28 NAA B356, 94: Major Ronald Glen to Sec. BPA 7 Jan. 1936.

raised again with both Parker and Everand threatening residents with the establishment of a reformatory station if they did not behave. Parker had informed them that a few malcontents were 'undermining the structure and writing surreptitiously to outsiders and causing a great deal of harm to the community at Lake Tyers', and he noted that he had urged 'the natives to let these malcontents know how much they disapproved of this unsportsmanlike attitude':

> Some years ago the Board had considered forming a second Station where the conditions would be much less attractive and work much harder. The Board was again seriously considering forming such a Station at Tortoise Head Island and if this was done mischief makers might find themselves there. In conclusion, Mr Parker urged all to play the game as a team as suggested by Mr Chapman so that the Station might continue to improve.[29]

Likewise, Everand told the Lake Tyers residents that the board was unanimous in its determination that 'certain people outside and sections of the press would not be permitted to undermine the good work being done and, if necessary, would move for the establishment of a small Station probably at Tortoise Head Island to deal with malcontents'.[30]

With Sprigg's criticisms in mind – the alleged flogging of two youths on the station was at this moment a charged subject – Under Secretary/Vice-Chairman Chapman, in August 1936, delivered another report: 'The situation is now that the aborigines have practically "called the bluff" of the management, and the Board must, in my opinion, provide some method of treatment to enforce more regard for its instructions and those issued by its officers to maintain and improve the general tone of the Station.' While rations could be withheld from men, and indeed they could be banished, neither was completely effective – rations supplied to wives and children were shared, and banishment meant 'the offender constitutes himself as a nuisance to local white settlers'. Again Chapman stressed the particular problem of discipline and punishment as it applied to women.

It is clear that Chapman was referring to discipline and punishment for what in the (white) justice system would be other than breaches of the law: he had in mind 'offenders against discipline and those guilty of misbehaviour on the Station'; those who did not heed the board's instructions 'and those issued by its officers'. He proposed 'a separate establishment', either a completely separate station or a fenced off area within the boundaries of Lake Tyers and he favoured the latter. He laid out the required institutional conditions: prison rations, unpaid sex-segregated manual labour, as much as possible unaided by machinery, locked sex-segregated cubicles. One obvious advantage was that 'it would have a most valuable effect particularly in relation to the

29 NAA B 314, 7: Report on visit of Messrs Everand & Chapman to Lake Tyers 16 Jan. 1936. Attachment to Minutes of Meeting of BPA 3 March 1936.

30 NAA B314, 7: Report on visit of Messrs Everand & Chapman to Lake Tyers 16 Jan. 1936. Attachment to Minutes of Meeting of BPA 3 March 1936.

behaviour of women'.[31] A discussion among board members ensued. Some were in favour; some had reservations. The chairman (chief secretary) then pointed out 'the danger of locking up any person in a separate station as natives were entitled to their liberty, and, if possible, favoured the transfer of offenders to another Institution for discipline'.[32] Remember that at this stage the board was made up largely of members of Parliament, not amateurs divorced from the principles of liberal government. But even here, in this note of restraint from the chief secretary – this one gesture to the fact that the principle of liberty *might* extend to 'natives' – this was not understood as precluding incarceration in another institution, for other than breaches of the law.

A separate reformatory station did not eventuate. For one thing, the board's preoccupation with discipline was interrupted by the first Commonwealth conference on 'Native Welfare', which shifted the agenda. The point to underscore is that up to the mid-1930s, the administration, in tandem with the government of the day, and indeed in tandem with its critics, thought 'the aborigine', including the young Aborigine, as properly the subject of discipline, punishment and indeed institutional incarceration on grounds separate and distinct from the non-Aboriginal population. But from 1937 onwards, the board would have to contend with a new line of sustained criticism. It questioned the legitimacy and legality of the board's practices. It pitted a new knowledge of the Aborigine informed by political and social science (including anthropology and psychology) against the assertion of an inherent racially deficient moral character which remained a fundamental justification for the administration's practices.

THE 1937 COMMONWEALTH CONFERENCE ON NATIVE WELFARE

The Commonwealth government convened a conference on native welfare, with then–Chief Secretary Bailey anticipating that the agenda would cover suggestions 'that the control of aborigines should be transferred to the Commonwealth Government'. Prior to the conference, he stated his position to the board: 'it does not seem to me that the welfare of the aborigines can receive the same degree of attention with a central administration housed at Canberra' and therefore 'the problem should remain the responsibility of the several States'. Victoria differed from other states in that, along with New South Wales, 'we have passed the stage at which the care of the native race presents real difficulties', given that 'at Lake Tyers the inhabitants have been living under civilized conditions for the last four generations and have nothing whatsoever in common with those in more remote parts of the continent'. In Western Australia, the Northern Territory, Queensland and other more remote parts of Australia, 'the problem is more acute owing to the later era of settlement'. These views were submitted by Under Secretary/Vice-Chairman

31 NAA B356, 91: Untitled report on discipline and misbehaviour at Lake Tyers, 15 Aug. 1936 (initialled L. L. C.).

32 NAA B314, 7: Minutes of Meeting of BPA 19 Aug. 1936.

Chapman in a document to the board at its February 1937 meeting. Chapman announced the chief secretary would represent Victoria at the conference even though the views in the document were initialled by Chapman himself.[33]

Russell McGregor observes that Victoria was the only state with ministerial representation – although Under Secretary Chapman was there too – the others from other states and territories being senior bureaucrats and a scientist.[34] Some interesting areas were covered, including the argument that chaining 'natives' around the neck was done on humanitarian grounds. Of particular interest was Chapman on the state of matters for Aborigines in Victoria. He began with the assertion: 'We are all agreed that the most urgent problem is the absorption of the quadroons and octoroons into the white community. The trouble is that conditions vary considerably as between one State and another.' For example, 'it is probably much easier for coloured girls in the Northern Territory to get white husbands than it would be for such girls in Victoria'. Likewise, Chapman claimed it was harder for half-castes to find employment in Victoria. In Victoria, unlike some other states, 'only full-blooded or half-caste natives who, by licence, reside on a station, or who apply for residence, come under our legislation'.[35]

But things start to sound a little contradictory from here on. Bailey and Chapman stated that the Victorian 'problem' was, comparatively speaking, hardly a problem at all. Bailey noted at one point that 'the full-blooded natives are not of much concern, really ... for they are so few in number'.[36] As far as the rest were concerned, the Victorian problem differed from that of other parts of Australia on account of the degree of 'civilisation' of its natives. And Chapman, who had always argued vehemently against any suggestion that the board's responsibility should extend to anyone who was not strictly Aboriginal under the Victorian Act, used something of that argument here to proffer the unique circumstances of Victoria. Those half-castes categorised as outside the terms of the act and living 'under civilised conditions' would be outraged at any attempt to bring them under the control of the board: 'In Victoria, many of the half-castes have been living under civilised conditions for five generations, and they would raise an outcry, in which they would receive support from white people, if any effort were made to deal with them on lines upon which it is proposed to deal with half-castes in Western Australia.'[37] Yet Chapman went on to describe the racial deficits that ostensibly persisted across generations and continued to be exhibited in the half-caste, the quadroon and the octoroon. Half-castes would work under supervision 'but they cannot be trusted alone'. He gestured to their 'lack of responsibility', 'the inability of the aborigines to fend for themselves'. He pointed to the quadroons and octoroons living around Framlingham, 'entirely without authority', and under 'deplorable' conditions (bark huts and beer bottles), quite contrary to the

33 NAA B314, 7: Minutes of Meeting of BPA 10 Feb. 1937, Attachment: 'Control of Aborigines', 20 Aug. 1936.

34 McGregor 2011. 35 Australia *c* 1937 (Aboriginal Welfare Conference [AWC]): 17.

36 Australia *c* 1937 (AWC): 20. 37 Australia *c* 1937 (AWC): 18.

standards of 'a civilised community'. It all led to the assertion that 'as the result of experience of five generations of natives living in contact with white people under these conditions, the promise of half-castes to maintain themselves is not very hopeful'.[38] The reader may be a little perplexed as to how this lined up with Victoria's stated position that it did not have a problem because of the civilised nature of its natives. What then was Chapman arguing *for*? He came close to arguing that half-castes, quadroons and octoroons were no good, and that any amount of Aboriginal blood carried inherent negative qualities that had to be met by an authoritarian response. So, force the issue? Declare them 'white', as the existing letter of the law required? Let them then exhibit their negative qualities to force a new response? Two decades on, the McLean Report, a new act and the practices it ushered in achieved an extension of the possibility of authoritarian and coercive practices upon those previously, by law, white and beyond the remit of the administration.

Bailey also spoke to conditions in Victoria at the conference and the difficulties of absorption of the half-caste. And again there was a rehearsal of the much-reiterated racial deficit, the inability to self-regulate. Bailey spoke in particular to the problem that had much vexed the board over the past decade: the half-caste girls' incapacity for moral self-regulation. The message was that despite all the care, attention and resources thrown in their direction, they would inevitably fall into situations of degradation, disease:

> Our principle difficulty is that as soon as a girl becomes competent to take a position as domestic servant and enters domestic service, it is no time before she comes back to the Lake Tyers Station either pregnant or, worse still, with two or three little children. It is difficult in a State with a large white population to prevent such things from happening . . . They all came under the influence of some hoboes and went off with them, with the result that not long after they came back to the Lake Tyers Station diseased. These are not the only examples I could cite; they are three outstanding cases which I have in mind and they exemplify the difficulty of absorbing this class of people amongst the whites in areas where there are large white populations. The half-castes get into the hands of degenerate whites, and that is the end; they go on breeding in the same way.[39]

The picture painted at the conference of the conditions in Victoria was one of benign supervision in an environment well resourced with facilities for health and for education. Nothing could be further from the truth.

SCIENCES OF CHILD DEVELOPMENT, AND THE ABORIGINAL CHILD

From the late 1930s the administration had to respond to a new group of non-Aboriginal critics – an alliance of various intellectuals and practitioners from various

[38] Australia *c* 1937 (AWC): 17–18. [39] Australia *c* 1937 (AWC): 12.

disciplines and professions (law and education were well represented). Eventually, the kinds of truths which contested the practices of the administration of Aborigines would become the basis upon which the 1957 McLean Report would set out its recommendations – most notably, developmental psychology largely displacing biological destiny as the basis from which to figure the problem of the Aborigine. Thus, the root cause of the problem lay in the aberrant psychology of the Aboriginal family, and the kinds of interventions recommended in the Barry Report are also recommended in the McLean Report – scientifically based professional intervention in family life. Further, the formal machinery of the Children's Welfare Department was to be made available for the reception of Aboriginal children when requirements extended beyond such intervention. But the reader should not think that it was enough to speak of pressure from a group of 'progressives' to explain such a paradigm shift, as if, according to some inevitable law of history, an enlightened truth would inevitably win out in the end. So how to explain, in the light of the archival evidence, the conditions for the eventual adoption of this new kind of logic beginning to be proffered? Might it be explained in these terms: this group, informed in one way or another by an emergent 'science' of psychological development which was fast emerging elsewhere – follows the modus operandi of that science? A rehearsal of a number of points established in Chapter 5 will help establish what was distinctive about that modus operandi at the time.

Until the early 1930s the CWDRS did not have a solution to the problem of the massing of that 'dangerous' cohort deemed mentally and morally deficient at the only state-owned and operated institution for children – the CWDRS's depot at Royal Park. The solution was to persuade the Mental Hygiene Department to take them on. The subsequent massing of a new cohort of white children under a psy-scientific gaze allowed two things to happen. First, a cohort was made available for statistical analysis overseen by psychiatric expertise and gradually that analysis revealed the ostensible facts upon which the Barry Report was to base its recommendations for the future of welfare-justice practices. Under a psychiatric clinical eye, it became apparent that those deemed mentally deficient did not necessarily exhibit the kind of problem moral conduct that until that point was understood to be part of their inherent make-up. Moreover, with the establishment of clinics such as that at the Children's Court, intelligence testing showed that most offending children were of normal intelligence – providing the conditions for refiguring the delinquent as born normal and made delinquent. Second, and at one and the same time, a cohort was made available for detailed case studies emanating from a range of clinical sites that began to map in detail the trajectory of the individual child from birth to the manifestation of offending conduct. This allowed for an articulation of the *process* of formation of delinquency in the context of family life and the identification of 'maladjusted' familial relations. By the mid-1950s the Barry Report (the inquiry itself overseen by a magistrate, a psychiatrist and an educationist) would recommend the psy-scientific oversight of, first, interventions at the level of the family to readjust maladjusted familial relations of the pre-delinquent, and second, re-involvement of the state in the establishment of juvenile training facilities for the fully fledged delinquent.

So by the early 1940s we have a clear point of contrast between the administration of the white child and that of the Aboriginal child. The white child, as the subject of welfare-justice, was increasingly understood in the circulation of knowledge between clinics, court and institution and between psychiatrist, educationist, the newly emergent professionally trained social worker, the probation officer and so on, as formative, and the white delinquent increasingly understood as an entity that 'develops'. Problem conduct was understood as emerging out of the contingency of its immediate conditions. And as noted, the machinery and the conditions – the establishment of special schools for the mentally deficient, the attachment of psychiatric clinics to such schools, the development of psychiatric clinics for problem children, of clinics to courts, of social workers to clinics and so on – excluded the Aboriginal child from any particular consideration. Welfare and justice as they pertained to the Aboriginal child were left largely in the hands of the chief secretary, the BPA and its officers and allied officials – the station schoolteacher, the station chaplain, the local police officer, the locally appointed medical officer – and we have already explored something of the logic from which they operated. At the same time as developmental psychology was gaining traction elsewhere, these officers and allied officials staunchly reiterated among themselves and to those who questioned their practices, the *fact* that Aboriginal children shared the inherent racial deficits of their parents, the latter inherently child-like. The Aborigine as an entity was born, not made. The nature of the Aborigine's conduct, child and adult alike, lay in their Aboriginality and had little to do with the contingencies of 'conditions'. The input of the likes of professionally trained social workers was unwelcome and unnecessary. There was a kind of ongoing tit-for-tat between the prevailing administration and its officers and allies, and those such as the Education Sub-Committee of the Victorian Aboriginal Group whose members wished to extend the fast establishing developmental paradigm to the Aboriginal child.

In 1943, the head teacher at Lake Tyers school replied to a request from Amy Brown of the Victorian Aboriginal Group for information regarding the schooling and general conditions of the children at Lake Tyers. There were, he noted 'no specially intelligent children who would profit from such instruction as you suggest'.[40] By way of explanation, he continued along what might be called social Darwinist lines: 'It can be taken as a general rule that the more progressive and/or aggressive types in any community are more likely to fend for themselves. Lake Tyers is no exception and the mental level of the children now left in attendance is not high.' The one possible exception in the teacher's experience over the past four years

[40] NAA B314, 7: J. Kelly, Head Teacher, Lake Tyers School, to Miss A. Brown, 3 Nov. 1943, attachment to Minutes of Meeting of BPA 1 Dec. 1943.

was a boy who, though he showed signs of higher intelligence, was 'incorrigibly lazy'. Anything beyond rudimentary technical training was of no use: 'The mathematical background for most other forms of technical training would be beyond the mental capabilities of the majority.' As regards the health conditions of children, he noted that sores were endemic. He was not sure about Brown's inquiry into any relationship between diet and low mentality; he did not think that there were any cases of malnutrition. Anyway, the prevalence of sores was entirely due to the 'moral deficiency' of the parents and if there were problems with diet, the parents were to blame here too: 'There is positively no doubt whatsoever that the present prevalence of sores is due to the laziness, lack of hygienic practice, and, more often than not, indifference of the parents to their children's welfare. In only a few cases is the ration issued used to the best advantage.' And he had little hope for Brown's suggestion for an alternative model of schooling along Fairbridge Farm lines as 'there is no guarantee that children, on leaving the group, will not return to the ways of their parents'. The teacher described the adults at the stations as hopeless: 'Most people familiar with the natives here would insist that it is a dose of discipline and hard work which is needed. See suggestion 1. No work no meal.' Having dismissed most of Brown's own suggestions, he ended on one of his own – improve the lighting as a 'well-lit village might go a long way to counter the moral laxity of these people'.[41] So the message was that Brown and like-minded critics spoke from ignorance of true knowledge of Aborigines as a people hopelessly morally and mentally deficient in the light of which improvement of conditions pertaining to health and to education would amount to naught.

Much the same kind of message was reiterated by Chief Secretary Hyland in a press statement of November 1943, by which time criticism of Lake Tyers, including the (perennially) charged subject of the presence of TB, had been raised in Parliament. The chief secretary himself had recently visited Lake Tyers and all was rosy. The inference was that those who criticised did so at a distance and had no first-hand knowledge of conditions: 'Mr Hyland said that he would advise anyone who was sincerely interested in the aborigines to visit the Station so that they could satisfy themselves, as he had done, that the State was doing its duty in providing for these people.' If the state of well-being of any of the residents of Lake Tyers was problematic, the root cause lay in a 'racial handicap', characterised as a moral deficit – an inherent vulnerability to the temptations that were outside the protective boundaries of the station:

> Experience had shown that many of them, because of racial handicap more than that of colour, could not successfully maintain themselves away from the Station or resist the temptations which civilization afforded. Time and again various families

[41] NAA B314, 7: J. Kelly to A. Brown 3 Nov. 1943, attachment to Minutes of Meeting of BPA 1 Dec. 1943. The first Fairbridge Farm School was established by Kingsley Fairbridge (founder of child migration scheme to British colonies) near Albany WA in 1913.

> had left the Station and engaged in private employment, but had failed to sustain the effort necessary to establish themselves in civil life. They had ultimately returned very often broken in health and neglected, and the Management at the Station had willingly undertaken the duty of treatment and encouragement to re-establish them on the reserve.[42]

What then, other than, or more precise than, the pressure of enlightened reform explained the eventual collapse of the old paradigm and the adoption of the new? As suggested previously it was less a case of the inevitability of humanist ideology winning out in the end than their modus operandi. There may have been no psychological clinic dedicated to inscribing the life trajectory of the Aboriginal child. But there were a number of Aboriginal people willing and able to use what opportunities existed and what allies were available to tell their story to underscore this or that injustice (as there had long been: the nuisance of the Aboriginal correspondent who would bypass the board for the ear of a higher authority had been a bugbear of the administration for decades). The board and its officers had fought a continuous battle over the years to attempt to control the flow of information emanating from station residents (intercepting mail, restricting visitors, overseeing contact between visitors and residents, proclaiming Aboriginal informants to be liars or mentally unbalanced and so on). From 1927 to 1937, Sprigg was fed information by Lake Tyers residents who managed to negotiate the barriers to communication foisted upon them by the board. They were accused of sneaking across the lake to meet him at night. What was distinctive about how that information was used was that Sprigg, as a principal available point of passage for Aboriginal claims to be heard, filtered that information through his own set of understandings, such that in the long run those claims served to substantiate the truth he shared with his opposition (the BPA) of a racially inherent moral deficit. That is, the information was used to push for more stringent controls of an inherently childish and morally weak race.

From 1937 onwards Aboriginal people had a newly available point of passage. What was distinctive about the period from 1937 to 1955 was that this new point of passage, in the form of intellectuals informed by a science of development of the human individual, shaped and filtered the information it received in terms of that developmental paradigm. It fell on the ear of a public increasingly attuning itself to a new orthodoxy of child development, emanating from the clinics and courts, education departments and welfare agencies at the time.

THE MAKING OF THE 'YOUNG DELINQUENT'

In February 1948 a public meeting was held at Box Hill on the topic, 'Living Conditions of Aborigines in Victoria'. The speakers were activists Anna Vroland,

42 NAA B314, 7: Letter to Press 26 Nov. 1943, attachment to Minutes of Meeting of BPA 1 Dec. 1943.

Cora Gilsenan and federal parliamentarian Doris Blackburn MHR. It occurred only a couple of weeks after the death of a young woman, M, at Lake Tyers whom Vroland and Gilsenan had befriended. They had accused the board and Lake Tyers management of inadequate care, of conspiring to block their access to M and of covering up the circumstances that led to her death. M's death, her case and the case of her sister, N, were represented at the meeting as pivotal and served to open discussion on conditions in general but also allowed for a particular focus on the circumstances of Aboriginal girls and young Aboriginal women. Hitherto, the young Aborigine, though long recognised as a disciplinary problem, was largely thought and acted upon as an entity to be properly managed by a discrete set of practices quite independent of administrative practices upon white youth, by virtue of Aborigines' particular inherent moral weakness. (Recall that only a year earlier the CWD had communicated to the board its reluctance to deal with wayward Aboriginal girls: they were 'the least public menace' at Lake Tyers and under the control the BPA.) Here, the story of M and in particular that of her sister N, pieced together by the white activists from the girls' own account, was translated in terms of the then well-established orthodoxy of the *making* of the young delinquent.

Vroland introduced the sisters' story: 'They go to gaol because they are not understood. They are by no means all criminals. Miss Gilsenan will tell you at least one girl did spend a great deal of time in gaol.'[43] The girl referred to was N. Gilsenan explained that M, near death, requested that she look after her sister. Gilsenan found N in gaol for non-payment of a £10 fine, which she paid. Gilsenan, who then had access to N's story, recounted it in detail at the meeting:

> Going back earlier in [N's] life, she was an orphan. The mother and father died, I think when the sisters were aged about 2 and 3 years. Usually, when left an orphan on Lake Tyers, a child is sent to a home around about the city. [M and N] were sent to various homes. I do not think there was, perhaps, the understanding there should have been. Perhaps they were isolated and nobody understood them. However, there was quite some trouble and the sisters resented some of the conditions and things that went on in those homes.

After a series of domestic situations N was sent back to the station where, accused of having sworn at the matron, she had an altercation with the manager:

> The next thing that happened was [N] was called into the office to apologise. She did not and would not apologise. She said to the manager 'She asked for it and made me say it; I am not going to apologise.' The manager said 'I think you will apologise.' [N] said 'No, I will not apologise.' They then got a strap and belted her. The manager hit her across the face and called her 'a little swine' which I do not think was anyway [sic] for a manager to speak.

43 NAA B356, 95: Transcript of Proceedings of Public Meeting at Box Hill 12 Feb. 1948: 2–3 (A. Vroland).

The police became involved:

> The manager informed [M] that [N]was going to Pentridge. I do not know what the charge was; I think there was to be a Charge usually before a person can be sent to Pentridge. Nevertheless, the manager informed [M] that [N] was going to Pentridge, and the police informed [M] she was going to a home.
>
> [N] was expelled from the station and the police took her to the police station, gave her lunch, 10/-, put her on the train and said 'Someone will be there to meet you.' She understood that someone would be there from the home to meet her; so when she arrived at Flinders street she got off the train and ran down the other end of the platform and boarded a train to Collingwood, where she stayed with some very fine aboriginal people who were previously on Lake Tyers. She stayed with them for some time but had no money. She then met up with some girls, some bad white girls from Fitzroy, and before she knew where she was she was up on a vagrancy charge and in Pentridge. When she came out of Pentridge after having served her time, there was no one to meet her and take an interest in her, and it was not long before [N] was back in Pentridge. Some months later [N] found she was going to have a baby. The baby was born in the Women's Hospital but lived only six months.

N then found herself in and out of Pentridge Prison – which is where Gilsenan found her. Before her release, Gilsenan gave the warden a lesson on the making of the delinquent:

> When I said to the warder 'I want to get [N] released' he was surprised and said 'You are an optimist.' I said 'How is that'. He said 'Do you know what I would do with that girl: I would have her exterminated!' I said 'That is a very rash statement you have made.' He continued on for quite some time so I asked him if he had ever heard [N's] story, to which he replied 'No.' I then told him her story, at the conclusion of which he said 'I am sorry; I had no idea. I will take back all I said; I am very sorry.' . . .
>
> After telling him about [N's] early experiences on Lake Tyers he said 'Maybe that is the reason for many of the aborigines leaving the station.'[44]

This example of youthful Aboriginal criminality, promiscuity and vagrancy became a case study for the making of the Aborigine as of the white delinquent. The term 'delinquent', up to this point, had been used rarely by the administration in relation to Aboriginal youth.

At the same meeting Doris Blackburn commented on a visit to Lake Tyers some years earlier:

> The things I saw were the same as those described this evening. Possibly, the two little girls of whom Miss Gilsenan has mentioned tonight, [M and N], were merely little school girls when I was there. After seeing the treatment that was being meted out to the people of Lake Tyers I came away feeling that there was a place for the

[44] NAA B356, 95: Transcript of Proceedings of Public Meeting at Box Hill 12 Feb. 1948: 17–23 (C. Gilsenan).

> making of delinquents . . . The background of [N] and [M], if they were then at the station, is easily understood . . . I have spoken to these people and they are afraid. It is their fear that makes them what they are and that sends them to Pentridge and such places.[45]

At the meeting, via the accounts of the speakers, N and M were bestowed a 'background' and made 'delinquent'.

The public meeting and the government's response were given press coverage. In the wake of the Box Hill meeting some members of the BPA were in favour of an official inquiry into Lake Tyers, although it was later reported in the press that it was a unanimous decision of the board to reject the suggestion.[46] The chief secretary (now Dodgshun in a new Conservative government) was in favour of a legal response in light of the 'reckless charges' raised at Box Hill. At that board meeting, the content of the files of N was presented:

> Case of [N]
>
> The case of [N] was referred to at length at the Box Hill meeting. Records showed that [N] was a half-caste orphan, who had been a ward of the Children's Welfare Department since she was three years of age until she attained her nineteenth birthday on 18/9/46. She had served several terms of imprisonment, and was released from gaol on 7/2/48 on her fine being paid by Miss Gilsenan. It was reported that she was now residing at Metung, and that arrangements were being made for her to broadcast from 3DB Station, Melbourne, on 23/2/48 on the subject of her life at Tyers.
>
> The Vice-Chairman was authorised to invite the attention of the manager of the Broadcasting Station to the record of this girl.[47]

Some pause for thought. In what kind of account does the truth most likely lie? Here the official record of the BPA was set against the account provided at the public meeting, with the suggestion that it would speak for itself, that the girl was *simply bad*. The official record did not contain the kind of continuity – that sense of *becoming* – the 'background' which was lent to her tale by her activist 'friends', and by the genre of the case study. The evidence showed that the kind of record keeping practices of the board – or lack thereof – helped prop up the administrative status quo and the logic of inherent racial deficits. In a sense, one cannot *become* or have a 'background' without the continuity of the individual case study. One of the conditions of becoming a delinquent was, in goodly part, the clinical case study which actually mapped the formation of the offender. When Vroland and her associates began to press, in mid-1950, for further details of further cases – specifically: 'How many convictions of part-aboriginal girls for vagrancy have taken place during

45 NAA B356, 95: Transcript of Proceedings of Public Meeting at Box Hill 12 Dec. 1948: 22–23 (Mrs Maurice [Doris]Blackburn MHR).

46 NAA B 356, 95: Press clipping: *Sun* 5 March 1948.

47 NAA B314, 8: Minutes of Meeting of BPA 18 Feb. 1948.

the past three years?'– the administration could reply with impunity: 'This is not known to the Board, as these girls would not be within its legal control. No special record would be kept by the Police Department, the girls being ordinary citizens.'[48]

THE DARK CHILDREN REPORT

By June 1951 Cora Gilsenan in the company of Dr Hilda Greenshields, 'a retired medical woman with special interest in child welfare', and Sister Millar, retired from a government position as industrial school matron in South Australia and with 'long experience in caring for Aboriginal children', had completed a fact-finding mission of the unofficial Aboriginal communal camps in country Victoria on the fringe of towns beyond Lake Tyers station. Their report was presented under the auspices of the WILPF and under the title 'Conditions of dark children in East Gippsland' (Dark Children report). An extract from Greenshields's observations encapsulates the content and orientation of the report, and, in particular, its focus on high rates of infant mortality:

> Do the people of Victoria realise that in the Gippsland area alone there are nearly 200 part-aboriginal children living under such appalling conditions that their very lives are threatened, the rate of mortality in some families being as high as 50%. The fundamental causes of death are ... attributable to exposure and malnutrition. Their winter accomodation [sic] is likely to be an unused shed standing in a sea of mud ... [with] no real shelter or warmth, and no cooking or bathing facilities ... [M]any of these children have an inadequate diet, insufficient warm clothing, too few blankets, no beds [and] many of them contract pneumonia ... The seasonal employment of the Fathers is the main reason for setting up these winter camps ... [O]nly casual labour is available to them, and they must move when the work changes. As Aboriginal parents will never leave their children they naturally all travel together. Although improved accommodation alone would save many childrens lives [sic], the mothers should also have the benefit of advice from the baby health centre. At present their attendance is discouraged, mainly owing to the unsympathetic attitude of local white people ... [W]hy cannot the mobile unit of this service contact these mothers, and give them the ante-natal, post-natal and child guidance which is their right.

The response to the report, Anna Vroland informed the chief secretary, 'depends largely on the community's care or neglect *now*'.[49] The chief secretary launched his own inquiry via the co-operation of the chief commissioner of police. Chapman,

[48] NAA B356, 97: A. Vroland to Miss M. A. Williamson, Hon. Sec. National Council of Women (NCW), forwarded to Chief Secretary 7 July 1950; Chief Secretary to M. A. Williamson, Sec. NCW, 25 July 1950.

[49] NAA B356, 97: WILPF (Australian Section) 'Conditions of dark children in East Gippsland, June 1951'; A. Vroland to Chief Secretary 8 Aug. 1951.

wearing his under secretary hat, *not* his BPA hat, penned the following direction, in which both the problem and the solution as expressed by the WILPF, underwent significant refiguring: 'The Chief Secretary desires inquiries to be made through the local police, and if they consider that the circumstances exist justifying action in having any children brought before the court as neglected children, that such action be taken accordingly.'[50]

By early September 1951 the Dark Children report had received press coverage and the matter was raised in Parliament, where the government vigorously defended its treatment of Aborigines and took the opportunity during the same debate to announce its decision not to be represented at the impending second Commonwealth-sponsored conference on native welfare.[51]

There are some general points to be made in order to capture the tenor of this second Commonwealth conference and to glimpse shifts in administrative policies and practices beyond Victoria. First, variations in terminology deployed in legislative bodies across Australia were proving problematic: 'At the present time, some anomalies are created by reason of the various definitions given to the terms "native" and "aboriginal".' So rather than attempt a legislated universal definition and/or uphold a legislated system in which those defined by such terms were 'regarded as constituting a different class of citizens by their very nature', the following was proposed:

> The more correct statement of our view is that those persons to whom the special legislation applies are wards of the State who, for the time being, stand in need of guardianship and who should automatically cease to be wards when they are able to assume to full citizenship to which they are entitled. This view could be given clear expression by amendments of existing legislation where necessary, so that, in place of attempts to define a native or an aboriginal, the legislation would be made to apply only to those persons deemed to stand in need of the provisions of such legislation for their guardianship and tutelage.[52]

No available evidence in the Victorian archival material explored to date shows any official statement or legislative framework that referred overtly to the Aborigine as a ward of the state. But certainly material dating from the 1860s onwards provides many examples from various administrative, government and non-government stakeholders alluding, directly or indirectly, to the child-like or childish nature of Aborigines. In 1862 the BPA described Aborigines as 'indeed but helpless children'; the 1877 royal commission heard testimony from pastoralist and chief inspector of sheep E. M. Curr that 'the native is a child'.[53] In this chapter we have already encountered Rev. Dobbinson's reference in 1928 to Aborigines as 'the most childish

50 NAA B356 97: L. L. Chapman, 17 Aug. 1951, note on corresp. A Vroland, Hon. Sec. WILPF (Aust. Sec.) to Chief Secretary 8 Aug. 1951.

51 VPD Session 1950–51 Vol 234 LA 4 Sept. 1951: 4280–82.

52 Australia 1951 (Native Welfare Conference [NWC]): 4 (Statement of Citizenship Status).

53 Victoria 1862 (BPA): 6; Victoria 1877 (RC): ME, 77.

and simple of races'. Lake Tyers chaplain G. A. Hancock explained the ostensible inability of Aborigines to adhere to the truth as 'due to a childish mentality'.[54] Such characterisations were not confined to the administration or its allies. Amy Brown, spokesperson for the (non-Aboriginal) Victorian Aborigines Group argued during a meeting with Chapman (acting in lieu of the chief secretary) that 'Aborigines brought up in segregation could not be expected to have anything but the moral standard of children. They were continually under surveillance and could not "grow up".' Chapman preserved Brown's characterisation, if not her reasoning, in his reply that 'for generations their ancestors had been nomads ... and it would be long years before industrious habits could be inculcated into these people'.[55] Now, at this 1951 Commonwealth conference, there was renewed legitimacy given to the child-like qualities of the Aborigine. Given that most wards of the state were children, the conference statement surely reinforced the long taken-for-granted child-like qualities of the Aborigine.

By 1951 governments and administrations had begun to adopt a new framework, fed, albeit indirectly, by developmental psychology, and first embraced and pushed by critics of the administration of the day. Developmental psychology had largely displaced the science of heredity in thinking the make-up of that other contingent of wards of the state – the neglected or delinquent child – and had certainly gained the ear of an administration. Now, the language was at pains to point out that those qualities necessitating *some* Aborigines to be provided for as wards of the state were not seen as qualities inherent to a race. Rather, it was as if Aboriginality was understood not as a deficit per se, but as a stage, like childhood, out of which the fully fledged citizen had the potential to develop, given (again, as the science of developing psyches had taught) the right environment, appropriate resources and appropriate guiding expertise. So, in the conference sections on education, although no overt statement put to rest theories of inherent inferior mental capacity, the general emphasis was on equivalence of standards of education 'and wherever practical and convenient, participation in the normal education facilities of the European community' though 'the inability of the aboriginal child to take his place readily, age for age, side by side with the European child because of general backwardness according to European standards and language' was acknowledged. The need for hostels to accommodate Aboriginal children seeking secondary education was underscored. When it came to the problem of adolescents, the influence of developmental psychology was seeping in:

> This problem may arise in two ways. There is the problem of the adolescent who is so backward that he cannot be catered for in the ordinary primary classes of the special native schools. Special provision must be made for him, as it is generally

54 NAA B356, 94: 'Report by the Chaplain, The Rev. G. A. Hancock, at Lake Tyers Aboriginal Station', undated, attachment to corresp. Archdeacon Weir, Administrator of Diocese of Gippsland to Sec. BPA 7 Nov. 1935.

55 NAA B356, 97: Notes of deputation from Victorian Aboriginal [sic] Group to Chief Secretary's Office 18 Aug. 1937.

> unwise to mix him with the lower age groups. Wherever possible, institutions specially catering for this type should be considered.[56]

Then there was the problem of the adolescent who had completed education 'as far as he or she can be taken' and 'is ready to enter employment either directly or as a trainee apprentice':

> This is probably the most dangerous stage of all. In many cases it involves moving in of youths from Missions and other isolated centres to settled communities in search of employment. Lack of experience, the sudden transition and the absence of a real home environment can easily combine to contribute to the demoralisation of these youths. Without the greatest care at this stage, years of patient endeavour and training can quickly be undone, and the development of an unsavoury poor class town type encouraged.[57]

Hostels appeared to be the answer to this problem – places where the adolescent 'in the transition stage from pupil to employee may be housed and cared for under good conditions and with good companionship, and given guidance and help in the choice of employment and in meeting the challenges which the new environment sets him or her'. There were calls at various moments throughout the conference proceedings for professionalisation of health and welfare workers. Teachers might require special training 'not usually imparted in the training of teachers for normal European schools'. Managers on stations might need to undergo 'special training and instructional courses'. All stations should have at least one trained nurse and the conference passed a resolution 'that there is an established need for welfare workers, who should be qualified nurses, to visit the white and coloured families in tropical Australia and it is recommended that such workers should be appointed'.[58] But Victoria was silent on all of this because it was not represented. We know, however, that the administration was vigorously resisting persistent calls from interest groups such as the WILPF for the involvement of social workers or welfare workers in station or off-station Aboriginal communities.

The matters raised in the WILPF Dark Children report were not successfully laid to rest. In mid-September, shortly after the Commonwealth conference, Anna Vroland pursued the subject with Sir George Knox MLA – a politician of considerable standing and influence. Knox had a long history of military command, represented Upper Yarra in the Victorian Parliament and was married to a prominent philanthropist. In the meantime, the police report on possible cases of neglect, instigated by the chief secretary in the wake of the Dark Children report appeared. It was several pages long and in two parts, and it contained local Constable Howlett's version of the history of the arrangements and circumstances that existed at the time, mixed with a good dose of pseudo-anthropological, yet familiar 'truths': 'It is common knowledge

56 Australia 1951 (NWC): 5–6 (Statement on Education and Agendum 4).
57 Australia 1951 (NWC): 5–6 (Statement on Education and Agendum 4).
58 Australia 1951 (NWC): Appendix p. 1, Resolution 9.

that once white blood has been introduced to the Australian Aboriginal it will eventually predominate, hence, it is only a matter of a few generations and there will then be no dark people despite the fact the progeny of the race is multiplying.'[59] Their 'desire to wander', to 'live simply from hand to mouth' along with the usual reiteration of the usual racial deficits – laziness, dirtiness, sexual precociousness, lack of perseverance, lack of self-control – were, according to Const. Howlett, all causal contributors to the conditions under which they lived. Regarding infant mortality specifically, he argued that the problem lay largely in the fact that they had too many babies, and they had those babies off the station (and hence were eligible for the 'baby bonus' – payment not available to station residents). Howlett performed his own spurious statistical analysis:

> Records obtained from station show that since the 1st June last there has been approximately 40 births on the station, and for the corresponding period only 5 deaths of children under 12 years of age. I would also like to point out that quite a number of births take place off the station because the mother then can obtain the baby bonus, where as, if the birth occurs on the station this is not received by the parents. Quite a number of children who have died have been taken back to the station by the parents when illness commences, to get the benefit of free medical treatment, hence, the births away from the station would be much greater than the deaths. After taking into consideration all the circumstances I consider the death rate among the children is remarkably low.

Recall that Under Secretary Chapman had requested specifically that the police look into possible charges of neglect. Constable Howlett, following an interview with the chairman of the Children's Court in his district, then argued that the living conditions generally of the Aboriginal people needed to be carefully studied before a defended case of a child or parent could be decided under the Children's Welfare Act. He pointed out that when a child was well fed and clothed, and the parents earned sufficient funds to keep the child that way, the mere fact of crude living conditions, especially with the housing shortage at that time, would not in itself constitute sufficient evidence. Because of these facts he considered it inadvisable to prefer any charges unless there was ample evidence for a conviction: 'Should any Defendant in such a case fight a charge, and with the aid of a solicitor be found not guilty, it would only tend to lessen the influence which is at present held by the police over these people.'[60]

This passage is remarkable on several accounts – most notably because it serves to reinforce a point underscored several times during the course of this work: that at least up to this point in time, matters pertaining to (white) children's welfare and matters pertaining to Aborigines were largely thought and acted upon as separate

59 NAA B356, 97: Victoria Police. Report of Senior Const. E. L. Howlett Relative to Aboriginal Children: alleged neglect in East Gippsland 14 Sept. 1951.

60 NAA B356, 97: Victoria Police. Report of Senior Const. E. L. Howlett Relative to Aboriginal Children: alleged neglect in East Gippsland 14 Sept. 1951.

and distinct. Beyond this, the passage is further testimony to the less than formal, less than transparent role of the police in the administration of Aborigines. The second part of Constable Howlett's report consisted of pages and pages of what looked, for all the world, like case notes on individual families, documenting in some detail the living conditions and circumstances of multiple families he interviewed. They documented family members – parents, children, caste, age and school grade of children; character; habits; health and employment status of parents; and conditions of their house. Constable Howlett's notes were occasionally augmented or corrected by Len Rule, then manager of Lake Tyers. It may well be that this was the first such exercise carried out among the Aboriginal population at Lake Tyers. Not only do they look like the case notes of, say, a social worker, but they would eventually become such. An undated note attached to a copy of Howlett's notes was to that effect:

> Sister Goldsworthy to study.
> Incorporate details onto cards
> Copies on family files.[61]

Clearly the postscript was added some years later. Sister Goldsworthy, a triple certificate nurse, was appointed by the newly constituted Aborigines Welfare Board in 1960 as one of its first welfare officers to work with 'aboriginal women and children in the Lakes Entrance [east Gippsland] district'.[62] The postscript signals the approaching transfer of authoritative knowledge from police to professional welfare workers. Together, Const. Howlett's report and the postscript signal a perceptible shift in *what* was being collected. Despite the board's best attempts up to this point to keep the social worker at bay, the kind of scrutiny and knowledge associated with that profession, by then an entrenched identity in (white) welfare agencies, had found its way in. Perhaps it is possible to think of it as having been dragged in, at least in part via the production of the 'Dark Children' report. Vroland, Gilsenan and others under the auspices of the Women's International League had ushered the professional welfare worker and the female doctor into the interiors of Aboriginal family life, and they reported what they found. The counter-investigation instigated by the board had, perhaps, little choice but to follow suit.

A NEW POINT OF ARRIVAL?

There was no board meeting in 1953. There was, however, an inspection report. To date, in the face of criticism of conditions on Lake Tyers, the previous government had claimed that conditions at the station including access to hospital and medical care, education and housing were exemplary. The inspection report was highly

[61] NAA B356, 97: Note attached to copy of Victoria Police: Report of Senior Const. E. L. Howlett Relative to Aboriginal Children: alleged neglect in East Gippsland 14 Sept. 1951.

[62] Victoria 1963a (AWB): 4.

critical of the state of the station, particularly its state of disrepair: 'The general impression was of unkempt buildings and a struggle to bring more land under cultivation.'[63] There were also questions about access to medical care and to education: delays in getting children admitted to hospital were reported, questions were raised about the board's role in the doctor-patient relationship pertaining in one case to a woman's fertility; the teacher reported 'none of the children showed scholastic promise', and he expected to be gone soon anyway. Church attendance was poor and although there was some provision for male sports there was little provision for recreation for young children and nothing for women and girls. Little to nothing was done in domestic training for women (other than that carried out on the matron's house), no cooking instruction or carpentry (much was made over past years of the excellent facilities for the system of handicraft-based education known as 'sloyd'). A critical administrative eye was also cast over the shanty communities outside the station, and the possibility of extending the administration's remit was at least raised here. Some of the issues raised at the 1951 Commonwealth Native Welfare Conference were entertained, among them hostels for access to higher education. On that point the official clergy began to show support. By this time a new term was beginning to find expression. In June 1953, Anna Vroland as representative of the WILPF produced a policy outline in which she urged a 'recognition of the human rights of aborigines'. The document opposed 'the policy of breaking up social and family life' and called for the substitution of 'a "mother and child" welfare system for the present practice of forcibly separating mother and child'. It called for a review of Aboriginal education policy, and 'an immediate anthropological and medical survey by independent experts'. It urged a royal commission with wide terms of reference including a 'review of the administration of justice'.[64] That same year the BPA's inspection report on Lake Tyers noted that as of January 1953 the gates of the station had been locked, with only non-Aboriginal residents holding keys![65]

In November 1954 Anna Vroland, again as representative of the WILPF, wrote to Premier Cain stressing, in the body of the letter, the league's connections with the UN and its intentions of informing the UN's Sub-Committee of the Human Rights Commission of the conditions under which 'the aboriginal people of Victoria' lived.[66] The letter was passed to the long-serving under secretary/vice-chairman of the BPA, L. L. Chapman, who provided the predictable reply:

> The persons referred to are not full-bloods, but of varying shades of colour from half-castes to octoroons, not resident on the Reserve. They are legally white citizens

[63] NAA B356, 92: Sec. BPA 6 May 1953, 'Report of inspection of Lake Tyers 28–30 April 1953'.

[64] NAA B 356, 97: WILPF, Aust. Sec., June 1953, 'Policy recommended by this Section regarding Australian Aborigines'.

[65] NAA B356, 92: Sec. BPA 6 May 1953, 'Report of inspection of Lake Tyers 28–30 April 1953'.

[66] NAA B356, 97: A. Vroland to Hon. John Cain, Premier, 30 Nov. 1954.

> entitled to all the benefits of our various social services and are subject to the same responsibilities as any other citizen, although they do not accept many of the latter.

Again, as was usual, Chapman intimated, in quite contradictory fashion, the enduring problem of racial deficit that lay at the heart of the problem – they were 'white' by law, but 'aboriginal' by nature:

> [T]he crux of the problem is how to make them engage in employment regularly and not sporadically and when they have money, to spend it wisely . . . The only real solution would be to place each individual family in the home of some citizen *who would have power to direct every phase of the life of the family* to ensure they work properly, observe reasonable standards of living, and discharge their proper responsibilities as parents.[67]

As the reader will discover, something akin to this solution would indeed be applied, bringing the Aboriginal family under the tutelage of professional welfare workers using the white family as a template.

By 1955 Chapman was gone, and board minutes following his resignation showed that the new under secretary no longer assumed the role of vice-chairman of the BPA. Anna Vroland wrote to the new under secretary enclosing the WILPF's policy statement. She asked him to discard the previous tenet of past administrations 'that if people are more than half-white (by descent) they ought to be able to fit into the general community without any special help to adapt' and to embrace 'the rising tide of realisation of the urgent need of a real change of attitude'.

SUMMARY

Up to the mid-twentieth century, the Aboriginal child was known and acted upon by an administration, first and foremost as 'aboriginal' and governed via a set of practices quite distinct from those by which the white child was administered. In the main, the Aboriginal person, irrespective of age, embodied a set of inherent racial deficits, moral and intellectual – childishness, laziness, untruthfulness, untrustworthiness, dirtiness, shiftlessness, animal cunning, inability to persevere, sexual promiscuity coupled with an animal fecundity and so on. These moral deficits were articulated by the various officers, government and administrative figures responsible for their control as the reason for a whole people's failure to achieve the necessary so-called ordinary standards of productive white citizenship, and they served to justify increasingly desperate and increasingly draconian attempts to control and to discipline the Victorian Aboriginal population. From the late 1920s, the Board for the Protection of Aborigines and, increasingly, the government of the day, faced sustained criticism of the administration of the Aboriginal population. At first, criticisms of the administration's 'failure' to

67 NAA B356, 97: Under Sec. L. L. Chapman 11 Jan. 1955, note on correspondence A. Vroland, Sec. WILPF to Hon. John Cain, Premier 30 Nov. 1954, emphasis added.

address a purported moral laxity among residents of Lake Tyers station served to reinforce the principle of inherent racial deficit according to which the administration justified its practices. But by the late 1930s a form of criticism, informed by the developmental turn in the psychological sciences, began to voice the so-called Aboriginal problem together with the 'case' of the problem Aboriginal child, as problems made rather than born of racial deficit, and made largely by the conditions imposed by the administration itself.

9

Government and Family

In 1956 the Report of the Advisory Committee on Juvenile Delinquency (Barry Report) recommended the state involve itself directly in the provision and control of institutions for delinquents. Other than its depot at Royal Park, renamed Turana Reception Centre in 1955, the state had long ago handed institutional control of reformatory inmates to voluntary organisations. As shown in Chapter 7 the Barry Report might well be represented as more a moment of arrival, an achievement, than of departure. It was more an exercise in collecting 'received opinion' primarily of state authorities than of anything else, and it did not recommend any radical departure from the course state authorities were already embarking upon. By the time the report appeared psychiatry had already consolidated its authority and the report's proposals for managing the so-called predelinquent and delinquent were a reiteration of logic that already underpinned, in principle, the administration of child welfare and justice. As to practices, prior to the Barry Report the government had already made some moves in reclaiming responsibility for institutions for delinquent girls, as will be shown shortly. Following the Barry Report, the state would gradually reclaim the territory ceded to charitable institutions in the late nineteenth century. Under a new 1960 Social Welfare Act the government embarked on a major overhaul of child welfare and juvenile justice ostensibly in line with the Barry Report.[1] For example, the Barry Report had been critical of overcrowding at Turana because it prevented proper classification of inmates. There was, it claimed, a lack of appropriate expertise and expert assessment 'of the child and his family situation [which was] a necessary preliminary to treatment or discharge', so as to overcome the situation then prevalent in which 'the offender is often returned to the same inadequate family situation which probably led to the delinquency'.[2] A new state-run Allambie Reception Centre began functioning in July 1961 and over the next twelve months of its operations came to replace Turana as the state's main reception centre, leaving sections of Turana available for other purposes. The specifics of the new Social Welfare Act and the administrative overhaul

[1] Victoria Social Welfare Act (No. 6651) 1960. [2] Victoria (J. Barry) 1956c: 59.

that followed will be discussed later in this chapter but by the mid-1950s new avenues were already opening up for the accommodation in state institutions of so-called problem children. This chapter traces the formation of those avenues and explores the governmental aspirations underpinning them.

Shortly after the Barry Report was released another government-commissioned report appeared, Charles McLean's 1957 Report upon the operation of the Aborigines Act 1928 and the Regulations and Orders made thereunder (McLean Report). Evidence presented in earlier chapters showed an enduring reluctance on the part of the administration overseeing children's welfare to accept Aboriginal charges from the Board for the Protection of Aborigines (BPA). As shown in Chapter 8 this reluctance persisted up to the mid-twentieth century with the Children's Welfare Department and Reformatory Schools (CWDRS) arguing the Aboriginal children, girls in particular, were not fit inmates for the existing privately run reformatories. Later sections of this chapter explore the means, via the McLean Report in particular, whereby the Aboriginal child was refigured in such a way that by the early 1960s Aboriginal children too could be mainstreamed along new avenues into new state-run institutions.

By the time of the Barry Report only a handful of institutions were available to the Children's Welfare Department for the placement of reformatory cases. For boys, the Salvation Army's Bayswater (No. 1) Home for younger and No. 2 Home for older boys were available to the department for the disposal of Protestant delinquents and after 1957 Tally Ho Boys' Village concentrated on delinquent cases from Turana. The Morning Star Training Farm would take delinquent Catholic boys. But the Barry Report noted, 'there is need for a male institution to take more hardened delinquent boys'.[3] By that stage the government had already moved to reclaim responsibility for delinquent girls via the establishment of Winlaton training and rehabilitation centre.

In the early 1950s a small number of juvenile delinquents under age seventeen was held by the Penal Department. Some were from the Children's Court, 'usually persistent absconders from institutions who cannot be held elsewhere'; in 1954 there were twenty under age seventeen dealt with by the Penal Department.[4] By then the plight of girls in gaol had received a lot of press attention. In September 1952, the *Argus* called attention to the plight of 'at least 20 girls of 17 and under who have been sent to Pentridge Gaol in the last two years'. The newspaper called for the establishment of a separate reformatory for female delinquents established, in line with contemporary expert opinion, on the principles of the cottage system.[5] Norval Morris, of the Criminology Department at Melbourne University, described Royal Park depot as a 'blocked sink' and the general state of child welfare in Victoria 'medieval'.[6] First, the government established Poplar House, a new section of the

[3] Victoria (J. Barry) 1956c: 60. [4] Victoria (J. Barry) 1956c: 60. [5] *Argus* 1952a, Sept. 6: 2.
[6] *Argus* 1952b, Oct. 1: 5; 1952c, Nov. 24: 7.

depot for senior delinquent girls in transit. At the same time it announced plans for Winlaton, a training and rehabilitation centre for delinquent girls which opened in 1956.[7] In three separate 'cottages the teenage girl requiring rehabilitation and training was to be taught 'how to live as a well-adjusted, self-reliant member of the community', a 'craft or skill', 'how to use her leisure hours' and 'to know and care for herself and, indeed, to care for others later on as a home-maker'.[8] It was perhaps appropriate or with remarkable foresight that the cottages at Winlaton were bestowed (ostensibly) Aboriginal names, as they had quickly filled up with Aboriginal inmates.

By 1958 Superintendent of Aborigines Welfare P. E. Felton had been appointed by a newly constituted Aborigines Welfare Board (AWB). His attention was drawn to Winlaton by the Women's Prison Council which had approached him on the wider matter of female Aboriginal prisoners. Mrs Frost of the Women's Prison Council was concerned at the relatively high proportion of Aboriginal women at Fairlea Women's Prison; 'on her last visit there were six aboriginal women out of a total of thirty-seven prisoners'.[9] By mid-1959 Dr Finney, medical superintendent at Turana and a member of the AWB, was pursuing investigations. By April 1960 the AWB received a report on Winlaton noting two types of girls were admitted: '"protection" cases, over fourteen' composed of 'girls who had become destitute because of family breakdown and the like' and 'court children' composed of two categories, those older than fourteen who had been declared wards of the state, and wards younger than fourteen 'who have proved to be uncontrollable in other (usually Church) institutions'.[10] One of the effects of the establishment of Winlaton then was to lift constraints imposed on the government by private institutions refusing charge of this or that inmate.

Much was made at the time of Winlaton's establishment of its embrace of the cottage system. The description in the report to the AWB however was very much that of a maximum security institution. There was no talk of cottages but of blocks. The three blocks were described as enclosed by a spiked, galvanised iron fence on top of which were rolls of barbed wire. But 'each of the blocks is surrounded by pleasant and spacious lawns which are expertly attended by the gardener'.[11] Girls entered Winlaton via the remand block, characterised by vigorous supervision, and a prison-like routine:

> In the Remand Section the girls are locked into their separate rooms each night and the bedrooms are kept locked during the day. The girls can, if they wish, be admitted to their rooms for a short time following the midday meal. During meal

7 Victoria 1954a (CWDRS): 5. 8 Victoria1957a (CWD): 11.

9 NAA B357, 109: P. E. Felton, Supt. Aborigines Welfare, AWB, 'Report: Women's Prison Council. Problem of female aboriginal prisoners at Fairlea Prison' 25 July 1958.

10 NAA B357, 109: (No author) 'Winlaton Visit' 27 April 1960.

11 NAA B357, 109: (No author) 'Winlaton Visit' 27 April 1960.

> times the door of the dining room is also kept locked, the meals being passed into the dining room from the kitchen servery.[12]

Time spent in the remand section was dependent upon 'her behaviour response (or . . . the number of girls being admitted)'. Girls graduated from greater to lesser austerity as they moved through the three blocks and eventually to a hostel on the grounds as the gateway to release:

> In the Remand Block the only article of furniture in the room is a bed. A wardrobe without a mirror is added to the rooms in the Second Block, while in the Third there is, in addition to the wardrobe, a dressing table with a mirror. The windows in the remand quarters also differ from those in the other two Blocks. In the latter are large windows which can be opened by the girls, while in the former the windows, which contain numerous small panes of glass, are fixed. There is evidence on every hand of past violence in the Remand Block – window panes are missing and a number of panel doors have had holes kicked in them.
>
> In each Block there is a lounge room very sparsely furnished with a number of wooden benches. As well, there is a large recreation room in each building. Each of these rooms was bare during my visit, except that in one there was a table-tennis table leaning against the wall and in another a stack of beds. The girls, I was told, have no recreation equipment because in the part [sic] articles of this nature have been destroyed . . .
>
> Apart from the three blocks described there is a hostel outside the compound, in which a number of girls, who have been discharged to employment, live. I was not shown this building. Two days after my visit a new Remand Block was officially opened. I did not see this building either.[13]

The visitor described the domestic training carried out – which amounted to the inmates' involvement in cooking and serving meals and cleaning the institution. Provisions for formal schooling amounted to a three-teacher government school for those between ages fourteen and sixteen, catering only for primary education, ill resourced and characterised as taking a 'rather dull, formal approach'. Some domestic science and needlework were included but these too were described as 'unimaginative'.[14]

The institution was under the supervision of a social worker – a Miss Pennington – who had declared herself interested in and willing to help the AWB regarding her Aboriginal charges. She had some thoughts, really only 'impressions', she noted, about how the Aboriginal girls differed from the whites:

> The aboriginal girls were lazier than the others. The Lake Tyers girls appear to be the 'heaviest' of all . . . The aborigines had a very poorly developed property sense and helped themselves freely to the possessions of the other girls . . . Stubbornness

12 NAA B357, 109: (No author) 'Winlaton Visit' 27 April 1960.
13 NAA B357, 109: (No author) 'Winlaton Visit' 27 April 1960.
14 NAA B357, 109: (No author) 'Winlaton Visit' 27 April 1960.

was displayed by both European and aboriginal girls but more consistently so by the latter.

... The girls (aborigines) displayed irresponsibility to a marked degree and appeared to have no conception of being members of a team ... Paradoxically, the aboriginal girls appeared to be less able than the whites to withstand group pressure. Also there is a strong desire by the Aborigines to 'cut down' to size any of their group who aspires to rise above the common level ... The girls were stated to be clean in themselves while at the Institution but outside, allowed themselves to drift into unhygienic ways. The sad case of one poor girl was mentioned; she showed an aptitude for peeling the hospital potatoes while seated on the floor.

Pennington thought the Aboriginal girls had a sense of superiority, as 'they commonly referred to whites as "white-rubbish"'. Finally, she ruminated that the Aboriginal girls possessed concepts at variance from those of the whites:

> This is a factor, no doubt, in the thinking of all delinquents of whatever race but Miss Pennington thought that the aboriginal girls were possessed of concepts and values, even different from delinquent white concepts. She tried to explain this by reference to a racial 'hang-over'. It perhaps could be related not to traditional aboriginal values but to the concepts commonly accepted by the aboriginal people of Victoria today – the concepts of a virtually segregated sub-culture.[15]

Yes, and already by 1960 Aborigines were over-represented at Winlaton.

With the 'success' of Winlaton under its belt, the government launched into a wider overhaul of juvenile justice and child welfare. The state government purchased the private children's home Kildonan and established Allambie on the site. It accommodated up to ninety children and by 1962 had overtaken Turana as the state's main reception centre. The residual population at Turana was reclassified. It would continue to accept infants and toddlers in a section devoted to their care, but the role and spaces left vacant through the establishment of Allambie would be filled by a Remand and a Youth Training Centre for boys. By 1962 a temporary Parkside Remand Centre was established in a building at Turana, with work well advanced on the conversion of another building for 'a permanent remand centre for boys between 14 and 17 years'. It would have a capacity for fifty and would 'permit appropriate segregation among the different categories of boys received on remand'.[16] It is clear that Turana provided a function that private reformatory institutions had not, until that date, been able to provide. It was acknowledged that 'the primary objective of the period of detention is rehabilitation', an aim 'more difficult to achieve under maximum security conditions' – hence the 'trend to "open" institutions of various kind'. Morning Star and Bayswater were the only two officially gazetted boys' reformatories at that time and both were privately run. Both would eventually be reclassified as Youth Training Centres according to the

[15] NAA B357, 109: (No author) 'Winlaton Visit' 27 April 1960.
[16] Victoria 1963b (Social Welfare Department [SWD]): 30–31.

dictates of new legislation, but both were farming communities and recognised as problematically open to absconding. One of the explicit functions of the new maximum security section at the state-run Turana was to accommodate 'persistent escapees from open institutions'. At Turana, 'the conditions vary from the maximum security of Poplar House to the family cottage under the supervision of cottage parents'.[17] Hence, from this point, the state did not simply *resume* a role in running reformatories, rejoining those private institutions to which it had delegated responsibility in the late nineteenth century. It *expanded the scope* of that role such that from that point conditions varied to include, under state management an officially designated maximum security institution for the detention of children.

Prior to the Barry Report, the state had also made a small move into establishing its own homes for younger children in the form of family group homes:

> The houses, ten in all, have been specially designed to serve as 'family group' homes . . . The houses, which will each accommodate eight children in the care of a cottage mother, are dotted here and there in the suburbs. The children will live under normal family conditions; they will be part of the local community; they will attend the local school, church, and Sunday school; they will mingle with and will be as other children in the neighbourhood; most importantly they will be in an atmosphere of 'belonging', and they will have the affection and the personal continuing care of their cottage mother, and indeed, where the cottage mother is married and her husband will share his leisure with the children, with a 'dad' also in the picture.[18]

By 1956 the state has also acquired Sutton Grange, 'a large spacious building set in picturesque grounds' at Mornington, with capacity for twenty-five children of both sexes. To this had been added Hillside Boys' Home, opened in mid-1959, 'to care for school-aged boys unacceptable to, or rejected by, voluntary children's homes'.[19]

PROBLEM CHILDREN, PROBLEM FAMILIES

In April 1960 the Bolte government introduced a social welfare bill into Parliament.[20] It amalgamated the Children's Welfare Department and the Penal Department through the formation of three new divisions – a Family Welfare Division, a Youth Welfare Division and a Prisons Division – all under a new Social Welfare Branch. The bill proposed that the new Social Welfare Branch fall under the directorship of the then director of penal services and operate out of the chief secretary's department. There were projected further divisions dealing with research, statistics, training, probation and parole. The Prisons Division would be substantially the existing Penal Department, but the young offender would be

[17] Victoria 1963b (SWD): 30–31. [18] Victoria 1957a (CWD): 8–9. [19] Victoria 1963b (SWD): 14.
[20] Victoria Parliamentary Debates (VPD) Session 1959–60 Vol 259 Legislative Assembly (LA) 6 April 1960: 2389–99.

removed from its remit. The bill, according to Chief Secretary Rylah, was characterised by a 'humane' and 'enlightened' approach. It would 'remove from the care of the Penal Department the young offender up to the age of 21 years'.[21] The young offender would be the responsibility of the Youth Division. On the face of it, this could be interpreted as an enlightened extension of the flexibility afforded young people by the criminal justice system inasmuch as it distinguished them from the 'criminal'. But in other respects the proposed legislation worked to fill a stopgap between the juvenile and adult offender, providing a new seamlessness which did not preclude the presumption of a continuing criminal career.

Recall that, according to the Barry Report, the juvenile delinquent and indeed the pre-delinquent could not be thought or acted upon out of the context from which they were understood to emerge – the family. Maladjusted families made delinquents. Prevention meant targeting the family rather than the child as the site upon which to base practices. The pre-delinquent was to be intercepted in the process of his or her formation by re-adjusting aberrant familial relations. The fully fledged delinquent, however, would require incarceration in a training facility. The state, having long ago ceded responsibility for training the delinquent to private reformatories, was now to resume responsibility for juvenile correctional institutions. Certainly some of those fundamentals made their way into the new bill. As to the state's responsibility, Chief Secretary Rylah noted:

> While we have made considerable progress with the family home proposition, and we see quite a lot of sunlight in the possibility of using existing institutions outside the care of the Department to take many children, we must still face squarely the fact that when it comes to the delinquent child the State must provide facilities which are not available at present ... [B]etter results and cooperation will be obtained from outside institutions if they are not given children who may be described as too difficult; they can handle the difficult ones, but not the very difficult, and the State must face its responsibilities and handle the latter problem.[22]

So, the proposed legislation would pave the way for the state to establish its own youth training centre with its own maximum security section that we saw established at Turana. For the pre-delinquent and its attendant problem family, the Department of *Children's* Welfare would disappear, replaced by a Division of *Family* Welfare. Rylah commented at one stage, 'In many cases the home is in need of greater attention than the child':

> I wish to mention an important part of the Department's work, namely, the keeping of the family together and preventing the children from becoming wards of the State at all. This is effected by financial assistance to the family, guidance to the family, and education of the parents in their obligations, and I firmly believe that it should be in the forefront of our minds in dealing with this problem. It is because of my

[21] VPD Session 1959–60 Vol 259 LA 6 April 1960: 2390.
[22] VPD Session 1959–60 Vol 259 LA 6 June 1960: 2392.

> earnest belief in the family unit as the foundation of our social structure that one division of the proposed new Social Welfare Branch is to be called the Family Welfare Division. This division will develop preventive work with families in an endeavour to maintain the family unit rather than wait until the stage is reached where the children have to be removed for care and protection.

As to the definitions of 'delinquent' and 'non-delinquent', Rylah explained: 'The position will be that any child under the age of fourteen years will not be regarded by the Children's Court as delinquent but rather as being in need of care and protection.'[23] Under the new arrangement of 'Family', 'Youth' and 'Prisons' divisions no administrative body had 'children' as its specified discrete responsibility. To know and to govern the child meant knowing and governing the family.

The resultant legislation would provide greater ease of entry of children into both 'care and protection' and correction. That much Rylah argued himself. The bill was necessary because 'there has been in the last four years an increasing number of children committed to the care of the Children's Welfare Department, either for delinquency or in need of care and protection'. The reasons, Rylah argued, were threefold: an increasing population, greater vigilance and efficiency on the part of police and social welfare services and an 'unfortunate increase in juvenile delinquency'.[24] Nowhere did Rylah name Aboriginal children or Aboriginal families in his speech. He did, however, make a pointed reference to them in the context of listing the factors that made the legislation imperative:

> I again emphasise the fact that . . . we are, owing to the vigilance and efficiency of members of the Police Force and others, finding in our care children who have only accidently come to the State of Victoria. It is obvious from the facts that have been brought to the notice of the Department that whether they come from Victoria, New South Wales, South Australia or anywhere else, we could not allow them to live under the conditions under which they were living on the banks of the River Murray and other streams in Victoria.[25]

If we are to understand the means by which Aboriginal children were governed, we need to look beyond the various acts and regulations that addressed, specifically, the Aboriginal population. Seemingly unrelated or indirectly related acts such as the Social Welfare Act could be manipulated to bring about racialised outcomes. Rylah's allusion to those 'living on the banks of the Murray and other streams' was a reference to the problem of unauthorised settlements of Aborigines, in particular on the river banks between the northern towns of Shepparton and Mooroopna that new 1957–58 Aborigines Acts and their attendant regulations had largely failed to bring under control. A bill which eased the way for problem children from problem families into both care and correction could well help.

23 VPD Session 1959–60 Vol 259 LA 6 April 1960: 2395.
24 VPD Session 1959–60 Vol 259 LA 6 April 1960: 2390–91.
25 VPD Session 1959–60 Vol 259 LA 6 April 1960: 2391.

The 1951 report, 'The Dark Children of East Gippsland' by Anna Vroland and the Women's International League for Peace and Freedom, though it did not include the river bank camps in the north of the state, firmed up the picture of appalling conditions of Aboriginal camps beyond Lake Tyers. As shown in the previous chapter, it drew particular attention to the health and welfare of children. Vroland's husband, A. W. Vroland, included the Shepparton-Mooroopna camps in his account in 1953 of the conditions confronting those living off-station across the state.[26] By 1953 the board's own inspection reports were calling for 'official interest' to be shown to those living under 'shanty' conditions, in part attributable, the report argued, to the board's own 'conflicting policies, of dispersal and assimilation on the one hand and insistence on residence on the Station as the prime qualification for protection and assistance on the other'. The report continued:

> In shelters constructed from the contents of some nearby rubbish tip which is all that is available to many of them, they exist for a while in increasingly unhygienic conditions to the detriment of their health and morals and to the annoyance of the surrounding white community. The children become dirty and unhealthy and consequently unwelcome at school. Eventually there is no alternative but to admit them to Lake Tyers to be rehabilitated.[27]

In the light of the BPA's refusal to own any responsibility beyond Lake Tyers Station and those few authorised residents on Framlingham Reserve, various parties had formed various alliances to deal with fringe communities in their districts. Organisations such as the Save the Children Fund began to lobby the government. By the mid-1950s the fund was coordinating its activities with other agencies including shire authorities and the police, to establish at least rudimentary welfare services in areas including the Murray-Goulburn river camps and the Dimboola-Antwerp communities. In the Dimboola-Antwerp area the fund had 'provided a house for one family and temporary small dwellings for two'.[28] At Robinvale the fund was running a kindergarten for Aboriginal children. At Mooroopna it had established a 'Welfare Hut' built among the campers on an area known as Daish's paddock with the help of the local New Deal committee and out of which operated a preschool centre and kindergarten, run by Sister Turner:

> Except for people like Sister Turner, of Mooroopna, and her helpers, the castes would be in a worse state than they are now. She and her helpers provide milk, clothes and food, and are interested in their welfare. When any children are being badly treated or neglected or ill fed, she comes to the police, who help where we can. Over the past two weeks we have had two half caste children, a boy of 12 years

26 NAA B356, 97: A. W. Vroland, 'Aboriginal Problems: Theory and Practice. Address in Australian Church Sunday January 25th, 1953', attached to correspondence A. W. Vroland to Chief Secretary (Galvin) 1 Feb. 1953.

27 NAA B356, 92: 'Report of inspection of Lake Tyers 28–30 April 1953', 6 May 1953.

28 NAA B408, 7: Hon. Sec., Dimboola Save the Children Fund Committee to A. Mansell MLC, 20 Feb. 1957.

and a baby girl of 10 weeks, committed to the care of the Children's Welfare Department. Other families are now under our supervision and probably more children will be committed to the care of that department.[29]

Another body becoming increasingly active in the field was the Apex Club. By 1955 the Apex Club had undertaken an Australia-wide fact-finding exercise as a prelude to its adoption of Aboriginal welfare as the focus of its National Service Scheme and had circularised its members accordingly and informed the chief secretary of its intentions.[30] The club prided itself on its social scientific approach: 'given that the problem of Aboriginal welfare is to be viewed as a "social disease" we have put ourselves in a Medical Practitioner's shoes':

Firstly – we establish the case history
Secondly – we make examinations of the patients in the light of the history established
Next – we make a diagnosis
Finally – we prescribe and endeavour to administer treatment
AT THE MOMENT . . . WE ARE AT STAGE ONE ONLY

A series of questions to Apex members followed regarding 'the "patient" in your areas', for example: 'How many abo. children (%) have primary education?'[31]

One extraordinary outcome of the amalgamation of shire authorities and voluntary organisations, independent of official state government involvement, was the Swan Hill District Native Children's Recreation Centre. Inasmuch as the title conjures up a playground it is a misnomer. Melbourne's *Age* newspaper noted a couple of years after its establishment that this 'new settlement has been described as the most complete in Australia'.[32] The centre was the brainchild of one Sergeant Feldtmann, a Victorian police officer, though the centre itself was across the Murray River state boundary, on its New South Wales (NSW) bank. *Dawn* magazine, the propaganda vehicle for the NSW Aborigines Welfare Board, described the Swan Hill centre as an initiative that grew out of white people's concerns over the number of Aborigines 'living in humpies and other primitive "makeshifts" on the banks of the Murray'. The plan was for a building divided into three rooms, one a well-equipped club room:

The two other rooms will be used as bedrooms and will be furnished with new furniture, good floor coverings, etc. They will be used by the children only and will be under the supervision of a responsible person. The parents of the children live in

[29] NAA B408, 4: Victoria Police (Sen Const. G. S. Haag, Mooroopna), 'Attached request for report upon the Administration of the Act and Regulations relating to Aboriginal welfare in Victoria and how such may concern those resident in the Mooroopna area', 23 March 1956.

[30] NAA B408, 9: A. G. Holden, Apex Club, Morwell to A. G. Rylah, Chief Secretary, 3 Nov. 1955.

[31] NAA B408, 9: Association of Apex Clubs, Australia. National Service Scheme 1955–57. Club Bulletin No. 2. 14 Sept. 1955; Press clipping, 'Apex towns to "adopt" aborigines', *Maryborough Advertiser* 27 June 1956.

[32] *Age* 1955, Dec. 24: 3.

> full view of the building whose doors face the 'dwellings' in which the parents live in very close proximity.[33]

So, in fact, the centre in its conception and construction was not so very different from arrangements in the early mission days of the previous century, according to which children lived in separate children's houses or dormitories under white supervision, as shown in Chapter 4. A newspaper used 'dormitories' in its description of the Swan Hill centre:

> Two aborigines with eight children living in a small 'humpy' made of bags and corrugated iron sheets gave a policeman in Swan Hill an idea. As a result, the family, with twenty other members of an aboriginal community living near Swan Hill, are today housed in cottages and dormitories taking only three children per room.[34]

The occasion of this press report was an award – the Victorian Chief Commissioner's Certificate – bestowed upon Feldtmann for his work. The centre certainly won the approval of the Victorian police, although it was not in his *official* capacity as Victorian police officer that Feldtmann 'supervised' the centre. The governor of Victoria and his wife had their photographs taken visiting the centre. It had approval and material support of the *New South Wales* AWB, which provided the materials for the erection of two cottages. There was no mention of the centre in the reports, records of meetings or correspondences of the Victorian BPA. Of course, according to the Victorian BPA, the centre catered for a group it defined as other than Aboriginal.

The sign at the front gate of the Swan Hill centre read 'No unauthorised person allowed'.[35] This raises the question of authority: how was control or supervision of the settlement authorised? A Victorian policeman headed a voluntary committee that supervised separate accommodations, just over the state border, for Aboriginal adults and children. Feldtmann's own description had it that after completion of the centre, 'the whole area was fenced in, and the aboriginal inhabitants were left wholly in charge of the settlement under my supervision'.[36] The centre remained under the watchful eye of Sergeant Feldtmann after his retirement from the police force and well into the 1960s, but more relevant to present discussion it came to the attention of both McLean and, following his inquiry, the newly constituted Victorian Aborigines Welfare Board.

SLUM CLEARANCES

By early 1956 McLean's inquiries got underway. In a procedure reminiscent of the 1860s, when the BPA surveyed leading citizens in the new state, McLean requested reports from interested members of the public. He also requested responses to

33 *Dawn* 1953: 6. 34 *Age* 1955, Dec. 24: 3. 35 *Dawn* 1956: Cover photograph.
36 NAA B408, 4: Victoria Police (Sgt A. H. Feldtmann, Swan Hill), 'Evidence for the Board of Enquiry into the Aborigines Act', 22 March 1956.

particular questions, via Chief Commissioner of Police S. H. Porter, of each of the eighteen police districts, both country and metropolitan, across the state.[37] A substantial return came from Sergeant Feldtmann, outlining the aspirations, substance and success of the Swan Hill centre.[38] The centre would feature favourably in McLean's eventual report. McLean considered housing the lynchpin for a successful overhaul of the administration in line with a policy of assimilation. He advocated a scheme similar to that already in place in NSW and likely to involve the Housing Commission in the supply of housing but he recommended that unlike the NSW system the Housing Commission should not be involved in the administration of the scheme.[39]

What seemed to most attract McLean to the Swan Hill centre was the template for close supervision offered by this combination of policeman-cum-philanthropist. McLean advised against anything more than 'two, or at most three, houses for aborigines either adjoining or in close proximity, in town areas'. But the newly constituted AWB did not, in its first foray into the provision of housing, adhere to this advice. The first settlement at Mooroopna would consist of ten cottages on land at some distance from town. As plans for this settlement took shape, the Housing Commission's Slum Research Officer J. H. Davey, appointed to the AWB as nominee of the Ministry of Housing, visited the Swan Hill centre: 'The Sergeant took the party over the centre and notes, sketches and photos of the buildings thereon were taken by Mr Patterson [of the Commission's architectural staff]. Further discussions with the Sergeant took place on Thursday morning before departure to Mooroopna.'[40]

Twelve months after the official opening at Mooroopna of the first of the Victorian government's Aboriginal housing settlements (named Rumbalara), it was noted 'rigid supervision' of these new communities was still needed and here reference was made again to the Swan Hill Centre: 'The private project at Swan Hill which Sergeant Feldtmann, with the assistance of a local committee, has been instrumental in establishing, consists of a settlement of four or five houses and, due to the supervision of the police sergeant, things have gone along very smoothly.'[41]

Prior to McLean launching his inquiries, various agencies including the police, voluntary organisations and committees and local government authorities had formed various alliances to deal with the perceived problem of the formation of unofficial and unregulated Aboriginal camps, including those in the Murray-Goulburn basin. The Rodney Shire Council, under which the town of Mooroopna fell, showed itself to be particularly impatient with state government inactivity. It had begun to communicate with state authorities beyond the bounds of

37 NAA B408, 4: Attachment to correspondence C. McLean to S. H. Porter, Chief Commissioner of Police, 27 Feb. 1956.

38 NAA B408, 4: Victoria Police (Sgt A. H. Feldtmann, Swan Hill) 'Evidence for the Board of Enquiry into the Aborigines Act', 22 March 1956.

39 Victoria (C. McLean) 1957b: 17–18.

40 NAA B357, 54: J. H. Davey, Slum Research Officer, Aboriginal Housing – Mooroopna, 8 Oct. 1957.

41 VPD Session 1958–59 Vol 257 LA 21 April 1959: 3209–11.

the chief secretary's department over a plan to have granted some form of 'permissive occupancy' of Crown land for a settlement. The plan was for a new area to be supplied with water and electricity (paid for by occupants) and 'a communal block of showers, lavatories and washing troughs'. The shire also requested that the minister for housing be approached to 'give permission to build sub-standard houses in the area by the people themselves'.[42] One can imagine the unease the term sub-standard might have caused. The envisaged houses were to be exempted from the building standards of the time. It was quickly replaced by the terms 'simple houses' or 'minimum requirement housing', although as it turned out 'sub-standard' was the more accurate descriptor of the buildings that eventuated and the original choice of terminology reflected an understanding that the housing needs of this and like communities of 'fringe-dwellers' in various locations across country Victoria were different from the standard needs of the non-Aboriginal population.[43]

About thirty Aboriginal families were living on a public reserve on the river bank under 'appalling conditions' and on a nearby site on higher land used as a rubbish tip (Daish's paddock). A parliamentarian P. V. Feltham recalled an earlier promise from the former minister for health that five houses would be allotted every year 'to aborigines out of a pool of housing estate houses' – an undertaking that had not been kept and that regardless was, according to Feltham, an ill-conceived plan: 'The process of assimilating the aborigines into Housing Commission houses would be a protracted one and has some unsatisfactory features. Their present conditions call for immediate relief.' Feltham explained that the New Deal Committee advised that the state provide no more than the land, electricity, water, 'communal ablution blocks and sanitary conveniences', and that the committee itself would manage the building of 'minimum requirement' housing with which municipal and health authorities would be happy, but a 'class of building' which would 'not necessarily conform to the requirements of the Housing Society'. From these, Aboriginal families 'could be drafted in due course into [Public Housing] Commission houses'. The proposal, Feltham noted, had been met with strong opposition from adjacent landowners, strongest from the Shepparton Pear Packing Company which had a factory nearby.[44] In the meantime, all hell broke loose among the non-Aboriginal residents of nearby townships over the 'use of Daish's paddock and river bank aboriginals'. Speakers at public meetings 'slated the "filthy," "unhygienic," "disgraceful," and "Communist breeding" conditions on Daish's paddock and in some cases condemned the local municipal bodies for their tolerance of a vice ridden and degrading environment'.[45] So in 1956, prior to the release of McLean's report, plans

[42] PROV VPRS 11563/P/0001 Unit 411 Item 58/475: J. E. Downer to P. V. Feltham 14 Aug. 1955.

[43] NAA B357, 54: T. N. Garnet, Acting Sec. AWB to Sec. Housing Commission 21 Nov. 1957.

[44] PROV VPRS 11563/P/0001 Unit 411 Item 58/475: P. V. Feltham to the Minister for Lands 23 Aug. 1955.

[45] PROV VPRS 11563/P0001. Unit 411 Item 58/475: Press clipping, 'River Bank Squalor Shocks Mooroopna Meeting', dated 16 Nov. 1955. Publication unknown, attached to correspondence P. V. Feltham (MLC, Northern Province) to Minister for Lands 21 Nov. 1955.

were submitted for a proposed subdivision of twenty-two rowed blocks.[46] Once again, it was envisaged that government and police would be supervising the whole operation. It is worth noting that up to this point the BPA had no official involvement in the scheme, having repeatedly declared the subjects of the scheme beyond its jurisdiction or responsibility (they were 'of aboriginal blood', but not *Aborigines*). The BPA nevertheless was willing to give support to the objections of the pear-packing company whose premises abutted the proposed settlement and which of course had a vested interest in an influx of cheap seasonal labour for the picking and packing seasons.

T. N. Garnet, who was then secretary of the BPA and had conducted a far-reaching study of the arrangements for oversight of Aboriginal peoples in New South Wales, wrote on behalf of the BPA to the secretary of the Forest Commission, noting the existence of the local 'committee of citizens' at Mooroopna, formed 'to take an interest in improving the living conditions of about 150 people of aboriginal blood camped on the river bank and at other places between Shepparton and Mooroopna'.[47]

MCLEAN'S SURVEY OF ABORIGINES

By the beginning of 1956 McLean had begun to launch his inquiry. But it was constituted in what must have been perceived by the chief secretary's department as a context alarmingly close to getting out of hand. Shire authorities had all but completed a deal involving the Ministry of Lands and the Forestry Commission and anticipating the involvement of the Housing Commission. An institution-like settlement for the accommodation of children had cropped up near Swan Hill under the unofficial authority of a local Victorian policeman. Meanwhile the public conscience had been pricked and public outrage had been aroused by reports of vice and squalor and the government had to meet demands for action from groups as diverse as the Country Women's Association and the Building Workers' Industrial Union. It was clear from the evidence that the Committee of Inquiry under McLean was launched as the first tactic in an overall strategy of containment. Its primary job may have been to contain the reported unruliness of the camps themselves but from the perspective of the chief secretary's department, an increasingly unruly number of players in the field of Aboriginal welfare also needed containing. That this was one of the anticipated roles of the inquiry is borne out by the fact that, post-McLean and with a new act in operation and a new Aborigines Welfare Board constituted, one of the first and ongoing roles assigned Superintendent of Aborigines Welfare P. E. Felton (an executive officer of the AWB) was to attempt to bring the various welfare

46 PROV VPRS 11563/P/0001 Unit 411 Item 58/475: Rodney Shire Engineer to Chairman Forestry Commission 22 June 1956.

47 PROV VPRS 11563/P/0001 Unit 411 Item 58/475: T. N. Garnet, Sec. BPA to Sec. Forest Commission of Victoria 18 Sept. 1956.

agencies in line and in tandem with the government's agenda. However, in early 1959 Felton reported to the AWB that his attempts to establish common ground among 'representatives of various aboriginal welfare bodies' had been a failure'.[48]

McLean's final report would draw on written submissions from a variety of government and non-government agencies and individuals. He also drew upon information gathered from his own fact-finding trips. Various comments and observations by McLean on his visits to camps and off-station Aboriginal residences reveal that relevant authorities had sometimes failed to give due attention to connecting Aborigines to social service or legal entitlements, and that his visit prompted some action in that respect. If he did not overtly admonish officials, McLean at least alerted them to the need to do their job. But McLean spent most of his time interviewing non-Aborigines; he inscribed in his notes *their* attitudes or prejudices or opinions without any clear sense to the reader that he maintained a critical distance from what he was told or that what he was told was taken as anything other than fact.

McLean had been given the job of addressing five specific subjects: His terms of reference included first, a working definition – 'those who are believed to be of not less than one-fourth part aboriginal blood' – with which McLean was to ascertain the 'number, distribution, and living conditions', including the employment status and prospects of Victorian Aborigines. Second, he was to ascertain Aborigines' capacities 'to maintain themselves and their families according to the general standards of the Victorian community'. Third, McLean was to inquire into the following:

The factors, if any, which militate against the absorption of people of aboriginal blood into the general community distinguishing between those which –

i) are peculiar to such people
ii) arise from the attitude of white citizens.

Finally he was to consider the future, if any, of Lake Tyers station and whether a discrete body for the administration of Aborigines was required, and if so 'what persons or classes should be deemed aboriginal for the purpose of the system'.

In late February 1956 McLean wrote to each of the superintendents of the state's seventeen police districts requesting a response to the first three terms of reference which he relayed word-for-word. The superintendents in turn passed the request onto local officers in the various sub-districts. First, there was the nonsensical mathematical precision with which police were to ascertain numbers and distribution 'of those who are believed to be of not less than one-fourth part aboriginal blood'. Upon this 'belief' officers were to hang a series of judgements and opinions as to capabilities, capacities and peculiarities – all relative to the central but unelaborated 'general standards of the Victorian community'.[49] The terms of reference may

48 NAA B314, 9: Minutes of Meeting of BPA 11 Feb. 1959.

49 NAA B408, 4: Attachment to correspondence C. McLean to S. H. Porter, Chief Commissioner of Police 27 Feb. 1956.

have been vague and imprecise, but in another respect they were built on firm limitations. McLean's inquiries allowed only a narrow prescription of the causal factors which 'militate against absorption'. Note the choices: either factors 'peculiar' to Aborigines *or* the 'attitudes' of 'white *citizens*' (emphasis added) – which rather left *government* or, for that matter, plain old poverty, outside the frame of reference in terms of contributory responsibility for the problematic situation under investigation. So, here was quite a challenge for the local police constable – but not an unfamiliar one. As shown in previous chapters the BPA had traditionally relied for many decades on the local police officers' knowledge of Aborigines, including that provided by police serving as officers of the board in the form of local guardians. The office of the last remaining local guardian, at Framlingham, had only been made redundant in the previous decade. More generally the board had long used the local constabulary to report on the deservedness or otherwise of this or that candidate for relief, and on population numbers, or indeed, in the more recent past, the circumstances and conditions of this or that whole community. Recall from the previous chapter Constable Howlett's extensive 1951 report, at the request of the BPA, on possible cases of child neglect in East Gippsland following the release of a report by its critics.

There was a surprising number of replies from country districts that reported no Aborigines: *no* 'full blood to quarter caste aboriginal persons', 'no experience of such persons', 'no Aborigines residing in this District thus there is no call for Welfare Work in that sphere', 'no persons of aboriginal blood under review residing permanently in this section of the state' and 'Inquiries ... have failed to locate any aboriginal natives.' Not so surprising were the number of returns from the suburban areas reporting no Aborigines and no knowledge of the matter. Other police reported no Aborigines in their areas but were keen, nevertheless, to offer their opinion on the capacities and capabilities of Aboriginal people. As to their capacities to measure up to the general standards of the white community, officers from country areas with fringe camps and where seasonal workers congregated, were generally adamant that 'these people' or 'the aborigine' sat below the standard of what was variously inscribed as 'Victorian people' or 'the ordinary community' and were incapable of reaching it. Here is the summary received from Northern Victoria, the area incorporating many of the fringe camps: 'The very great majority of people of aboriginal blood are incapable of maintaining themselves and their families according to the general standards of the Victorian community.'[50] Some officers added explanations of racial heredity to these expressions of character. There was a fair sprinkling of allusions to heredity. Sergeant Kennedy of Mildura (but formerly of Mooroopna) provided a Darwinist-infused anthropological account:

[50] NAA B408, 4: Supt A. Donnelly, Shepparton, to Chairman, Aboriginal Welfare Board of Inquiry 27 March 1956.

> The aboriginal was only a hunter, he never worked and when not hunting lay around the camp. He was never a builder, as being a hunter he was always on the move and his shelters were only of the crudest that could be built. This coupled with the fact that the whites who first associated and still associate with these people of aboriginal stock, were people of poor character, lazy and shiftless. This is the stock from which the present generation of half-castes come and it can be seen that there is nothing hereditary to fit them into the present day life. Their absenteeism from work and laziness probably comes [sic] from their wanderlust which was a 'walk-about' with their aboriginal ancestors.[51]

Others (several officers) used the term 'inferiority complex' which, though it might sound like a more modern concession to the influence of environmental factors on the development of the psyche, was not in fact proffered as such. The superintendent of A District, incorporating the inner-Melbourne suburb of Fitzroy, named, as one of the factors peculiar to Aborigines, and militating against absorption, 'Inferiority complex due no doubt to unfortunately having aboriginal blood in their veins.'[52]

It is difficult to tell how much McLean set store by these replies. As will be shown, he would have other experts to feed the inquiry particulars regarding the IQ and educability of Aborigines. The final report displayed a decided shift away on McLean's part from the logic of heredity and towards that of developmental psychology – a shift away but not an outright rejection. Traits such as 'unreliability' and 'irresponsibility' previously connected to colour or bloodlines were certainly inscribed in the report as characteristic of Aborigines, but for the most part these traits were to be understood as grounded in environmental factors which had led to the development of an Aboriginal psychology:

> Some of the characteristics militating against economic progress to which I have referred, such as lack of thought for tomorrow, have a racial or traditional origin, but I have no doubt that many of them are at least fostered to some extent by two principal factors. Firstly, deficient education and mental training – the unreliability and irresponsibility of the mentally backward is well recognised. Secondly, the psychological effect of their environment, with a consciousness of being regarded as outcasts in the community. Both tend to develop in them an acceptance of their position as an 'inferior' race, leading to apathy and lack of initiative. Seeing no hope for the future, they live for the present, and to some extent that attitude is at least understandable.[53]

As to that part of the exercise that was about determining numbers and distribution of those 'believed to be of not less than one fourth part aboriginal

[51] NAA B408, 4: Victoria Police (Sgt F. T. Kennedy, Mildura) 'Attached file re Board of Inquiry into Aborigines Act etc.', 8 April 1956.

[52] NAA B408, 4: Victoria Police (Supt Hutchinson A District 24 May 1956, Addendum to Sgt Biddington, Fitzroy), 'Aboriginals in the Fitzroy Sub District' 20 April 1956.

[53] Victoria (C. McLean) 1957b: 10.

blood', an important thing to note about the exercise is that it underscored the very liquid contours of an administrative category of being, still in the process of its (re)formation. Certainly those who were being counted were not those who once counted as Aborigines. A survey produced by Sergeant Feldtmann in August 1955, and which made its way into McLean's papers, gave a total of 796 Aboriginal persons in Victoria.[54] But these, still, were only *possibly* to be counted, officially, as Aborigines. In the process of McLean's inquiries numbers were disputed, failed to tally, were crossed out and re-entered. Was it the subjects of the count who had shifted, as many an officer complained they *would* do – more than one officer noted with annoyance the difficulty of counting people who moved in and out of their jurisdiction as seasonal work and/or their ostensible wanderlust dictated. Alternatively, was it the criteria that shifted from count to count? McLean would note in his final report that the figures provided to him needed qualification as they included 'some who were fairly obviously of less than one fourth aboriginal blood'.[55] McLean would finally decide that those who were counted, but who were outside the initial criterion of 'not less than one fourth aboriginal blood', were just as relevant to the inquiry, given they were 'brought up by their mothers in aboriginal communities' and were 'generally regarded, by themselves and others, as aborigines' and hence 'present the same problem'.[56]

But there was something else beyond the problem of who should count and how to count them – another kind of instability that became evident through this police survey. It has been noted previously that up to and through most of the first half of the twentieth century, Aboriginal children were known and acted upon, first and foremost as *Aboriginal*. Until the mid-twentieth century they were only reluctantly thought of by children's welfare authorities and related agencies as appropriate inmates of institutions for white children. There was an earlier instance, in 1951, when the BPA called upon the services of the police to check reports of unsatisfactory conditions for 'dark children' of East Gippsland. Constable Howlett, of Orbost, was sent to check for possible cases of neglect. Recall from the previous chapter his conclusion that the 'mere fact of crude living conditions' did not constitute grounds for committing a child to the CWD, and to do so would have lessened 'the influence ... held by the police over these people'. Besides, the children 'appeared well fed and happy'. And no action was taken. There was nothing to suggest conditions for Aboriginal people had changed for the better or worse at Orbost. But now in 1956, that same officer, Constable Howlett, reported to McLean on conditions in that same area, 'the women and children are covered with white sores which I believe are some form of scabies caused by filth'. Their living conditions

54 NAA B408, 4: Victoria Police (Sgt R. Feldtmann, Swan Hill), 'Survey of Aborigines of Various Centres in Victoria (Excluding Lake Tyers)', Aug. 1955.

55 Victoria (C. McLean) 1957b: 6.

56 Victoria (C. McLean) 1957b: 6.

'have to be inspected to be appreciated'.[57] It is unlikely, had he included such a description in 1951, he could have justified the conclusion he reached then.

So in the midst of McLean's inquiries and in the context in which it was launched, it had become increasingly difficult to argue as Constable Howlett had argued only a few years earlier, that Aboriginal children should be excluded from mainstream child welfare practices. Mclean mentioned in his final report that 'shortly after my visit there, twenty-four of the younger children were, at the instance of the police, taken from these "homes" and committed to the care of the Children's Welfare Department'.[58] A long-entrenched reluctance to recognise the Aboriginal child as the proper subject of formal (white) child welfare practices would seem to be shifting.

THE PSYCHOLOGIST AND THE ABORIGINES

Submissions to McLean's inquiry by organisations and individuals were a pretty mixed bag. The executive of the Liberal and Country Party expressed an interest in breeding out the 'genetic patterns' that supposedly determined the 'peculiar characteristics that distinguish the Aboriginal': administrative policy, it argued, should be directed to encouraging the those of mixed blood to move out of the areas of partial segregation where opportunity existed to change the physical type by the re-infusion of European characteristics.[59] McLean himself nudged pretty close in his final report to this notion of the breeding in and breeding out of undesirable characteristics. On the other hand a Mr and Mrs Margaret and Percy Holmes of Seymour claimed 'prejudice in the minds of White People against Mixed Bloods' must be tackled first:

> The widespread belief that Moral And Cultural background and poor Educational ability is [sic] a product of Biological Inheritance, when in truth the Social Inheritance which we Whites could so very easily change for them is so overwhelming that few of us would be likely to overcome it ourselves if we had a really unfavourable start to life.[60]

Two pieces of work which found their way to McLean's desk are of particular note. Both were from psychologists. Neither piece was commissioned by McLean and in both instances McLean was alerted by a third party as to their existence. One was from Keith Cathcart, psychologist at the Mental Hygiene Authority's Travancore Clinic and the other from J. R. Hall of the Psychology and Guidance Branch of the Education Department.

57 NAA B408, 4: Victoria Police (Sen. Const. D. K. Downie, Orbost), 'Persons of aboriginal descent residing in or frequenting Orbost', 16 March 1956.

58 Victoria (C. McLean) 1957b: 7.

59 NAA B 408, 6: Liberal and Country Party (undated), 'Aborigines or Those People of Mixed Descent. For Presentation to the Hon. the Chief Secretary'.

60 NAA B408, 9: Mr & Mrs P. Holmes to Chairman, Aborigines Welfare Board [sic: BPA] 23 Feb. 1956.

In September 1954 Hall undertook a survey of children at the Framlingham school, primarily carrying out intelligence tests.[61] Framlingham school, along with that at Lake Tyers, was run by the Education Department as a state school. Framlingham was still designated a reserve and hence an authorised place of residence for a number of people deemed Aborigines but it was also the unauthorised place of residence for a number deemed quadroons and octoroons (i.e. according to the BPA, non-Aborigines) living in various 'camps' and 'shacks' in and around the reserve. Together, their children formed the population of Framlingham State School pupils. Among McLean's papers are Hall's own record of his work at Framlingham and McLean's rough notes pertaining to that record. McLean noted of Hall's work that 'owing to poorness of oral expression limited vocabulary of children, the ordinary tests were no good. Therefore didn't use some of the verbal tests but did use some of the performance scales.'[62] The outcome of Hall's survey was that, according to McLean's notes 'the spread of results very similar to white children'. So, if not intelligence levels, where did the problem lie? McLean's notes again:

> Factors militating against progress – if they see themselves as failures no job prospects they have no initiative – parents unskilled occupations – & they are timid, insecure, shy. No cultural levels in homes. 'Psycho. Climate' of homes is bad. Children absorb this atmosphere from their environment & contacts, which in normal cases are their parents.[63]

And in the body of Hall's record:

> The influence of the depressed home environment of these children is apparent at school in two ways – one physical, one psychological. Physically the children are unclean in their persons and in their dress, though this is less true of some than of others. In view of the reported absence of laundry and bathroom facilities in their homes, the efforts being made by the school will have only limited success. The psychological effect of their background is shown in their marked shyness and timidity, which, though it results in a school which is easy to handle, is a definite social handicap and a barrier to effective learning.[64]

[61] NAA B408, 4: Victoria Police: Statement of G. T. Atkinson, Schoolteacher, Framlingham Settlement, Purnim, 23 March 1956; NAA B408, 9: Psychology Branch, Education Department. State School No. 4532, Framlingham Settlement. Report of Special Survey. Sept. 1954.

[62] NAA B408, 9: Unsigned notes (McLean) 17 July 1956, 'J. R. Hall – Psychologist & Guidance Officer Education Department, 17 July 56' attached to report 'Psychology Branch, Education Department. State School No. 4532, Framlingham Settlement. Report of Special Survey. September 1954.'

[63] NAA B408, 9: Unsigned notes (McLean) 17 July 1956, 'J. R. Hall – Psychologist & Guidance Officer Education Department, 17 July 56' attached to report 'Psychology Branch, Education Department. State School No. 4532, Framlingham Settlement. Report of Special Survey. September 1954.'

[64] NAA B408, 9: Psychology Branch, Education Department. State School No. 4532, Framlingham Settlement. Report of Special Survey. Sept. 1954.

Hall concluded with some general advice about encouraging 'the exercise of initiative and of expression' and 'personally encouraging worthwhile effort'.[65] But McLean's notes on Hall's record end on a different note:

> Educn Dept has (1) sixty odd 'opportunity classes' mostly in Melb, but in some country places. (2) About 8 'Remedial centres' in Melb, Ballarat + 1 Bendigo, for normal, but educationally retarded for various reasons, not dullness. Also special schools for mentally defective in Melb, B'rat, B'go. There are also schools run by Mental Hygiene Dept. Admission to (1) and (2) is by recommendation of trained psychologist.[66]

Cathcart also produced a record of testing carried out on Aboriginal children attending a state school, this time in Robinvale and at the behest of the Save the Children Fund. Again, informed of its existence, McLean requested a report from Cathcart which arrived in July 1956.[67] From a list of twenty-six children, thirteen children between ages five and fourteen, from five homes, were examined. Cathcart mentioned, specifically, intelligence tests. His record did not provide any IQ scores as such, although he noted that individual results were to be forwarded by Dr Trood. Instead, Cathcart used the categories 'very dull', 'dull', 'dull-normal', 'low normal' and 'normal'. Only two of the children were pronounced 'normal', the rest inhabiting the 'very dull' to 'low normal' range, with the exception of one for whom testing was suspended on account of the 'disturbed' attitude of the child. On the record Cathcart admitted: 'The use of intelligence tests was rendered, to some extent, unreliable by the attitude of the children to a stranger', which, he noted, though a factor in all psychological testing, was 'extreme' among this cohort. So, the results of the intelligence tests were dubious and Cathcart admitted longer and periodical testing was required.

But at the same time as the children's lack of co-operation with him was underscored to caution against the reliability of the results pertaining to intelligence, that same behaviour was used to help confirm diagnoses on his part of 'emotional disturbance', 'maladjustment' and 'inadequate personalities'. The latter was a diagnosis of the *parents* of one of the children, quite remarkable given that by Cathcart's own account, 'No house was visited, and the only contact with families was when one of the mothers attended with a child to be examined, and later when Mrs Ostmeier [welfare worker, Save the Children Fund] gave Dr Trood and myself the opportunity of visiting a Parents' Group and also prepared notes on the various

65 NAA B408, 9: Psychology Branch, Education Department. State School No. 4532, Framlingham Settlement. Report of Special Survey. Sept. 1954.

66 NAA B408, 9: Unsigned notes (McLean) 17 July 1956, 'J. R. Hall – Psychologist & Guidance Officer Education Department, 17 July 56' attached to report 'Psychology Branch, Education Department. State School No. 4532, Framlingham Settlement. Report of Special Survey. September 1954.'

67 NAA B408, 9: Keith M. Cathcart, Inspector, Mental Deficiency Training (Mental Hygiene Authority) to T. N. Garnet, Sec. BPA, 'Report Re Aboriginal Children, Robinvale. Datum of Examinations: 6th–9th September 1955', 13 July 1956.

families.' So a brief encounter with an un-cooperative child coupled with notes provided by a welfare worker allowed the psychologist to conclude the following:

> [X] has a different name from that of the couple where she lives, her blood relationship to them is not indicated in the notes. However, it would appear that she is rejected in the home. (Father) very rude to [X] – seems to resent her – (Mother) very unintelligent – thrashes [X]. The child's behaviour during the examination suggested marked emotional maladjustment. The parents of [X] and her brothers are, on the notes provided, inadequate personalities.[68]

These two exercises were performed by two psychologists well trained in the (white) orthodoxies of child-and-family psychology, which had by then firmly rooted itself in the discourse of child welfare and juvenile justice as it applied to non-Aborigines. As shown in Chapter 7 the 1955 Barry Report on juvenile delinquency was an expression of that achievement but its deliberations excluded Aboriginal children. These two limited psychological exercises would travel. They were given a central and pivotal place in the McLean Report. It was upon them that McLean placed what served as an at least *official* full stop to the idea of hereditary racial intellectual defect:

> As to their mental capacity, most authorities now agree that there is no innate racial inferiority of intelligence in the aborigine ... I sought information from various sources on this subject. Close surveys have been made by Health, Mental Hygiene and Education Departmental officers of the mental capacity of part-aboriginal children in various schools.[69]

In introducing the new Aborigines bill to Parliament Chief Secretary Rylah would cite McLean on this point.[70] We now know the extent (or rather, the limitations) of the 'close surveys' by the Mental Hygiene and Education Department. But what was meant by 'close surveys' by the Health Department? There is no evidence of any commissioned or hefty research provided McLean by the Health Department. McLean's papers regarding Health Department surveys were limited to a letter to a Dr E. F. McKenzie of the General Health Branch of the Health Department, who forwarded McLean some work by a Miss Pennington on the conditions for Aboriginal people at Shepparton, carried out some years earlier. It was 'very useful', perhaps because it allowed McLean to speak with the apparent weight of Health Department research behind him. Other than that, it was these two exercises by Hall and Cathcart that McLean drew upon closely and quite substantially to make his point, paraphrasing more than once Hall's concept of the 'absorption' of the home 'atmosphere':

68 NAA B408, 9: Keith M. Cathcart, Inspector, Mental Deficiency Training to T. N. Garnet, Sec. BPA, 'Report Re Aboriginal Children, Robinvale. Datum of Examinations: 6th–9th September 1955', 13 July 1956.

69 Victoria (C. McLean) 1957b: 8.

70 VPD Session 1956–57–58 Vol 251 LA 30 April 1957: 344.

> Though difficulty was experienced in applying the recognised intelligence tests, due to the children's timidity and suspicion, and their limited vocabulary, leading to some doubt as to the reliability of results, the general spread of those results was not markedly dissimilar to those expected of white children ...
>
> It is certainly the fact that most aboriginal children from sub-standard environment [sic] do not in fact progress beyond the lower grades before they leave school, but the reasons for this scholastic backwardness must be sought in other directions ... While at school, they entirely lack the encouragement to learn given to most white children by their parents and from a comparatively early age they absorb the psychological atmosphere of their homes.[71]

From this point on, the problematic psychology of the Aboriginal family became something of a leitmotif throughout the McLean Report: The 'psychological effect of their environment' militated against economic progress: 'Having become infected, during their formative years, by the discouraging and unhopeful atmosphere of their homes ... the young people ... display a marked tendency to idle around the camps.' And McLean recommended the closure of Framlingham and Lake Tyers State schools: mixed schools would provide 'incentive to progress', counteracting the 'retarding influence of their home environment'.[72]

It is worth recalling that prior to the 1886 Half-Caste Act, a great deal of energy was put into education provided by the mission schools and in proving the educability of the half-caste. Before half-caste children of school leaving age could be forced from the missions, they had, as a group, to be legitimately understood as able to 'do for themselves'. One way of legitimising the act was to bestow upon these children 'intelligence ... quite equal to the standard required from children of the same age in the State schools of the colony'.[73] Something similar was happening here – a lack of educability led to a kind of nihilism. It would present a barrier to any administrative attempt to shift those problematic congregations of mixed-blood quadroons and octoroons on the supposed borderland between Aborigine and white, and geographically, occupying neither of the racialised territories of town or reserve. How to shift these camps was one of the fundamental preoccupations that saw the government commission McLean's inquiry. One of the achievements of the McLean Report was, with the aid of the psy-sciences, to bestow educability on 'children of aboriginal blood' as a prerequisite for new legislation and a new set of practices on the horizon.[74] There was one fundamental difference however. In the period leading up to the 1886 act an investment in the educability of mission children helped legitimate the forced removal of young half-castes from their families. In the wake of the McLean Report whole families were to be dispersed among the white community in the name of assimilation. In 1956 on the eve of the release of the McLean Report the BPA, then in its final days, declared its support for 'the principle of dispersal under which only two or three town houses in close

[71] Victoria (C. McLean) 1957b: 9–10. [72] Victoria (C. McLean) 1957b: 10, 19.
[73] Victoria 1882 (BPA): 6. [74] Victoria (C. McLean) 1957b: 8.

proximity are provided'. A few years later, Lake Tyers, once the focus of a policy of concentration, became the focus of the policy of dispersal with the new AWB agreeing that 'Lake Tyers families be dispersed as quickly as possible'.[75]

That same psychological science that was beginning tentatively to move on the Aboriginal child, and just beginning to enfold that child in a discourse of 'maladjustment' and 'emotional disturbance' and so on, also dictated that the child could not, at least conceptually, be removed from the family. The suggestion that the children actually be removed to institutions was certainly broached both in McLean's notes pertaining to Hall's work and in the body of Cathcart's work but as the Aboriginal child began to take on some of the contours and dimensions of the white child, so the Aboriginal family would move with it. Already, in Cathcart's work, along with the emotionally maladjusted child went the parents' inadequate personalities. The Aboriginal family had to take on the shape of its white counterpart – it had to become a recognisable family *unit* – at one and the same time as it became the subject of administrative dispersal.

The Aborigines Bill was introduced into Parliament in April of 1957.[76] The 1957 Aborigines Act allowed for the establishment of the new Aborigines Welfare Board. It was later repealed and substituted with the 1958 Aborigines Act to allow for the ongoing operations of the AWB.[77] The template for the structure of the new AWB was taken largely from the NSW system, as detailed by T. N. Garnet after his study tour, and as advised by McLean. The composition of the AWB included two Aboriginal members, Pastor Dougal Nicholls MBE and Mr Harold Blair, as well as the anthropologist Dr Donald Thompson OBE, the medical practitioner (and medical superintendent at Turana) Jannette Finney, Housing Commission Officer J. H. Davey and an Education Department representative. However, there would be no representative of the Police Department, as there was in the NSW system. The newly established Aborigines Welfare Board noted in its first annual report:

> There are now no distinctions whatever in the laws of this State as between aborigines and other citizens. It is important to stress that the aborigines of Victoria now have all the normal rights and obligations of citizenship which are shared by other citizens. They have the franchise; the right to own property; freedom of movement; can sue or be sued, and are protected by all the normal industrial and social legislation. Victoria is the only State of the Commonwealth where this condition applies.[78]

While a sense of progressive pride may ring from this statement, from this point on the government was particularly circumspect in its dealings with Aborigines, whom, as a group, it recognised as generally not meeting the required standard of

75 PROV VPRS 11563 Unit 411: Sec. BPA to Sec. Forest Commission 18 Sept. 1956; NAA B314: Minutes of Meeting of AWB 14 Sept. 1961.
76 VPD Session 1956–57–58 Vol 251 LA 30 April 1957: 342–47.
77 Victoria Aborigines Act (No. 6086) 1957; Victoria Aborigines Act (No. 6190) 1958.
78 Victoria 1958b (AWB): 3.

citizenship, but, nevertheless, a group upon whom it had bestowed all the rights of citizenship and against whom, having declared its hand, it must not be *seen* to discriminate. Clearly this paradox remained a preoccupation of this new administration: despite its overt declaration of rights, including 'freedom of movement', like the previous administrative body it too had to find a means of curtailing as much as possible the 'wandering habits' of Aborigines:

> The Board is of the opinion that it is not in the best interests of aborigines that indiscriminate camping on river frontages and Crown areas be permitted to continue unregulated and uncontrolled. More rigid supervision and, perhaps, the introduction of camping permits, would tend to curb the wandering habits of some families and encourage them to settle permanently in one place.[79]

The regulations pertaining to the new Aborigines Act were gazetted in the following year.[80] They effectively regulated for two populations – or rather *only effectively* regulated for one – those residing on Lake Tyers, which would remain, under this period of review, along with Framlingham, a designated Aboriginal reserve. (The administration was on less sure ground when it came to formally regulating the lives of Aborigines who chose to live off-station.) The manager of a reserve remained responsible 'for the enforcement of discipline and good order' (Regulation 5) and all residing on the reserve 'shall obey the instructions of the Manager'. During the course of his inquiries, McLean discovered that the licensing system for reserve residents, though still legally in operation under the 1928 act, had fallen into disuse, with Major Glen reporting that the last licence had been issued in 1937 but had, to the best of his knowledge, been discontinued 'because of the amount of clerical work involved'.[81] By February 1959 it was reported that a written permit system 'regulating admission to Lake Tyers Aboriginal Station was now in operation':[82]

> Applications by [PG] on behalf of himself and his wife and Miss [WH], both of Harrisfield, for admission to the Lake Tyers Station were submitted by the Superintendent with the recommendation that they be refused. RESOLVED: That the Superintendent's recommendation be approved.[83]

Unauthorised persons who failed to leave a reserve when requested, including those whose permits had been cancelled, 'may be removed by a Member of the Police Force' and fines for misconduct could be imposed by the manager.[84] But it was not at all clear that the police had the power to arrest anyone on Lake Tyers, given that,

79 Victoria 1958b (AWB): 6. 80 Victoria 1958a (Government Gazette): 2978–81.

81 NAA B408, 1: 'Notes on Mr McLean's Visits to Lakes Entrance, Lake Tyers Aboriginal Station and Orbost District, accompanied by Dr P. J. White, Health Department, Major Glen, and Board Secretary: Lake Tyers Station, 27th June, 1956'.

82 NAA B314, 9: Minutes of Meeting of AWB 11 Feb. 1959.

83 NAA B314, 9: Minutes of Meeting of AWB 11 March 1959.

84 Victoria 1958a (Government Gazette): 2979, Regulation 16.

according to the local constabulary, it was not a 'public place'. AWB Superintendent of Aborigines Welfare P. E. Felton begged to differ: 'Surely the Police have a duty to arrest any person committing such an offence, whether it is under the Police Offences Act or otherwise.'[85] The AWB requested advice from the Crown solicitor and was told that Lake Tyers was probably not a public place, and hence, under the Police Offences Act, only if there was an offence against the law could an arrest be executed without a warrant. Otherwise, a warrant was required, by which time, of course, unauthorised persons might well have disappeared.[86]

The AWB's authority to use formal legal means to enforce regulations relating to conduct (other than those that clearly constituted a crime), and indeed to trespass, remained in doubt. In 1961 the manager at Lake Tyers was still reporting 'having difficulty in obtaining co-operation from the Lakes Entrance Police' in apprehending those who came onto the station without authority.[87] The question of using police powers to enforce restrictions regarding permits was never completely resolved during the AWB's existence. As to other aspects of discipline of the population within reserve boundaries, they continued much as they did before the new legislation. Rations continued to be allocated and policed. In 1960 the manager reported 'the detection of three cases where aboriginal residents had attempted to send a portion of their rations in parcels to persons living off the Station' and the board delivered a 'general warning'.[88] In the context of a problem concerning the repair of footwear, the board approved a decision to supply women with 'more durable shoes ... A lace-up military type appeared to be the most satisfactory.'[89] A mundane point, but as well as speaking to an administrative mindset that understood Lake Tyers to be an institution, the architecture and design of the designated shoe spoke to the ostensible destructive character of the Aborigine and the indelicate nature of the Aboriginal woman. It is the kind of assumption that would be expressed more generally in decisions about the architecture and design of Aboriginal housing. On this, domestic arrangements and facilities remained rudimentary. The old communal bathhouse remained in operation – or it would if, as had been its history, it was not in a continual state of disrepair. The board was still considering (not for the first time) 'proposals for the reticulation of water to the aborigines cottages' and in 1960 the supply of electric light for cottages was still only a matter of consideration.[90]

By mid-1961 it had become apparent that the attempt to preserve, and in some ways reinforce, a pre-1957 model of the imposition of discipline upon the Lake Tyers population, through the permit system for example, was clearly at odds with the administration's commitment to an overall policy of assimilation through dispersal.

85 NAA B357, 3: P. E. Felton, 'Power of Police to Arrest on Lake Tyers Aboriginal Station' 16 Jan. 1959.

86 NAA B314, 9: Minutes of Meeting of AWB 11 Feb. 1959; NAA B357, 3: T. N. Garnet, Sec. AWB to Crown Solicitor 23 Feb. 1959; Thomas F. Mornane, Crown Solicitor to Sec. AWB, 25 March 1959.

87 NAA B314, 9: Minutes of Meeting of AWB 8 March 1961.

88 NAA B314, 9: Minutes of Meeting of AWB 9 March 1960.

89 NAA B314, 9: Minutes of Meeting of AWB 8 April 1959.

90 NAA B314, 9: Minutes of Meeting of AWB 19 Aug. 59; 9 March 1960.

It was then the AWB's objective 'to provide houses and employment for men with younger families away from the station in order that their children will be brought up under the same conditions as other children'.[91] As noted earlier, where once the target of practice for older models of absorption had been the station's youth, the target at Lake Tyers, as elsewhere, was the 'young family'. By that stage, however, an 'old school' station manager in the person of Mr Miles was entrenched at Lake Tyers, with his wife as matron. Miles was formerly superintendent of the Cape Barren Island Reserve for half-castes off the coast of Tasmania.[92] The general approach of the matron and manager at Lake Tyers had come under increasing criticism by the AWB, and at its May 1961 meeting the board's dissatisfaction was openly expressed and recorded. Superintendent of Aborigines Welfare P. E. Felton devoted a large section of his report to the unsatisfactory situation at Lake Tyers. He criticised the 'paternal and directive' approach there, noting that despite its being part of the policy of the board to prepare residents for life beyond the station 'there is no real programme of training in operation' and 'in practice the aborigines at Lake Tyers are still being taught dependence'. Felton doubted whether the current manager and matron 'really believe that the aborigines at Lake Tyers can be trained as better citizens'. They were not open to constructive criticism and 'view the aborigines generally with distaste and distrust, and regard the aborigines' problems with cynicism', preferring 'force and compulsion; hence they stress their authority and would impose their rule over the aborigines' lives'.[93]

THE MULTIPLE 'FAILURES' OF THE ABORIGINAL FAMILY

The production of statistics and records of the various comings and goings and strengths and weaknesses of the client group that was the Aboriginal population of Victoria continued to be an essential apparatus of their governing body, the Aborigines Welfare Board. The J family was described as 'stable', J himself a 'fine type of man'. He paid his rent, was in steady employment and aspired to better living conditions; he had a wife and two children. Consider here that in the wake of the McLean Report Aborigines as a group were to be considered the subjects of an exercise in rehabilitation: 'the Board regards aboriginal rehabilitation as one of the major social problems of the State'.[94] There was no single central register ranking Aboriginal families in terms of their rehabilitative progress: it existed, mostly, in amorphous fashion, within the monthly reports of welfare officers and those of Superintendent Felton. In those reports the AWB was advised as to the success or failure of individual families to achieve the next stage in their progress towards assimilation.

91 NAA B314, 9: Minutes of Special Meeting of AWB (Lake Tyers) 29 Aug. 1961.
92 VPD Session 1962–63 Vol 268 LA 23 Oct. 1962: 995–96.
93 NAA B357, 166: Report by Mr P. E. Felton for the Month of May 1961.
94 NAA B357, 55: Acting Sec. AWB, to Sec. Housing Commission 14 March 1958.

In these now quite recent times, the process of ranking Aboriginal families began with the selection of tenants for the ten-cottage Rumbalara settlement at Mooroopna, at which time J. H. Davey, in consultation with the Save the Children Fund and shire authorities produced a list, ranked one to ten, of prospective tenants who were then living on the river bank. Mr and Mrs A with their three children, fifteen months to seven years, were 'expected to make the grade'. But the selectors were more equivocal about others: the familial boundaries of some would need redefining before they were deemed suitable:

> Mr & Mrs [JH] – 6 children – 5 to 19 years.
> Also son in family, 22 years, but evidently problem and could live elsewhere.[95]

Those who had lived for some time on the river bank but did not bear the appropriate signs of yet being a 'good family' would be moved into the better huts vacated by the better families, unless they were old-age pensioners – their presence would 'resolve itself eventually'. Among the huts to remain was that of GA and LB: 'Undeserving – both drink heavily and real problems'.[96] Once established in the settlement tenants were scrutinised as to their progress: 'The next matter to be decided at Mooroopna is whether the best families at "Rumbalara" should be housed in the town through the Housing Commission channels, or whether the Board will acquire land and build houses in the town.'[97] In December 1958 Felton forwarded a draft 'Conditions of Tenancy' to the Crown solicitor for advice as to its suitability and the AWB's authority to apply such. The document itself articulates the signs by which the AWB and its officers would rank the progress of the family towards rehabilitation: tenancy was from week to week (at a rate of 15 shillings) and could be terminated under the following conditions:

> If the tenant –
>
> a) fails to pay the rent on the due date;
> b) refuses or neglects to give the Board on demand any information required by the Board concerning the tenant or his family or as to the earnings of the tenant members of his family or other persons residing in the house
> c) makes any false or incorrect statement on his application for tenancy or to any inquiry made by the Board; or
> d) fails to comply with any of the following conditions.

Many of those conditions concerned keeping the interior of the house clean, tidy, vermin free and in good repair, but it extended to the grounds, which were required to have a 'proper' appearance:

95 NAA B357, 55: J. H. Davey, 'Mooroopna Houses', 26 March 1958.
96 NAA B357, 55: J. H. Davey, 'Mooroopna Houses', 26 March 1958.
97 NAA B357, 55: P. E. Felton, 7 July 1958.

e) cultivate and maintain in a proper manner the garden area about the house and the nature strip between street footpath and channel so that the premises shall present a neat and tidy appearance.

They also required the tenant to give virtually unlimited access, certainly to information as indicated in regulation b), but also to the interior of their homes, to those authorised by the board:

> 9. The Board shall be at liberty by its officers agents or workmen to enter upon the house to inspect the state of repair and cleanliness at all times and to execute repairs or to make alterations or additions.

As well as a series of strictures as to what the tenant could or could not do with the house, from hanging pictures – the tenant could not 'suffer or permit pictures to be hung otherwise than on picture hooks of a pattern approved by the Board' – to keeping lodgers or boarders 'unless with the express permission of the Board', the agreement extended to the conduct of residents:

> 8. The tenant shall be responsible for the orderly conduct of his children so that no nuisance or annoyance will be caused to the other tenants of the Board or members of the public. He shall not make or permit to be made on the premises thereon any disturbances noise or annoyance whatsoever prejudicial to the premises or to the comfort of any occupier of the adjoining premises or of any other inhabitants of the neighbourhood or of any member of the public.[98]

With more officers in the field and the demand for housing growing, welfare officers reported regularly on the achievement (or otherwise) of this or that family in measuring up as tenants, itself a gauge of their success or otherwise in approaching the goal of assimilation.

Some attempt was made at a formal register of those 'headed towards assimilation' or not, and the stage at which they were, according to the kinds of signs rehearsed in welfare officers' notes.[99] As to the nature of those signs, in the years that saw their establishment in the field of Aboriginal welfare, professional welfare officers continued to scrutinise and judge the Aboriginal family according to the long-held and much-rehearsed list of deficits that *Aborigines* had largely (with exceptions) failed to overcome, among them, insobriety, immorality, imprudence, laziness, lack of hygiene and cleanliness and, perhaps above all, a failure to impose and maintain the appropriate limits of kinship as expressed in the 'normal' (white) family unit.

98 NAA B357, 3: 'Rumbalara Housing Settlement Mooroopna: Conditions of Tenancy', attachment to correspondence P. E. Felton to Crown Solicitor 8 Dec. 1958.

99 NAA B357, 192: AWB Field Notes – Murray Valley Survey of Aborigines, June 1961.

MAKING UP ABORIGINAL FAMILY UNITS

From the date of its constitution, the AWB recognised the size of the Aboriginal family as an issue. It was not overtly Malthusian nor even overtly critical but the fact that large families were both typical and problematic (they caused overcrowding, they were difficult for the breadwinner to support) was cause for more than one comment in the AWB's first report on the shack dwellers in river bank camps: 'these shacks in which parents and as many as six or more children live are rarely more than 20 feet by 12 feet, sometimes less. There is little privacy, insufficient beds, and furniture generally is sparse and poor.'[100] Among those families who had entered into arrangements with the Housing Commission prior to the AWB's involvement: 'Some of them ... experience difficulty in maintaining their rental commitments because of spasmodic employment and large families.'[101]

Meanwhile, the Apex Club pursued its aspirations of developing and overseeing the distribution of housing. First, it explained, 'by use of the knowledge and experience of those in close contact with the families comprising the groups, family units can be selected'. But 'all dark families would not be suitable'; they had to '*desire* to get away from the humpy town'. Once the scheme was established, 'the family must be supervised, aided and encouraged in a very personal and close manner until such time as the assistance of Apexians and their wives is no longer necessary'.[102] The AWB would work with the Apex Club in some instances, incorporating the club's sponsorship of a few Aboriginal families into its overall scheme of dispersal through re-housing. But beyond that scheme the AWB also invested in the concept of the family unit as the desired administrative entity. From its inception, Rumbalara was to function as a theatre for an administrative eye to scrutinise and to judge chosen residents' performance as families, divided, as they then were – or rather, as they were *required to be* – into distinguishable family units. The small cottage-size and lay-out of the houses provided at Rumbalara imposed material restrictions on the number of residents, restrictions supplemented by regulations forbidding unauthorised visitors. Much was made of the achievements (or indeed failures) of families in fencing off and maintaining the yards and boundaries of their individual cottages: 'tenants have already effected improvements in their surroundings with gardens and fences provided by their own effort'.[103] In 1965, with a second settlement established at Robinvale, the AWB noted that although it would 'continue rehousing families from these two Settlements who make the grade there is always the possibility that they will serve a useful purpose as places of last resort to which families who fail in conventional housing can return'.[104] However, over the

100 Victoria 1958b (AWB): 10. 101 Victoria 1958b (AWB): 6.
102 NAA B408, 9: Association of Apex Clubs. National Service Scheme – Aboriginal Welfare. White Paper. Undated *c* March 1956: 10–11, emphasis in original.
103 VPD Session 1958–59 Vol 257 LA 15 April 1959: 3070. 104 Victoria 1967 (AWB): 14.

seven years after the establishment of Rumbalara only five families 'progressed to town housing . . . and four at Robinvale over five years'.[105]

Health still remained one dimension according to which Aboriginal parenthood could be deemed a failure. There were reported instances of Aboriginal parents' failure to attend, specifically, to the health of their children constituting grounds for child removal. A more general achievement, in the wake of McLean Report, was the constitution of the means by which the Aboriginal population failed to achieve the contours of the normal family unit. The 'bad home', judged by the presence of visitors and/or the absence of a clearly defined unit of married couple and appropriate number of children and/or a proper house was articulated as the grounds for child removal. There are almost no instances of *recorded* forced removal of Aboriginal children on the grounds of neglect in the period under review. The AWB itself would note, in its report for 1963:

> It should not, however, be thought that there is a great body of consciously neglectful aboriginal parents. Few aboriginal children become State Wards on the grounds of neglect. From time to time, unqualified observers and well-meaning persons make the suggestion that aboriginal children from sub-standard homes should be made State Wards and be brought up in Institutions or in the care of foster parents. Quite apart from the fact that legal proceedings of this nature are not taken because there is no evidence of neglect, it must be pointed out that in the vast majority of cases there is a strong sense of family and a deep affection for children. It is quite obvious that it is far more satisfactory for their emotional well-being that such children should be brought up in their own family circle, and that efforts of welfare workers and health visitors should be directed at the general improvement of all aspects of social adjustment and health.
>
> Constantly, Board staff have to balance between the need to give some material aid and the risk that parents will feel absolved of responsibility for the health and care of their offspring. The Board desires at all costs to avoid being paternal so that people become wholly dependent upon it. It desires to encourage self-reliance and responsibility.[106]

Once again, this raw accounting needs explanation. First, though forced removals on the grounds of neglect might have been uncommon at this time, the AWB's welfare officers were nevertheless involved in other arrangements for the removal of children in circumstances deemed unsatisfactory. These included arranging fostering and adoption. Second, if as asserted few Aboriginal children were being made wards on the grounds of neglect, they were nevertheless being made wards in disproportionate numbers. Note this statement from the AWB's annual report just two years on: 'Aboriginal children are much more likely to become State Wards. A very high proportion of these children come into care as State Wards at some time in their lives.'[107] But by what means? In the 1930s the administration had acknowledged

[105] Victoria 1967 (AWB): 14. [106] Victoria 1964 (AWB): 8. [107] Victoria 1967 (AWB): 5.

the fact that 'it is extremely difficult to place coloured children with advantage in Institutions or white homes'. The remark was made in the context of admitting having no choice but to allow a half-caste woman living off Lake Tyers to 'foster' members of her own family.[108] In 1958 the AWB attempted a census of Aboriginal children in state care and in other institutions. In October 1958 it could count only seven Aboriginal wards of the state as boarded-out.[109] But pathways into foster care within white households were beginning to open up for Aboriginal children, a move for which non-Aboriginal Victorians saw fit to congratulate themselves. Debating the new Aborigines Bill, Mr Doube MLA was pleased 'to note in today's press a story of a Brighton family who had taken into their home a group of aboriginal children'.[110] There is little evidence that the AWB was hesitant about the practice. Its welfare officers were regularly reporting on finding white foster parents for children as part of their role. Sometimes, foster arrangements were made so that children could receive specialist services in the city. Sometimes children would, after a prolonged stay in hospital, be 'discharged . . . to a foster family'.[111] This was a moment of achievement in itself: by the 1960s it was no longer difficult, as it was once difficult, to place Aboriginal children in white homes – other than as servants. So, we can already see that, in the late 1950s and early 1960s, adoption and fostering were opening up as alternative means of an administration removing children from Aboriginal families or from circumstances deemed, in one way or another, unsatisfactory. While this did not lead directly to their becoming wards of the state, one could hypothesise that failed fostering arrangements, and adoptions that did not endure, could see children made wards.

What of the other means, such as being made wards directly by means of offences against the law? Aboriginal youth crime did not appear as a problem beyond the usual complaints about failure to achieve productive citizenship and their 'gainless existence', or that the young were 'happy to "make do" on social services'.[112] References were made to 'wayward young aborigines' and 'unattached young men' drawn, as an unauthorised and unwelcome presence, to Rumbalara.[113] At the April 1959 board meeting Dr Finney referred to reports of serious delinquency among young people at Mooroopna and suggested that sporting activities and classes be arranged.[114] In its 1963 report the AWB noted:

> Great concern is felt about the large number of teenagers and single persons up to the early twenties who are virtually unemployed . . . A particularly difficult problem

[108] NAA B337, 540: Under Secretary to J. R. Henry, Sec. CWD 9 Sept. 1931.
[109] NAA B357, 155: 'Summary of Children in Institutions and Hospitals, Etc. October 1958'.
[110] VPD Session 1956–57–58 Vol 252 LA 28 May 1957: 1116.
[111] NAA B357, 166: Report of Sister Goldsworthy (AWB welfare officer) for the month of May 1962.
[112] NAA B357, 166: Report of A. West (AWB welfare officer) for the month of October 1961.
[113] NAA B314, 9: Minutes of Meeting of AWB 8 June 1960; NAA B357, 166: Report by Mr H. W. McDonald (AWB welfare officer) for the Month of Dec. 1960.
[114] NAA B314, 9: Minutes of Meeting of AWB 8 April 1959.

> is the situation confronting aboriginal children who are State Wards when they are discharged from Institutions and Children's Homes. While this is primarily a problem for the Social Welfare Department, the Board's advice and help is [sic] often sought. These children often have no home to return to. They may eventually return to unsatisfactory living conditions from which they were removed at an earlier age, or else drift into the company of delinquents and start to follow a similar life until they are brought under the notice of the Law as juvenile offenders. There is simply no satisfactory place for such children to live if they desire to seek employment away from home or if they have no home to return to. In consequence, the youths often develop idle habits, learn to drink to excess and become involved in offences against the law, such as the illegal use of motor cars. The girls and young women tend to become promiscuous and sometimes have illegitimate children before settling down at an early age to a more or less stable relationship, which may or may not lead to marriage.[115]

But there was nothing particularly new about Aboriginal children and youths being charged with an offence. It happened frequently enough under the BPA's years of administration. And given that those legally known as Aborigine pre-1957, and those legally known as Aborigine post-1957 differed, it is well-nigh impossible to claim with any statistical certainty that more Aboriginal children were finding their way, at least directly on account of their offending against the law, into state care. What can be asserted is that Aboriginal youth, though recognised as a problem were not *primarily* understood as a *delinquency* problem.

So what evidence do we have that might give insight into the conditions that made it possible for most Aboriginal children, by 1965, to become wards of the state at least for a period of their lives? What changed? Or, first, did anything change? Some statistical evidence supports the claim that prior to the 1957–58 acts, relatively few Aboriginal children were wards of the state. As noted, McLean attempted a count during his inquiry – using his wide definition of Aborigine. He came up with the figure of eight children in the care of the CWD in December 1956.[116] To this must be added another twenty-six committed following his visit to Mooroopna.[117] Shortly after its constitution the AWB attempted a census including a count of Aboriginal children in institutions. In October 1958 it came up with a figure of seventy-two wards of the state, sixty-five of whom were in children's homes and seven boarded-out.[118] There was not a full set of replies corresponding to the list of institutions approached, but among the replies from individual institutions, Ballarat Orphanage had seventeen children, all wards of the state. Among the existing replies, there was only one from a reformatory – Morning Star, run by the Franciscans since the early 1930s. It noted 'we have no aborigines or part aborigines at the home'. As a private

[115] Victoria 1964 (AWB): 6. [116] NAA B408, 4: Unsigned note, 'Dec [Xmas] 1956'.
[117] NAA B408, 4: (Initialled) T. N. Garnet, 'Children committed to Children's Welfare Depmt between 14 April 56 and 31 July 56', 1 Aug. 1956.
[118] NAA B357, 155: 'Summary of Children in Institutions and Hospitals, Etc. October 1958'.

reformatory, it had the freedom to accept or reject this or that prospective inmate, as did all private homes. The BPA always had to battle long and hard from the second decade of the twentieth century through to the end of its administration to persuade increasingly reluctant private institutions to accept its disciplinary problems. Right up to the time of the McLean Report, non-government institutions were still showing a reluctance to have particularly older Aboriginal children as inmates, and when they were persuaded to take them on, showed a reluctance to keep them on account of inability to fit in. Up to the eve of the McLean Report, apart from Turana, the main Children's Welfare Department depot, there were only private institutions. But we know that by the time McLean had completed his report the situation had begun to change: the state was no longer reliant on non-government institutions. Making an Aboriginal child a ward of the state was one thing; having the means of disposal of that child as a ward was another. The means were increasingly at hand.

What remains to examine is to outline a process whereby Aboriginal children, though they might not have primarily been known in terms of neglect, nor primarily a problem in terms of delinquency, came to be known increasingly as problem children, with all the nuances bestowed upon the term by the psychological sciences. This process came into place at a time when, post–Barry Report, new avenues were opening up for the management and disposal of the problem child – whom, we know, was a product of the problem family. In addition, new legislation in the form of the Social Welfare Act (1960) was geared to manage problem children, problem families, delinquent youth and adult criminals all under the one administrative body, which achieved a lifting of constraints imposed upon the disposal of Aboriginal children. Recall too that when introducing the bill to Parliament the chief secretary had specifically, if not overtly, the wider 'Aboriginal problem' in his sites.

MAKING UP THE ABORIGINAL PROBLEM CHILD

We know that by the 1950s the (white) problem family was well established as the context out of which was formed the problem child. The Barry Report based its recommendations for a reshaping of juvenile justice practices upon this given. While the fully fledged delinquent child might properly be the subject of removal to an institution, identification of the pre-delinquent maladjusted child should, it concluded, be followed by action upon the family as a whole. We know too that the term 'problem family had come to be applied to the Aboriginal population. But it applied, more or less, to the *whole* of the Aboriginal population. AWB board member Dr Finney would make that point succinctly enough. Fresh from a study tour of New South Wales she would arrive at the newly constituted AWB having convinced herself that 'these dark skinned folk ... are just the same as problem white families that are uneducated, ignorant and ... unable to help themselves.'[119] In the decade following the McLean Report, Aborigines were largely acted upon as problem families in an envisaged population-wide process of rehabilitation.

Some limited, direct involvement of the psychological sciences had taken place in the mid-1950s in matters to do with Aboriginal children. Children in schools at Framlingham and Robinvale had become the subject of psychological testing; Dr Finney, through her report of her travels in NSW, had argued that 'children should come under the Child Welfare Department and have all the facilities for the emotionally subnormal, the maladjusted, etc., which are at the disposal of Child Welfare'.[120] By August 1959 the school psychologist J. A. Hall had submitted a report to the board after testing schoolchildren at Lake Tyers. Hall named 'lack of cultural stimulus and home support' as their fundamental problem, and he advised against directing efforts at achieving entrance to secondary education: 'instead the aim should be that of developing basic educational, personal and social skills to the highest possible level'.[121] By the early 1960s the network of clinics and institutions developed for problem children were beginning to open up to Aboriginal children. A child would be escorted for psychiatric testing at Travancore or was found a place in a special school. Even when children had committed an offence, it was beginning to be understood as a manifestation of problematic familial relations:

> [BP]: a thirteen-year old lad who has been successfully defying his parents at Framlingham for a long time arrived in Melbourne during the month and was quickly taken into custody by the police. A protection application to the Children's Court was approved and [BP] has now been placed in the care of the Family Welfare Division ... [BP] (14 years) of Framlingham appeared in the Court of Petty Sessions, Fitzroy before Mr Slattery SM on a larceny charge. Mr O'Brien, Chief Attendance Officer gave evidence in this case. [BP] was committed to the care of the Children's Welfare Department.[122]

In the wake of the Barry Report and under a new 1960 Social Welfare Act the entry to an institution for delinquent boys was no longer conditional on a non-government superintendent's agreement. At the same time new means were opening up for the disposal of children neither charged with a specific offence nor necessarily identified as outright victims of neglect. Under the 1960 act the new Social Welfare Department was operating a span of institutions for children and adults. A state-run reception centre was in operation, channelling children into a growing range of state-run institutions, certainly for delinquents, also for those neglected by their parents, but also for those who bore the signs of pre-delinquency – problem children from problem families. Among them were children previously 'unacceptable to, or

119 NAA B357, 169: Dr J. Finney, 'The Aboriginal Problem', 1958: 4–5.
120 NAA B357, 169: Dr J. Finney, 'The Aboriginal Problem', 1958: 12–13.
121 NAA B314, 9: Minutes of Meeting of AWB 10 Feb. 1960.
122 NAA B357, 166: Report by Mr West (AWB welfare officer) for the month of Aug. 1961.

rejected by, voluntary children's homes'.[123] In the wake of the McLean Report conditions were ripe, as it were, for new kinds of expert interventions upon Aboriginal children. The professionally trained welfare officer, sent from the city out into the field, was free to read the Aboriginal child in terms of developmental psychology, maladjustment and the making of delinquency, to send the child along a newly cleared pathway into state care, and to anticipate mainstreaming the child's fellows down that same avenue This from AWB welfare officer A. McDonald in November 1962:

> The Bendigo Women Police, on a request from us, investigated the case of [VM], 11 years, of Rumbalara. This girl has been running wild since her mother died in June last and the father was finding it hard to care for her and as a result she got herself into a few scrapes and in one case was involved in an 'indecent assault' case. Her school attendance has been very poor and as a result action has been taken against her father by the School Attendance Officer.
>
> In October arrangements were made by this office to have her examined by a psychologist at Travancore. [V] gave very little co-operation at this examination but the psychologist reported that it would be advisable to place her in some Home where she would get a good training and discipline. Efforts were made to place her but without success. As her case appeared to be urgent the police were called in to investigate in order that something be done to protect the child from further moral danger. After investigation the police proceeded against her and as a result she was admitted to the care of the Social Welfare Department and has been placed at 'Allambie'.
>
> Similar requests for investigation have been made in the cases of the [W] children of Barmah and the [A] children at Echuca. So far no reports on these cases have been received.[124]

[123] Victoria 1963b (SWD): 14.

[124] NAA B357, 166: Report of Mr McDonald (AWB welfare officer) for the month of Nov. 1962.

Summary and Conclusions

This book has reviewed the operation of welfare and justice systems as they pertain to Indigenous and non-Indigenous children in the Australian state of Victoria over a 100-year period. Taking as its two main initial points of purchase the establishment of the Central Board to watch over the Interests of the Aborigines in the Colony of Victoria in 1860 and the Neglected and Criminal Children's Act of 1864, the work addresses a number of questions about the categories used to govern children through legal and extra-legal means.

CRIMINALIZING WHITE CHILDREN

One strand of research has traced the emergence across the period under review of a number of key categories used to apprehend the problem the non-Indigenous child presented to the state. Of early categories – neglected and criminal children – the evidence shows that in the immediate wake of the 1864 legislation those categories proved highly unstable with a certain degree of arbitrariness apparent in the practices of disposal of 'innocent' cases of welfare and of those considered in need of correction via a nascent juvenile justice system. Just a few months after the first legislation on children was passed in the Victorian Parliament, the Crown Law Office was directed by the minister of justice to instruct magistrates not to send neglected children to a reformatory school or, conversely, children who had committed a crime to an industrial school. Clearly, magistrates were not always following the legislated system of disposal of these two categories of child. But beyond the apparent arbitrariness of judicial determinations, the three decades following the initial legislation display an incremental increase in the extra-legal power of the executive in determining which child was in need of correction and which child was not. An 1878 amendment to the original act had provided the executive with new powers to send children committed to a reformatory to an industrial school, or to send children committed to an industrial school to a reformatory, and this flexibility of disposal was maintained. Assessments of an individual child's habits and conduct sat over and against grounds of an offence committed, in determining the disposal of the child, and the judgement of the executive now sat over and against that of the judiciary. By the late 1880s, at the same time as the government was being congratulated for new legislative moves to better separate the 'criminal' from the 'purely unfortunate' and 'perfectly innocent', the evidence of the *actually existing* administrative practices at the state's clearing house, the Royal Park Children's Depot, shows that administrative decisions allowed an individual case to be dispatched to a welfare or a correctional environment, within or beyond the depot, depending on that administration's assessment of the child's conduct: children misbehaving in a 'welfare' setting could be dispatched to a more punitive correctional setting on the advice of the depot's superintendent with the approval of the minister. Further amendments to the law allowed for a series of caveats and crossings over, some certainly at the discretion of the courts but others, increasingly, at the discretion of superintendents of institutions. The period leading up to the twentieth century is marked by a reduction in the significance of an offence as the main variable in decision making on the disposal of a child, and a corresponding increased focus on the 'morality' of the child, a decreasing impact of court decisions with a concomitant increased significance of administrative officers' decisions about disposal of offending and neglected children.

Early shifting around of spaces in the new mid-nineteenth-century legislative environment reflected a change of mind on the role of large institutions for properly caring for the child in state care. A grand, barrack-style home potentially holding 500 children was closed a few years after it opened in the late 1870s, in favour of boarding-out of children to families. In the early 1890s too 'prison-like' state reformatories were closed and responsibility for children deemed in need of correction was ceded to privately run institutions. These arrangements later stumbled into more difficulties as a result of an inability to handle the increased numbers of children categorised as neglected. Early in the twentieth century the charities gave way to a professional cadre created after the setting up of the Children's Court in 1906. These shifts were implicated in a sharing of functions between those concerned with neglect and those concerned with correction. The apparatus around children's offending inherited from the adult justice system, including senior personnel and some of the innovations including indeterminate sentencing. Voluntary child supervisors would more systematically link the activities of courts, police and families. Charity workers were brought under the aegis of the court system which set about authorising agents to do the work previously undertaken by philanthropy but now to be performed by a more regulated group of honorary probation officers, followed by stipendiary probation officers, appointed under its jurisdiction. Justice administration and child welfare had clear lines of connection rather than separation. The evolving networks were significant preconditions for the collection of social information on children and families, and the soon-to-appear calculative regime of the pathological family. In the nascent juvenile court system, as in the institutional setting, a space began to open up for extra-legal 'petty' judgements of the child, occupied by an increasingly professionalised set of experts mediating between the child and the law. An examination of that intermediary space across the first half of the twentieth century reveals the growing influence of an incipient positivist science – medicine, followed by psychiatry and psychology – on decisions about the disposal of children and more generally on procedures involving neglected and offending children, given that the range of likely trajectories of the children who would occupy correctional or other spaces hinged increasingly on the outcomes of the question, 'What kind of person are you?'

The influence of the medical and psychological sciences from early in the twentieth century changed the way in which children in state care were apprehended in the assessment and counting agencies taking shape during this period. Medical expertise was given new authority in the context of a new attention to the problem of infant mortality, itself enmeshed in a national worry about a decline in the quality of the population as were anxieties over particular kinds of disease including syphilis. The flight of children suspected of carrying diseases into the Royal Park depot reshaped what earlier had been calculated as separate categories – neglected and criminal – into a mix of suspected carriers of infection. It changed the personnel, forms of knowledge and practice, and the categories that were used to think through the problem of children and the modus operandi of the central agencies managing the disposal of problem children. The enmeshment of physical and moral contagion saw the psy-sciences become a major contributor to the production of knowledge of the relationship between mental deficiency and crime. Building on moral panic around a newly discovered epidemic of 'feeble-mindedness' in children in the early twentieth century, an emerging psy-science of children sought to forecast a hardening of links between mental capacities and criminal conduct. Criminality had enfolded the whole of the population of children coming into state care, to the extent that even those who did not bear the signs of actual criminality had to be scrutinised for the possibility of bearing its potential. By the end of the 1920s neglected and offending children alike had come to share the same profile of mental and moral misfit.

The category of 'mental defect' enjoyed some prominence for a few decades as the cause of delinquency, but its time would come. The proliferation of psy-scientific expertise operating within the depot and under the aegis of the Children's Welfare Department was concurrent with a proliferation of new clinical sites beyond that department's remit, constituted under a number of authorities, including the Mental Hygiene Department and the Children's Court itself. Under pressure from the Children's Welfare Department, keen to disburden itself of a population deemed 'a danger to themselves and others', the Mental Hygiene Department began to take responsibility for 'control' of those deemed mentally defective. But by the late 1930s under a dedicated psychiatric eye, established truths about the mentally and morally deficient began to show signs of instability. Under clinical scrutiny those exhibiting problem conduct were found to be not necessarily of sub-normal intelligence and those deemed sub-normal did not necessarily display the kind of problem conduct associated with delinquency. At the Children's Court itself informal clinical activity independent of psychiatric oversight took a more sociological bent, and here too the effect was to destabilise the truth about mental deficiency and crime. Under testing regimes instigated there most delinquents revealed themselves as within the normal range of intelligence and an analysis of reports of delinquency around Melbourne revealed delinquency was most concentrated in slum areas. But with Mental Hygiene fast capturing the field of the problem child, extending its clinical activity and the authority of psychiatry to the Children's Welfare Department and the Children's Court, any conclusion that poverty itself might be the root cause of delinquency was effectively waylaid: the problem of delinquency lay not in the slum but in the 'slum-minded' and what could possibly have been conceived of as primarily a social and economic problem was instead reshaped and recontained as primarily a psychological one. A psychology of the normal child began to be activated. Under the growing influence of psychiatry as an authoritative voice in the administration of child welfare and juvenile justice the primary problem was no longer the mentally defective but the juvenile delinquent. Unlike the mentally defective the juvenile delinquent was made, not born. The matter of distinguishing the problematic mentally defective from the largely unproblematic child of normal intelligence gave way to that of distinguishing 'pre-delinquents' from within a cohort of children of mainly normal intelligence and preventing their development into the 'frankly delinquent'. The private family home, once a key solution to the problem of child welfare became the primary site for the development of maladjustment in children as the first signs of a career into delinquency. By the second half of the twentieth century it became an established truth that the psychology of the family contributed more to delinquency than any other cause, including poverty, heredity and pathology. Where once large scale institutional separation of the mentally defective was proposed as the necessary cornerstone of an effective child welfare system and a means of preventing crime now the solution lay, certainly in waylaying the development of delinquency via expert intervention at the level of the family but also in the state reclaiming responsibility for a cohort of children now deemed fully developed – fully formed in their delinquency – and as such beyond the pale of the more 'open' private reformatory institutions to which the government had ceded responsibility in the late nineteenth century. By the early 1960s the state had not simply reclaimed responsibility for the institutional incarceration of a cohort of children marked by their criminality but had expanded the scope of that role to include an officially designated 'maximum security' institution for the detention of children.

CRIMINALIZING ABORIGINAL CHILDREN

As Ian Hacking, David Armstrong and Nikolas Rose have all observed, childhood in modern times is perhaps the most intensely governed sector of the population.[1]

[1] Armstrong 2002; Hacking 1991; Hacking 2004; Rose 1999: 235.

Children were one of the first social groups to regularly appear in modern institutional spaces – schools, clinics and hospitals – and were readily available to be inspected, measured, calculated and assessed. Children became the focus of increasing economic productiveness, social order and cohesion. At varying historical moments, the modern family became the preferred site of education, moral guidance and protection, along with the traditional functions of wealth transfer. But as Donzelot has noted, the family had joined other explicitly governmental agencies concerned with a developing 'disciplinary society', acting as a checkpoint and measuring stick of a self-governing, entrepreneurial self.[2] These aspirations were not always met, or met equally, as could be expected. So while modern sociology may speak confidently of the family as a 'social institution' in these terms, in the nineteenth and into the twentieth centuries, the institution and the family home sat at each end of a spectrum of spaces that reflected, by those occupying them, differential stages of capacity for self-government accompanied by differing kinds of social worlds. Early attempts by the Board for the Protection of Aborigines to know Aborigines in order to govern them throw into relief settler society's determination to apply the language and parameters of family responsibility to the social world of Indigenous people under its remit.

The Central Board to watch over the Interests of Aborigines in the Colony of Victoria was constituted on the eve of implementation of the first piece of child welfare legislation directed at white children in Victoria, in which categories of vulnerable children were formally differentiated. The problem of the non-Aboriginal neglected child was being shaped in the context of the management of the vagrant and the offender and in the context of the prevention of crime. The 'innocent' destitute and orphaned child had become the object of philanthropy with the government resisting any move that might encourage parents' perceived readiness to abandon their children if they knew that the state would provide for them. By 1864 neglected children would be known by signs of abandonment inscribed in the legislation: 'found begging . . . found wandering . . . not [having] any home'.[3]

In its earliest ruminations the board expressed concern over 'the many black and half-caste children throughout the colony' and sought authority 'to order . . . as to the disposal of orphan and deserted children'.[4] But the administration's attempts to apply the language of neglect, abandonment and destitution to the Aboriginal child threw up a number of paradoxes. For one thing we know that from the time of the constitution of the board little distinction was made between Aboriginal children and Aboriginal adults: fed by its responses to surveys of leading colonists' views the BPA soon after its constitution declared Aborigines to be 'indeed, but helpless children',[5] a racialised characterisation that persisted in one form of iteration or other until well into the twentieth century and a 'truth' that served to legitimate a

[2] Donzelot 1979. [3] Victoria Neglected and Criminal Children's Act (No. 216) 1864 s 13.
[4] Victoria 1861 (BPA): 11. [5] Victoria 1862 (BPA): 15.

denial of Aboriginal powers of sovereignty and self-government. Further, the word 'neglected' was commonly enough used by the board itself as a descriptor for the Aboriginal population as whole: in 1864, for example, the board noted that its allocation of funds to support this or that project needed to take into account 'the neglected condition of the blacks in Victoria'.[6] In this sense while signs of neglect might distinguish non-Aboriginal children from their peers, for Aboriginal children, being neglected was a condition of their being Aboriginal and while non-Aboriginal parents' all-too-readiness to cede responsibility for their children's welfare to the state had to be guarded against, Aboriginal parents' reluctance to part with their children was seen by white administrators as a problem that had to be overcome. As to the care of 'orphans and destitute children', the administration was repeatedly confronted with the inappropriateness of attempts to apply the white imperative of family responsibilisation to the social world of the Aborigine: 'There is no fear of an orphan child being desititute ... A child always has two fathers and two mothers, or five or six ... so that, according to the views of the natives, there are no orphans at all.'[7] From the mid-1860s onwards, two quite distinct sets of administrative yardsticks were used for intervening in the lives of Aboriginal and non-Aboriginal children: 'welfare' and 'justice' as they applied to Aboriginal children across the period under review were applied in the name of quite different aspirations underpinned by quite different logics and administered by quite a different authority than welfare and justice as they pertained to the non-Aboriginal child.

The decision to establish a mission system to contain and control Indigenous peoples reflected a hardening of racial thinking throughout the colony: difference was to be understood as deficiency. Aborigines were deficient in their 'natural' capacities and were to be regarded as remnants of an about-to-be-extinct race. Coranderrk mission station was a case in point. The board chose to blame the appalling death rates which came to light soon after its establishment on Aborigines themselves; their 'thoughtless exposure' of themselves to the elements or their 'drunkenness and debauchery' might explain the prevalence of a mysterious 'disease of the lung peculiar to natives'. The board chose to ignore advice from the government's own chief medical officer that there was no mystery – high mortality and morbidity rates were principally the effect of ill-constructed dwellings, bad drainage and overcrowding. But the 'fact' of a naturally declining population persisted into the twentieth century and went hand-in-hand with the engineering of that decline. Forty years on, approaching the third decade of the twentieth century, Lake Tyers had been chosen as the single station on which to concentrate all Victorian Aborigines. One of the more remote encampments, it was characterised as a natural enclave, where 'the blacks' would be free to hunt and fish, protected from white intrusion, 'for the rest of their natural lives'. At the same time, under 'the services of a first class engineer' Coranderrk could be made to realise its potential for (white)

[6] Victoria 1864a (BPA): 11. [7] Victoria 1877 (Royal Commission): Minutes of Evidence, 49.

development. The absence of anything engineered was represented as justly and properly distinguishing the world of the Aborigine from the white world beyond and served to reinforce the 'fact' that nature, not government, was doing the work of reducing a population to the point of extinction. Of course the exclusion of the application of medical science and sanitary engineering to the well-being of the Aboriginal population helped engineer a reduction in population numbers. It is on the basis of that understanding that we arrive at a fundamental disparity according to which the 'child' and the Aboriginal child were figured differentially as the subjects of welfare. White children found deprived, in poor health or pitiful circumstances justified intervention. They became the object of reform and protection and were sent to special homes until strong enough to be sent to a 'good country home'. For the half-caste Aboriginal population quite the opposite occurred. In contrast to white children, neglect and distress among the Aboriginal children were signals that they should not be intervened upon given that the leadership of Aboriginal policy in Victoria increasingly thought of the mission station as a place in which to die. Might not a girl be allowed to remain on Lake Condah, though she had reached the age at which half-castes were compelled to leave? Her widowed mother needed her 'but apart from this the girl is consumptive, her brother and three sisters having already succumbed to the disease'.[8]

While racial deficit might be used to explain the 'natural decline' to extinction of so-called 'full-bloods' the problem of growing numbers of so-called half-castes could not be subsumed under the same logic. As early as 1862 the board was alert to the fact that 'the half-castes, though numerically small, are increasing'[9] and by the 1877 Royal Commission on the Aborigines questions of *degrees* of Aboriginality had come to the fore. Did Aboriginality lie in colour and could it be bred out, allowing for 'absorption' or did it lie at some more fundamental level of nature such that despite appearances, half-castes, when put to the test, would reveal the same racial deficits as their darker-skinned forebearers? By the turn of the twentieth century while the BPA was noting a steady decrease in numbers of Aborigines from year to year and a corresponding decrease in 'the expense of managing them . . . from year to year' its confident forecast that in 'another twenty years they will probably be extinct'[10] could only be made in the context of an administrative fiat in the form of the 1886 Aborigines Protection Act which effectively reversed the definition of Aboriginality in the 1869 protection act to exclude from its new definition of Aboriginality those included in the original act, namely, 'every aboriginal half-caste or child of a half-caste'.[11] In the lead up to the new act the board was charged with figuring half-caste children anew as having the potential to make do in, and to 'merge' with settler society. Here, schooling would play a role on a number of fronts. Schooling had been early recognised as a means of drawing children, with their parents to follow,

8 PROV VPRS 1694, Unit 1: J. H. Stähle to Vice Chairman BPA 13 Oct. 1890

9 Victoria 1861 (BPA): 11 10 Victoria 1902b (BPA): 5–7.

11 Victoria Aborigines' Protection Act (No. 349) 1869 s 8.

onto the missions. The 1877 royal commission had advocated strongly for all mission schools to be brought under the control of the education department, and once under its control the standardised measures of scholarly success could be used to proclaim the educability of the mission child and hence bolster the legitimacy of a policy of merging the half-caste with the white population. Beyond that, the mission school, complete with dormitories, became a means of impinging on relations between the older and younger generations, separating children from the Aboriginality of their parents within the mission grounds, inculcating them with appropriate (non-Aboriginal) habits and 'protecting' girls in particular from their own understood promiscuity. State education, whatever else its advantages, was enmeshed in a programme of 'merging' the Aborigine, helping to legitimise the forced departure of youths from the station at school leaving age by refiguring half-castes as having the capacity to 'do for themselves'. With the 1886 legislation firmly in place, the earlier enthusiasm displayed by mission station managers for bringing their charges up to educational par with white children quickly dissipated and was followed by decades of an increasingly desultory attitude to station education. Indeed, running down school amenities and then highlighting the lack of satisfactory educational facilities was used more than once by the BPA as a ploy to better bring problematic Aborigines under control.

As a consequence of the government's aspirations regarding the Aboriginal population as a whole, young Aboriginal people cast out from the mission to 'do for themselves' were thrown into relief as troublemakers as were their kin who supported them by providing shelter on the mission and/or sharing rations, and as indeed were parents who refused to cede control of the fate of their children to the board. At the same time as welfarist policies of building support for the norms of non-Aboriginal family life were coming into operation, 'misconduct' in the form of the wilful maintenance of kinship ties within the Aboriginal population was being shaped as a punishable offence, with the mission stations taking on more and more of the operations of a correctional institution.

By the turn of the twentieth century it was a truism in government policy circles that non-Aboriginal children did not belong in institutions, home and institution being understood as contrasting parameters, defining and articulating the trajectories of both neglected and reformatory children. The non-Aboriginal child might be compelled to move from home to institution in the name of welfare and/or justice but it had become an entrenched principle (however questionable the actualities of the contrast) that the private home rather than the institution catered for the nature of childhood and the institution did not. But those parameters 'home' and 'institution' were not the parameters that held and gave shape to the Aboriginal child. With the establishment of government encampments overseen by the Board for the Protection of Aborigines there was no 'home' for Aboriginal children that was not conceived of by white administrators as, in essence, a correctional institution for Aboriginal parents and children alike. As noted in the body of this work, a distinction must be drawn between, on the one hand, the aspirations of an administration intent on scrutinising and controlling every aspect of conduct of Aborigines and the experience and understandings of Aborigines themselves, including their resistance to categories, rules and regulations imposed by an administration which regarded the Aboriginal home as an institutional space rightfully open for scrutiny and subjection to its authority. On the missions the BPA administered a justice welfare system in which conduct was tightly controlled via a disciplinary regime that bore a strong resemblance to disciplinary regimes of correctional institutions. From time to time the board resorted to formally transferring young charges deemed disciplinary problems to the department for Neglected Children and Reformatory Schools/ Children's Welfare Department and from time to time it engaged the services of the police and the courts in bringing miscreants under control. But for the most part managers were instructed by the board to deal with problems 'in house' as much as possible. Across the first half of the twentieth century private reformatories were voicing a reluctance to receive children formally transferred from the BPA. Nevertheless the BPA showed itself ready and willing to invoke the threat of DNCRS/CWD involvement as a strategy for managing station residents. Further, given that it had the power to banish station residents and to force relocations from one station to the other, its choice from time to time not to involve child welfare authorities in forced child removals by no means represented less coercive, less violent actions upon Aboriginal families.

With the decision taken in 1917 to close all but Lake Tyers and to 'concentrate' the Aborigines there the board was aware that it had lost an important weapon in its correctional arsenal: 'Before the days of concentration when we had other Stations under control we could transfer malcontents and offenders as a punishment. The plan is closed to us now.'[12] But 'concentration' also gave rise to new problems of control and containment that extended beyond the boundaries of the station and beyond the remit of the BPA. By 1917 any meaningful distinction between half-castes dwelling beyond station boundaries and full-boods within those boundaries had collapsed. On the eve of the first attempts to execute a policy of concentration and in the context of the BPA's increasing frustration over the Indigenous people's refusal to acquiesce to the imposed administrative categories Aboriginal/half-caste, to 'merge' and to disappear, the board once more changed the standard according to which individuals would count as falling under their administrative control in an attempt to shore up its authority and the mission boundaries. A new distinction would be drawn between those who were 'half-caste and up to full blood' and those who were deemed 'less than half-caste'. The former would be ushered into Lake Tyers; the latter, as legally white, would be beyond the board's remit and left to fend for themselves. Spurred on by criticism of moral laxity within station boundaries and limited by the growing reluctance of private reformatories to take troublesome

[12] NAA B356, 93: No author. Response to Report of Bishop of Gippsland re Lake Tyers 10 Sept. 1928.

charges off its hands, the board ruminated on more and more draconian means of bringing a station population to heal: a purpose-built reformatory station; a sectioned off area of Lake Tyers with all the trappings of a labour camp? Meanwhile many who were not living on Lake Tyers station were living a marginalised existence, subsisting in community camps on the fringe of country towns where they were largely ignored, or tolerated as a source of cheap, mobile seasonal labour, their children beyond the margins of the various departmental concerns with welfare, with health, with governing, educating and policing children.

By the mid-1950s the influence of the psy-sciences in figuring the relations between poverty, the family, child welfare and juvenile delinquency underpinned the logic of administering *sections* of a non-Aboriginal population. By the 1950s the primary problem facing the mainstream welfare justice system was juvenile delinquency; the juvenile delinquent was made, not born and the aberrant psychology of the family was firmly understood as the primary site for the production of maladjustment and delinquency. But up to that time there was not a word among the various departmental stakeholders and related agencies – the Children's Court, Mental Hygiene or the CWD itself – on Aboriginal children. Aboriginality was born not made, and expressed itself in a set of moral and intellectual racial deficits – childishness, laziness, untruthfulness, untrustworthiness, dirtiness, shiftlessness, animal cunning, inability to persevere and sexual promiscuity coupled with animal fecundity – rehearsed and reiterated among the board, its officers, and allied agencies including the police, church officials, education and medical officers as the reason for a whole people's failure to achieve the so-called ordinary standards of productive white citizenship. Aboriginal welfare and child welfare were understood by government as 'diverse' administrative matters.

In the light of the BPA's refusal to own any responsibility for fringe communities in country districts various parties formed various alliances to lobby the government, to establish rudimentary welfare services and to devise various means of bringing perceived out-of-control river camps under white supervision. Growing criticism of the government's failure to act on these camps joined criticism informed by the developmental turn in the psychological sciences which began to voice the so-called Aboriginal problem, together with the 'case' of the problem Aboriginal child as problems made rather than born of racial deficit, and made largely by conditions imposed by the administration itself. The logic was still underpinned by a recognition of a whole people's failure, but that failure now came to be understood in terms informed by developmental psychology as largely the product of the immediate social and familial environment: 'Aborigines brought up in segregation could not be expected to have anything but the moral standard of children. They were continually under surveillance and could not "grow up"'.[13] Developmental psychology

[13] NAA B56, 97: Notes of deputation from Victorian Aboriginal [sic] Group to Chief Secretary's Office 18 Aug. 1937.

would formally displace biological destiny as the basis upon which the 1957 McLean Report recommended the government proceed. The root cause of the problem lay in the aberrant psychology of the Aboriginal family and the forms of intervention as recommended in the 1956 Barry Report and that were taking hold in the reshaping of the mainstream child welfare-justice system were to be applied to Aborigines – scientifically based professional intervention in family life backed up by a newly available spectrum of state-run institutions when requirements extended beyond such interventions. McLean redefined Aboriginality to include 'all persons with an admixture of aboriginal blood', given that inasmuch as they were 'brought up by their mothers in aboriginal communities' and were 'generally regarded, by themselves and others, as aborigines' they 'present the same problem'.[14] The extension of the definition allowed the government to extend efforts to control unauthorised camp communities. In the decade following the McLean Report Aborigines were largely acted upon as problem families in an envisaged population-wide programme of 'rehabilitation' geared towards assimilation via 'dispersal'. Intervention at the level of the family meant teaching Aborigines to live like normal (white) families, a role delegated to an army of professional welfare workers of one ilk or another under a new Aborigines Welfare Board. Subjected to the scrutiny and conjecture of this flood of expertise, Aborigines either measured up to the norm or failed and the consequences of failure included such actions as child removal.

In 1960 the Victorian government introduced a social welfare bill into Parliament which would see an amalgamation of the Children's Welfare and Penal departments. In introducing the bill, Chief Secretary Rylah aligned its contents with the recommendations of the Barry Report. He professed his 'earnest belief in the family unit as the foundation of our social structure' and while the government had made 'considerable progress with the family home proposition' in its attempts to waylay the development of delinquency, the state 'must still face squarely the fact that when it comes to the delinquent child the state must provide facilities which are not available at present', especially for those children deemed not suitable for 'outside [non-government] institutions'. Aborigines were not named as targeted by the legislation but in listing the reasons why the new legislation was imperative Rylah made specific reference to the unauthorised seasonal river camps: 'we could not allow them to live under the conditions under which they were living on the banks of the River Murray and other streams in Victoria'.[15] A couple of years on, the Aborigines Welfare Board while underscoring 'a strong sense of family and a deep affection for children' noted a necessary wariness on the part of its officers in recommending material aid to Aboriginal people living in 'sub-standard' conditions for fear 'that parents will feel absolved of responsibility for the health and care of their off-spring'.[16] And a couple of years after that the children of a whole people

14 Victoria (C. McLean) 1957b: 6.
15 Victoria Parliamentary Debates Session 1959–60 Vol 259 Legislative Assembly 6 April 1960: 2389–99.
16 Victoria 1964 (AWB): 8.

were marked out by the likelihood of their removal from their families into state care: 'Aboriginal children are much more likely to become State wards. A very high proportion of these children come into care as State wards at some time in their lives.'[17]

This book has placed under examination white modes of governing: the conduct of white rule helped shape the social worlds of the governed, whether behind the fences in the wooden encampments set up for those who lost the war of occupation, or in the brick institutions that sprang up in the city to house the white children, whether neglected or offending or both. Of course, governing Indigenous or non-Indigenous peoples presupposes more or less organised responses and resistance on the part of the governed, and there exists a substantial literature in this field. The overwhelming display of white power and its continuous deployment for more than a century of direct institutional oversight of Aboriginal peoples in Victoria – the power to make bodies move – nevertheless set conditions of possibility for the kinds of institutional confinement presently used for both Indigenous and non-Indigenous people.

INTO THE PRESENT

The regular reporting of statistics on present matters of welfare and justice is mostly from two main organisations in Australia, the Australian Institute of Health and Welfare (AIHW) and the Australian Institute of Criminology (AIC). The AIHW recognised some years ago that there was a level of 'dual involvement' of children and youth in both the welfare and justice systems. It has become commonplace to draw a statistical picture of analyses of children and young people in both welfare and justice institutions – an early example were Australian Law Reform Commission studies from 1997 showing that up to 70 per cent of children and young people convicted of a criminal offence were already 'know to the welfare'.[18] In more recently published AIHW reports, young people in the child protection system were reported as fourteen times as likely as the general population to be under youth justice supervision in the same year. In 2014–15, more than 5 per cent of children between the ages of ten and seventeen who were in the child protection system were also under youth justice supervision in the same year (although not necessarily at the same time), compared with just 0.4 per cent of the general population in the same age group. The level of dual involvement was 8 per cent for those under care and protection orders, 6.3 per cent for those in out-of-home care and 4.1 per cent for those who were the subject of an investigated notification – meaning there was strong evidence of harm to children.[19] Indigenous children were seven times as likely as non-Indigenous children to be receiving child protection services and Indigenous

[17] Victoria 1967 (AWB): 5. [18] Australia (Law Reform Commission) 1997b.
[19] Australia (AIHW) 2016c: vi.

young people in the child protection system were more than twice as likely to be under youth justice supervision as non-Indigenous young people (10.4 per cent compared with 4.3 per cent).[20]

Conversely, young people under youth justice supervision were fifteen times as likely as the general population to be in the child protection system in the same year. In 2014–15, the percentage of those under youth justice supervision who were also in the child protection system was 32.4. Two in five (40 per cent) of those in detention were involved in the child protection system in the same year, which is nineteen times the rate for the general population. The level of child protection involvement for those under community-based supervision in 2014–15 was also high: with about one-third (32.1 per cent) also in the child protection system. The younger someone was at his or her first youth justice supervision, the more likely that individual was to also be in child protection: of those under youth justice supervision in 2014–15, three in five (60.0 per cent) of those age ten at their first youth justice supervision were also in child protection in 2014–15, compared with 9.4 per cent of those age seventeen.[21] The authors of the AIHW report offer some speculative assessments of the underlying systemic circumstances that may lead to such dual involvement, citing an Australian Institute of Family Studies survey:

> Procedures used within the child protection and youth justice systems can also facilitate involvement of one system with the other. For example, contact with youth justice agencies may lead to a child protection notification being made if abuse or neglect is suspected by, or reported to, agency staff. This highlights the importance of better understanding the characteristics and pathways of children and young people who are both in the child protection system and under youth justice supervision. This information can assist support staff, case workers and policy makers to get the best outcomes for children and young people.[22]

Despite numerous and continuing inquiries into increasing levels of incarceration and Indigenous child removal since the 1960s, rates of Indigenous imprisonment have doubled from 14 per cent of the prison population in 1991 to 27 per cent in 2015. Indigenous adults are now fifteen times more likely to be jailed than non-Indigenous adults, Indigenous women are thirty times more likely, and Indigenous children are twenty-six times more likely.[23] What is laid down in this book is documentation and analysis of some of the preconditions for making up the present that are found articulated in the differing ways in which the provision of welfare and

[20] Australia (AIHW) 2016b: vii; Australia (AIHW) 2016c: vi. [21] Australia (AIHW) 2016c: vi.

[22] Australia (AIHW) 2016c: 1.

[23] Australia (AIC) 2016a: Chapter 5. In 2013, the Indigenous imprisonment rate (2,359 per 100,000) was 19 times higher than the non-Indigenous rate (126 per 100,000). Between 2003 and 2013, Indigenous imprisonment rates increased, while non-Indigenous rates decreased. The rate of Indigenous offender imprisonment was 29 per cent higher than that recorded in 2003, while the rate of non-Indigenous offenders had decreased by 3 per cent. Indigenous prisoners comprised 27 per cent of the total prisoner population in 2013, compared with 21 per cent in 2003.

justice is attempted. The assumptions or unspoken taken-for-grantedness underpinning present-day governmental actions upon children shape what is possible if in policy terms these assumptions remain unchallenged by the leadership and those who contribute to policymaking over time.[24] The present operation of the justice and welfare systems in Victoria and across Australia produce a range of outcomes for children that are seen by many Australians as concerning, particularly the seemingly ever-increasing rates of incarceration of young persons and the highly disproportionate rates of Indigenous child removal and incarceration. Subsidiary events affecting health and well-being of Australian children are the increasing rates of illness of children in remote areas, increasing rates of suicide even among relatively young children, and increasing drug use across all social groups.

INQUIRY AFTER INQUIRY

Grief and loss are the predominant themes of this report. Tenacity and survival are also acknowledged. It is no ordinary report. Much of its subject matter is so personal and intimate that ordinarily it would not be discussed. These matters have only been discussed with the Inquiry with great difficulty and much personal distress. The suffering and the courage of those who have told their stories inspire sensitivity and respect. The histories we trace are complex and pervasive. Most significantly the actions of the past resonate in the present and will continue to do so in the future. The laws, policies and practices which separated Indigenous children from their families have contributed directly to the alienation of Indigenous societies today. For individuals, their removal as children and the abuse they experienced at the hands of the authorities or their delegates have permanently scarred their lives. The harm continues in later generations, affecting their children and grandchildren. In no sense has the Inquiry been 'raking over the past' for its own sake. The truth is that the past is very much with us today, in the continuing devastation of the lives of Indigenous Australians. That devastation cannot be addressed unless the whole community listens with an open heart and mind to the stories of what has happened in the past and, having listened and understood, commits itself to reconciliation.[25]

Twenty years on the recommendations of the Bringing Them Home Report, cited here, have in most instances not been carried out. Neither have most of the recommendations of the Royal Commission into Aboriginal Deaths in Custody Report, thirty years ago.[26] Major representative bodies such as the Aboriginal and Torres Strait Islander Commission (ATSIC), the body recommended by the Bringing Them Home Inquiry to develop a framework 'for the implementation of self-determination in relation to the well-being of Indigenous children and young people' in collaboration with the Council of Australian Governments, was closed down by the same minister responsible for the Northern Territory Intervention. The

[24] Bacchi 2009. [25] Australia (M. Dodson and R. Wilson) 1997a: Introduction.
[26] Australia (E. Johnson) 1991.

Human Rights Commission in 1998 noted the closing of ATSIC represented the central government's withdrawal of efforts at self-determination that had been tried by earlier governments – 'a radical change in the way government and non-government organisations consult, engage with and support Aboriginal people'. The Bringing Them Home Report further recommended that within the parameters of the act, 'Indigenous communities are free to formulate and negotiate an agreement on measures best suited to their individual needs concerning children, young people and families'; and 'the transfer of legal jurisdiction in relation to children's welfare, care and protection, adoption and/or juvenile justice to an Indigenous community, region or representative organisation'.[27]

In a recent speech to the Australian Bar Association in Melbourne, the Australian Attorney-General George Brandis announced a new inquiry into the increasing rates of Indigenous incarceration. He pointed to the doubling of incarceration rates since the Royal Commission into Aboriginal deaths in custody in 1988–91, which he argued showed that attempts by successive governments to address the issue had failed: 'Those statistics of course paint a stark picture – a picture of failed initiatives and flawed or incomplete reform efforts which, despite the best intentions, often deliver little by way of tangible progress and indeed, as those statistics reveal, we have gone backwards.' A Western Australian Labor senator Pat Dodson, an Indigenous Yawuru man who sat as a member of that Royal Commission, recently commented to the *Guardian* newspaper that any fresh inquiry would have to be accompanied by real action to combat the cynicism felt by many in the Indigenous community who had seen inquiry after inquiry pass without change: 'in this case at least they've done something ... The effectiveness of it has yet to be seen, of course.'[28]

The inquiry was announced a week after Dodson had criticised Indigenous Affairs Minister Nigel Scullion, for 'amnesia over past inquiries into Indigenous incarceration'. Dodson argued that the Royal Commission into Aboriginal Deaths in Custody had produced 339 recommendations, very few of which had been enacted: '[The Minister] may have peered through the window into the morass in front of him and got a bit of a fright ... I am not confident that there is a real sense of zeal about this.' Reforms such as scrapping mandatory sentencing laws in Western Australia and paperless arrest laws in the Northern Territory would reduce incarceration, he said, but were outside of federal government control: 'the social policy settings are as crucial as any reform to the legal situation, and that's something the federal government does control', Dodson told *Guardian Australia*, pointing to the shared system of governance of Indigenous matters in Australia. Nevertheless, Indigenous leaders have cautiously welcomed plans for a fresh inquiry into the high rates of Indigenous incarceration, providing it delivers tangible changes in government policy.[29]

27 Australia (M. Dodson and R. Wilson) 1997a: Recommendations 43a; 43b 2; 43c 1.
28 *Guardian* (Australian edition) 2016, Oct. 27.
29 *Guardian* (Australian edition) 2016, Oct. 27.

A report by the Community Council of Australia released in the same week has, according to one newspaper report, 'shattered perceptions that Australia is a country of the "fair go", finding it is less fair, less safe, and with a higher incarceration rate than comparable OECD nations'.[30] *The Australia We Want* was released at a National Press Club address by World Vision Australia's chief executive, Tim Costello, pointing to rising inequality, suicide rates and above-average carbon emissions. The report's author, the Community Council of Australia's chief executive David Crosbie, said he was shocked that Australia rated so poorly against other developed countries. The total national incarceration rate increased by 6 per cent to 196 people for every 100,000 in 2015, higher than any country in Western Europe. In the Northern Territory, imprisonment rates are four times the national average, at 885 for every 100,000, and higher than the rate of imprisonment in the United States. Again, Indigenous child removal and incarceration were particularly in focus. The Australia-wide Indigenous incarceration rate was fifteen times the national rate, at 2253 for every 100,000 in 2015. Crosby reported to the *Guardian* that incarceration rates 'are like the canary in the coalmine, they tell you how your most vulnerable are being treated'; he said it was disingenuous to suggest the imprisonment rate was connected to crime, because only 25 per cent of prisoners had been convicted of a violent offence. In 2015 almost 10,000 prisoners had not been convicted at all and were on remand awaiting court dates. 'The incarceration rates are entirely a product of policy we implemented and enacted', he said, 'They are not an accident.'[31]

The decision to establish a series of government encampments to contain and control Indigenous people in Victoria lasted about one hundred years and was premised on the view that Aborigines were not able to govern themselves, a view perpetuated in the present. The opening sections of this book discussing the shaping of black/white relations in Australia, especially those established as a consequence of the Northern Territory Intervention, have a stark familiarity. As one Indigenous elder said of the Intervention in a frustrated attempt to explain to government why Aborigines were dismayed at the hostility and the patronising nature of the attack on their people, 'Much exertion brought to bear on naughty children. We are not naughty children.'[32] The Intervention, which harnessed Aboriginal child welfare to the pursuit of political power, at the same time tapping into the unease and latent racism existing among white Australians, was not simply history repeating itself, and, as we have discovered, not so 'exceptional'. Rather, it is an expression of the ongoing contingent and unstable nature of freedom of self-determination under the exercise of contemporary liberalism, an illustration of the vulnerability of particular social groups to decision making about who is eligible for self-government and who is not and testament to 'actually existing liberalism' – to the thread of authoritarianism that runs through contemporary liberal rule and which exposes those deemed

[30] *Guardian* (Australian edition) 2016, Oct. 27.
[31] *Guardian* (Australian edition) 2016, Oct. 27.
[32] Concerned Australians 2010: 21.

incapable of self-government to despotic practices quite counter to contemporaneous ethical norms espoused in the liberal philosophy of the 'fair go'.[33]

ACTUALLY EXISTING LIBERALISM

In 2013 the Victorian Government launched a bipartisan Parliamentary Committee Inquiry into the handling of Child Abuse by Religious and other Non-Government Organisations. It exposed evidence of the failure of such organisations to adequately prevent and respond to the criminal abuse of children. A wide range of organisations under scrutiny 'had taken steps with the direct object of concealing wrongdoing'. It had also provided the opportunity for the personal experiences of 'victims' to be publicly acknowledged. The Inquiry noted that victims said 'they were seeking justice for what they often felt to be the loss of their innocence as a child' and acknowledged the unjustified guilt they carried. Most instances considered were 'perpetrated more than twenty years ago', but organisational and individual responsibility could not be relegated to the past.[34] In this kind of exercise, the past was to be opened for historical scrutiny but the 'child' at the centre of the Inquiry was not. No official definition of 'child' was offered. The primary question for the Inquiry was how, given this entity, non-government organisations failed to act appropriately.

That same year the Australian government launched a Royal Commission into Institutional Responses to Child Sexual Abuse. It would take in a wide range of non-government and government bureaucracies, agencies and institutions, including child protection agencies and juvenile justice centres. The commission abides by the definition of 'child' provided by the 1989 UN Convention on the Rights of the Child, of which Australia is a signatory, namely, it explains, 'a person below the age of 18 years' who is both the bearer of human rights and one who, it is recognised 'may need special care and attention where adults may not'.[35] It opened at the County Court in Victoria in April of 2013 and at the time of writing is still proceeding.

As with the Victorian inquiry, much media coverage and commentary has been given, via commission hearings, to the attempts of organisations, including the Catholic church, to conceal abuse. In regional Victoria a retired bishop's admission that he 'didn't do enough' was derided in the press: 'He actually did plenty – all of it wrong and all of it sacrificing the innocence of the child for the reputation of the Church.'[36] At a Sydney Hearing, criticism of the church hierarchy by a US expert in cardinal law was met with 'loud applause': 'there's no office in the Catholic Church or anywhere else so important that it justifies sacrificing the welfare of one innocent child. Period'.[37]

One effect of these inquiries is to bring to the fore the 'innocent child' as an unqualified fixed point against which the guilty history of various individual and

33 Dean 2007; Hindess 2001. 34 Victoria 2013a: xxvi–xxviii, 4–5.
35 Australia (Royal Commission) 2013: 2, 13–14. 36 *Age* 2017c, April 5: 3.
37 *Newcastle Herald* 2017, Feb. 7.

administrative crimes and misdemeanours is judged. At the time of writing of this book the commission has yet to move to the scrutiny of juvenile justice centres.

In November 2016, following a reported 'riot' the Victorian state government transferred 15 juvenile detainees from the site of the old Royal Park Children's Depot in Melbourne, now a 123-bed Parkville juvenile justice facility. Inmates were to be transferred to a wing of the state's adult high security prison at Barwon in regional Victoria. This was not the first time the government had made such a move. A 2013 report of the Victorian ombudsman investigated the circumstances of five children, two of them Indigenous, transferred by the Youth Parole Board from Parkville to an adult prison in mid-2012. The children were afforded no legal representation. The ombudsman noted: 'The children were locked in their cells on their own for 23 hours a day. They were allowed one hour in the exercise yard per day and during that time they were in handcuffs. The children remained in solitary confinement for a number of months.' One child had a serious mental illness, of which the authorities were aware but he too was made to endure these conditions for several months. The ombudsman emphasised the children's vulnerability in the adult prison environment, noting in particular their vulnerability to sexual assault.[38]

A later decision in 2016 to transfer children to an adult prison was met by a legal challenge on human rights grounds. The Supreme Court ruled that it was illegal to house juvenile detainees in an adult facility. The government held firm, noting that, since it had recently gazetted part of the prison as a youth justice facility and remand centre, and had improved facilities there, it had addressed the court's concerns.[39] In January 2017 further trouble at Parkville saw the deployment of police dogs and another seven Parkville detainees transferred to Barwon and to the Malmsbury Youth Justice Centre in regional Victoria. Later that month, following a 'mass break-out' from Malmsbury of fifteen detainees, all under 18, the government announced plans for a new 'fit-for-purpose' high security youth detention centre. It later confirmed that staff from the adult prison system, equipped with extendable batons and capsicum spray, would be deployed at the Malmsbury and Parkville centres. It confirmed shortly thereafter that capsicum spray had been authorised and deployed against juvenile inmates held at Barwon. Tear gas had been used at Malmsbury.[40]

Reports of unrest in the juvenile justice system ran simultaneously with reports of a 'youth crime wave' involving armed robberies, home invasions and car-jackings attributed to the so-called 'Apex gang', understood as primarily Sudanese in its make-up but more recently inclusive of Pacific Islander and 'caucasian' members. Connections were quick to be made between the 'riots' and the 'crime wave'.[41] Connections were further forged with broader political concerns to do with national

[38] Victoria (Ombudsman) 2013b: 3–4. [39] Victoria (Ombudsman) 2017.

[40] Australian Broadcasting Corporation (ABC) 2017b, Jan. 31. [41] *Australian* 2016, Dec. 2: 13.

identity, border security and immigration. A 'growing trend of out-of-control South Sudanese youth' revealed an 'obvious truth' about Sudanese refugees, vindicating moves by a conservative government, a decade earlier, to reduce its intake of refugees from Sudan and Somalia and reinforcing the veracity of a 'culture clash'.[42] The Victorian Leader of the Opposition stated that those who were not Australian citizens had 'worn out their welcome and should be deported.'[43] A police spokesperson confirmed that, via 'established process with the Australian Border Force' a number of Apex members had been deported.[44]

The government's response to unrest in its juvenile justice centres was, it admitted, 'confronting', but counsel for government argued in court that the rights of those at Barwon 'were not limited', and '[e]ven if they were, there was a clear case of justification' given they had 'the size and strength of men': 'We're talking about 16- and 17-year-old boys, we're not talking about young children.'[45] The premier noted the government was 'dealing with a group of violent offenders that the youth justice centre was never meant to deal with', and with behaviour 'more akin to the sorts of events and experiences that prison officers are trained to deal with'.[46] Other stakeholders were more pointed, a Police Association spokesperson notocing, 'People that commit armed robberies, assaults and car jackings to escape custody are not kids whatever their age . . . They are dangerous criminals that need to be arrested quickly before they can cause further harm.'[47] These, then, are no innocent children. Indeed, in their offending they are not children at all. Neither, suggestion would have it, are they *our* children and hence they can be excluded justifiably from the kinds of protections afforded those deemed to inhabit childhood proper.

The above sketch is introduced to juxtapose two very different but contemporaneous investments by government in the category of the child. *Here* the 'child' is afforded an apparent inviolable stability around which government must operate. Simultaneously, *there*, the 'child' is up for political grabs. Following Hindess, it may be suggested that this is something other than 'a simple matter of liberal hypocrisy', something other than a *simple* case of government saying one thing – committing to the rights of children – and doing another. 'Liberty and domination', Hindess argues, 'are joined in liberal thought like two sides of a single coin: the value of one may appear on the face, but the figure of the other is firmly stamped on the reverse'.[48] Under liberalism, freedom to make choices is granted to those who may be trusted to make the right *sort* of decision. By this account, all children become the legitimate subjects of less liberal rule, given that they are all in-the-making, so to speak. But some, it seems, are more readily recognised as liberalism's others, as types lacking what might be termed an ideal readiness for the inculcation of habits of self-restraint as a precondition of the granting of the freedom of self-government. (Regarding the Victorian juvenile justice scene, we are reminded that the

42 *Herald-Sun* 2016, Dec. 1: 13. 43 ABC 2016, Dec. 6. 44 *Age* 2017a, Jan. 19.
45 *Age* 2016, Dec. 16: 6. 46 ABC 2017a, Jan. 27. 47 *Age* 2017b, Jan. 27. 48 Hindess 2001: 94.

government is dealing with a group of atypical 'hardcore' juveniles.)[49] Particular cohorts of children, it seems, continue to be made up in the context of a range of aspirations to do with population, territory, national security and racial identity, and as legitimately subject to administrative practices counter to contemporaneous ethical norms embedded elsewhere in the logic of governing childhood 'proper'.

49 *Australian* 2017, April 20: 2.

References

BOOKS, CHAPTERS, ARTICLES

Age 1955. 'Award for work for Aborigines'. December 24: 3.

Age 2016. 'Teenagers held at Barwon Prison "have the size and strength of men", court hears'. December 16: 6.

Age 2017a. 'Police and Border Force to deport a number of Apex gang members'. January 19. At www.theage.com.au/victoria/police-and-border-force-to-deport-a-number-of-apex-gang-members-20170118-gtu7f6.html

Age 2017b. 'Malmsbury riot. Besieged government promises major youth justice shakeup'. January 27. At www.theage.com.au/victoria/malmsbury-riot-besieged-government-promises-major-youth-justice-shakeup-20170126-gtz2hv.html

Age 2017c. 'Ronald Mulkearns takes his secrets – and his guilt – to the grave'. April 5: 3.

Anderson, W. 2002. *The Cultivation of Whiteness: science, health and racial destiny in Australia*. Melbourne University Press.

Anderson, W. 2009. 'From subjugated knowledge to conjugated subjects: science and globalisation, or postcolonial studies', *Postcolonial Studies*, 12 (4): 389–400.

Andrews, S. 1963. 'Victoria', in Murray, W. (ed.), *The Struggle for Dignity*. Melbourne: Council for Aboriginal Rights.

Argus 1878. 'The Royal-Park Industrial School. By A Visitor'. June 8: 9.

Argus 1879. 'Royal-Park Industrial School'. October 14: 7.

Argus 1880a. 'Saturday, June 19, 1880'. June 19: 6.

Argus 1880b. 'The Industrial Schools'. September 23: 7. [Published Report of Industrial Schools Committee to Chief Secretary]

Argus 1894. 'Neglected children'. January 29: 6.

Argus 1908. 'Abandoned child'. January 10: 6.

Argus 1911. 'Treatment of disease. A malady to be fought'. July 11: 5.

Argus 1952a. 'When a girl goes to gaol – the fault's ours'. September 6: 2.

Argus 1952b. 'State "stingy" to children'. October 1: 5.

Argus 1952c. 'Our child welfare ideas "medieval"'. November 24: 7.

Argus 1954a. 'The sink of human decency is also blocked'. July 19: 4.

Argus 1954b. 'Children not "left to rot"'. July 21: 11.

Ariès, P. 1965. *Centuries of Childhood: a social history of family life*. New York: Vintage Books.

Armstrong, D. 2002. *A New History of Identity: a sociology of medical knowledge*. New York: Palgrave Macmillan.

Ashford, B. and Morgan, R. 2004. 'Criminalizing looked-after children', *Criminal Justice Matters*, 57 (1): 8–9; 38.
Attwood, B. 1986. 'Off the mission stations: Aborigines in Gippsland 1860–1890', *Aboriginal History*, 10 (2): 131–51.
Attwood, B. 1989. *The Making of the Aborigines*. Sydney: Allen & Unwin.
Australian 2016. 'At the Apex of a crime wave in Melbourne'. December 2: 13.
Australian 2017. 'Victorian youths in hardcore wave of violence'. April 20: 2.
Australian Broadcasting Corporation 2016. News, December 6. At www.abc.net.au/news/2016-12-04/statistics-raise-questions-about-calls-to-deport-youth-offenders/8087410
Australian Broadcasting Corporation 2017a. News, January 27. At www.abc.net.au/news/2017-01-27/additions-staff-to-secure-malmsbury-and-parkville-youth-centres/8217566
Australian Broadcasting Corporation 2017b. *The World Today*, January 31. At www.abc.net.au/news/2017-01-31/tear-gas-used-in-vic-youth-detention-centre/8226396
Australian Legal Information Institute. 'R. v Ballard or Barrett [1829] NSW Supreme Court 26'. At www.austlii.edu.au/au/cases/nsw/NSWSupC/1829/26
Bacchi, C. 2009. *Analysing Policy: what's the problem represented to be?* Frenchs Forest NSW: Pearson.
Barry, A., Osborne, T. and Rose, N. 1996. *Foucault and Political Reason: liberalism, neo-liberalism and rationalities of government*. London: UCL Press.
Barwick, D., Barwick, R. and Barwick, L. 1998. *Rebellion at Coranderrk*. Aboriginal History.
Bourdieu, P. 1977. *An Outline of a Theory of Practice*. Cambridge: Cambridge University Press.
Broome, R. 2005. *Aboriginal Victorians: a history since 1800*. Sydney: Allen and Unwin.
Buchan, B. 2005. 'The empire of political thought: civilization, savagery and perceptions of Indigenous government', *History of the Human Sciences*, 18 (2): 1–22.
Burchell, G., Gordon, C. and Miller, P. 1991. *The Foucault Effect: studies in governmentality*. London: Harvester Wheatsheaf.
Campbell, A. 1994. *Victorian Aborigines: John Bulmer's recollections 1855–1908*, Occasional Paper No. 1. Melbourne: Museum of Victoria.
Canberra Times 2007. 'Brough labels ATSIC a "fraud"'. June 2: 8.
Carrington, K. 1993. *Offending Girls: sex, youth and justice*. Sydney: Allen and Unwin.
Carrington, K. 2011. 'Punitiveness and the criminalization of the other: state wards, unlawful non-citizens and Indigenous youth', *Somatechnics*, 1 (1): 30–48.
Chesterman, J. 2005. *Civil Rights: how Indigenous Australians won formal equality*. St. Lucia, Qld: University of Queensland Press.
Clark, I. 2013. *Goulburn River Aboriginal Protectorate: a history of the Goulburn River Aboriginal Protectorate Station at Murchison, Victoria, 1840–1853*. Ballarat, Vic.: Ballarat Heritage Services.
Combined Aboriginal Organisations of the Northern Territory. 2007. *A Proposed Emergency Response and Development Plan to Protect Aboriginal Children in the Northern Territory: a preliminary response to the Australian Government's proposals*. At http://apo.org.au/files/Resource/2787_cao_report_8_july.pdf
Concerned Australians. 2010. *This Is What We Said. Australian Aboriginal People Give Their Views on the Northern Territory Intervention*. East Melbourne: Concerned Australians.
Davies, S. 1987. 'Aborigines, murder and the criminal law in early Port Phillip, 1841–1851', *Australian Historical Studies*, 22 (88): 313–35.
Dawn 1953. 'Swan Hill's New Centre. Police Sergeant Helps', *Dawn. A Magazine for the Aboriginal People of New South Wales*, 2 (11): 6.

Dawn 1956. 'Swan Hill Native Children's Recreation Centre [Cover photograph]', *Dawn. A Magazine for the Aboriginal People of New South Wales*, 5 (8).
Dean, M. 1999. *Governmentality: power and rule in modern society*. London: Sage.
Dean, M. 2002. 'Liberal government and authoritarianism', *Economy and Society*, 31 (1): 37–61.
Dean, M. 2007. *Governing Societies: political perspectives on domestic and international rule*. Maidenhead: Open University Press.
Dean, M. and Hindess, B. eds. 1998. *Governing Australia. Studies in Contemporary Rationalities of Government*. Cambridge: Cambridge University Press.
Derham, A. 1919. 'Notes on pneumonic influenza, with special reference to the medic epidemic', *Medical Journal of Australia*, January 25: 65–66.
Donzelot, J. 1979. *The Policing of Families*. New York: Pantheon.
Dutton, M. 2009. '911: the after-life of colonial governmentality', *Postcolonial Studies*, 12 (3): 303–14.
Elias, N. [1939] 1994. *The Civilizing Process*. Oxford: Blackwell.
Elias, N. and Scotson J. [1964] 1994. *The Established and the Outsiders: a sociological enquiry into community problems*. Teesside, UK: Sage.
Ellinghaus, K. 2001. 'Regulating Koori marriages: the 1886 Victorian Aborigines Protection Act', *Journal of Australian Studies*, 25 (67): 22–29.
Ewald, F. 1990. 'Norms, discipline and the law', *Representations*, 30: 138–61.
Finnane, M. and Garton, S. 1992. 'The work of policing: social relations and the criminal justice system in Queensland 1880–1914: Part I', *Labour History*, 62: 52–70.
Fitzpatrick, P. and Joyce, R. 2007. 'The normality of the exception in democracy's empire', *Journal of Law and Society*, 34 (1): 65–76.
Foucault, M. 1979. *Discipline and Punish: the birth of the prison* (Trans. A. Sheridan). Harmondsworth: Penguin.
Foucault, M. 1991. 'Governmentality' (Trans. P. Pasquino), in Burchell, G., Gordon, C. and Miller, P. (eds.), *The Foucault Effect: studies in governmentality*. London: Harvester Wheatsheaf.
Foucault, M. 2003. *Abnormal: lectures at the College de France 1974–1975* (Trans. G. Burchell). London: Picador.
Foucault, M. 2004. *'Society Must Be Defended': lectures at the Collège de France 1975–76* (Trans. D. Macey). London: Penguin.
Foucault, M. 2007. *Security, Territory, Population: lectures at the Collège de France, 1977–1978* (Trans. G. Burchell). Basingstoke: Palgrave Macmillan.
Foucault, M. 2008. *The Birth of Biopolitics: lectures at the Collège de France, 1978–79* (Trans. G. Burchell). Basingstoke: Palgrave Macmillan.
Ford, L. 2010. *Settler Sovereignty: jurisdiction and Indigenous people in America and Australia, 1788–1836*. Cambridge, Mass.: Harvard University Press.
Gadda, A. 2008. 'Rights, Foucault and power: a critical analysis of the United Nation Convention on the Rights of the Child', *Edinburgh Working Papers in Sociology*, 31.
Garland, D. 1985. *Punishment and Welfare: a history of penal strategies*. Aldershot: Gower.
Garland, D. 1997. '"Governmentality" and the problem of crime: Foucault, criminology, sociology', *Theoretical Criminology*, 1 (2): 173–214.
Garton, S. 1988. *Medicine and Madness: a social history of insanity in New South Wales, 1880–1940*. Sydney: New South Wales University Press.
Grimshaw, P. 2008. '"That we may obtain our religious liberty . . .": Aboriginal women, faith and rights in early twentieth century Victoria, Australia', *Journal of the Canadian Historical Association/Revue de la Société Historique du Canada*, 19 (2): 24–42.

Guardian (Australian Edition) 2016. 'Call for fresh inquiry into Indigenous incarceration gets cautious welcome'. October 27.

Hacking, I. 1983. *Representing and Intervening: introductory topics in the philosophy of natural science*. Cambridge University Press.

Hacking, I. 1986. 'Making up people', in Heller, T., Sosna, M. and Wellbery, D. (eds.), *Reconstructing Individualism*. Stanford University Press.

Hacking, I. 1991. 'The making and molding of child abuse', *Critical Inquiry*, 17 (2): 253–78.

Hacking, I. 2004. *Historical Ontology*, Cambridge, Mass.: Harvard University Press.

Hanson, K. 2016. 'Separate childhood laws and the future of society', *Law, Culture and the Humanities*, 12 (2): 195–205.

Herald 1899. 'Improper behaviour leads to imprisonment'. January 21.

Herald-Sun 2016. 'Andrews was right about Sudanese crime. Where are the apologies?' December 1: 13.

Hindess, B. 1996. 'Liberalism, socialism and democracy: variations on a governmental theme', in Barry, A., Osborne, T. and. Rose, N. (eds.), *Foucault and Political Reason: liberalism, neo-liberalism and rationalities of government*. University of Chicago Press.

Hindess, B. 2000. 'Democracy and the neo-liberal promotion of arbitrary power', *Critical Review of International Social Political Philosophy*, 3 (4): 68–84.

Hindess, B. 2001. 'The liberal government of unfreedom', *Alternatives*, 26 (2): 93–111.

Hindess, B. 2004. 'Liberalism: what's in a name?', in Larner, W. and Walters, W. (eds.), *Global Governmentality: governing international spaces*. London: Routledge.

Hindess, B. 2008. 'Political theory and "actually existing liberalism"', *Critical Review of International Social and Political Philosophy*, 11 (3): 347–52.

Hindess, B. 2009. 'Liberalism and history', Keynote Address, *Foucault: 25 Years On. Proceedings of Conference hosted by the Centre for Post-colonial and Globalisation Studies*, Adelaide, 25 June. Underdale, SA: Hawke Research Institute, University of South Australia. At www.unisa.edu.au/hawkeinstitute/publications/foucault-25-years/hindess.pdf

Hirst, P. 1981. 'The genesis of the social', *Politics and Power*, 3: 67–82.

Hogg, R. and Carrington, K. 2001. 'Governing rural Australia: land space and race', in Wickham, G. and Pavlich, G. (eds.), *Rethinking Law, Society, and Governance: Foucault's bequest*. Oxford: Hart Publishing.

Horton, J. 2010. 'The case of Elsie Barrett: Aboriginal women, sexuality and the Victorian Board for the Protection of Aborigines', *Journal of Australian Studies*, 34 (1): 1–18.

Howard-Wagner, D. 2010. 'From denial to emergency: governing Indigenous communities in Australia', in Fassin, D. and Pandolfi, M. (eds.), *Contemporary States of Emergency: the politics of military and humanitarian interventions*. New York: Zone Books.

Hunt, A. 1992. 'Foucault's expulsion of law: towards a retrieval', *Law and Social Inquiry*, 17 (1): 1–38.

Hunt, A. and Wickham, G. 1994. *Foucault and Law: towards a sociology of law as governance*. London: Pluto.

Hunter, I. 2007. 'Natural law, historiography, and Aboriginal sovereignty', *Legal History*, 11 (2): 137–68.

Jaggs, D. 1986. *Neglected and Criminal: foundations of child welfare legislation in Victoria*. Melbourne: Centre for Youth and Community Studies, Phillip Institute of Technology.

Kercher, B. 1995. *An Unruly Child: a history of law in Australia*. St Leonards, NSW: Allen & Unwin.

Latour, B. 1988. *The Pasteurization of France*. Cambridge, Mass.: Harvard University Press.

Massola, A. 1973. *Coranderrk: a history of the Aboriginal Station*. Lowden Publishing.

McCallum, D. 1982–3. 'Eugenics, psychology and education in Australia', in Teese, R. and Wickham, G. (eds.), *Melbourne Working Papers 4*, University of Melbourne, 17–33.
McCallum, D. 1990. *The Social Production of Merit: education, psychology and politics in Australia 1900–1950*. London: Falmer.
McCallum, D. 1993. 'Problem children and familial relations', in Meredyth, D. and Tyler, D. (eds.), *Child and Citizen: genealogies of schooling and subjectivity*. Nathan, Qld: Institute for Cultural Policy Studies, Griffith University.
McCallum, D. 1997. 'Mental health, criminality and the human sciences', in Peterson, A. and Buntine, R. (eds.), *Foucault, Health and Medicine*. London: Routledge.
McCallum, D. 2004. 'Law and norm: justice administration and the human sciences in early juvenile justice in Victoria', *Newcastle Law Review*, 7 (2): 62–71.
McCallum, D. 2005. 'Law and governance in Australian Aboriginal communities: liberal and neo-liberal political reason', *International Journal of Children's Rights*, 13: 333–50.
McCallum, D. 2006. '"Merging" the Aboriginal population: welfare, justice, power, and the separation of Aboriginal children in Victoria', *Health Sociology Review*, 15 (1): 29–37.
McCallum, D. 2007. 'Informal powers and the removal of Aboriginal children: consequences for health and social order', *International Journal of the Sociology of Law*, 35 (1): 29–40.
McCallum, D. 2008. 'Representing and intervening in child abuse: law, statistics, community', *Communication, Politics & Culture*, 41 (1): 63–77.
McCallum, D. 2009. 'Punishing welfare: genealogies of child abuse', *Griffith Law Review*, 18 (1): 114–28.
McCallum, D. 2014a. 'Bio-child: human sciences and governing through freedom', *Journal of Sociology*, 50 (4): 458–71.
McCallum, D. 2014b. 'Criminal neglect: tracing the category of the Aboriginal "neglected child"', *Social Identities*, 20 (4–5): 379–90.
McGregor, R. 1997. *Imagined Destinies: Aboriginal Australians and the doomed race theory, 1880–1939*. Carlton: Melbourne University Press.
McGregor, R. 2011. *Indifferent inclusion: Aboriginal people and the Australian nation*. Canberra: Aboriginal Studies Press.
McLean, W. 1904. 'The declining birth-rate in Australia', *Intercolonial Medical Journal of Australasia*, 9 (3): 109–26.
Mauss, M. 1973 [1935]. 'Techniques of the body', *Economy and Society*, 2 (1): 70–88.
Medical Journal of Australia 1918. 'Neglected children of Victoria', *Medical Journal of Australia*, May 4: 380–81.
Meuwese, S. et al. eds. 2007. *100 Years of Child Protection*. Oisterwijk, NL: Wolf Legal Publishers.
Minson, J. 1985. *Genealogy of Morals. Nietzsche, Foucault, Donzelot and the Eccentricity of Ethics*. New York: St Martin's Press.
Morning, A. 2014. 'And you thought we had moved beyond all that: biological race returns to the social sciences', *Ethnic and Racial Studies*, 37 (10): 1676–85.
Muldoon, P. 2008. 'The sovereign exceptions: colonization and the foundation of society', *Social and Legal Studies*, 17 (1): 59–74.
Nanni, G. and James, A. 2013. *Coranderrk. We Will Show the Country*. Canberra: Aboriginal Studies Press.
Newcastle Herald 2017. 'Royal Commission into Institutional Responses to Child Sexual Abuse: Day 2'. February 7. At www.theherald.com.au/story/4450889/royal-commission-into-institutional-responses-to-child-sexual-abuse-day-two/

Nicholson, A., Harris, M. and Gartland, G. 2010. *Loss of Rights – The Despair of Aboriginal Communities in the Northern Territory: a submission to the UN Committee on the Elimination of Racial Discrimination – Australia*. East Melbourne: Concerned Australians.

O'Malley, P. 1998. 'Indigenous governance', in Dean, M. and Hindess, B. (eds.), *Governing Australia: studies in contemporary rationalities of government*. Cambridge University Press.

Paisley, F. 1997. 'Race and remembrance: contesting Aboriginal child removal in the inter-war years', *Australian Humanities Review*, November.

Parton, N. 1991. *Governing the Family: child care, child protection and the state*. London: Macmillan.

Pavlich, G. 2001. 'Transforming images: society, law and critique', in Wickham, G. and Pavlich, G. (eds.), *Rethinking Law, Society, and Governance: Foucault's bequest*. Oxford: Hart Publishing.

Pepper, P. with de Arauga, T. 1980. *You Are What You Make Yourself To Be: the story of a Victorian Aboriginal family 1842–1980*. Melbourne: Hyland House.

Pepper, P. with de Araugo, T. 1985. *The Kurnai of Gippsland*. Melbourne: Hyland House.

Platt, A. 1969. *The Child Savers: the invention of juvenile delinquency*. Chicago University Press.

Platt, A. 2008–9. 'The child savers reconsidered', *Current Issues in Criminal Justice*, 20: 123–28.

Pratt, J. 1997. *Governing the Dangerous: dangerousness, law and social change*. Leichhard, NSW: Federation Press.

Read, P. 2003. 'How many separated aboriginal children?', *Australian Journal of Politics and History*, 49 (2): 155–63.

Reiger, K. 1985. *The Disenchantment of the Home: modernising the Australian family 1880–1940*. Melbourne: Oxford University Press.

Reynolds, H. 1996. *Aboriginal Sovereignty: reflections on race, state, and nation*. St Leonards, NSW: Allen & Unwin.

Reynolds, H. 2010. 'Time immemorial', *Australian Book Review*, April 7, 320: 7.

Rorty, R. 1993. 'Oxford Amnesty lecture on Human Rights, 1992', in Shute, S. and Hurley, S. (eds.), *On Human Rights: the Oxford Amnesty lectures, 1993*. New York: Basic Books.

Rose, N. 1985. *The Psychological Complex: politics, education and psychology 1850–1990*. London: Routledge & Kegan Paul.

Rose, N. 1990. *Governing the Soul: the shaping of the private self*. London: Routledge.

Rose, N. 1996. 'Governing "advanced" liberal democracies', in Barry, A., Osborne, T. and Rose, N. (eds.), *Foucault and Political Reason: liberalism, neo-liberalism and rationalities of government*. London: UCL Press.

Rose, N. 1999. *Powers of Freedom: reframing political thought*. Cambridge: Cambridge University Press.

Rose, N. 2005. 'Government', in Bennett, T., Grossberg, L. and Morris, M. (eds.), *New Keywords: a revised vocabulary of culture and society*. Oxford: Blackwell.

Rose, N. and Valverde, M. 1998. 'Governed by law?', *Social and Legal Studies*, 7: 541–51.

Rowse, T. 2006. 'Towards a history of Indigenous statistics in Australia', in Hunter, B. (ed.), *Assessing Recent Evidence on Indigenous Socioeconomic Outcomes: a focus on the 2002 NATSISS, CAEPR Monograph No. 26*. Canberra: ANU Press.

Rowse, T. 2009. 'Official statistics and the contemporary politics of indigeneity', *Australian Journal of Political Science*, 44 (2): 193–211.

Rowse, T. 2012. *Rethinking Social Justice: from 'peoples' to 'population'*. Canberra: Aboriginal Studies Press.

Ryan, L. 2010. 'Settler massacres on the Port Phillip Frontier, 1836–1851', *Journal of Australian Studies*, 34 (3): 257–73.

Sandison Yule, J. 1914. 'The census of the feeble-minded in Victoria, 1912', *Australasian Medical Congress. Transactions*: 722–27.
Sandor, D. 1990. '"Protecting" *Aboriginal Children: segregation, assimilation and collusion*'. Unpublished paper.
Scott, D. and Swain, S. 2002. *Confronting Cruelty: historical perspectives on child protection in Australia*. Melbourne University Press.
Scraton, P. 2008–9. 'Criminalization and punishment of children and young people: introduction', *Current Issues in Criminal Justice*, 20: 1–13.
Tedmanson, D. and Wadiwel, D. 2010. 'Neoptolemus: the governmentality of new race/pleasure wars?', *Culture and* Organization, 16 (1): 7–22.
Thornton, M. 1990. *The Liberal Promise: anti-discrimination legislation in Australia*. Melbourne: Oxford University Press.
Thorpe, D. 1994. *Evaluating Child Protection*. Buckingham: Open University Press.
United Nations. 1948a. General Convention on the Prevention and Punishment of the Crime of Genocide, December 9, Article 2.
United Nations. 1948b. The Universal Declaration of Human Rights.
United Nations. 1989. General Assembly Resolution 25, Session 44. Convention on the Rights of the Child.
United Nations. 2007. General Assembly Resolution 61/295. Declaration on the Rights of Indigenous Peoples.
Van Krieken, R. 1992. *Children and the State: social control and the formation of Australian child welfare*. Sydney: Allen and Unwin.
Van Krieken, R. 2000. 'Legal informalism, power and liberal governance', *Social and Legal Studies*, 10 (1): 5–22.
Weatherburn, D. and Holmes, J. 2010, 'Rethinking Indigenous over-representation in prison', *Australian Journal of Social Issues*, 45 (4): 559–76.
Wells, K. 2011. 'The politics of life: governing childhood', *Global Studies of Childhood*, 1 (1): 15–25.
White, R. and Habibis, D. 2005. *Crime and Society*. South Melbourne: Oxford University Press.
White, R. and Haines, F. 2008. *Crime and Criminology* (4th ed.). South Melbourne: Oxford University Press.
Wickham, G. 2006. 'Foucault, law, and power: a reassessment', *Journal of Law and Society*, 33 (4): 596–614.
Wright, K. 2012. '"Help for wayward children": child guidance in 1930s Australia', *History of Education Review*, 41 (1): 4–19.

GOVERNMENT DOCUMENTS

Australia (W. Ernest Jones) 1929. Report on Mental Deficiency in the Commonwealth of Australia. Canberra: Government Printer.
Australia (no date) *c* 1937. Aboriginal Welfare: Initial Conference of Commonwealth and State Aboriginal Authorities held at Canberra 21st to 22nd April 1937, Canberra: Commonwealth Government Printer.
Australia 1951. Native Welfare. Meeting of Commonwealth and State Ministers held at Canberra, 3rd and 4th September. Canberra: Commonwealth Government Printer.
Australia (E. Johnson) 1991. Royal Commission into Aboriginal Deaths in Custody. Canberra: Australian Government Publishing Service.

Australia (M. Dodson and R. Wilson) 1997a. Bringing them Home: Report of the National Inquiry into the separation of Aboriginal and Torres Strait Islander children from their families. Sydney: Human Rights and Equal Opportunity Commission.

Australia (Law Reform Commission) 1997b. Seen and Heard: priority for children in the legal process. Sydney: Human Rights and Equal Opportunity Commission.

Australia (M. Brough, Minister for Families, Community Services and Indigenous Affairs) 2007. Media Release: National Emergency Response to Protect Aboriginal Children in the NT. June 21. At www.formerministers.dss.gov.au/3581/emergency_21june07/

Australia (Human Rights and Equal Opportunity Commission) 2008. Social Justice Report No. 1, 2007. Report of the Aboriginal and Torres Strait Islander Social Justice Commission to the Attorney General. Sydney: HREOC.

Australia 2013. Royal Commission into Institutional Responses to Child Sexual Abuse: Formal Opening of the Inquiry, April 3. At http://www.childabuseroyalcommission.gov.au/documents/transcript-3-april-2013.pdf

Australia (Australian Institute of Criminology) 2016a. Australian Crime: Facts and Figures 2014. At http://www.aic.gov.au/publications/current%20series/facts/1-20/2014.html

Australia (Australian Institute of Health and Welfare [AIHW]) 2016b. Child Welfare Series No. 63: Child Protection Australia 2014–15. Canberra: AIHW.

Australia (AIHW) 2016c. Data Linkage Series No. 22: Young people in child protection and under youth justice supervision 2014–15. Canberra: AIHW.

Northern Territory (R. Wild and P. Anderson) 2007a. Ampe Akelyarnemane Meke Mekarle. Little Children Are Sacred. Summary Report of the Northern Territory Board of Inquiry into the Protection of Aboriginal Children from Sexual Abuse. NT Government Printer.

Northern Territory (R. Wild and P Anderson) 2007b. Ampe Akelyarnemane Meke Mekarle. Little Children Are Sacred. Report of the Northern Territory Board of Inquiry into the Protection of Aboriginal Children from Sexual Abuse. NT Government Printer.

Victoria 1861. 1st Report of the Central Board to Watch over the Interests of the Aborigines in the Colony of Victoria. Victorian Parliamentary Papers [VPP] 1861–62, No. 39.

Victoria 1862. 2nd Report of the Central Board to Watch over the Interests of the Aborigines in the Colony of Victoria. VPP 1862–63, No. 11.

Victoria 1864a. 3rd Report of the Central Board to Watch over the Interests of the Aborigines in the Colony of Victoria. VPP 1864, No. 8.

Victoria 1864b. 4th Report of the Central Board to Watch over the Interests of the Aborigines in the Colony of Victoria. VPP 1864–65, No. 19.

Victoria 1866. 5th Report of the Central Board to Watch over the Interests of the Aborigines in the Colony of Victoria. VPP 1866, No. 13.

Victoria 1869. 6th Report of the Central Board to Watch over the Interests of the Aborigines in the Colony of Victoria. VPP 1869, No. 47.
Victoria 1871. 7th Report of the Board for the Protection of Aborigines in the Colony of Victoria. VPP 1871, No. 41.
Victoria 1872. 8th Report of the Board for the Protection of Aborigines in the Colony of Victoria. VPP 1872, No. 60.
Victoria 1873. Industrial and Reformatory Schools. General Regulations (Approved by the Administrator of the Government in Council on the 7th July 1873) VPP 1873, No. 80.
Victoria 1875. 11th Report of the Board for the Protection of Aborigines in the Colony of Victoria. VPP 1875–76, No. 26.
Victoria 1876. 12th Report of the Board for the Protection of Aborigines in the Colony of Victoria. VPP 1876, No. 25.
Victoria 1877. Royal Commission on the Aborigines: report of the commissioners appointed to inquire into the present condition of the Aborigines of this colony, and to advise as to the best means of caring for, and dealing with them, in the future. VPP 1877–78, No. 76.
Victoria 1878. 14th Report of the Board for the Protection of Aborigines in the Colony of Victoria. VPP 1878, No. 71.
Victoria 1879a. Aborigines. Report and Correspondences Relative to the Mortality amongst the Residents of the Aboriginal Stations of Victoria, Etc. VPP 1879–80, No. 86.
Victoria 1879b. 15th Report of the Board for the Protection of Aborigines in the Colony of Victoria. VPP 1879–80, No. 68.
Victoria 1880a. Industrial and Reformatory Schools. Reports of the Visiting Committee to the Industrial and Reformatory Schools of Victoria with the Correspondence relating thereto. VPP 1880–81, No. 12.
Victoria 1880b. Industrial Schools. Regulations. *Victoria Government Gazette* No. 83. July 30: 1944–54.
Victoria 1880c. Neglected and Criminal Children's Amendment Act 1874: regulations for generally regulating the apprenticing, licensing out, and boarding out of children from Industrial Schools. VPP 1880–81, No. 15.
Victoria 1880d. 16th Report of the Board for the Protection of Aborigines in the Colony of Victoria. VPP 1880–81, No. 29.
Victoria 1882. 18th Report of the Board for the Protection of Aborigines in the Colony of Victoria. VPP 1882–83, No. 78.
Victoria 1883. Department of Industrial and Reformatory Schools. Report of the Secretary for the Year 1881. VPP 1883, No. 16.
Victoria 1884. 20th Report of the Board for the Protection of Aborigines in the Colony of Victoria. VPP 1984, No. 94.
Victoria 1885. Department of Industrial and Reformatory Schools. Report of the Secretary for the Year 1884. VPP 1885. No. 75.

Victoria 1887. Department of Industrial and Reformatory Schools. Report of the Secretary for the Year 1886. VPP 1887, No. 75.

Victoria 1890a. Regulations Under the Neglected Children's Act 1890. *Victoria Government Gazette* No. 69, 22 August: 8849–71.

Victoria 1890b. 26th Report of the Board for the Protection of Aborigines in the Colony of Victoria. VPP 1890, No. 212.

Victoria 1891. Department of Neglected Children and Reformatory Schools. Report of the Secretary for the Year 1890. VPP 1891, No. 121.

Victoria 1892a. Department for Neglected Children and Reformatory Schools. Report of the Secretary for the Year 1891. VPP 1892–93, No. 105.

Victoria 1892b. 28th Report of the Board for the Protection of Aborigines in the Colony of Victoria. VPP 1892–93, No. 158.

Victoria 1892c. Royal Park Reformatory School for Protestant Girls (Receiving Depot). *Victoria Government Gazette* No. 76. May 27: 2168.

Victoria 1893a. Department for Neglected Children and Reformatory Schools. Report of the Secretary for the Year 1892. VPP 1893, No. 35.

Victoria 1893b. Matron of Reformatory School. *Victoria Government Gazette* No. 4. January 3: 118.

Victoria 1894. 30th Report of the Board for the Protection of Aborigines in the Colony of Victoria. VPP 1894–95, No. 21.

Victoria 1895. 31st Report of the Board for the Protection of Aborigines in the Colony of Victoria. VPP 1895–96, No. 78.

Victoria 1899. 35th Report of the Board for the Protection of Aborigines. VPP 1899–1900, No. 59.

Victoria 1900a. Department for Neglected Children and Reformatory Schools. Report of the Secretary and Inspector for the Year 1899.

Victoria 1900b. 36th Report of the Board for the Protection of Aborigines. VPP 1900, No. 42.

Victoria 1901a. Department for Neglected Children and Reformatory Schools. Report of the Secretary and Inspector for the Year 1900. VPP 1901, No. 30.

Victoria 1901b. 37th Report of the Board for the Protection of Aborigines. VPP 1901, No. 42.

Victoria 1902a. Department for Neglected Children and Reformatory Schools. Report of the Secretary and Inspector for the Year 1901. VPP 1902, No. 24.

Victoria 1902b. 38th Report of the Board for the Protection of Aborigines. VPP 1902–3, No. 12.

Victoria 1903a. Department for Neglected Children and Reformatory Schools. Report of the Secretary and Inspector for the Year 1902. VPP 1903, No. 30.

Victoria 1903b. 39th Report of the Board for the Protection of Aborigines. VPP 1903, No. 36.

Victoria 1904a. Department for Neglected Children and Reformatory Schools. Report of the Secretary and Inspector for the Year 1903. VPP 1904, No. 22.

Victoria 1904b. 40th Report of the Board for the Protection of Aborigines. VPP 1904, No. 39.
Victoria 1905. 41st Report of the Board for the Protection of Aborigines. VPP 1905, No. 56.
Victoria 1906a. Department for Neglected Children and Reformatory Schools. Report of the Acting Secretary and Inspector for the Year 1905. VPP 1906, No. 14.
Victoria 1906b. Penal Establishments and Gaols. Report of the Inspector General for the Year 1905. VPP 1906, No. 21.
Victoria 1906c. Royal Commission on the Victorian Police Force. Report on I. – The Efficiency of the Police Force in Connexion with the repression of Crime; II. – The Present Condition, Organization, and Administration of the Said Force. VPP 1906, No. 10.
Victoria 1906d. 42nd Report of the Board for the Protection of Aborigines. VPP 1906, No. 44.
Victoria 1907. 43rd Report of the Board for the Protection of Aborigines. VPP 1907, No. 47.
Victoria 1909a. The Children's Court Act. Report of the Chief Probation Officer for the Year 1908. Melbourne. [Pamphlet: State Library of Victoria.]
Victoria 1909b. 44th Report of the Board for the Protection of Aborigines. VPP 1909, No. 3.
Victoria 1910. 46th Report of the Board for the Protection of Aborigines. VPP 1910, No. 57.
Victoria 1911a. Department for Neglected Children and Reformatory Schools. Report of the Secretary and Inspector for the Year 1910. VPP 1911, No. 20.
Victoria 1911b. 47th Report of the Board for the Protection of Aborigines. VPP 1911, 2nd Sess., No. 13.
Victoria 1912a. Department for Neglected Children and Reformatory Schools. Report of the Secretary and Inspector for the Year 1911. VPP 1912, No. 25.
Victoria 1912b. 48th Report of the Board for the Protection of Aborigines. VPP 1912, No. 60.
Victoria 1913. Department for Neglected Children and Reformatory Schools. Report of the Secretary and Inspector for the Year 1912. VPP 1913–14, No. 57.
Victoria 1914a. Aborigines Act 1890. Department of Chief Secretary. Residence of Aborigines Prescribed. *Victoria Government Gazette* No. 93. July 1: 2628.
Victoria 1914b. Department for Neglected Children and Reformatory Schools. Report of the Secretary and Inspector for the Year 1913. VPP 1914, No. 21.
Victoria 1915. Aborigines Act 1890. Department of Chief Secretary. Residence of Aborigines Prescribed. *Victoria Government Gazette* No. 57. May 12: 1703.
Victoria 1916. Aborigines Act 1915. Regulations. *Victoria Government Gazette* No. 198. November 1: 4257.
Victoria 1918. Department for Neglected Children and Reformatory Schools. Report of the Secretary and Inspector for the Year 1917. VPP 1918, No. 20.

Victoria 1922. 49th Report of the Board for the Protection of Aborigines. VPP 1922, No. 6.
Victoria 1923a. Department for Neglected Children and Reformatory Schools. Report of the Secretary and Inspector for the year 1922. VPP 1923–24, No. 17.
Victoria 1923b. 50th Report of the Board for the Protection of Aborigines. VPP 1923–24, No. 8.
Victoria 1924. Department for Neglected Children and Reformatory Schools. Report of the Secretary and Inspector for the Year 1923. VPP 1924, No. 28.
Victoria 1928. Children's Welfare Department and Department for Reformatory Schools. Report of the Secretary and Inspector for the year 1927. VPP 1928, No. 40.
Victoria 1930. Report on the Children's Courts for the year 1929. Unpublished. Children's Court Offices, July 1. State Library of Victoria.
Victoria 1931. Report on the Children's Courts for the year 1930. Unpublished. Children's Court Offices, July 1. State Library of Victoria.
Victoria 1932. Report on the Children's Courts for the year 1931. Unpublished. Children's Court Offices, July 1. State Library of Victoria.
Victoria 1933. Report on the Children's Courts for the year 1932. Unpublished. Children's Court Offices, July 1. State Library of Victoria.
Victoria 1934. Report on the Children's Courts for the year 1933. Unpublished. Children's Court Offices 2 July 1934. State Library of Victoria.
Victoria 1935. Report on the Children's Courts for the year 1934. Melbourne: Government Printer.
Victoria 1936. Report on the Children's Courts for the year 1935. Melbourne: Government Printer.
Victoria 1937a. Children's Welfare Department and Reformatory Schools. Report of the Secretary and Inspector for the Year 1936. Melbourne: Government Printer.
Victoria 1937b. Report on the Children's Courts for the year 1936. Melbourne: Government Printer.
Victoria 1938a. Department of Mental Hygiene. Report of the Director for the year ended 31 December 1937. VPP 1939, No. 9.
Victoria 1938b. Report on Children's Courts for the Year 1937. Melbourne: Government Printer.
Victoria 1939a. Department of Mental Hygiene. Report of the Director for the year ended 31 December 1938. VPP 1940, No. 6.
Victoria 1939b. Report on the Children's Courts for the year 1938. Melbourne: Government Printer.
Victoria 1940a. Department of Mental Hygiene. Report of the Director for the year ended 31 December 1939. VPP 1940, No. 6.
Victoria 1940b. Report on the Children's Courts for the year 1939. Melbourne: Government Printer.
Victoria 1941a. Department of Mental Hygiene. Report of the Director for the year ended 31 December 1940. VPP 1941, No. 11.

Victoria 1941b. Report on the Children's Courts for the year 1940. Melbourne: Government Printer.
Victoria 1943a. Department of Mental Hygiene. Report of the Director for the year ended 31 December 1942. VPP 1943, No. 6.
Victoria 1943b. Report on the Children's Courts for the year 1942. Melbourne: Government Printer.
Victoria 1944. Report on the Children's Courts for the year 1943. Melbourne: Government Printer.
Victoria 1945. Report on the Children's Courts for the year 1944. Melbourne: Government Printer.
Victoria 1947. Department of Mental Hygiene. Report of the Director for the year ended 31 December 1946. VPP 1947–48, No. 9.
Victoria 1949. Department of Mental Hygiene. Report of the Director for the year ended 31 December 1948. VPP 1949, No. 17.
Victoria 1950a. Department of Mental Hygiene. Report of the Director for the year ended 31 December 1949. VPP 1950–51, No. 21.
Victoria 1950b. Report on the Children's Courts for the year 1949. Melbourne: Government Printer.
Victoria (A. Kennedy) 1950c. Report to the Minister for Health on Mental Health and Mental Hygiene Services in the State of Victoria. Melbourne: Government Printer.
Victoria 1951. Department of Mental Hygiene. Report of the Director for the year ended 31 December 1950. VPP 1951–52, No. 1.
Victoria 1953. Report of the Mental Hygiene Authority for the year ended 30 June 1952. VPP 1952–53, No. 8.
Victoria 1954a. Children's Welfare Department and Department for Reformatory Schools. Report of the Secretary for the Years 1951 and 1952. VPP 1954–55, No. 16.
Victoria 1954b. Children's Welfare Department and Department for Reformatory Schools. Report of the Secretary for the Year 1953. VPP 1954–55, No. 21.
Victoria 1954c. Report of the Mental Hygiene Authority for the year ended 30 June 1953. VPP 1954–55, No. 1.
Victoria 1956a. Children's Welfare Department and Department for Reformatory Schools. Report of the Secretary for the Year 1954. VPP 1955–56, No. 23.
Victoria 1956b. Children's Welfare Department. Report of the Director for the Year 1955. VPP 1955–56, No. 36.
Victoria (Justice John V. Barry) 1956c. Report of the Advisory Committee on Juvenile Delinquency. VPP 1955–56, No. 38.
Victoria 1956d. Report of the Mental Hygiene Authority for the year ended 30 June 1955. VPP 1955–56, No. 34.
Victoria 1957a. Children's Welfare Department. Report of the Director for the Year 1956. VPP 1956–58, No. 25.
Victoria (Charles McLean) 1957b. Report upon the operation of the Aborigines Act 1928 and the Regulations and Orders made thereunder. VPP 1956–58, No. 18.

Victoria 1958a. Aborigines Act 1957 – Regulations. *Victoria Government Gazette* No. 80, 27 August: 2978–81.
Victoria 1958b. Report of the Aborigines Welfare Board for Year Ended 30 June 1958. VPP 1958–59, No. 19.
Victoria 1963a. Report of the Aborigines Welfare Board for Year Ended 30 June 1961. VPP 1962–63, No. 33.
Victoria 1963b. Social Welfare Department. Annual Report for Year Ended 30 June 1962. VPP 1963–64, No. 4.
Victoria 1964. Report of the Aborigines Welfare Board for Year Ended 30 June 1963. VPP 1963–64, No. 37.
Victoria 1967. Report of the Aborigines Welfare Board for Year Ended 30 June 1965. VPP 1966–67, No. 25.
Victoria 2013a. Betrayal of Trust. Inquiry into the Handling of Child Abuse by Religious and Other Non-Government Organisations. VPP 2010–13, No. 275.
Victoria (Ombudsman) 2013b. Investigation into children transferred from the youth justice system to the adult prison system. VPP 2010–13, No. 293.
Victoria (Ombudsman) 2017. Report on Youth Justice Facilities at the Grevillea Unit at Barwon Prison, Malmsbury and Parkville February 6. VPP 2014–17, No. 323.

ACTS

Australia Racial Discrimination Act (No. 52) 1975. An Act relating to the Elimination of Racial and other Discrimination.
Australia Anti-Terrorism Act (No. 127) 2005. An Act to amend the law relating to terrorist acts, and for other purposes.
Australia Appropriation (Northern Territory National Emergency Response) Act (No. 1) 2007–8 (No. 126) 2007. An Act to appropriate money out of the Consolidated Revenue Fund for the ordinary annual services of the Government in relation to the Northern Territory National Emergency Response, and for related purposes.
Australia Appropriation (Northern Territory National Emergency Response) Act (No. 2) 2007–8 (No. 127) 2007. An Act to appropriate money out of the Consolidated Revenue Fund for certain expenditure in relation to the Northern Territory National Emergency Response, and for related purposes.
Australia Families, Community Services and Indigenous Affairs and Other Legislation Amendment (Northern Territory National Emergency Response and Other Measures) Act (No. 128) 2007. An Act to amend laws in order to respond to the Northern Territory's national emergency, and for related purposes.
Australia Northern Territory National Emergency Response Act (No. 129) 2007. An Act to respond to the Northern Territory's national emergency, and for related purposes.

Australia Social Security and Other Legislation Amendment (Welfare Payment Reform) Act (No. 130) 2007. An Act to amend the social security law, and for other purposes.

New South Wales Habitual Criminals Act (No. 15) 1905. An Act to provide for the detention and control of habitual criminals.

Victoria Neglected and Criminal Children's Act (No. 216) 1864. An Act for the amendment of the Law relating to Neglected and Criminal Children.

Victoria Aborigines' Protection Act (No. 349) 1869. An Act to provide for the Protection and Management of the Aboriginal Natives of Victoria.

Victoria The Neglected and Criminal Children's Amendment Act (No. 626) 1878. An Act to further amend the Law relating to Neglected and Criminal Children.

Victoria The Aborigines Protection Act (No. 912) 1886. An Act to amend an Act intituled 'An Act to provide for the Protection and Management of the Aboriginal Natives of Victoria.'

Victoria The Neglected Children's Act (No. 941) 1887. An Act to amend the Law relating to Neglected Children.

Victoria The Juvenile Offenders Act (No. 951) 1887. An Act to amend the Law relating to Juvenile Offenders and for other purposes.

Victoria Aborigines Act (No. 1059) 1890. An Act to consolidate the Laws relating to the Aboriginal Natives of Victoria.

Victoria Crimes Act (No. 1079) 1890. An Act to consolidate the Law relating to Crimes and Criminal Offenders.

Victoria Children's Court Act (No. 2058) 1906. An Act to establish and regulate Children's Courts.

Victoria Indeterminate Sentences Act (No. 2016) 1907. An Act to provide for Indeterminate Sentences and for the Detention and Control of Habitual and other Criminals.

Victoria Infant Life Protection Act (No. 2102) 1907. An Act to amend the Infant Life Protection Act 1890.

Victoria Aborigines Act (No. 2255) 1910. An Act to extend the powers of the Board for the Protection of the Aborigines.

Victoria Aborigines Act (No. 2610) 1915. An Act to consolidate the Law relating to the Aboriginal Natives of Victoria.

Victoria Children's Maintenance Act (No. 3001) 1919. An Act to make provision with respect to certain Children without Sufficient Means of Support and for other purposes.

Victoria Children's Welfare Act (No. 3654) 1928. An Act to consolidate the Law relating to Children's Welfare and to the Protection of Infant Life.

Victoria Children's Welfare Act (No. 4152) 1933. An Act to amend Sections Eighteen and One hundred and nine of the Children's Welfare Act 1928.

Victoria Children's Welfare Act (No. 5817) 1954. An Act to provide for and promote the Welfare, Protection and Care of Children and Young Persons.
Victoria Aborigines Act (No. 6086) 1957. An Act relating to the Aboriginal Natives of Victoria and for other purposes.
Victoria Aborigines Act (No. 6190) 1958. An Act to consolidate the Law relating to the Aboriginal Natives of Victoria, and for other purposes.
Victoria Social Welfare Act (No. 6651) 1960. An Act to establish a Social Welfare Branch of the Chief Secretary's Department and to make Provision with respect to the Functions of that Branch and for other purposes.

VICTORIAN PARLIAMENTARY DEBATES (VPD)

VPD Session 1928 Vol 177, Legislative Assembly 11 October 1928.
VPD Session 1950–51 Vol 232, Legislative Assembly 9 August 1950.
VPD Session 1950–51 Vol 234, Legislative Assembly 14 November 1950; 4 September 1951.
VPD Session 1956–57–58 Vol 251, Legislative Assembly 30 April 1957.
VPD Session 1956–57–58 Vol 252, Legislative Assembly 28 May 1957.
VPD Session 1958–59 Vol 257, Legislative Assembly 15 April 1959; 21 April 1959.
VPD Session 1959–60 Vol 259, Legislative Assembly 6 April 1960.
VPD Session 1962–63 Vol 268, Legislative Assembly 23 October 1962.

ARCHIVAL SOURCES

National Archives of Australia

NAA B314, 7. Minutes of Meeting of Board for the Protection of Aborigines [BPA] (1921–46).
NAA B314, 8. Minutes of Meeting of BPA/Aborigines Welfare Board [AWB] (1946–58).
NAA B314, 9. Minutes of Meeting of AWB (1959–61).
NAA B337, 540. Aboriginal Case Files: D. M.
NAA B337, 56. Aboriginal Case Files: E. B.
NAA B337, 253. Aboriginal Case Files: E. and R. F.
NAA B337, 635. Aboriginal Case Files: M. R.
NAA B337, 689. Aboriginal Case Files: A. S.
NAA B356, 90. Lake Tyers – inspections (1931–34).
NAA B356, 91. Lake Tyers – inspection reports (1935–38).
NAA B356, 92. Lake Tyers – inspection reports (1939–62).
NAA B356, 93. Lake Tyers – outside/unofficial reports and complaints – Mr Gordon Sprigg (Baptist Union of Victoria) (1935–37).

NAA B356, 94. Lake Tyers – outside/unofficial reports and complaints – Mr Gordon Sprigg (Baptist Union of Victoria) (1935–36).
NAA B356, 95. Lake Tyers – outside/unofficial reports and complaints (general) (1948–65).
NAA B356, 97. Lake Tyers – outside/unofficial reports and complaints – Mrs Anna Vroland (Women's International League for Peace and Freedom).
NAA B357, 1. Acts and Regulations 1957–58 Aborigines Bill.
NAA B357, 3. Acts and Regulations 1958–65: Correspondence.
NAA B357, 54. 1957 Districts: Mooroopna.
NAA B357, 55. Mooroopna 1958.
NAA B357, 109. Correspondence: Institutions.
NAA B357, 155. Correspondence Files Health: Children in Hospitals and Institutions.
NAA B357, 166. Social Workers' Reports 1961–64.
NAA B357, 169. Dr Finney's Report 1958.
NAA B357, 192. AWB Field Notes – Murray Valley Survey of Aborigines.
NAA B408, 1. McLean Inquiry – notes on country visits.
NAA B408, 4. Police Reports and Population Details.
NAA B408, 6. McLean Inquiry – correspondence of inquiry board (1).
NAA B408, 7. McLean Inquiry – correspondence of inquiry board (2).
NAA B408, 9. McLean Inquiry – correspondence 1954–57.

Public Records Office of Victoria (PROV)

PROV VPRS 266, Unit 630. Inward Registered Correspondence (1852–1938). Law Department.
PROV VPRS 1579, Unit 1. Circulars from Crown Law Office, Melbourne (1865–1914).
PROV VPRS 1694, Units 1–11. Board for the Protection of Aborigines: Correspondences.
PROV VPRS 5694, Unit 1. Annual Reports Children's Welfare Department 1925–61.
PROV VPRS 6345. Health Department Central Administration Files. General Correspondences:
  Unit 72. Item 236. Psychiatric Clinic for Children.
  Unit 95. Item 82. Mental Hygiene Branch: Children's Court Clinic – Transfer to Mental Hygiene Branch.
  Unit 102. Mental Deficiency Act: Accommodation of retarded children and Children's Welfare at Royal Park.
PROV VPRS 10309 P0001. Secretary's Letter Book 1905–7.
PROV VPRS 11563 P0001 Unit 411 Item 58/475. Shepparton PO [Permissive Occupancy] Areas Aborigines Welfare Board re Camps on Forest Land.

Victorian Children's Aid Society Records. State Library of Victoria. La Trobe Collection. MS 10051.

Box 1/2 (a). Annual Report of the Presbyterian Society for Neglected and Destitute Children, 1893–94.

Box 1/2 (b). Reports and statements of accounts for the years 1897–1908.

Box 1/5. Minute book for committee meeting 1902–8.

Box 4/1. Minute book of sub-committee April 1895–December 1901.

Box 4/4. Casebook Vol 1. November 1893–September 1894.

Box 18/10. Register of foster parents including copies of departmental inspectors' reports.

Box 19/4. Applications for foster children 1894–1921. Box 21/2. Correspondence re reports on children November 1902–May 1933.

Index

Books in the Series

Diseases of the Will
Mariana Valverde

The Politics of Truth and Reconciliation in South Africa: Legitimizing the Post-Apartheid State
Richard A. Wilson

Modernism and the Grounds of Law
Peter Fitzpatrick

Unemployment and Government: Genealogies of the Social
William Walters

Autonomy and Ethnicity: Negotiating Competing Claims in Multi-Ethnic States
Yash Ghai

Constituting Democracy: Law, Globalism and South Africa's Political Reconstruction
Heinz Klug

The Ritual of Rights in Japan: Law, Society, and Health Policy
Eric A. Feldman

The Invention of the Passport: Surveillance, Citizenship and the State
John Torpey

Governing Morals: A Social History of Moral Regulation
Alan Hunt

The Colonies of Law: Colonialism, Zionism and Law in Early Mandate Palestine
Ronen Shamir

Law and Nature
David Delaney

Social Citizenship and Workfare in the United States and Western Europe: The Paradox of Inclusion
Joel F. Handler

Law, Anthropology and the Constitution of the Social: Making Persons and Things
Edited by Alain Pottage and Martha Mundy

Judicial Review and Bureaucratic Impact: International and Interdisciplinary Perspectives
Edited by Marc Hertogh and Simon Halliday

Immigrants at the Margins: Law, Race, and Exclusion in Southern Europe
Kitty Calavita

Lawyers and Regulation: The Politics of the Administrative Process
Patrick Schmidt

Law and Globalization from Below: Toward a Cosmopolitan Legality
Edited by Boaventura de Sousa Santos and Cesar A. Rodriguez-Garavito

Public Accountability: Designs, Dilemmas and Experiences
Edited by Michael W. Dowdle

Law, Violence and Sovereignty Among West Bank Palestinians
Tobias Kelly

Legal Reform and Administrative Detention Powers in China
Sarah Biddulph

The Practice of Human Rights: Tracking Law Between the Global and the Local
Edited by Mark Goodale and Sally Engle Merry

Judges Beyond Politics in Democracy and Dictatorship: Lessons from Chile
Lisa Hilbink

Paths to International Justice: Social and Legal Perspectives
Edited by Marie-Bénédicte Dembour and Tobias Kelly

Law and Society in Vietnam: The Transition from Socialism in Comparative Perspective
Mark Sidel

Constitutionalizing Economic Globalization: Investment Rules and Democracy's Promise
David Schneiderman

The New World Trade Organization Knowledge Agreements: 2nd Edition
Christopher Arup

Justice and Reconciliation in Post-Apartheid South Africa
Edited by François du Bois and Antje du Bois-Pedain

Militarization and Violence Against Women in Conflict Zones in the Middle East: A Palestinian Case-Study
Nadera Shalhoub-Kevorkian

Child Pornography and Sexual Grooming: Legal and Societal Responses
Suzanne Ost

Darfur and the Crime of Genocide
John Hagan and Wenona Rymond-Richmond

Fictions of Justice: The International Criminal Court and the Challenge of Legal Pluralism in Sub-Saharan Africa
Kamari Maxine Clarke

Conducting Law and Society Research: Reflections on Methods and Practices
Simon Halliday and Patrick Schmidt

Planted Flags: Trees, Land, and Law in Israel/Palestine
Irus Braverman

Culture under Cross-Examination: International Justice and the Special Court for Sierra Leone
Tim Kelsall

Cultures of Legality: Judicialization and Political Activism in Latin America
Javier Couso, Alexandra Huneeus and Rachel Sieder

Courting Democracy in Bosnia and Herzegovina: The Hague Tribunal's Impact in a Postwar State
Lara J. Nettelfield

The Gacaca Courts and Post-Genocide Justice and Reconciliation in Rwanda: Justice Without Lawyers
Phil Clark

Law, Society, and History: Themes in the Legal Sociology and Legal History of Lawrence M. Friedman
Robert W. Gordon and Morton J. Horwitz

After Abu Ghraib: Exploring Human Rights in America and the Middle East
Shadi Mokhtari

Adjudication in Religious Family Laws: Cultural Accommodation, Legal Pluralism, and Gender Equality in India
Gopika Solanki

Water On Tap: Rights and Regulation in the Transnational Governance of Urban Water Services
Bronwen Morgan

Elements of Moral Cognition: Rawls' Linguistic Analogy and the Cognitive Science of Moral and Legal Judgment
John Mikhail

A Sociology of Transnational Constitutions: Social Foundations of the Post-National Legal Structure
Chris Thornhill

Mitigation and Aggravation at Sentencing
Edited by Julian Roberts

Institutional Inequality and the Mobilization of the Family and Medical Leave Act: Rights on Leave
Catherine R. Albiston

Authoritarian Rule of Law: Legislation, Discourse and Legitimacy in Singapore
Jothie Rajah

Law and Development and the Global Discourses of Legal Transfers
Edited by John Gillespie and Pip Nicholson

Law against the State: Ethnographic Forays into Law's Transformations
Edited by Julia Eckert, Brian Donahoe, Christian Strümpell and Zerrin Özlem Biner

Transnational Legal Process and State Change
Edited by Gregory C. Shaffer

Legal Mobilization Under Authoritarianism: The Case of Post-Colonial Hong Kong
Edited by Waikeung Tam

Complementarity in the Line of Fire: The Catalysing Effect of the International Criminal Court in Uganda and Sudan
Sarah M. H. Nouwen

Political and Legal Transformations of an Indonesian Polity: The Nagari from Colonisation to Decentralisation
Franz von Benda-Beckmann and Keebet von Benda-Beckmann

Pakistan's Experience with Formal Law: An Alien Justice
Osama Siddique

Human Rights under State-Enforced Religious Family Laws in Israel, Egypt, and India
Yüksel Sezgin

Why Prison?
Edited by David Scott

Law's Fragile State: Colonial, Authoritarian, and Humanitarian Legacies in Sudan
Mark Fathi Massoud

Rights for Others: The Slow Home-Coming of Human Rights in the Netherlands
Barbara Oomen

European States and Their Muslim Citizens: The Impact of Institutions on Perceptions and Boundaries
Edited by John R. Bowen, Christophe Bertossi, Jan Willem Duyvendak and Mona Lena Krook

Environmental Litigation in China
Rachel E. Stern

Indigeneity and Legal Pluralism in India: Claims, Histories, Meanings
Pooja Parmar

Paper Tiger: Law, Bureaucracy and the Developmental State in Himalayan India
Nayanika Mathur

Religion, Law and Society
Russell Sandberg

The Experiences of Face Veil Wearers in Europe and the Law
Edited by Eva Brems

The Contentious History of the International Bill of Human Rights
Christopher N. J. Roberts

Transnational Legal Orders
Edited by Terence C. Halliday and Gregory Shaffer

Lost in China?: Law, Culture and Society in Post-1997 Hong Kong
Carol A. G. Jones

Security Theology, Surveillance and the Politics of Fear
Nadera Shalhoub-Kevorkian

Opposing the Rule of Law: How Myanmar's Courts Make Law and Order
Nick Cheesman

The Ironies of Colonial Governance: Law, Custom and Justice in Colonial India
James Jaffe

The Clinic and the Court: Law, Medicine and Anthropology
Edited by Tobias Kelly, Ian Harper and Akshay Khanna

A World of Indicators: The Making of Government Knowledge Through Quantification
Edited by Richard Rottenburg, Sally E. Merry, Sung-Joon Park and Johanna Mugler

Contesting Immigration Policy in Court: Legal Activism and Its Radiating Effects in the United States and France
Leila Kawar

The Quiet Power of Indicators: Measuring Governance, Corruption, and Rule of Law
Edited by Sally Engle Merry, Kevin Davis and Benedict Kingsbury

Investing in Authoritarian Rule: Punishment and Patronage in Rwanda's Gacaca Courts for Genocide Crimes
Anuradha Chakravarty

Contractual Knowledge: One Hundred Years of Legal Experimentation in Global Markets
Edited by Grégoire Mallard and Jérôme Sgard

Iraq and the Crimes of Aggressive War: The Legal Cynicism of Criminal Militarism
John Hagan, Joshua Kaiser and Anna Hanson

Culture in the Domains of Law
Edited by René Provost

China and Islam: The Prophet, the Party, and Law
Matthew S. Erie

Diversity in Practice: Race, Gender, and Class in Legal and Professional Careers
Edited by Spencer Headworth and Robert Nelson

A Sociology of Transnational Constitutions: Social Foundations of the Post-National Legal Structure
Chris Thornhill

Shifting Legal Visions: Judicial Change and Human Rights Trials in Latin America
Ezequiel A. González Ocantos

The Demographic Transformations of Citizenship
Heli Askola

Criminal Defense in China: The Politics of Lawyers at Work
Sida Liu and Terence C. Halliday

Contesting Economic and Social Rights in Ireland: Constitution, State and Society, 1848–2016
Thomas Murray

Buried in the Heart: Women, Complex Victimhood and the War in Northern Uganda
Erin Baines

Palaces of Hope: The Anthropology of Global Organizations
Edited by Ronald Niezen and Maria Sapignoli

The Politics of Bureaucratic Corruption in Post-Transitional Eastern Europe
Marina Zaloznaya

Revisiting the Law and Governance of Trafficking, Forced Labor and Modern Slavery
Prabha Kotiswaran

Incitement on Trial: Prosecuting International Speech Crimes
Richard Ashby Wilson

Criminalizing Children: A History of Welfare and the State in Australia
David McCallum